THE SCOTTISH MOUNTAINEERING CLUB JOURNAL

| Vol. XLI | 2011 | No. 202 |

STONE TEMPLE PILOTS

By Peter Macpherson

EILIDH CLINGS to me like a limpet, her warm chubby arms tight around my neck, unwilling to let go. 'Night night Sweetheart. Be good for mum and I'll see you tomorrow.' Only three and a half years old, my daughter can't understand why I'm going climbing before she goes to bed. I'd usually leave early morning, but this occasion wasn't usual. As I give Niccy and our unborn baby a big hug she implores me to be careful. My edginess and distant stare tell her this is no ordinary adventure. I head out into the night with only one thing on my mind; a new route on the mighty Shelter Stone.

The seed had been sown last winter on the long walk out from a big new route on Creag an Dubh Loch. Comparisons had been made between our new route and the great winter routes on the Shelter Stone which Guy had done in years gone by. The conversation quickly moved on to potential new lines, and Guy mooted the possibility of a 'Super Directissima' up the front of the main bastion linking a whole stack of steep, hard summer pitches. It was typical of Guy to come up with such an audacious idea and if it wasn't for the bounty of recent hard routes under my belt I might have shrunk away at the thought of it. I had met Guy the previous winter while climbing in the Cairngorms, and it was clear we shared a passion and relentless drive for winter climbing that crossed the border into obsession. We seemed to 'gel' quickly due to our similar backgrounds, and our sardonic sense of humour helped to relieve the tension often felt on hard winter routes. In a very short time we had forged a strong and equal partnership. All we needed was the right weather and conditions to get a chance at our dream.

The alarm rings at 0130 hours, smashing my sleeping-pill-induced limbo. A couple of Chelsea Buns, two pots of Ambrosia Creamed Rice and a yogurt are demolished in minutes. A few metres away, Guy is crammed in the back of his car going through the same routine and

Opposite: Shelter Stone Crag, Loch Avon Basin, on the day of the ascent (28 January 2011). Robertson & Macpherson are the tiny figures in the centre. Photo: Brian Duthie.

before we know it we're suited, booted and off out over fields of perfect névé. A full moon and canvas of stars serenade us, glowing with excitement at the prospect of the long night and day ahead. Despite the unearthly hour, we chat non-stop like fishwives.

0520 hours, and racked up and ready for action Guy has opted for the breakfast pitch. Our plan is to take on the challenge of technical rock both in the lower corners of *Steeple* (E2) and on the steep middle walls left of *The Needle* (E1). Higher up Guy is intent on gaining and trying to climb the awesome cracks on the headwall of *The Spire* (E4). True to a shared spirit of adventure, the guidebook is at home; it's many years since either of us has climbed here in summer.

The long opening pitch is tricky and bold in the darkness, the thin cracks choked with ice and the right wall blanketed in snow. The climbing is delicate and complex; a stressful early lead. An hour or so later, the first embers of sun nudging the horizon, Guy reaches the belay. I second quickly, hooking anything for speed, and arrive at the belay to big smiles – conditions are first class. Up above us the great concave sweep of *The Bastion* extends relentlessly to the sky, progressively thicker with white the higher and steeper it gets. Succeed or fail in our quest, we've hit the jackpot of opportunity.

The second pitch continuing up the corner is easier, though still absorbing to climb. The vertical left wall provides a continuous shoulder-high crack which I gladly feed with nuts and cams, mono-points tip-toeing crampons up helpful rugosities on the slab to my right. Within minutes I'm belayed and Guy is giving the corner the same gentle treatment it deserves. Across the glen, Hell's Lum Crag lies sheathed in ice, bathed in a peachy orange glow. We make short work of the turfy steps leading to the overhanging rock band barring access to the upper Bastion. The first summer crux of *Haystack* (E3) looms above, and although this is our favoured path we're open-minded about the route, choosing to rely on instincts and go wherever the placements take us. We share a vague idea that this section may prove to be the crux.

Much needed sustenance is taken in the form of Jelly Babies and Lucozade, as I arm myself to the teeth with an enormous rack. Like the proverbial Chieftain's pre-battle speech, Guy fires me up with talk of 'historic moments' and 'the first time the headwall has been breached in winter'. I head off making my way steadily up towards the impending fault, the ground steepening steadily with every move. A mixture of fear and exhilaration swirls round in my head, held in place by total focus and conviction. The cracks are perfect, swallowing protection and picks easily, increasing my confidence. I need to concentrate on one move at a time though, as the sight of what lies above is too overwhelming to take in. The hooks get thinner and the rock tips beyond vertical as my head darts left and right trying to find edges for crampons to bite on. With a tiny, wobbling hook for my left tool, I thrust a cam into a crack and make the clip, but in the blink of an eye the hook pops and I'm hanging in space, my right tool still lodged precariously above. A tirade of foul language would be my usual course of action at this turn of events but anger here is my enemy; I must maintain focus and get straight back in the saddle! Months of training is paying dividends now as pumping arms are kept at bay, pulling through a fierce-yet-delicate bulge clipping an old peg en route. At last the angle eases where a ramp leads up right. Short of gear and low on resolve I choose to belay awkwardly on a small ledge.

Seconding hard pitches can be a frustrating business, and Guy curses both his numb hands and handicapping rucksack as he makes his way to my perch. His words from below sum it up typically succinctly – 'Holy Shit, this is proper hard!' Hard enough, it seems, to leave me in a state of post-traumatic euphoria. The sky above is crystal clear except for the odd wisp of cloud floating by on the gentle wind. The air fills my stretched lungs like invisible peppermint ice cream. The cold, however, is penetrating hard, eating into my hands as I try to be useful and organise ropes.

Thoughts drift back to Inverness, where my wife and daughter are probably still fast asleep under warm duvets, dreaming peacefully, happy and content. At least that's how I imagine them from my shivering little

Peter Macpherson embarks on the summer crux pitch of Haystack.. Photo: Guy Robertson.

perch. (I'm kidding myself though. Deep down I know Niccy is probably up and about after another restless sleep. She's nearing the end of a particularly difficult pregnancy and my absence will surely be compounding her burden. As always though, my perennial selfish streak won out over a guilty conscience. I remember a day the previous season, arriving back late with Iain Small after a day on Beinn Eighe. Niccy had playfully reminded me of my hollow promise to cut back on my winter climbing, to which Iain had replied, 'Well Niccy, a climber is a bit like a junky – his word is only as good as his last hit!' So here I am again, disengaged from the fight, torn as ever between the family I love so dearly and the climbing adventures I yearn for so helplessly. But being blessed with the chance to try a line like this on one of Britain's premier cliffs, and still get home to family duties the same day seems to strike a perfect balance. As the sun reaches its high point and the effervescent Mr Robertson cruises upwards to my stance, I realise this is exactly where I should be. I'm in my element.

After a flurry of exchanged gear Guy attacks the ramp leading right, teetering crampons up creases with axe picks gently locked in a crack on the left. All of a sudden he grinds to a halt, neck craning up trying to suss out the way forward. A futile and increasingly frustrated question-and-answer session takes place as we try to work out where the hell the route goes. Do we continue up the ramp or do we head left to what looks like a big ledge? With limited daylight at our disposal we can't afford time-draining dead ends. So Guy tosses an imaginary coin in his head and plumps for the ledge out left, a shout of 'safe!' confirming it's a good choice. But when I join him I'm dismayed to discover a steep crack above blanking out into a bulging wall, devoid of any cracks or edges. It's clear we're into virgin territory now, and the clock is ticking loudly.

Negotiating past the belay is easier said than done, with crampons inches from Guy's worried face. Luckily the crack is a sinker and I soon have bomber gear, but it soon peters out and with stark blankness above I'm forced to grope left onto a high sloping foothold, leaving my right axe in the crack behind me. A wide, bottomless crack winks tantalisingly six feet round the edge to my left, but it's out of reach and my last runner is now low enough that I'll land on the belay should the unthinkable happen. After a period of soul-searching, a tiny rounded foothold below and left presents the only vague solution. 'Watch me man – this is fucking scary; watch me, waaaaatch…me!' I've no choice but to crimp a small edge with gloved fingers and span delicately left, hoping my crampon finds that rounded hold. And it does. A big cam and a nut in the wide crack bring relief, but this is short-lived as it slowly dawns that I'm now missing one of my axes! Somehow, inexplicably, I'm reunited with both tools, and with a bit of turbo-boosting up easier ground, arrive at the airy perch below the huge upper Bastion.

Guy on the ramp.

Two hundred metres up the Stone, the view is immense. Straight ahead lies a frozen Loch Avon, framed on the left by Stag Rocks and Stac an Fharaidh, and on the right by Beinn Mheadhoin. Hanging over my right shoulder, like a belligerent giant, lurk the castellated buttresses of Càrn Etchachan. After six extremely hard pitches, with at least two more to come, this is surely one of the most spectacular and intimidating winter belay spots in Britain.

It's 1430 hours when Guy appears at my belay. Giving me the jacket and sack, he racks up slowly in silence. We're both muted by the difficulty and exposure of his next lead. I usually relish the thought of leading hard pitches but I don't envy him this one. We've been climbing hard for nine hours and now here are thirty metres of gently overhanging rock in the most intimidating position imaginable.

Gingerly, he steps out into the fray. Despite his visible concern and occasional request to 'watch me like a hawk!' I'm in awe of his ability to stay so calm and focused in such a scary, oppressive place. He stops every now and then, calmly shaking out cramped muscles, and I'm well aware that I'm witnessing my own 'historic moment'. But this doesn't

stop me selfishly willing him to get a bloody move on. The thought of seconding this pitch in the dark before leading the final 5b summer pitch of *The Steeple* fills me with gut-wrenching apprehension.

'TIGHT!' I scream hopelessly. He's sitting somewhere up above me with a warm, contented glow. He's done his work and he knows it. But no such luck for me, I'm struggling with it. My hands are now so cold I can't feel my axes. Looking down between my feet I can see the bottom of the crag seven hundred dizzying feet below; looking up, the verticality continues, relentless. My stretchy axe lanyards are wrapped confusingly several times round the ropes and I've just climbed past a piece of gear which has pulled me to a halt. I'm getting increasingly desperate; 'KEEP ME TIGHT!' I curse, fumble and fight my way up the wall until a final pull over a capping overhang gains what should be our last belay. My head is spinning with adrenaline as I get to my feet and offer heartfelt respect.

What I really need now is a nice, easy pitch to warm down, but instead I'm reliably informed the last pitch is 'a sturdy grade 8'. I really don't need this! With the light fading, I hand myself over, the protection plentiful but the wide and parallel cracks hard and tenuous to climb. As far as strength goes, this is the bottom of the barrel but with a sustained bout of guttural 'power-screaming' somehow I torque onto the ledge above. After what seems an eternity, the climbing gradually eases off, cracks leading left to the exit groove of *Citadel* and sharply up onto the plateau. Just in time for total darkness to arrive.

Sitting up there, totally spent of every calorie, my mind is swimming with emotion. It's as if pure opium is coursing through my veins. I'm atop arguably the ultimate winter cliff, having just climbed the most incredible route of my life. It's funny, but in more flamboyant countries climbers at moments such as this might jump about and scream and whoop, embrace their partner and give them a mighty 'high five'. But not us Scots. We're made of more reserved stuff. As a smiling Guy reaches the top and quietly unties from the rope, a simple 'nice one lad' and a firm handshake are all that's needed. I guess we struggle to find words enough to describe the perfection in such moments.

It's 2130 hours when I pull the car up outside my house, looking forward to a wee dram to savour my contentment. As the front door opens, the dog launches himself skywards, turning cartwheels with excitement. A small, excited voice calls down from the top of the stairs 'Daddy you're home! I waited up for you!' 'Come here and give your old man a hug' I reply. She clings to my neck like a monkey and, turning her nose up at my smelly clothes, she says, 'did you have a nice climbing?' To which I reply, honestly, 'Aye – one of the best, Eils, one of the best'.

Opposite: Guy Robertson on pitch 7 of Stone Temple Pilots (X,9) during the first ascent. Photo: Peter Macpherson.

A NIGHT IN THE BIG BEDROOM

By Bob Richardson

WHEN THE EVENING twilight lies across the north it is no time to be under a roof. So I drove up to the North Face car park and walked up to the CIC in the sunshine of a June afternoon. The air was fresh and warm, my pack was light and I could take my time and enjoy the scenery. None of the slight tension that precedes a climbing trip; this time I was going to enjoy just being in the glen below those familiar cliffs.

Later, after a leisurely meal, I took a chair and a glass of wine outside and watched the changing light of evening play across the ridges and buttresses. I was waiting for the double sunset as the sun disappears behind Càrn Dearg, only to reappear and send another shaft of warmth up the glen before continuing its track towards the Rough Bounds. A sight that only the summer devotees of the CIC are privy to.

Then, packing my sack only with bivvy bag, mat and sleeping bag and with a bottle of water and some biscuits, I crossed the burn and walked up the glen in the evening air. The top of the Orion Face was glowing pink. (A poor imitation of the Chamonix Aiguilles – but our own.) The glen was slowly darkening and the lower rocks becoming grey and then black as I followed the grass until it died out below the slabs running down from Coire Leis. Here there is a small alp of sheep-grazed grass with the tower of North-East Buttress on one side and the sweep of the Càrn Mòr Dearg Arête skyline on the other. The grass is short and fairly level, the infant Allt drains out of Coire Leis and murmurs down the slabs. Long ago I had picked out this spot as ideal for a summer bivouac – a place to lie snug and feel the mountain air flow over my face as I watched the gradual changes of light and colour in the sky. I found a place to roll out my mat and bivvy bag, got into my sleeping bag and lay facing the Ben; relaxed and comfortable in my own little corner of what Johnny Cunningham called 'the big bedroom'.

The rocks were familiar, scene of many days of tension, occasional fear and joy in success. But, over there just a couple of hundred metres away at the foot of the buttress, was the place where one February evening, after a day of delight in good ice and a fine route, we found a friend dying. And, further down where the boulder field spilled out of Observatory Gully, I had the seen the blood-spattered snow after two climbers fell from the top of Slav Route. But I was not here to remember the good times or the bad, only to absorb the peace of the mountain on a summer night.

Our emotional response to landscape is complex. How is it that inanimate geology and a thin skin of vegetation can arouse a feeling which makes you so conscious of your own existence? The mountain is only rock but from within ourselves we project meaning and character on to it – what Neil Gunn called 'this psychic stuff'. All my remembered life I have been conscious of what you might call an empathy with mountain landscapes: but how can you empathise with the inanimate? It is more than an appreciation of form and colour, there seems to be a deep atavistic response which makes time spent among the high hills (especially solitary time) so emotionally satisfying. And there is no better way of experiencing it than a bivouac on a fine summer night.

The colours of a clear simmer-dim sky are almost impossible to describe – faint pinks shading into delicate blues and greys before the clear pale blue of the pre-dawn. I lay there feeling the cool katabatic breeze drifting over my face, warm in my down bag, no sound or trace of any other living being. It was not my intention to sleep, a night like this was too precious, but I must have dozed because the unmistakable sharp crack of a high-velocity rifle round startled me awake to a clear blue sky. I looked at my watch – three o'clock. Someone else was out on the mountain taking advantage of the pre-dawn light.

Soon the sunlight was beginning to come over the Arête, casting a pink glow on the upper part of Tower Ridge. After an hour or two watching the changing play of light across the higher rocks, I packed up and wandered slowly downwards. I stopped opposite Observatory Gully to see it as few people ever see it, with the morning light flooding in from the left. Rocks which rarely felt the sun were being thrown into relief. Observatory Ridge, normally so shy and retiring against the sweep of the cliffs, was standing out like a stone knife held against the throat of the mountain, Rubicon Wall was half in sunlight and the left flank of Tower Ridge was bathed in light. After a while I continued on down to the Hut in the silence and warmth. The frying pan was waiting.

ADVENTURES ON CREAG MHÒR

By Desmond Rubens

'CREAG MHÒR is one of the remotest mountains in the Southern Highlands … From no point on any public road can one get a clear view of it.' (*The Southern Highlands*, D.J. Bennet 1991.)

Adventure, the emotional heart of mountaineering, can be harder to come by these days. We are supported by a tumult of electronic wizardry, unsporting weatherproof clothing and fast highways and cars that have reduced times to the hills to negligible proportions compared to former times. All this progress would have astonished the ancients (Marshall, Campbell, Smith et al.), whose suffering in the cause of mountaineering is now unfathomable to the modern generation.

For those of us keen on maintaining some uncertainty in their mountaineering outcomes, there are ways of redressing the balance away from that of complete predictability. These include:

1 Growing older.
2 The rejection of innovation, preferably by loyalty to the technology which existed when one started climbing. For example, with care, one can continue to deploy one-inch-to-the mile maps (ideally costing 8/- or less) for many years.
3 Adopting an unfamiliar mode of transport in the hills.
4 Eschewing company.

Regarding the practical approach to the above methodology, none are difficult although the first requires a little patience. Some come naturally. I am generally inclined to give new technology around a couple of decades to bed in while teething problems are ironed out by others. However, I did recently invest in ski-mountaineering skis as a way of adding interest to ascents of our hills and satisfying condition 3 above. Finally, although not unsociable, I recognise that occasionally it is good to go it alone (particularly as some of us grow more cantankerous as we age).

Having had a desultory interest in 'Munro Bagging' for the last thirty years and conscious that the risk of failing to complete the playing of the 'Long Game' increases exponentially with age, I decided this year to become more purposeful about completing my final fifteen or so. I therefore planned to increase my rate of bagging to around three annually. I estimated that this rate would give me a more than evens chance of winning the game (hopefully).

Creag Mhòr and Beinn Heasgarnich were my last Munros in the Glen Lochay area. I realised that I had never even seen these two peaks, at least not consciously. On my first attempt in mid-February of this year, I roped in Cairns Dickson as company and we travelled up from the Central Belt on roads foggy and mysterious throughout. As the car negotiated snow-generated tramlines on the ascent of the very minor road east of Heasgarnich, blue skies, sunshine and Alpine snowfields magically materialised. We were able to pull off and stop just as the car exhaust was in danger of being seriously compromised. We geared up in quiet sparkling sunshine while the summit of Heasgarnich called to me distantly over an intervening white hummocky tableland. I had brought my skis but Cairns, foolishly, had decided that he would be as fast on foot. In these snow conditions, the inevitable happened. I glided over the surface of two feet of perfect snow and then idled for him to catch up. Within an hour, Cairns faced the inevitable and retreated.

Continuing alone, I gloried in skinning up a shallow corrie to the summit plateau, solitary in a deep white realm, surrounded by the peaceful hills of Breadalbane. This pleasant state of affairs was terminated on cresting the wide summit ridge which coincided with the descent of a thick grey mist. This being Scotland, I was expecting such a setback and was therefore relieved that no further awaiting of the weather deterioration was necessary. After half an hour or so of diligent searching, I discovered the summit and continued my journey to Creag Mhòr. The pleasures of skinning up rhythmically on powder were now substituted with erratic upper body motions, inner and spontaneous swearing and sudden deep intakes of breath. This was caused by skiing the corrugated iron of the summit ridge in the ever denser mist. I consulted the map. Becoming aware of a hidden and alarming drop on my right, I abandoned the attempt to ski to Creag Mhòr. Shortly afterwards, I abandoned the attempt altogether as being pointless in the conditions. This was a bit weak, but was justified by there being no further pleasure to be had in the process and having at least reduced the Munro deficit by one. I negotiated a mainly but not entirely unpleasant descent to Glen Lochay by the mountain's southern slopes, met Cairns and returned to Edinburgh.

A month later, I determined to finish the job. For a change, and having just the one Munro to dispatch, I decided to approach from Auch, near Bridge of Orchy. Departing late to allow some bad weather to clear, I left the road about midday, again taking skis and, it being a weekday, on my own from the start.

Here let me mention the 'Three Hour' rule of Munro bagging, which saves a deal of tedious planning time. This simple rule states that the great majority of Munro summits are three hours from the car. If one rules out the obvious exceptions such as the Glenshee hills (too close) and the odd Cairngorm and Fisherfield Forest hill (too far), you will find the rule works very well and I applied it on this occasion.

I put my skis on just beyond the railway viaduct and enjoyed a gentle ski up a newly constructed road, which, along with other excavations,

Looking back to Beinn Odhar during the second unsuccessful attempt on Creag Mhòr.

detracted from the scene. However, round the spur of Beinn a' Chaisteil all man-made artifacts disappeared as I approached the Scottish watershed and I felt exhilarated to be alone in this land. As on the previous occasion, the hills were deep in snow which was wonderfully highlighted by the sun, particularly the gullies and ridges on Beinn Odhar behind me. I cautiously zigzagged up to a ridge to reach the col between Creag Mhòr and Cam Chreag, its satellite Corbett.

Even on skis, the going was slow. As before, a dense mist descended. I skinned up from the col to an outlying top of Creag Mhòr, spent time satisfying myself that I had found the thing and then continued along the ridge to the main summit. As most of the snow had been blown clear of the ridge, I carried the skis as far as the col before the main summit. At this final col, which was not a particularly obvious feature in these conditions, I decided that there was no point in carrying the skis any further. I would make a quick dash for the summit, which was obviously not far away. Before leaving the skis, I did a time check and was surprised to find that the three hour rule had been well out in the case of Creag Mhòr. It was so far out, in fact, that issues of darkness were beginning to enter my mind. Never mind, I thought, it would be a quick nip up and a rapid ski down. Nevertheless, I thought it wise to give myself a deadline of five o' clock to turn back. I set off at a fast determined pace along the faint well-rimed path. Five minutes later, I was most disappointed to come across a deep bank of snow of about a hundred feet in altitude. I ploughed up this thigh-deep to easier ground and continued up. Three minutes later I came across an identical feature although this time with a prominent rocky nose just discernable at its upper limit. I was excited to know that I was now within reach of the summit. Sometime later, the rocky nose having proved false, I was peering around a plateau, Creag Mhòr continuing to toy with its victim. Five o' clock had come and gone. Darkness and the possibility of not finding my skis were also entering my head. I was also increasingly conscious of being on my own, in conditions of poor visibility and a long way from anywhere. I gave myself a talking to and decided that retreat was essential.

There were a few slightly anxious minutes until the skis were found again. I changed gloves and then traversed for several minutes before stopping to check my bearing. Crumbs! Where in heaven was the compass? Probably lying in the snow at the last stop. Unpleasant newspaper headlines came to mind. 'After a Full-Scale Search of Two Days, The Rescue Team Leader Expressed Surprise to Find Mr. Rubens at Loch Lyon.' A systematic search of my sack revealed the instrument attached to the previous gloves. Relief. A very unpleasant moment.

There were some good, albeit brief, experiences. I came below the mist, the scenery around the remote west end of Loch Lyon beautifully monochromatic in the failing light. I enjoyed some fine though careful skiing. I decided not to repeat the upward journey but traverse round the northerly spur of Cam Chreag and descend gently to the watershed. The lie of the land, however, forced me much further downhill, leaving me with a wearisome pull back up. There being a surface of long and tussocky grass, the tips of the skis catapulted me forward on several occasions to form a heaped tangle from which it became increasingly tiresome to extricate myself. I confess to feelings of weariness latterly. I reached the road some hours later than the original estimate.

As you see, Creag Mhòr is proving a worthy adversary. However, further adventures on this mountain are no longer required. I am considering the purchase of a GPS and a new map, revising my planning methods, a possible companion and maybe just nipping up on a fine summer's day by the shortest route. And I will continue to scan the Youth Elixir advertisements in the tabloid press.

FOLLOWING IN FATHER'S FOOTSTEPS

By Peter Biggar

'The Creation is pairfect in every respect, it's only man…'[1]
[Archbald Hannah]

I NEVER REALLY got to know my father. I met him a few times as a child – a huge giant of a man he seemed to me then who would come into my bedroom and laugh his uproarious rich laugh and tell me tales of his life in the fabulous north where he spent his time watching birds, stealing osprey eggs, dodging keepers, fighting elections and flouting authority. I remember once going to a hotel somewhere in the Highlands with my mother and her sister, and my father took me for a walk in the woods; at one point he took a quite mature sapling in his bare hands and wrenched it from the earth. I think he wanted to impress me. He also taught me how to cross boggy ground by crushing down the rushes to step on; I remember this lesson every time I do it.

I met him only once later on in life when I was a gawky teenager in Edinburgh; he was still a big man and surrounded by a numerous family, but he seemed less overpowering. We had a civilised meal and discussed literature, politics and sport. He used to write to me occasionally – I still have his letters – in one of the last, he described how one of his sons had been fatally injured in a car crash and had spent some time in a coma. The family had sat round his bedside playing his favourite music in the hope of stimulating his brain, but all to no avail. The relevance of all this may become apparent in what follows.

Quite recently I had to go through old diaries at the behest of my own son Richard, who, for obscure purposes, wanted to know what hills and routes he had climbed earlier in life. I was quite surprised by how much we had done together, but it was also rather interesting to note the pattern of it all, especially the natural cut-off point at which climbing or walking with Dad became a less favoured option, just as, of course, it should. I remember a rather dismal day's walking in the Fannaichs when he charged ahead with a whoop of delight and I thought, no, I just don't want to compete any more. I remember his justified disgust when we failed on some easy rock route on Blàbheinn. When I refused to let him embark on the upper pitches of *Ghlastail GTX* in Strathconon he wouldn't speak to me all the way home.

---

1   Archie Hannah was a member of the Club. He should have made this remark on his last visit to the CIC when he was 76, but I think it was somewhere else. He was looking up at the stars when he said it.

The pattern changes. The young man goes on his first Alpine trip; Dad proffers what he hopes is sage advice and worries quietly, till he comes back having done more and harder routes than his Dad ever did. Then come trips to Canada and Australia and big routes on the Ben with this and that new partner poor old Dad has never heard of. And one listens to each new bulletin feeling sort of pleased and jealous and humble all at once. And reports of one's own modest doings occasionally merit a word of praise. ('Good effort.') Some of the wonderful partners swirl through the house accepting hospitality with gracious condescension:

'You used to climb yourself, I hear?'

'Och well, I still try to do a bit…'

The fresh-run fish sweep on up the river while the kelts flop about in shallow pools.

Later on, the gradual realisation dawns – perhaps with the coming of marriage (or, more likely, partnerships), and even more with the raising of children, – that it is just possible that the younger generation too are a bit like Socrates: not in their wisdom, but in their mortality, – and a more tolerant view is taken of those who, by this time, might be grandparents.

'I wonder if the Old Man would like to go climbing?'

Richard lives in Aberdeen, I live on the Black Isle; we met at Invercauld. We had bicycles and a tent. His bike was a marvel of technology with quietly clicking gears and purring oiled chainwheels; it was bright red. Mine was as grey as my hair and rather cantankerous – a bit like old Archie from whom I bought it many years ago, but, like him, it kept going. My son looked askance upon this machine and produced a folding pump and a miniature oilcan.

We must have made an interesting sight riding up Gleann-an-t-Slugain, Richard in shiny black and yellow lycra, and me in heavy blue climbing breeches. His brightly-coloured sack was small; my ancient blue one looked enormous. Through the trees and up by the Fairy Pools, the track gets rough, and, just after bumping through a shallow burn, there was an ominous crack from beneath my seat and I lurched backwards. The bolt which secured my saddle had sheered in two. Like a duck with a broken wing I waved the useless saddle at the retreating back of my companion and then started to push the bike uphill. When I caught up with him, Richard nobly insisted that I should ride his bike and he would ride mine – without sitting down. He still went faster than me because I couldn't get the hang of his gears at all and my feet went round and round like demented windmills.

In this strange fashion we reached the junction of high and low tracks round the ruins of Slugain Lodge and agreed that this was as far as the bikes could go. I dumped mine in disgust behind the first peat hag, but Richard carried his a long way up the hillside to keep it safe from prying eyes.

The day was dour and grey with a fine drizzle, and cloud was edging along the cliff tops. The thread of the well-mended path unrolled endlessly over the moor, and a cold wind made us put on extra clothing. It was a Cairngorm wind, sharp and insistent, from one direction only. A high pressure system was expected, but it hadn't come yet. Tiny spurts of red gravel shot up from Richard's trainers as I followed his footsteps up the glen. Our chances of climbing looked remote.

Of course we'd had romantic notions of camping in the Garbh Choire, but now, with the wind in our faces and heavy weights on our backs, we realised that if we took the tent down into the corrie, we should only have to carry it back up again, so we settled for the most sheltered site we could find down by the river, just under Clach a' Chleirich where the path runs up to the Sneck. We'd had enough of the wind. Even putting up the tent was a challenge – the more so because one of its bendy hoops was broken and had to be encased in a metal sleeve and taped in position. Then both segments of the tent had to be zipped together in a fashion I couldn't master, but Richard is technically minded and thrives on this sort of problem. We were glad to put boulders on top of the guy pegs.

The corries on the far side of the valley were dark and mysterious and the wind was screaming over them. Richard used up several matches and some patience before his little gas stove would light: the cylinder was too full; if he turned it on too much, the flow of cold gas put out the flame. Suddenly he grinned:

'Do you still carry that old Primus through Knoydart?' Memories of following Mum and Dad on interminable bothy trips.

'Och yes. You know, considering how many other things you can get in the tin, it's not that heavy.' He smiled indulgently. I listed the little bottle of meths, the tin-opener, the spare tea-bags, the little black film container of salt; all this as well as matches, a pan handle, the dismantled stove, its legs, a spanner, a nipple spanner and the vital set of nozzle prickers still encased in the same grimy, greasy, yellowing paper sleeve they came in. He laughed: parents ought, after all, to remain much the same, though getting greyer and ghostlier, until they just vanish, like the Cheshire Cat, leaving nothing but a grin. After all, hadn't Richard's grandfather gained an intimate knowledge of these very hills, spending days in small tents while trying to comprehend the behaviour of greenshank, snow bunting and dotterel? In an odd way, just being here was part of a family tradition.

As the drizzle had stopped and the cloud risen a little, we took a turn up the hillside towards one of the corries. Here were muted shades of granite and lichen, dripping black slabs, walls and gullies with the wind eddying round them, and delicate patterns made by mosses on the gravel beds. A small group of hinds and young stags moved away uphill. We didn't linger.

On the way down I tried to explain why I think Scotland should be fully independent. For me it has nothing to do with economics; it's about national maturity, about accepting responsibility for ordering one's own affairs.

'After all,' I argued, 'who on earth, once they're grown up, wants to go on living with their parents? You want to branch out, do your own thing…' The analogy seemed pertinent, but, while he listened thoughtfully, he wasn't convinced. Although he was born in Aberdeenshire, Richard spent about nine years growing up near Liverpool. Perhaps, in these circumstances, one doesn't so easily develop the same emotional attachment to one's native country? There again, like many young people, he's very much an individualist and tends to see himself, if I understand it right, as a kind of solitary survivor in a harsh environment. Clubs and other organisations are viewed with caution if not suspicion… a wee bit like his grandfather maybe?

Food and drink can unite or divide the generations. He had brought the main meals. Pasta. Two different kinds of little shells: one with spinach and one with sun-dried tomatoes and little pots of sauce to pour over them.

'Which will we have tonight?' he asked.

'Why not mix them – half each?'

Soon they were bubbling happily in the light-as-air pan. Very tasty, very economical to carry, but there wasn't enough to satisfy a hungry mouse. Fortunately I had brought some sensible extras: digestive biscuits, a big lump of red cheese and a large slab of fruit cake.

'I knew you'd bring lots of food,' he remarked cheerfully, between mouthfuls.

The wind rattled the tent against our faces as we lay in our bags. I hadn't dared to bring a dram for fear of disapproval. Alcohol, it seems, is bad for serious climbing – I wouldn't really know about that – but one's offspring have great moral authority, so, when they take you out for an airing you'd better be on your best behaviour.

It rained heavily in the night. Richard, protected by ear-plugs, slept through it. I looked out at 6.30; the wind was still strong. I spoke but there was no answer. He eventually woke at 8.30; after all, it was summer and there was no hurry. Breakfast was traditional: a bowl of porridge, a large mug of hot, sweet tea and a thick bacon sandwich. I tend to suffer from nervous apprehension before climbing and the butty was a struggle, but it made a greasy passage to my stomach.

Up at the Sneck the wind was fierce, but the sky was a clear, bright blue. I'd been there twice before and seen nothing. It was Richard's first time. Through watering eyes we peered down into the corrie, an awe-inspiring place, then, leaving as much as we could in our sacks and stashing these behind boulders, we jingled our way down a repulsively loose gully, and turned left to make our way under a famous wall which, in the guidebook Richard gave me for Christmas twenty years ago is called 'impossible' and, in the lovely old red guidebook my adoptive father gave me forty-six years ago, isn't even mentioned.

We scrambled up into a bay in the rocks where a crack-line runs up to a shoulder left of an arctic sea of grey slabs. Removing socks and getting the gear on was bitter in the shadows and my hands were stiffening by the time we were ready.

'How do you feel about leading this?' he asked.

'I'd like to, but it's cold and you'll be quicker.'

It was the right decision. I carried the mini-sack with the footwear and the water. When my turn came, I was glad the rock gave so much friction for the feet, because my hands had almost lost sensation, but light was creeping towards us over the slabs, greyness was turning to silver, apprehension to hope and even confidence.

My careful reading of the photocopied page was useful on the first stance. Richard was puzzled by a reference to climbing up the arête, but I rightly guessed that our start had been more direct and missed that bit out. Above us, over the rim of an overhang, angels might edge their way, but ordinary mortals stepped, a little gingerly, down onto nuggets of quartz and traversed to ledges. I was so engrossed in working this out that I didn't realise that we were now climbing in golden sunlight and the wind was dropping away. Richard was grinning hugely as I reached the stance.

Easy, spiralling motion brought him to the final difficulties. Some comments floated down:

'This is old-fashioned climbing, Pete,' (he almost never calls me Dad; when I had darker hair people sometimes mistook us for brothers). 'There's a steep crack with no gear!'

But that wasn't quite accurate, because he had managed to place a small nut and a small cam. The cam I removed with a struggle, but the nut was stuck. After much jiggling, I did what he said and left it. Then, to get started up the crack, I had to hand-jam. This was fine, but I don't do hand-jams. Thereafter I found a couple of frictiony steps and I embraced a huge block with big holds on either side. The position was airy, but so secure I even posed for a photograph. Beneath my feet *Squareface* plunged to the dark screes. We had talked about doing it for years. Now I could sit at peace in the sun and watch the expert abseil nonchalantly to free the stuck nut. I was having happy little thoughts of wandering up to the top of the mountain, free from the cares and stress of climbing:

'I think we should go and do Mitre Ridge,' he said.

Standing at the bottom of the Direct Start to *Mitre Ridge* – whose imposing granite tower soared into the blue sky above – and watching

Squareface, Garbh Choire, Beinn a' Bhùird: *The author follows the Severe variation on the top pitch.*
Photo: Richard Biggar.

carefully as the ropes inched out behind my son, I could sense that the difficulties here were of a different order. An occasional midge appeared, just to remind us that, after all, this was August in Scotland.

When I stepped onto the slab I knew at once that this pitch was going to be really hard. Difficulty is relative to ability, and I've never been very confident on steep rock. Yet, from below, it didn't look that bad: a gently steepening, rough slab running up to join a bounding wall on its left, with a nasty-looking wet, mossy step to be crossed higher up. Richard grunted something about 'climbing on little pockets'. What this seemed to mean was that there weren't any real holds. Finger ends clawed at tiny edges and feet were held in place by microscopic spines of granite.

The whole trend of the pitch manoeuvred one leftwards. From below that looked good, because, surely, there would be good holds where slab and wall converged? But when I got close, it was only to realise with horror that wetness was oozing from the crack all over slab. The closer I got the more slippy it became, but I had to go there anyway because he had placed a nut or two in the mossy slit. Every move I made was minute and gasping. At one point the sack threatened to stick me fast against the wall. I never asked for a tight rope – I didn't have to.

'Hard Severe!' I spluttered as he dragged me up onto the stance, my fingers dirty and sore.

'Mmm, maybe it should have a technical grading,' he remarked judiciously.

Poor old Dad reckoned that V.S. wouldn't be out of place. After all, that wonderful granite slab *Ardverikie Wall* is also Hard Severe, but much gentler. At this point Richard might have said: 'You're not just as young as you were, Pete.' But, being a good man at heart, he didn't.

Above this Neanderthal pitch, *Mitre Ridge* is said to become a little easier, and Richard shot off along a winding, grassy ledge. When I joined him he was peering up at what looked like an executioner's block which had been jammed in a steep chimney. He moved up:

'The guidebook really ought to mention this chockstone!' he gritted out as he levered himself upwards.

'Oh, but it does!' Dad muttered, 'And I know where.' A glance at the guide on the next stance showed that we had included the first pitch of *Cumming-Crofton Route* on our itinerary, and I had a bruise on my knee for weeks afterwards to prove it.

After this little diversion our route went by an old-fashioned gully, slithery traverse, awkward corner and deceptively difficult wall, with generous helpings of heather and grass, until we came to the little col between the First and Second Towers. Above us loomed the last difficulties, and, as I was starting to feel just a little weary by this time, I hoped they wouldn't be too bad. There seemed to be only two

Looking across to Squareface from Mitre Ridge, Beinn a' Bhùird.   Photo: Richard Biggar.

alternatives: to the left an evasive, ledgy scramble (perfect, I thought), and in the middle a steep, blocky chimney.

'Ah but,' he said with a smile that was truly Mephisophelean, 'the best way is round the corner: it's called Bell's Variation!' And he vanished before I could protest. My heart sank. I much prefer Brahms's variations to those of Dr Bell:

'Any fool can climb clean rock...' I intoned as the ropes ran out. When my turn came, I stepped nervously round the edge of the tower expecting to find a slimy, woodrush-sprouting crack, but found instead a spine of perfect grey granite which even had sharp holds and little resting places. Up above, Richard was lolling against the rock and smiling with delight as he took in the rope. It felt so secure that I could pause and relish the space between my feet and the corrie floor.

Chatting happily we wandered back to the sacks, drank water and devoured some sandwiches, for we'd had almost nothing since breakfast which now seemed a very long time ago. In that miserable summer how strange and beneficent that the wind had dropped and the sun come out:

'You just have to try to spot these little weather windows coming,' said Richard, 'and go for it and take a chance.' He bent down and removed a crisp packet from a glassy pool. I felt so pleased that he was utterly different from me and yet so much the same.

But, as Archie Hannah said, nothing human is ever perfect, and, of course, the rest of the day was absolute hell! When we got back to the tent, the midges came out in clouds and we had to pack and flee. We could have had a pleasant dinner and a chat. Instead of which we had a hurried bite, a long walk and a truly ghastly cycle ride back to Invercauld in the dark. Back at the car park there was nothing for it but to pack and go our separate ways. Richard, looking after me to the last, produced a muesli bar. As the lights of his car receded into the dark, I was left to reflect on the strange and wonderful quality of providence, for my father's son, my half-brother, the one who never recovered from his car accident, was also called Richard; but we never knew that when we named our son.

CORBETT'S DROP CRITERION[1]

By Robin N Campbell

SINCE ITS APPEARANCE in Munro's Tables in 1953, Corbett's 'List of Scottish Hills 2,500 and under 3,000 feet in Height' has been announced as selected by the criterion that each listed hill has a drop of 500 feet on all sides. However, this criterion was never stated by Corbett[2]. Instead, the editors John Dow and Jim Donaldson[3] *deduced* that this was Corbett's criterion, which 'has obviously been exhaustively applied and rigidly adhered to', said Dow. I believe that this deduction was incorrect.

The 'zoomable' digital map of Scotland accessible through the National Library website provides a convenient means of examining the hills included by Corbett, and those left out, in relation to the map data available at the time. The zoom passes through the 'Popular' One-Inch Survey to the Six-Inch Survey, and these are the same maps that were available to Corbett. I presume that I have to thank Ordnance Survey copyright restrictions, as well as the National Library, for access to this useful historical tool.

An examination of the hills included in the 1952 List in relation to the Popular Map shows that all of them had at least 10 contour lines intervening between the drop-determining col and the summit. An examination of those hills excluded from the 1952 List shows that all of these had 9 or fewer contour lines between col and summit. Corbett's drop criterion was therefore 'at least 10 contour lines intervening between drop-determining col and summit', and it is this criterion which was 'exhaustively applied and rigidly adhered to'. The Popular Map plotted contour lines at 50-foot intervals, and so 10 contour lines enclose 450 feet. Effectively, then, Corbett's drop criterion was '450 feet or more'.

Naturally, the application of this criterion will result in the inclusion of some hills with between 450ft and 500ft of drop. Five 10-contour hills were removed from the List in 1981 and a sixth in 1984, because they failed to meet the drop criterion of 500 feet. But these deficiencies of drop did not result from any relevant change in the mapping of these hills. Data was available in 1952 (though it is unlikely that Corbett

---

1 A longer version of this note, with more detailed argument and discussion, appeared as 'Corbett's Criterion' in *The Munro Society Journal*, No. 2, 2010.

2 Dow's introduction to the first published version in 1952 makes this clear (SMCJ, 25, 45–52).

3 Jim Barton (SMCJ, 41, 36) showed that it was E.W. Hodge who originally made this deduction.

consulted it) to associate these six hills with drops between 450ft and 500ft. Dow and Donaldson, had they noticed this in 1952, would have concluded that Corbett's drop criterion was 450 feet, rather than 500 feet.

If Corbett had consulted Six-Inch col heights, and/or contour-interpolated One-Inch col estimates, his list would have been a different one, whatever height-specific drop criterion he had in mind, if any. In fact, there is no evidence that he looked at any data except the summit heights and the contour markings of the Popular Map.

As a consequence of these observations, and if it is desired to keep faith with Corbett's intentions, the List of Corbetts should be revised to include 21 new or reinstated hills with current drops between 500 feet (152.4m) and 450 feet (137.2m). These are the first 21 hills in the list on page 27 of Alan Dawson & Dave Hewitt's booklet *Corbett Tops and Corbetteers* (TACit Press, 1999). A slightly different possibility, less precise but perhaps more in keeping with Corbett's actual criterion, would be to add those Corbett Tops which exhibit at least 15 contour lines intervening between drop-defining col and summit on current maps. Since 15 ten-metre lines enclose 459ft, this is effectively a slightly more severe criterion than Corbett's. Its application would add only 19 new or reinstated Corbetts.

CAMPED THERE IN THE COLD

By Iain Smart

The temperature was below zero. Near enough, for the purposes of this story, to the 50 below when the man from the creeks stumbled into the din and the glare of the Malemute Saloon prior to the shooting of Dangerous Dan McGrew. We were 15° further south in the rain shadow of the Coast Range of British Columbia somewhere between Lytton and Lillooet. I write of an event that took place some sixty years ago when this area was still fairly empty and a faint whiff of the old frontier lingered on; the people of the First Nation still retained a presence in this backwater.

We left the car at the end of a long dirt road and started off through a land of cactus and sagebrush that lined the valley bottoms where the rain shadow was deepest. This gave way to a pleasant forest of Ponderosa pine. Higher up the open pine forest turned to increasingly dense spruce plugged with deep dry unconsolidated snow. After a few hours of struggle we reached our first flowery alpine pasture, at this time of year covered by a couple of feet of floury snow. We could see our ridge leaving the trees a few hundred feet above the thinning trees leading to a shapely summit.

By now the sun was sinking over the western peaks. The temperature started to fall; things were about to get serious. Under these conditions it is wise to bivouac early so you can see what you are doing. We headed for a thick island of spruce, one of several dotting the ragged edge of the tree line, here to make a des. res. for the night. The islet was particularly well favoured. It had three taller trees at its centre and the space around them was protected by a dense hedge of smaller trees. The central space was snow-free and level. Once we had got our sleeping bags out and a candle burning on a knife stuck in a tree trunk and the Primus roaring, we had a sheltered home and dined in comfort. Outside our nook the silence was deep and the stars glittered in a black, black sky. Something – hopefully a coyote or a wolf, rather than something less tangible – howled from time to time from different locations in the surrounding forest primeval.

It was the first time we had tried out this type of bivouac. We were following the advice of a patient of mine, a Red Indian, by the name of Murdo MacDonald who had explained that this was standard practice among his people when out on a winter hunting expedition. He also gave me the helpful advice that if attacked by a bear you should get your back against a tree, hold your knife in your right hand point upwards and throw your left arm across your throat to protect your windpipe and great vessels. When the bear embraces you its claws dig into the tree rather than you. Before its teeth can do too much damage to your left arm, you stab upwards with the knife under its rib cage into its heart. This is anatomically a plausible procedure and may even work. His camping advice was certainly sound but, thankfully, I never had the chance to test his technique with an uppity bear.

The next morning we started late. It was cold outside and a strong wind was blowing. Our refuge remained sheltered, a warm microclimate filled with the comforting aroma of coffee and pine resin. We lay in our sleeping bags listening to the wind in the branches until the sun was well up in a bright blue sky. When we eventually did get going the wind cut to the bone and travel through the spindrift and deep unconsolidated powder was slow and painful. We could see long plumes of silver dust streaming from our ridge all the way to the summit. It must at least be snow-free up there and we prepared for a battle along a windy corridor. To get shelter from the wind for as long as possible we returned to the trees and gained the lee side of the shoulder leading to our ridge. The price of the lee was deeper snow and denser forest as we were crossing into the climatically different Pacific slope.

I emerged from a dense thicket into a clearing. A few seconds later I was facing an Indian pointing a rifle at me. Then two other Indians materialised also with rifles. They seemed vastly relieved at something. But not half as relieved as we were when we learned they were on the point of shooting us as deer. However, something about our progress was un-deer-like and had made them pause. They spoke little English but the message was the same as you get for spoiling the sport of a stalking party anywhere in the world.

We pointed uphill and asked 'Okay?' They gestured us on and we continued our struggle. The incident had been a close call. A lot of people get shot by mistake in the hunting season. In some areas farmers have been known to put white smocks on their animals with 'COW' or 'HORSE', as appropriate, written on the side in large black letters. We were lucky to encounter experienced hunters on their native heath. Townie palefaces tend to shoot anything that moves or even rustles. All this showed our double inexperience: the woods are dangerous in the hunting season and the new unconsolidated snow of November is best avoided.

We continued on to the foot of the ridge but after leaving the trees we were into wearing wind and waist-high spindrift. The ridge was longer than it looked from below and after a hundred feet or so of exposure to the wind hypothermia set in; it would be easy to die pointlessly in this unforgiving land. We wisely retreated to descend a couple of thousand feet through the spruce to the kindly belt of whispering Ponderosa pine.

Here we found a sheltered spot floored with pine needles instead of snow. We made a modest campfire and after our bacon and beans, mandatory fare in this context, reclined in happy comfort beneath bright stars twinkling in a black sky undiminished by the glow of urban electricity. My companion was moved to quote from *The Shooting of Dan McGrew*:

Were you ever out in the Great Alone, when the moon was awful clear,
And the icy mountains hemmed you in with a silence you most could *hear*;
With only the howl of a timber wolf, and you camped there in the cold,
A half-dead thing in a stark, dead world, clean mad for the muck called gold;
While high overhead, green, yellow and red, the North Lights swept in bars? –
Then you've a hunch what the music meant... hunger and night and the stars.

Okay, so we weren't hungry, there was no music, no moon, no aurora and the wandering thing that had howled in the darkness the night before seemed to be elsewhere, but the rest of the *mise-en-scène* was there: the icy mountains hemmed us in and there was silence... and night... and the stars.

Sociological Note

The above episode happened almost sixty years ago. We were young and romantic at the time and much given to reading Robert Service. We saw the West through his eyes. We were very immature. To be fair, in the early fifties of last century, there was still a faint sense of the old frontier in British Columbia, outside the towns at any rate. There were still prospectors left over from the gold rush days living in shacks up Tranquille Creek near where we lived and they would tell tales of the wild times in the old times when the west was predominantly a footloose male society. For example, the first time we went into a pub in BC we walked up to the bar, leant on it and asked for two beers. Everybody laughed and someone said, 'You guys must have been fresh off the train this morning.' At that time in a bar in BC you couldn't drink standing up. You had to order while sitting at a table; you were limited to two glasses of beer at a time; the glasses were small, less than half a pint if I remember correctly and they were brought to you at your table. So we sat down at a table and raised two fingers to indicate we were hard drinkers and wanted the maximum.

In remoter parts of the Province virgin land was still on offer from the Government at 25 cents an acre, provided you lived on it and cleared an acre a year; after five years it became yours. I forget the various obligations but they weren't onerous for a young man to fulfil. We thought seriously of combining homesteading with prospecting. Surely in a few years up some remote valley in the interior ranges of British Columbia we would strike it rich, find a mother lode and remedy our lack of wealth. I had taken instruction in prospecting procedures and had actually acquired a Free Miner Certificate that gave me the right to stake a claim and affix my own numbered 'claim plates' to mark it and later register it at the appropriate government office; it would then be mine for five years.

A technique Murdo MacDonald had told me about sounded interesting; it was to wait until a likely river froze and dig out the ice at the bottom of the waterfalls and then mine the gravel at the foot. This is where the heavy gold would have accumulated over the years. Come the spring, the stockpiled gravel could be washed at leisure and the nuggets recovered.

Alas, that is as far as it went; you need real courage to take wing and leave the cage. I was at the time a civil servant ingloriously employed by the BC Department of Health. We worked a five-and-a-half-day week with two weeks holiday a year with the occasional Monday off. After fifteen years service you qualified for an extra week of annual leave; this in an area of spectacular unclimbed mountains, all far too big for a day-and-a-half expedition. Even the above long weekend was insufficient. The dimensions of Scotland are more suited to someone who needs the belay of secure employment.

The west face of Naranjo de Bulnes.
Photo: Andy Tibbs.

AMISTAD CON EL DIABLO
– NARANJO DE BULNES

By Alan Wilson

IN SEPTEMBER 2009 I and two colleagues from work decided we needed a short climbing holiday to recharge the batteries and also present ourselves with a challenging climb in a new, for us, location.

Neil Smith had long coveted the towering peak of Naranjo de Bulnes in the Picos de Europa, of Northern Spain, so we decided this was as good as anywhere, if not better, and Spanish limestone too, it would have bolts every six feet, so we could cut down on gear that way, we guessed.

I admit to leaving much of the planning and logistics to the other two, Neil Smith (SMC) and Craig Lonsdale (from Sheffield, but that's not his fault). We three were busy working offshore together, so a lot of the planning and discussion took place in the smokers' tea-shack, and, not being a smoker, I let them get on with it.

Our two-weeks-on-and-off rotation meant early September would be the ideal time, hopefully the Picos summer crowds would be gone, the hut still open and the snow still a month or two away. Neil and I booked flights from Prestwick and arranged to meet Craig at Stansted for the onward leg to Santander. From there it was a rental car and a couple hours drive into the hills.

A quick bite to eat and a stop to stock up on hill food and we headed into the evening sunset westwards towards Asturias. As darkness fell the road turned narrower and twistier as it climbed through the presumably picturesque limestone canyons. I knew there were steep and deep ravines, because occasionally the headlights offered disturbing glimpses of black voids and the tops of trees beyond the concrete barriers. Having driven with Neil on some of the more challenging Highland roads, surely there was nothing to fear as he threw the Seat around like a rally driver, but I recall telling him there was no rush and this was not an X Box game. It was the least I could do. I suspect he enjoyed the drive more than I.

After an hour or so following the rising hairpin bends we eventually arrived at the pretty village of Sotres de Cabrales, which sits at 1045m, and found a local tavern, Casa de Cipriano, which was run by a local guide and former Himalayan climber. We thought we might enjoy a beverage or two and then find a bivvy site nearby. Over drinks, however, we discovered the tavern had spare rooms, and for a reasonable price we could get a comfortable bed, shower and breakfast too. Naturally, being hard core, rufty-tufty North Sea tigers we opted for the room rather than hunting in the darkness for an empty barn. Craig produced a fine single malt, whereupon we retired to our quarters and settled down for the night.

Next day dawned sunny and warm, we enjoyed breakfast and fuelled up on fresh squeezed orange juice and pints of coffee. From Sotres it was a fairly short but winding drive to the trail head which leads to the hut, Refugio Julián Delgado Úbeda (or Vega Urriellu). The walk in was pleasant, through lush green, alpine-like meadows and passing ruinous shielings on the way. After an hour or so, the grey and white limestone peaks began to close in and we caught our first glimpse of the Naranjo. Rising up like some Iberian Devil's Tower, it looked every inch the Last Great Problem, although we knew there were many routes on all its faces, none of which fell below an interesting 4b (British) grade.

Naranjo de Bulnes, also known as El Urriellu locally, is not the highest peak in the range, but it is definitely an impressive sight. This monolith rises more than 300m above the surrounding terrain to a height of 2519m, and with its steep faces and lack of any easy scrambling routes, it resembles a marooned, inland sea stack. First climbed via the south face in 1904 by Pedro Pidal and local guides, there are now numerous routes on all sides, many of which have been climbed in winter too. El Naranjo is the jewel in the crown of the Picos de Europa and for Spanish climbers it may be likened to our Old Man of Hoy as a 'must do' attraction.

After a while the gap between me and my companions widened. I was not aware of putting on any significant turn of speed, and was also stopping for pictures and admiring the views ahead and behind, so wondered what could be wrong. I worried for them, perhaps breakfast or the Dalwhinnie had not agreed with them?

My fears were soon put to rest however. I found myself at the door of the hut, and it had actually started to rain, so I made my way in, rather than wait in the wet for the lads to catch up. We had no booking, such was the quality of our planning, but it was such a big hut, so surely there would be room? Not knowing much Spanish I employed my best Québecois French, hoping that there would be enough linguistic similarities to get my message across. That, and a bit of sign language, led to success, and I secured three places for four nights, but we had to be out by el weekend, as it would be busy then. The reason for my friends' delaying tactics then became clear, the hut guardian required both my passport and a credit card to be handed over as security, so now all expenses incurred would be reflected on my account. Clever lads, very shrewd move, if only I had smoked!

That evening it dried up somewhat, and after our evening meal I went out for a bit of a recce stroll. Directly behind the hut towered the enormous and dizzyingly steep west face. Originally, the lads had chosen to go for a long route up this side, but reality soon kicked in, and the scale and unrelenting verticality combined with the prospect of three on a rope, not to mention at least one pendulum section made me pause for thought. I scrambled up a nearby top which looked across a wide gully to

Beneath the east face of Naranjo de Bulnes.
Photo: Neil Smith.

the tower and soon had a good view of the east face. Although still a massive sweeping wall, this friendlier looking side would be in the sun early and would dry out quicker from the recent rain. Armed with this insight, I returned to the hut, where I enjoyed some of the fine red wine I was going to pay for.

As luck would have it, a party of Welsh trekkers was installed in the refugio as well. Neil and Craig had established they were staying in the area for a few days and one of their number fancied a route. It was decided that Craig and our new friend would partner up, while Neil and I would form the other pair. I then broached the subject of the east face, and met with little objection, surprisingly. By end of the evening we had sorted kit out and chosen our respective routes, Neil and I opting for the fine looking *Amistad con el Diablo*, a 250m route which would go at around E1 5a/b, apparently.

The morning brought some low cloud and cool air. The hut warden however assured us that round the corner on the east side it would soon burn off and we would be bathed in sunshine, which was more than enough encouragement for us. We shouldered our sacks and set off. Within an hour we found ourselves below the tremendous pale wall of limestone which formed the east face. True to the guardian's word, the sun now shone brightly on the wall, which looked magnificent. Our route was identified, and it looked a fine line indeed, taking a fairly direct and elegant way up the centre of the face, which grew progressively steeper with each pitch. This route was first climbed in 1980, so it is of fairly modern vintage too.

Neil opted to belay first, and received no arguments from me. The rock looked inviting and I was keen to get moving. There is always something exciting about climbing on a new crag for the first time, the senses seem sharper, the eyes a little more focused. There may have been an element of nervousness and trepidation on my part, not knowing the local grading or style of climbing required, but it was great to get moving upwards at last. I felt I was meeting a new friend and starting to get acquainted.

The initial slabby pitch went at around Severe I felt and offered good but spaced protection. The rock was sharper than I had expected, but the friction was excellent. Looking up from the base it had been difficult to judge distance, and as I arrived at the belay, a horizontal ledge atop a large flake, I was surprised to find there was only five metres of rope remaining. The flake offered plenty of choice for gear though. Some bomber anchors were set up and Neil was soon following.

The second pitch was a little steeper. Neil moved confidently, but did remark on the lack of protection. Where were all those Spanish bolts we wondered? Perhaps they would show up on the upper, steeper pitches. The rock at this lower section was riddled with little solution channels or

Neil leads Pitch 2. Photo: Alan Wilson.

canalizos and small pockets, the edges of which were sharp and unforgiving on the fingers, and also difficult to protect, tending to be all similar in size, so that once the couple of appropriate-sized bits of gear was used, then nothing else tended to fit very well.

On the third pitch the angle started to increase from slab to wall, and the gear got a little harder to find. A few shaky nuts offered at least psychological protection as I ran out many metres of rope above a decent Friend. I recall looking down and thinking the distance between pro was more in line with a winter route. As is usual in such situations Neil shouted occasional words of encouragement to spur me on, which I largely ignored. There was nothing for it but to accept that this was the style of the climb, keep calm, and carry on. Friction played a big part on this climb, and by this point we had learned not to waste too much time seeking the really positive incut hold or elusive jug, as they did not exist. A good deal of the moves were not in themselves difficult, just linking many of them together with little in the way of solid protection was often the challenge. In some ways it reminded a little of the Arrow Wall climbs in Glen Coe, sort of E1 V Diff style, but steeper.

Neil led the fourth pitch in fine style, cheerfully ignoring the exposure he managed to fiddle in a few nuts and even included a couple of chicken heads for variety. I was impressed. As I departed the belay to join him the clouds moved in and the temperature dropped. Continuing upwards, I could see neither Neil nor the ledge below. The grey mist swirled around me and created an almost winter-like atmosphere. Hopefully it would clear enough for us to identify the line of the next pitch.

We exchanged gear at the stance and consulted our photocopied topo. There appeared to be a traverse under some flake-like feature followed by a fairly blank section of wall. I headed up and soon found an undercling traverse off to the right, which was fairly positive for the hands if not the feet. I did fiddle in a couple of solid nuts though, which improved my outlook. Above this I set off into the mist, scanning for a bolt. There are a few spaced out along the length of the route, but with poor visibility and the grey rock it was always hard to spot them at any distance. After forty cloudy metres I at last arrived at the hanging belay, complete with chain and bolts. I could feel rather than see the exposure below me, and was glad to find a good hex placement to back things up. Calling down to Neil to follow, I felt a bit of a chill set in. 'Weather like this we can get in Scotland' I thought.

Neil arrived soon enough. We probably both had a sense of unease at the conditions, being unfamiliar with the weather patterns one can expect in the area. He wasted no time in gearing up, anxious perhaps to push on in case the situation continued to deteriorate. It looked like we could expect at least close to a full rope length, after which the guide was a bit vague. However, several routes also seemed to converge at that

Alan looks for a bolt.   Photo: Neil Smith.

point, so perhaps the way above would be clearer then. Our spirits remained high though. We felt confident that we had cracked it, and the face held no more surprises for us, now that we knew this was no bolt-ridden 'holiday climb'.

After some time, with a few pregnant pauses of rope movement in between, I at last heard a muffled shout to follow. He seemed so far away, which made sense of course, there being only a few metres of rope remaining. With condensation dripping off the end of my nose I headed off, initially continuing up the blank slabby wall, then my way was barred by a small bulging overhang. The rope led off to the right and I spied a good runner, one of the first really sound bits of gear in quite a while. This overhang then turned into a steep little semi-corner feature, which, after the open slab and wall below caught me off guard somewhat. There was a bit of off-balance thrutching and reaching up high, fingers searching for a good slot in the back of the corner. After a few such moves the rock eased back somewhat into more open and friendly territory.

I moved up quickly, not having to pause too much to clean gear, so Neil had obviously rattled up that section in confident mood. The ropes were taken in smoothly, and I wondered if we were within a pitch of the top yet. Soon enough what looked like a little niche or sentry box feature came into view, which would explain the distant sound of Neil's earlier shouts. Suddenly, I could see into the slot, and could barely believe what I saw. The niche was actually a complete passage through the wall,

Neil follows Pitch 5.
Photo: Alan Wilson.

beyond which lay the south face, cloud free and bathed in sunlight and warmth. This passage was like some golden eye of the needle in the mountain, entirely unexpected and very welcome.

Neil was ensconced on the other side, roll up jammed in the corner of his mouth, looking deservedly satisfied. What a spectacular pitch to lead. He must have been as surprised as I had been. I removed my sack and handed it through the gap, then followed myself. From the belay we could see it was an easy steep scramble to the summit ridge. The bright sunlight reflected off the pale rock, and we had to shield our eyes as we looked up and across those final fifty metres.

After coiling the ropes, we beetled up, dumping the sacks en route at a set of sturdy chains which marked the first of four long abseils down the south face. We were soon on the summit, complete with little Madonna statuette. Excellent views across the Picos and beyond out to the distant blue Atlantic, obscured here and there by patches of low cloud below, such as we had just climbed through. Following pictures and handshakes, we set off back to the anchors, wondering if we would be able to get back to the hut in time for supper. Our stomachs were rumbling, but we faced a 200m abseil. Not a good time to relax yet or let our guard down.

The descent was routine and uneventful, though the belay points were in a direct line and close to a full rope length apart. As the sun was starting to dip, the mist moved in again, and soon we were back in the murk, but also on the ground, so all was good. Collecting the spare gear we had left at the base, we trotted off in the direction of the refugio. Above us we could hear the shouts and the clank of karabiners and climbing gear in the fog, the sound of other climbers descending. We shouted up words of encouragement and offered to eat their supper if they were not back soon. Neither of us speaks Welsh, so I have no idea if the response was good or bad.

Back at the hut we enjoyed a good meal and a bottle or three of wine. A well earned repast for our efforts. Craig and our Welsh friend arrived in time to eat after all, but unfortunately had abseiled off below the summit, not knowing they were within a rope length of the golden eye and the top.

The next day Neil and Craig headed back to the south face, and climbed the voie normale in grand conditions, so I was pleased Craig reached the summit after all. A successful outcome for everyone then. I spent some time scrambling on the nearby peaks, enjoying the rough limestone and marvellous vistas. In the following couple of days we enjoyed a PD ascent of the Picos's highest summit, Torre de Cerredo at 2648m and, following another night in the Casa Cipriano, a great trek through the deep Cares Gorge complete with a swim in the cool green river, before heading home and back to the offshore grind, but at least we now had something new to talk about in the tea-shack.

STRANGE HAPPENINGS AT BEN ALDER COTTAGE

By Paddy Buckley

JUST AFTER THE Great War of 1914–18 Joseph McCook, a deer forester, left his lonely and isolated cottage on the north-western shore of Loch Ericht, where he and his family had lived for almost forty years. He loaded his few possessions into a boat and rowed nine miles up the loch to Ben Alder Lodge, where he spent the last years of his working life before retiring to Newtonmore. He died there at the Cottage Hospital on 4 July 1933 at the age of 85.

'He was a very fine type of Highland stalker, level-headed and sensible.' Thus wrote the Reverend Archibald Eneas Robertson, Minister for the parish of the Braes of Rannoch from 1907–20. Robertson, in 1901, was the first man to complete the Munros, and became President of the Scottish Mountaineering Club from 1930–2. During his journeys into the Badenoch hills, he would occasionally stay with the McCooks at Ben Alder Cottage, having called there for the first time in 1893. One of McCook's granddaughters, Nan Michael, who lived at the Cottage until she was 15, remembered the visits of a Minister, on a walking trip from Rannoch to Dalwhinnie, who gave her some round shiny metal objects. Never having seen coins before she threw them into the stream!

Ben Alder Cottage around 1905, with McCook, his wife and their youngest daughter outside.
Photo: SMC Image Archive (A.E. Robertson Collection).

By the early twenties the uninhabited cottage had deteriorated. No one was willing to live in such an isolated place. A new head stalker, Finlay McIntosh, came to Ben Alder Lodge on 3 June 1920, and he had the Cottage put into good repair. He installed a watcher, Magnus McLeod, from Skye, but Magnus found it too lonely. So the Cottage was lived in only occasionally by the Estate gillies and stalkers, and more frequently by travellers – tramps, walkers, fishermen, poachers – and bit by bit the woodwork vanished into their fires.

By the end of the Twenties a new sort of traveller was on the move around Loch Ericht; the navvy. In September 1928 Balfour and Beatty began work on the vast Grampian Electricity Scheme, and over 1000 men, mainly from the Western Isles and Ireland, started boring tunnels and building dams on Lochs Rannoch, Ericht and Tummel. Construction camps were erected at both ends of Loch Ericht, the western camp incorporating a Roman Catholic chapel. The old right of way from Rannoch to Dalwhinnie (shown on Roy's map of 1755) became busy once again, and Ben Alder Cottage became a regular halfway house, where tramps and navvies met and swapped stories by the bothy fire. And very soon there were ghosts in the cottage where McCook had lived for forty years.

A good account of these times was given in *Happy Hawkers* (1937) by Elizabeth and Ian McPherson. Ian had been a ghillie on the Ben Alder Estate, and in order to frighten away unwelcome travellers, had invented a ghost at McCook's Cottage.

> The house was haunted by a woman who once took refuge there from a storm. She was storm-stayed until hunger crazed her and she killed and ate her child. She was seen passing through Rannoch so wild-eyed with despair that no one dared to cross her path. Some said that she returned to the wastes of Rannoch, driven by remorse, and was lost in the morasses of that place.

The stalker Finlay McIntosh could see the value of such a story. When asked by a navvy for his opinion, he replied;

> The truth of it, how can I tell? She went past here with the child that's truth I know. She had no child when she came to Rannoch, that's truth I've heard. What happened to the child?

Finlay's daughter, Eileen MacPherson, who kept the Dalwhinnie shop in 1988, was adamant that it was her father who propagated the story of the 'Ghost House' as a ruse to deter unauthorised visitors. She grew up at Ben Alder Lodge, and she and her husband Johnnie, a former stalker on the Ardverikie Estate, were both familiar with the local history and legends. Elizabeth McPherson (later Mrs Bremner of Nethybridge) admitted that at the time *Happy Hawkers* was published, she and her husband were freelance writers keen to sell their stories wherever they could. A good story was more important than scholarly research.

Thus after centuries of peace and quiet the Badenoch hills were visited by new groups of travellers. First the working men, the surveyors engineers and navvies, and then as the Twenties gave way to the Thirties, came those out of work, or those seeking some brief escape from hard times in the towns and cities. (The atmosphere of this period is preserved in Alastair Borthwick's classic account, *Always a Little Further.*) The hills were being used as places for recreation.

In 1938 Bob Grieve (then an apprentice civil engineer but later Sir Robert Grieve, Chairman of the Highlands and Islands Development Board) went into Ben Alder with his friend Tom Robertson, who had heard of a loch at over 2000ft where marvellous trout could be caught. They stayed at Ben Alder Cottage for almost a week, found the famous loch, and fished it to their hearts' content. On the last night of their stay they were disturbed by strange sounds at midnight for which they could find no explanation. Similar uncanny noises were heard on another visit, years later, and three groups of friends also reported happenings that could not be explained. I spoke to Bob on 5 December 1987 at the SMC Dinner and asked him about his visits to Ben Alder Cottage. That one trip in 1939, almost 50 years ago, was still etched in his memory. In essence the story he told me was the same one he had recorded on tape in 1973 for Chris Brasher, then Editor of *Mountain Life*, and which Chris later published in the Dec '73/Jan '74 issue, assuring his readers that although the author's name had been concealed 'because he is fed up with having his leg pulled', this was no leg-pull.

Some additional information came up during our conversation. The note from F. McIntosh, Head Stalker, which Tom had found on Bob's rucksack, had been kept by Tom. It said, 'You must leave this house immediately – you are not permitted to stay here'. Bob conceded that the note could have been placed on his sack during the day when they were out fishing the loch, and that he could perhaps have failed to spot it when they returned. Head stalkers are forthright men, and if Finlay had called there in the evening he would surely have confronted the two trespassers and told them to leave.

Ben Alder Cottage stands at the junction of two ancient rights of way; one a low-level route along Loch Ericht to Dalwhinnie; the other a high track going over Bealach Cumhann and Bealach Dubh and down to Culra and Glen Pattack. The present Ben Alder Cottage probably dates back to 1871 when Sir John Ramsden, owner of Ardverikie and Ben Alder estates, inaugurated a vast programme of building and renovation, road making, fencing and tree planting. But there had been a bothy at Ben Alder Bay in former times, and certainly during the period just after Culloden. Prince Charles Edward Stuart was said to have spent one night in a bothy known as 'Doom's Smoky Place' before meeting Cluny McPherson. Bob Grieve claimed that in 1938 he could trace the outlines of an older building at Ben Alder Cottage, on the same site but at an angle to the present structure, and that this could have been 'Doom's Smoky Place'. If there are ghosts there perhaps they sprang up after Culloden.

Bob related another strange occurrence. Some years after the Great War a former officer in the Royal Engineers was walking from Rannoch to Dalwhinnie, and he stayed overnight at Ben Alder Cottage at a time when it was inhabited by a stalker and his wife. During the night he heard what seemed like footsteps in the adjacent room. Next morning the wife explained that a semi-tame stag was in the habit of banging its antlers on the outside walls, but she told this story so unconvincingly and with such a look of guilt upon her face that the visitor was sure that she was covering up the real truth, which was that the cottage was haunted. A nice tale, but after McCook left, circa 1920, no other family ever lived at Ben Alder Cottage.

Bob Grieve's original story first appeared in print in 1951, in *Undiscovered Scotland*, written by Bob's friend and fellow SMC member, Bill Murray:

> …the previous tenant, a stalker named McCook, had hanged himself on the back of the front door.

Bill was quoting Bob Grieve, who told me (December 1987) that the suicide story was 'common knowledge among climbers at that time', although he was not aware of it when he first visited Ben Alder Cottage.

The alleged suicide caused great distress among McCook's descendants, and Murray published an apology in SMC Journal Vol. 24, No 142, April 1951, p. 355:

> I have been informed by the Rev. A. E. Robertson that the rumour, current among climbers for many years past and quoted in my book, "Undiscovered Scotland," connecting the name of the stalker McCook with the alleged suicide at Ben Alder Cottage, is without foundation. McCook died in his bed at Newtonmore, honoured and respected. Mr Robertson assures me that he was a very fine type of Highland stalker, level-headed and sensible.

By this time the Rev A.E. Robertson had died (1870–1958; an obituary notice appeared in the SMC Journal Vol. 26, pp. 362–6, May 1959), but his widow, Winifred, was ever vigilant in the cause of truth. In a letter published in the Scotsman on 1 August 1973, p. 6, she wrote from 17 Cluny Gardens, Edinburgh on 28 July 1973:

> Sir, I much enjoyed 'To the wilderness and back' in the Scotsman today, until I came to the repetition of the cruel untruth of Mr McCook's suicide. Sixteen or eighteen years ago this appeared under the hand of W H Murray. My late husband, the Rev A E Robertson was greatly shocked and asked W H Murray to make a public apology, which was done, I think in your columns. Mr McCook, in old age, died in his bed in either Kingussie or Newtonmore, I forget which. My husband, when minister of the Parish of Braes of

Rannoch, frequently stayed with the McCooks at Benalder Cottage. There is a theory that certain workmen on a very large 'scheme' were enjoying large scale poaching and purposely circulated the suicide tale to deter visitors.

A similar disclaimer appeared in the *Scotsman*, but this failed to kill the rumour. A centrepiece spread called 'To the Wilderness and Back' was published in the *Weekend Scotsman* on 28 July 1973. Author Harry Reid did not actually visit Ben Alder Cottage, but wrote:

> The cottage is notable chiefly from the fact that it is haunted, a stalker called McCook being alleged to have hung himself there.

There are a couple of similar tales concerning the local Doctor's visits to the Cottage. On one occasion the Doctor was said to have arrived in such a state of exhaustion that he had to be put to bed and Mrs McCook had to perform the operation herself. On another, Mrs McCook was in childbirth; the Doctor came in blizzard conditions, saved the child, but was unable to save poor Mrs McCook. The true source of these mythical exploits can be found in the archives of the Carnegie Hero Fund Trust. Joseph McCook aged 61 became seriously ill with pneumonia; his daughter walked out in terrible conditions to fetch the Doctor, Donald MacDonald from Laggan. The Doctor set out at 7 a.m. on 9 January 1910, but because of severe gales, swollen streams, snow and ice, did not reach his patient until 6 p.m. He stayed overnight to see his patient through the crisis, and for his efforts was awarded a medal by the Carnegie Trust. The truth yields an even better story than the rumours, although equal credit should perhaps have gone to the daughter, who must have made the double journey in very difficult conditions.

I should interject here a note about the longevity of the McCooks. Joseph was 85 when he died, his mother Betsy was 97, his sister Hannah was 84, his wife Annie was 84, her father Donald was 82, and her mother Jane was well over 80 when she died. The fresh air of Badenoch was undoubtedly beneficial!

Sid Scroggie was a mountaineer who was blinded during the last war, but who still managed to tramp the Scottish hills. His first visit to Ben Alder Cottage was in November 1963. During the night he and his companion heard a series of tappings, scratchings, footsteps and groans, which although mysterious did not appear 'in any way frightening'. The next morning Sid experienced a poltergeist phenomenon, in which a packet of biscuits flew across the room from the mantelpiece to the opposite side of the room. Sid has explained this as a manifestation of the tension between him and his companion. On a later visit with his daughter Mary, some tension had grown up between them, giving rise, Sid believes, to another poltergeist phenomenon; the bothy door crashed open for no obvious physical reason.

Ben Alder and Ardverikie were the estates of the Duke of Gordon until about 1794, when they were exchanged with Cluny McPherson for land in Speyside. In 1836 the Marquis of Abercorn leased Ben Alder and cleared off the sheep. In 1844 he took a further lease on Ardverikie and cleared it of sheep also. Thus he had an enormous forest but it was poorly stocked with only about 100 of the original wild deer. His head forester was James Cattanach – 'one of the most honest and experienced foresters' – who doubled the size of the herd, bringing in deer from another area. In 1844 Queen Victoria and Prince Albert visited Ardverikie, and at one stage were interested in buying it. In the year of the Queen's visit, the proprietor, out of a total estate rental of less than £2000 received £1360 for the deer forest alone. In 1850 he made over the leases to Lord Henry Bentinck, who kept the forests until his death on the last day of 1870. Sir John Ramsden bought Ardverikie in 1871 and in 1873 added the adjacent Strathmashie estate erecting a deer-proof fence on the eastern march between Loch Ericht and Loch Laggan, thus preventing the deer from straying on the cultivated lands along the valley of the Spey. In 1874 he split the huge estate into Ben Alder and Ardverikie. Between 1871 and 1883 he spent £180,000 on 76 miles of internal fencing, 43 miles of march fencing for which the expense was shared by the neighbouring estates, 473 miles of drains, 20 miles of carriage road and 18 miles of pony paths and walks; 18 new houses were built and 13 restored. He began planting Ardverikie in 1875 and by the end of the Great War, the plantation had reached 10,500 acres. In 1883 Ardverikie employed seven foresters on 28,000 acres.

Joseph McCook, born towards the end of 1849 at Newtonmore, was the second of two children born to George McCook and his wife Elizabeth Grant. George was the son of a gamekeeper and was born at Insh in 1804; he was a blacksmith and carried out his work in Newtonmore where he died of phthisis at the age of 57. Joseph went to school in Newtonmore. By 1871, at the age of 21, he was working as a mason's labourer at Ardverikie Lodge, one of 24 tradesmen; stone quarriers, masons, joiners, labourers, a blacksmith and a carter; who were at work for Sir John Ramsden on a major improvement of the estate. One of Joseph's mates was a lad of 18, Alexander Bain. Three miles away at the farm of Gallovie, working as a servant, was Alexander's older sister, Annie Bain. Ten years later, Joseph had become a deer forester, living with his widowed mother at the 'Forester's House Ben Alder', i.e. Ben Alder Cottage. In 1884 Joseph married Annie Bain, the third of ten children born to Donald Bain and Jane McDonald. They lived at the isolated cottage on the shore of Loch Ericht, a long way from anywhere, and raised three children. The Census reveals that they and their parents all spoke Gaelic. Annie died in 1931 at the age of 84; Joseph died two years later, at the age of 85. Their grandchildren still live in the Spey valley, at Laggan, Newtonmore, and Kingussie, showing a family of at least six generations living in the same small area.

CHEATING THE REAPER

By John Burns

SO THIS IS HOW it feels. Dying I mean. It ends here, alone, afraid, crouching on a ledge, struggling for breath, vomiting quietly. A rock, a metre square, lands on the ledge beside me, exploding on impact. The next one won't miss. I don't have long. Close by a twenty-metre rock gendarme topples slowly forward like a drunken old man and collapses. And there is the noise. The roar all around me, so loud the mountain trembles and my ribs reverberate. The rope pulls hard at my waist, a reminder that it leads down to Steve's lifeless body. He has already stepped into the darkness, I wait at the threshold. A leaf brushes my face, just the gentlest of touches, looking up I see a tree falling past. Hurled to its death by the monster it reaches out to me with its finger tips. Through the fog of terror and despair that clouds my brain, a thought struggles to be heard. I am not dead, I realise, not yet. Somehow I have survived the last ten seconds. Perhaps, just maybe, I can survive the next.

I had always thought that birds were dumb, not that I gave the matter any thought, I'm no ornithologist. One of many things I learned that day is that they are smarter than they look. We were descending, the hot sun had thawed the ice making it too unstable. I relaxed – no more hard climbing today – and looked out, across a thousand snow-capped peaks of the Canadian Rockies. I looked down and noticed, with mild curiosity, that in the forest, a thousand feet below, a line of birds was flying away through the tree tops. There were brown ones, white ones, fat ones and thin ones – eagles, sparrows and pigeons, all were leaving the forest at the foot of the climb in a ragged line. They were flying away, I now realise, as fast as their feathers could carry them, because they knew something I didn't. They were smarter than me. They knew that in the snow basin, way above the ice climb, a crack had ripped across the face of the snow pack. A monster was coming, and the birds knew it.

I dreamed ice in those days, lived it, breathed it, and spent long summers waiting for the first kiss of frost to turn the glens sparkling white. I began my climbing in the Northern Corries of the Cairngorms, survived my novice years and endured the endless weekdays waiting for Sundays on Lochnagar, Creag Meagaidh or Ben Nevis. My days in the winter hills were Technicolor, days that lived bright in the memory, shining amongst the grey every day. *Green Gully*, *Zero*, *Emerald*, *The Curtain,* these were gifts from the mountain Gods on rare bright days when the sunlight seemed to splinter on the ice. The disappointment of damp black winters led Steve and me to look far afield for places where the ice God lived. Canada was the place, we decided, in Canada it would be cold and we would have all the ice we dreamt of. Reality, and global warming, conspired to disappoint and we caught the warmest Canadian winter for twenty years, a fact that had sealed our fate.

I noticed something else unusual as I was watching the birds leave, that sunlit Canadian day, it was going dark. I remember thinking how odd that was, curious, peculiar perhaps, but of no real concern. It was warm, way warmer than it should have been and water was dripping from the surface of the ice as we climbed the lower pitches. We had forgotten to check the avalanche warnings and as we climbed our ice screws melted out. The mountain had tried to tell us but we had not listened. The signs were all there but we couldn't see them. We had tunnel vision; all we could see was the shining ice that had drawn us thousands of miles from Scotland. The seeds of catastrophe are frequently found in a collection of small inconsequential errors. I was watching the birds scatter when Steve called out, as I turned to reply... the mountain exploded.

At moments like these, time becomes distorted and the memory a series of disjointed moments. The monster leapt over the cliff hundreds of feet above us and landed on top of us bringing with him tonnes of wet snow, shattered ice, rocks and trees. He vented his wrath on anything that stood in his way and we were very definitely in his way. I was just to the side of the icefall and Steve was retreating down the climb towards me, one rope clipped to a runner behind him with our second rope as back-up, when the monster grabbed him and hurled him from the mountain. I watched in horror as he disappeared into the maelstrom and thousands of tonnes of rock and ice poured down on top of both of us. Moments later I knew he must be going over the cliff below us, I had to stop him. I'm not a brave man, I knew that if I locked off the belay the shock would hit me and if the belay failed I'd be catapulted into oblivion. I hesitated, transfixed by fear while the battle within me raged. Then something happened. I watched, as though from somewhere far away, as my arm swung across my body and locked off the belay. I had been on a winter climbing course at Glenmore Lodge and they told me to use a body belay, to hold a fall by gradually slowing the climber down in order to protect the belay from a sudden shock. What they hadn't told me is what it feels like to hold a falling climber in the grip of a monster. The moment I locked off the rope I was convulsed with pain, the rope tried to separate my pelvis from my chest. It cut deep into my body cracking my ribs. Just when I could hold on no longer the rope broke and I collapsed on to the ledge, gasping and vomiting, waiting for death.

I learned something then. When it gets really bad, surviving the whole thing feels too much, so I broke it down into small chunks, bite-sized pieces of survival. Just get through the next ten seconds, I thought, then worry about the rest. I was pressed hard against the rock face whilst the monster hurled everything it could at me. Rocks, trees and wet slab thundered down. The certainty of death was replaced by some glimmer of hope. I spotted a peg I'd missed before and stepped out from the meagre shelter afforded by the stance to clip into it, anything to maximise the chance of survival. If you have seen the film *Saving Private Ryan* you'll have some idea of what it was like breaking cover. Remember the scene when they land on the beach and step out into a hail of fire. That's exactly what it was like. As I clipped the peg a rock playfully bounced off my right hand breaking a couple of fingers but, much worse, bringing a temporary paralysis. I will never know how I wasn't killed clipping that peg, in retrospect it was probably a mistake but there was only one mantra going through my mind at the time, 'protect the belay'.

As quickly as it had arrived the monster departed, its mischief done. The sun came out and the birds returned. It was hard to believe that, moments before, I had been fighting for my life. It was as though nothing had happened apart from the fact that the ice climb we had come up no longer existed, at the foot of the crag was a huge cone of debris. The first rope had broken but the second had held, it pulled at my waist, still attached to Steve's body. It seemed so utterly pointless, so stupid, to have come all this way to die on a piece of ice. I didn't call down to Steve, after all there is no point in shouting at a corpse. I tied a prusik knot around the remaining rope and set down to find the remains of my friend, dreading what I was about to meet. Just beneath a small overhang I found him grinning like a baboon, but obviously alive. He had had the presence of mind to roll under the overhang. His lung was punctured, he was bloodied but alive. I will never be more surprised or relieved than I was at that moment. A Park Ranger had been amongst the cars that had stopped on the highway below to watch the spectacle unfold. He called in a helicopter. Twenty minutes later Steve was in hospital and I was standing on a helipad trying to stop shaking.

Every time you tie on, every time you make the first move, you take that chance. If it had ended there, would it have been worth it? The years of climbing in Scotland, seeing the starlight sparkling on the summit of the Ben, the mates, the laughs we had, the good times and the bad, would all have ended there. Somehow we had cheated the Grim Reaper, he had us on his list but we escaped him. I doubt if he was troubled, after all, I'm sure he has pencilled us in for another day. Next time I'm climbing, if I notice it's going dark and, looking down, I see the birds are leaving, I'll know... the Reaper's back.

CAIRNGORMS SIX AND EIGHT TOPS SKI TOURS

By Roger Wild

ADAM WATSON STARTED it all so we have him to thank for our snowy wanderings. Adam's cyberspace alias is 'chionophile' – snow lover, like the ptarmigan and mountain hare. A snow lover he certainly is and his 1962 trip has inspired many other chionophiles to relive his day in the Cairngorms with a variety of differing routes.

Adam's account of his 1962 trip, entitled *Cairngorm Langlauf*, was published in SMCJ 1963 and is well worth reading. His style of writing paints a vivid picture and puts the reader on the hill, sharing the experience with him. The following line from his article demonstrates this style, 'The sun was flooding in a rosy glow over the great bulk of Beinn a' Bhuird and down into the old green mushroom pines of the Quoich.'

Adam recently sent me copies of the photographs which he took on the day and one of these illustrates this article. I must admit to a spine-tingling moment when I received the photographs from Adam by e-mail. When they were taken nearly fifty years ago, I was a primary schoolboy in Lancashire, hardly aware of mountains and knowing nothing of the Cairngorms or ski touring. In our e-mail exchanges we discussed the joy of skiing in the Cairngorms and Adam commented, 'There is nothing to beat the feeling of skiing on good snow with light Scandinavian skis and boots, magical snow slippers and memorable sounds from them!'

Looking towards Ben Macdui and Cairn Toul from west of Beinn a' Bhuird, April 1962.
Photo: Adam Watson.

Adam's route started at Invercauld and took in Ben Avon, Beinn a' Bhuird, Ben Macdui, Cairn Gorm, Braeriach, Cairn Toul and finished in Glen Luibeg. He had skied the well known Four Tops in 1958 and had now added Ben Avon and Beinn a' Bhuird to create the Six Tops ski tour.

It was eighteen years later in the spring of 1980 before the Six Tops were again skied in a day. The trip by Graham Boyd and Graham Keir of the Etchachan Club is recorded in SMCJ 1981. Speaking to Graham Keir thirty years later, his enthusiasm was evident as he recalled the trip which was done while he was a student at Aberdeen University. Graham provided the following timings which are not shown in the SMCJ article:

05.40 Departed Luibeg Bothy
10.15 Cairn Toul
12.00 Braeriach
15.00 Cairn Gorm
16.20 Ben Macdui
17.20 Hutchison Hut
20.00 Beinn a' Bhuird
22.20 Ben Avon
00.20 The Howff

Graham used Fischer Europa 99 Nordic skis with three-pin bindings and leather boots.

Adam published a note in SMCJ 1983 in which he responds to the notes of the above 1980 trip. He provides some useful comments for any aspiring tourers – top tips which still apply today. One comment says,

As long as the weather is not downright bad, snow conditions are more important than weather. Even in good weather a tour is difficult on snow too soft, too hard, a continual mixture of both, or too ridged. Snow was good on most of my 1962 tour, but bad on some parts. Much better conditions occasionally occur over a big area and altitude range. In the best conditions, skiing is almost effortless, but such conditions are rare in Scotland; I have seen them only on one trip in the last three years.

On Easter Sunday 1984 Raymond Simpson and Rob Ferguson completed a round trip of the Six Tops in 24 hours from Derry (which included 5 hours sleep at Corrour!). Skis were carried at times although all the downhill sections were skied. Nordic skis were used. Further details and timings are shown in SMCJ 1984.

In February 1986 Blyth Wright and I completed a round trip in just under 24 hours. The snow cover was so complete that we removed skis only to go into Corrour bothy and for fitting skins. The following is a summary of the trip written from memory two decades later.

I was at Glenmore Lodge having just finished a course, when I heard that Blyth was planning a long ski tour in the Cairngorms. I was curious to know what he had in mind and when I asked him about the trip he kindly asked me along. We agreed to meet at midnight, drove to Coire Cas car park and made our way up through the ski resort to Cairn Gorm summit.

It was a clear cold night as we set off and followed a long traversing descent across the lips of the Northern Corries to reach the Lairig Ghru near the foot of Sròn na Lairige. The snow was quite deep and we had to break a trail up to Braeriach, arriving as the red dawn lit up the rim of the Garbh Coire. It was spectacular to be up here at first light with the whole of the Cairngorms covered in pristine snow. Inspired by the views and the magnificence of our surroundings we soon reached Cairn Toul and the descent down Coire Odhar to Corrour bothy. A brief stop for refreshments propelled us upwards by the Allt Clach nan Taillear (Tailors' Burn) to the summit of Ben Macdui where we bumped into Allen Fyffe with a Glenmore Lodge group.

This was the point which Blyth had previously identified where we would need an 'injection of moral fibre'. However, the weather and snow conditions were superb and we were feeling fresh so no additional fibre was required to send us swooping down to Loch Etchachan and Glen Derry. More food and drink was taken and a short steep climb brought us to the high ground of the Moine Bhealaidh and superb conditions for Nordic 'kick and glide' technique. We soon reached Beinn a' Bhuird and continued on soft snow down to the Sneck. We left our rucksacks here for the final climb up to Ben Avon. The snow cover was so complete that we could easily ski to the top of the highest tor.

We returned from Ben Avon to the Sneck and climbed up towards Beinn a' Bhuird, cutting off before the summit to head towards the Fords of Avon. The mist came down as we descended and we saw very little from this point onwards. From the Fords of Avon the snow was knee-deep even on skis and we had some difficulty deciding whether we had reached Loch Avon. It was misty and dark and pre-GPS technology so one of us stood still while the other skied around in a wide circle to see if the ground was flat. It was flat and so we concluded that we had reached Loch Avon. Careful compass work and tired legs took us to The Saddle and then up to Ciste Mhearad and our start point.

The round trip had taken 23 hours 25 minutes. We both used Nordic skis with 3-pin bindings and leather boots. Blyth's skis were Rossignol Descente and mine were Fischer Europa 99.

The following year, in April 1987, Kenneth MacIver completed a traverse of the Six Tops from east to west. The trip took 15½ hours. His route started at Linn of Avon and finished at Achlean in Glen Feshie. The trip is recorded in SMCJ 1988. Speaking to Kenneth over twenty years later, he referred to Adam's article about his 1962 trip in which he mentioned that the grand finish to his tour would be a downhill run to

Glen Feshie. This was the inspiration for Kenneth's traverse. Kenneth used Rossignol Chamois skis with 3-pin bindings and leather boots.

Alastair Hubbard skied the Six Tops from Cairn Toul to Ben Avon in April 2001. He started at Linn of Dee and finished at the Keiloch by Invercauld Bridge. The trip took 16 hours. The timings were:

Linn of Dee	Hours
Derry Lodge	1¼
Corrour	2½
Cairn Toul	4
Sgòr an Lochain Uaine	4½
Braeriach	6
Lairig Ghru	6½
Ben Macdui	7½
Cairn Gorm	8¾
Fords of Avon	10¼
Beinn a' Bhuird	12½
Ben Avon	13½
Keiloch	16

Alastair used Atomic skis and leather Alico boots and he reports:

There was snow down to the Lairig Ghru, some walking was needed from the Saddle to Fords of Avon and on the approaches in and out. Good spring snow in settled high pressure conditions (firm underfoot at first with early morning inversion which gave way to sunshine for most of the day).

In May 2001 Ian Murray and Colin Bruce completed a trip starting from Corrour bothy and finishing at Loch Builg where they were picked up by motor vehicle. Ian recollects that they had a poor night's sleep at Corrour due to late arrivals and mice rustling about in the bothy. They set off at first light after a breakfast of coffee and bacon rolls and ascended Cairn Toul, Sgòr an Lochain Uaine and Braeriach before descending to the Lairig Ghru and climbing up to Ben Macdui. Ian recalled that he left his ice axe on Ben Macdui and returned alone to collect it. The skies were blue and visibility was perfect. He distinctly remembers hearing the crunch, crunch sound of footsteps on gravel despite the fact that the plateau was entirely snow covered. Was this Am Fear Liath Mòr, the big grey man of Ben Macdui?

Eight Tops

The Six Tops tour takes in the five highest summits plus Ben Avon which is the eighth highest. Not included in the Six Tops is Beinn Mheadhoin which is higher than Ben Avon. Beinn Mheadhoin is conveniently on the way between Ben Macdui and Beinn a' Bhuird and adds only an extra hour so it is a logical step to include it. Sgòr an Lochain Uaine was promoted to Munro status and hardly adds any time. So with a fairly minor addition to the original Six Tops route a traverse over the eight highest Munros can be made, hence the Eight Tops. The round trip covers 60 kilometres and 4000 metres ascent.

I've had a few goes at skiing the Eight Tops during the recent snowy winters. The snow conditions in April 2008 were stunning, with a good covering of firm snow which gave very fast going. Unfortunately the light easterly winds which provided generally superb conditions also shrouded much of the high ground with white-out conditions slowing progress. Being inside a ping-pong ball is a good description. I bailed out at the Lairig an Laoigh and enjoyed a relaxing ski back to Loch Avon and on to Coire Cas.

In February 2010 the whole of the Cairngorms were plastered with a thick cover of snow, much of it in the form of five centimetres of surface hoar. I set off from Cairn Gorm at 6 a.m. and almost floated down on the surface hoar to the Lairig Ghru at the foot of Sròn na Lairige. Trailbreaking up the trackless snow to Braeriach was delightful and soon I was gazing across to Sgòr an Lochain Uaine and Cairn Toul. The whole of the Lairig Ghru was completely covered and the view across to the eastern plateau was stunning. It was a day to be savoured. The thick covering of surface hoar was not conducive to fast travel but it was a joy to ski over, with every stride extending a brand new track which had never previously existed and would never exist again. At times like this it is fascinating to think of the process which produced the conditions I was enjoying and how it would all disappear, make its way to the sea and then, hopefully, reappear in future winters. The descent into Coire

Cairn Toul from Braeriach, February 2010.   Photo: Roger Wild.

Odhar was great fun and a straight line took me directly to the foot of the Allt Clach nan Taillear (Tailors' Burn). Time for tea. The 24-hour concept faded away somewhere to the back of my mind as I brewed up and gazed around in the glorious sunshine and the white wonderland. Where else could one possibly wish to be?

A direct line took me to Ben Macdui and a good glug of water from the bottle which I had filled in the Lairig Ghru. Unless I stopped to melt snow on the stove, there would be no more water from here until reaching the River Avon, several hours away. An easy descent took me to Loch Etchachan and the climb up to Beinn Mheadhoin. I had seen nobody all day and I had this huge white wilderness all to myself. A sliver of moon had risen in the dusky sky as I dropped down the eastern slopes and negotiated one of the steepest descents of the tour, down to the Lairig an Laoigh. This slope had previously been quite testing on Nordic gear but this evening it was straightforward with soft snow on a firm base. I considered stopping to brew up in the Lairig but was reluctant to break the mystical spell cast by hours of gliding over the fairy tale snow. My skis had become Adam's magical snow slippers with their memorable sounds. As I crossed the Moine Bhealaidh the moon and stars provided some light and then the night sky clouded over and the world became a torch beam. Some focus was needed to keep the spell going on the long climb up to Beinn a' Bhuird and it almost ebbed away while negotiating the Sneck prior to the climb up to Ben Avon. This eighth and final top was reached 18 hours after leaving Cairn Gorm. All that remained was to turn west to Loch Avon and the final climb back to Cairn Gorm. The day had been magical, mystical and perfect but the trail-breaking had taken its toll. The final leg back to Cairn Gorm took 9 hours and it was fortunate that the magical snow slippers continued to weave their spell as I followed the torch beam along the way.

Reflecting on the stories of these trips, what comes through is that the challenge of the route is secondary. The main event is the landscape and the intimacy with it from travelling light and fast over long distances. Recent winters have provided some outstanding conditions and we can only hope for more to come. Speaking in February 2010 Kenneth MacIver said, 'We thought it was all over – but recent winters have shown that it is firmly back on the agenda.'

The final words are left to Adam Watson with a quotation from his article in SMCJ 1983:

'Settled conditions occur nearly every spring, and you need only one day of them!'

(I apologise to any six or eight tops ski tourers who have not been mentioned. Please get in touch – I would be delighted to hear from you).

THE MEMORY OF WHAT HAS BEEN

(Exploring Longbow Crag in the winter of 1979)

By Gordon Smith

Into my heart an air that kills
From yon far country blows:
What are those blue remembered hills…?[1]

Now, it just so happens that when a south-facing Cairngorm crag is known to be dry, and therefore ill-suited for conventional ice climbing, early in the season and buried in powder snow, it may yet provide excellent winter possibilities. East-facing Hell's Lum Crag, as I was aware from climbing on it during several winters previous to 1979, has seeps of water that trickle down its slabs. These floods freeze well in a cold snap, building up into tremendous ice climbs that can last throughout the winter. On the other hand the slabs on the front face of Longbow Crag, just down the way from Hell's Lum at Stag Rocks, between Amphitheatre Gully and the east end of the crag, are not wet and they lose any snow and ice that has collected on them and dry quickly even under a mid-winter sun. But, in a good winter, early on the days tend to be dark and cold and snowy, and bags of powder snow and a little ice can cling a while under those conditions even to the driest south-facing crags. Thus it was in the cold, dark, snowy days of early December '78, when the Cairngorms were buried deep, the fog was down close to the level of Loch A'an, and the wind was howling, that I wandered alone over the back of Cairngorm to survey those dry Longbow Slabs. And do you know, there were indeed fine winter climbs to be had there after all, of a mixed nature of course; and, moreover, those pretty winter slabs were virgin. I would be the first!

I cannot but remember such things were,
That were most precious to me.[2]

So it was that I opened up the winter's Longbow Campaign by scampering that day up a fine little corner system, buried deep in powder snow, on the arete bordering the right-hand side of Stanky Gully. Many years later I discovered from the guidebook that I had started up the first two pitches of the summer V. Diff *The Tenements* and then continued up a brand new finish, let's call it the 'The Easterhouse Finish', to that route, climbing directly a shadowy corner between Stanky Gully and the 'open

---

1   Alfred Housman, 'Into my Heart an Air That Kills', *A Shropshire Lad*.

2   William Shakespeare, 'MacBeth' Act 4, Sc. 3.

Stag Rocks, Loch Avon Basin . Photo: Andy Nisbet.

corner' pitch of the normal route, followed by a convex granite slab, scarred by cracks and coated in a skim of powder and an inch of windslab, that bulged out of a snowy terrace above the corner and which was tenuous and difficult just to get on to. And, as Grande Finale, there was a steep and hoary buttress, a little on the right, that reached directly to the plateau and almost, it seemed, into the swirling sky. By and by I also spotted that day on my wanderings, three more lines, these on the main slabs to the left, with which to satisfy a later, less solitary, appetite.

The first of those lines, up the 'Wigwag' slab between the vegetated central depression and Stanky Gully, went in late December for I had bumped some place or other into Englishman Mick Fowler, a man of vaulting ambitions indeed and a man always looking for action. Today he may be Michael Fowler Esq., Senior Official with the Department of

Longbow Crag is the dark face to the right of the bottom of Diagonal Gully.

Inland Revenue and World Famous Mountaineer, but then he was just Mick the Tax Man and one of my pals from alpine climbing. Now tell me, what better thing is there to do to an English Tax Man than to make him thoroughly miserable at Christmas time by dragging him through deep drifts of powder snow across the Cairngorm plateau and introducing him to the idiosyncratic techniques and attitude required for Difficult Cairngorm Mixed? Best of all on a foul and stormy day! Although the day was as wild and windy as I could have wished, it turned out to be a superb day of roaring up turfy grooves and tiptoeing scarty granite slabs deep in powder, and swinging bravely over bare overhangs through the driving snow. And of course Mick, hard as nails and not just any old English Tax Man, loved every minute of it; damn his English eyes!

Early, therefore, we two monkish figures, red coated against the bleary grey morning gloaming, left the Fiachaill a' Coire Chais behind and marched resolutely across the plateau. We marched pressed along by shrieking snow squalls and ploughing a trail through the drifting powder, burdened with our gear and cowled against the stinging snow-spray and that blasted wind. We got safely to the bottom of our slab, however, and there, at the foot of a cul-de-sac filled deeply with snow on the right-hand side and not so far from the bottom of Stanky Gully, we started climbing. A few feet up our cul-de-sac we arrived at a rocky blockage which encouraged us to abandon the easy snow and launch ourselves up the main slab on the left. Once on the slab we sneaked around and over bare overhangs, and we scratched our way up snow-choked grooves patched with frozen turf overlooking the vegetated central depression. Thus we forced our passage through falling snow and spindrift slurries and drifted powder towards the left side of a great barrier wall, hidden in the stour, that stretched across the 'Wigwag' slab.

Halfway up the climb, at that barrier wall, and caked like a snowman on the go, Mick climbed up a pedestal and into a niche under an overhang and there he huddled. I can see him even now in my mind's eye; the shivering bureaucrat-in-the-making sporting a long and frozen dreepy hanging from his neb, and cowering in his grotto. While the Tax Man sheltered himself thus, I was directed by that budding executive to get myself back out into the blizzard and up and over the overhang blocking our way. To the left there was a fortunate spot that looked less than the rest. This, therefore, was where the overhang was despatched with axe and hammer stretched out and hooked over the top, and with a mighty, scratching heave and belly roll. Then, climbing on up the snowy grooves and walls and corners above, and chilled and buffeted by rough winds and flying spindrift, I was ready when the rope ran out to claim the recess underneath the next great overhang as my own shelter. This, of course, forced our Tax Man to collect the subsequent dues on his own account, facing up to that horrid final roof with its nasty overhang and awkward, leaning corner above and then the evil weather out in the open. Thereafter, moderate mixed climbing for a rope length or two up the flank of a slabby face patched here and there with frozen turf, blanketed in snow, and blasted by winter gale, led us to the dusk-grey plateau and victory; and the long, deep flog home.

Later, I was faced down by a hulking and irate New Zealander, my colleague at work and recent partner from several dark and stormy adventures on Aladdin's Buttress (new route adventures although at the time we didn't know), flexing his muscles and waving his bushy blond beard and flashing his round blue eyes at me.

'What's this I hear, you little rat. You've been out a-climbing. I heard that you did a new route over at Stag Rocks, you sneaky devil! The shop's closed next Monday so I take it that's where we're going!'

It doesn't do at all, it would seem, for a little rat like me to sneak away and pick off new routes with any old chap while The Big Cat is doing his bit at work and desperate to get out on the hill.

A few days later and it was time to patch things up with Gary Ball, the impatient Kiwi. I forged, together with Gary the Kiwi, therefore, a weary path through the dark chill and clinging snow over the great humpback shoulder of Cairngorm, and back again to the foot of the Longbow Slabs. We had made, over the New Year, plans to pocket for ourselves a Scottish Plum; and there it was, barely seen through morning half light, mists, and falling snow. For right down the ice-glazed, snow-drifted and wind-scoured 'Sand-Pyper' slab between the central vegetated depression and the 'water washed' depression of the summer route *Longbow Direct* was the second of the lines I had spotted before; a slender smear of very thin ice that had wept out of a faint ribbon of cracks with just an occasional wisp of grass and one or two tiny frozen turf divots sticking out of the ice to show where the cracks lay. But for all we could see the world ended in mist, where grey and shadowy overhangs closed in over the slab. It looked hard, very hard and very bold. But difficult and bold were what we had told ourselves we wanted, and so there were no excuses for us in that.

Through the mist and the lightly falling snow that first pitch up the slab was indeed tough and tenuous. Teetering like a drunken gerbil scratching tiptoe step by tiptoe step the steep and slender thread, here a little overlap awkwardly was grappled, there blades of grass delicately were pecked; here half an inch of knifeblade runner was tied off, there an inch of frost and some ice were scraped away and a little Chouinard Stopper slipped behind a tiny flake of granite. Until the ice ahead faded completely and a way forward, and somewhat to the right as it emerged, to more cracks and flakes and bits of ice and patches of snow, had to be scratched out of glazed frosting and patched powder. But there, beyond the bare bit and standing on a snowy flake in the middle of the glazed and powdered slab, and with the rope almost out (and contemplating a numbingly uncomfortable belay half standing on my flake, half hanging from pegs and chocks) despair took the better part of valour. My eye was drawn ever farther away from the straight line towards those grey and shadowy overhangs above, and towards instead a small, snowy clump of turf to my right which was clinging deliriously to the left edge of the central vegetated depression. That clump first had seduced my eye; and then had whispered insistently and magically and, it must be said, quite falsely in my ear,

'Here am I, and I am a Very Fine Belay Stance!'

And thus a horizontal, snow-stenciled crack was shuffled so that that small, snowy, and largely faithless clump of turf could be occupied.

Now, take note of this: as the poet says, there is always one particular thing to keep in the forefront of one's mind before taking a step when its outcome might prove perilous:

> From hence, ye beauties, undeceiv'd,
> Know, one false step is ne'er retriev'd,
> And be with caution bold.[3]

It is, perhaps, a good thing as that wisest of men Mr Whymper once said always to be cautious; to reflect that courage is naught without prudence; to look well to each step and to beware the carnage that awaits the careless. But the traverse to that clump decried prudence! It demanded unthinking boldness! Indeed, it fairly bellowed it out!

'Be a man!' It cried. 'Stand up and step out!'

'Grasp the nettle, you fool!' It pressed.' Don't bother about the consequences; just do it!'

Whilst I may not be so very bold I am, as so many clever people have pointed out, nothing if not a fool. Therefore foolishly I did what was required; that is to say I stood up and I stepped out. A series of wobbling crampon scrapes across the crack were accomplished with all the grace and confidence, I like to think, of a Tai Chi Master and it was done. But the welcoming bosom of that clump of snowy turf,

'A wee bit heap o' leaves an' stibble',

and a poor peg backed up by half a MOAC sort of wedged into a crack, expanding and ice-encrusted, provided dubious comfort. Then Gary, not being so stupid, tried the crack low and on his hands and knees like a chimpanzee instead of standing up like a man and on his feet. With knees knocking against blank granite, and crampons scratching at thin patches of powder below the crack, and with bare hands clawed with the cold and hooked into the snowed-up sloping shelves of the crack itself, his axe and hammer hanging from their strings and doing nothing so much as get in his way, he eyed me balefully from a few feet out.

'And why the bloody hell did you not put in a runner, you Scotch fool?' he cried in his anguish; for he had been looking at a heart-stopping swing across the vegetated snow of the depression and into the granite wall at its other side. And me tied to my poor peg and half a MOAC and standing on a wilting dollop of snow that hid an unfortunate little piece of mismanaged turf. And laughing at him!

'Oh, you're a silly, silly man! he muttered and with his eyes almost popped out of his head, and screaming with excitement, he lurched and scrabbled to me and gasped, so happy to be still alive,

'You'd better lead the next pitch, mate. My hands are fucking frozen.'

So it was that Gary, the big Kiwi, was reduced and the Little Rat, puffed up with pride, was able to retain the mantle of leadership.

---

3   Thomas Gray, 'Ode on the Death of a Favorite Cat, Drowned in a Tub of Goldfishes'.

The next pitch was a short affair, some mousy scrabbling from snowy turf to snowy turf, some nit-picking at cracks and scratching at powder-glazed walls, to reach the leftmost edge of a plump and snowy ledge straight above. And beneath a large overhang. From here the way ahead was hidden by the overhang; but hope, as they say, was springing eternal. Gary again declined the offer of the sharp end of the rope:

'My hands are still frozen, you stupid bugger. I can't believe you didn't put in a runner. It was bloody hard hand-traversing the crack, you know! If I'd come off we'd both have died! And why didn't you tell me it was easier to go high, instead of just laughing at me like a howling ghoul?'

The third pitch, like the first, was another long and difficult and wandering business. And it started boldly enough, bridging out over the large overhang. Gary's eyes, up-cast from his perch below where he was snugged up tight under the roof were big and round and worried.

'Hey there mate, will it go?'

'Can you do it?

And then the plaintive bleat

'What does it look like above?'

It looked bad, although the overhang itself went quickly enough on the left (and a hint for those that might follow: you move left under, you bridge right over, and from there it's a doddle), followed by a short rightwards escape around a blank wall, guarding the exit from a snowy trap, up a frosted grassy crack on the right that belongs, so the original guidebook apparently indicates, to the diagonal fault of the old SandPiper route. From a few moves up the crack, and still looking out for directness and difficulty, I slipped back hard left across a glassy slab but changed my mind, like a fanciful young girl, and came back hard right again under yet another overhang. Thence I found the remainder of the pitch, a great slab, rearing above my head, oppressive, steep, and technical. With this second overhang safely under my belt but the gristle gone out of my feeble backbone, somewhere up the steep crack above and facing yet another little overhang right in front of my nose and tier upon tier of huge overhangs apparently ranged far ahead and across the top of the slab, I stepped back down again, and in a hurry! And, because I didn't like to go back up again, I stepped instead to the left, like a piker led on or like a soldier dressing the wrong way on parade, and onto a turfy ledge somewhere above that second overhang. I shivered, or perhaps it is more true to say that I trembled.

Just so it was that I forfeited a more direct way up the steep and iceless slab glistening grey and apparently rimmed by huge overhangs; and, having scampered across my ledge and up a shallow corner, and drifted across the snowy top of a curious bottomless block strangely glued to the wall, and then up a rocky little corner further along, I took an easier, roundabout way up the wintery *Sand-Pyper Direct* corners on the left. Thus I had hoped to avoid those sobering overhangs, but we were tempted by events to go back rightwards into a huddle on a ledge at the top of that iceless slab. Thus it was, later, that I found myself, on a moderately difficult pitch above the iceless slab, standing on snowy ledges directly beneath some of those very same huge overhangs which I'd seen from the crack low down on the slab and which had scared me off. Gary the Kiwi was at my side.

'Hmm. Looks awfully hard, mate. Where'd you think you can get over them?' he asked, pointedly.

Thus, the astute reader will have noted, Gary still had expressed no interest in assuming the sharp end of the rope. By now the snow had stopped, the clouds and fog had cleared, and a cool and watery afternoon sun had come out. It should have been cheerful, eating a wee bit jeely piece and taking our ease reclining in the snow with the early afternoon sun warming the cockles of our hearts just a little. But the overhangs above looked so big and dark; they cast a chill and an ominous pall upon our doubting spirits.

'Och well, Jimmy, I suppose I'll just wander up and have a wee peek.'

It was easy enough to approach a cave in the middle of the overhangs, scratching up reasonably-angled, snow-encrusted granite slab and treading over tufts of turf sticking out of the snow. But, from the rocky shadows at the back of the cave, overcoming the overhang looked quite desperate. Of course, if it had been nowadays the modern climber would gracefully have dry-tooled his elegant and practiced way out across the crack that separated roof from right-hand wall, torqueing and can-opening and heel-hooking and what have you, hanging like bat or ballerina from his bent shafts and banana picks and mono-points and heel spurs. But instead we primitives took off our Dachstein mittens, facing the battle barehanded and rattling our blunt and battered old Salewa Adjustables at the difficulties.

I must say that I tried and I tried to use the banana pick of my Chacal marteau-piolet, the serendipitous prototype of its race, the very first of its sort, as a sort of reversed hook behind a large flake at the back of the cave. I tried facing outward; I tried facing inward; I tried it right-handed; I tried it left-handed; but I couldn't make head nor tail of it. It just seemed to do no good at all. And so I resorted instead to the old ways, and hooked and clawed my way out along the crack with numb fingers hooked and clawed into the icy crevice, and crampons scraping and scratching where they could at roof and right wall and flailing in air where they couldn't. Axe and hammer and Dachsteins hung down, tangling around each other and getting in the way. A fat MOAC jammed in the crack two thirds of the way out, leading to the last frantic moves under the roof, made progress at least seem safer once clipped by nipped and nerveless fingers. I hereby admit, however, to that last move around the lip as being a cheating move, a modern move, a move made with the curved pick of my French Simond Mustang piolet hooked French-Free into whatever bits of snow and ice and frosted turf and frozen cracks there were hidden around the lip, and its shaft permitting a final screaming French heave:

'Oooh la la!'

From the easy ground above the roofs a short pillar plastered in snow lay between us and the plateau. Not far below the top, and blocking the exit from a corner, there was still another overhang to be dealt with;

'Oh God! Will these overhangs never end?' Gary the Kiwi called up.

But the fight had gone out of the climb by now and the overhang was bypassed easily to gain the plateau drenched in the last of the sun. The evening walk home dipped into night and a last, cursing, scrabble down the Fiachaill a' Coire Chais in the dark to the chairlift car park and the skiers' happy road that descends in curves and spirals, through the snow banks, towards the venal city lights of Aviemore; Aviemore with its reeking bars and discotheque dance floors. And and its chip shops.

Several years later, in the early eighties, I happened while passing by Glenmore upon Blyth Wright, then beginning the process of assuming the post of 'Minister of Scottish Avalanches' or some such position (from the perspective of the rescuer, so they tell me, and not the victim), and he told me that Rab Anderson and Rob Milne had gone out to repeat my routes the previous winter. And they had said, so he said, that the route Gary and I had done wasn't so very hard after all! They couldn't, as he claimed, understand Gary's fuss (I gather that Gary had fussed about our Scottish Plum). Not a Scottish Plum but a Piece o' Cake it was, apparently; and No Big Deal.

From the new guidebook, however, it is clear that they'd been after the trite and the obvious while Gary and I had been after instead the hardest and the boldest. Thus it would appear that they had made, in fact, the first ascent of the guidebook's vegetated central depression, a route now called *Central Route*. Meanwhile, Gary the Kiwi and I, for our sins, had climbed a nameless, forgotten, and meandering horror that had reached up the glazed slabs and snowy corners and absurd overhangs to its left. We could, in irony, have given at least our route a name and called it perhaps *A Piece o' Cake*; in irony because I do declare that never was it such a thing at all. But anyway, 'for a' that an' a' that', it really was A Scottish Plum that we pocketed for ourselves that day! And I guarantee it!

But Mousie, thou art no thy lane,
In proving foresight may be vain:
The best-laid schemes o' mice an' men…[4]

4   Robert Burns 'To a Mouse, on Turning Her up in Her Nest with the Plough'.

A few days after our wild excesses on the second of the three lines, I made my way, hotfoot in my excitement, back to those Longbow Slabs with Gary in tow in order to finish off the campaign by adding the last of the lines to my tally before the powder snow and what little ice there was disappeared. We climbed, therefore, a pitch up the 'water washed fault' of the *Longbow Direct* route and belayed beneath a beetle-browed wall that bristled with outrageous little overhangs and corners gathered together by unlikely blocks of granite.

Now, it just so happened that a significant weep of water had leaked down that bulging wall and cemented those unlikely blocks with a thin veneer of ice garnished, wherever there were overhangs, with fringes of icicles. The whole had been draped in a coat of early winter powder still sticking to the granite with an impressive air of determination.

Gary, in his infinite wisdom, had reserved for me pole position for this pitch by volunteering to lead the first up the 'water washed fault'. This had been somewhat banked out with temptation and easy snow at its foot. The bulging wall itself, however, was of an entirely different tenor to that first pitch. Right from the starting line tentative, but inordinately strenuous and definitely irreversible, moves led to the first of the outrageous little overhangs.

Now, ponder upon this: the term commitment can have many shades of meaning; from the commitment of marriage wherein the spectre of divorce hangs over one half and more of those committing to such contracts, to the commitment of hanging about in the middle of a bulging mixed pitch from axe and hammer hooked delicately into thin ice or tiny frozen divots over the top of a rocky roof, and looking something like a miniature gorilla hanging from his airy branch and not quite in the mood for seppuku. This show, as I can testify, demanded a commitment entirely unlike that of marriage; rather it demanded a commitment like the constancy of true love; an ever fixed mark, as the poet tells us, that alters not with his brief hours and weeks,

But bears it out even to the edge of doom.[5]

You see, this show just had to go on. There could be no going back, for the sharp edge of doom was there at my neck and I had no runner below to which I might have resorted; 'in extremis', as the saying goes. I was completely committed to carrying on. I had no choice. Indeed, that hackneyed old-fashioned aphorism

'The leader must not fall!'

was exquisitely suited to this pitch. Murray, MacKenzie, Bell, their friends and their forebears well would have understood my pickle!

From that first overhang a wall, streaked with ice, led to more of the

---

5   William Shakespeare, Sonnet 116.

outlandishly misset blocks of granite that created vertical right-angled corners packed with powder and verglas and steep, shallow grooves lined with ice; and also, to be sure, more of the unlikely fringed and tasseled overhangs. And the fringes and tassels were, even as I climbed, starting to drip for, although the morning still felt cold, the bright yellow light of a midwinter sun was turning those south-facing slabs into warm and brassy gold. At last a clear crack, at the start of a short rightwards traverse, invited a MOAC; a gesture, immediate, to security and to an easing of the dreadful, knee-trembling panic.

The belay stance close alongside the Longbow Roof, and at the end of the short traverse, on the other hand, although snug inspired a lasting contentment for the sun smiled down and there was a solid little flake, quickly draped with rope, and there were cracks for little chocks and MOACS. And just above there was a fine-looking corner to climb, from the top of which the way ahead looked easy.

'Oh happy, happy day! We have it in the bag now, whatever happens; and it's Gary's turn to lead.'

But before he could lead the next pitch Gary still had to follow the last; and following that second pitch he straightaway fell off the first overhang. Twice he fell off that first overhang before he accepted a small tug on the rope and climbed on. I, being nasty as I am, of course pointed out;

'Och there Jimmy, don't worry about it. If I'd a had a rope above me I'd have fallen off too.'

Just so I pulled his pecker. More falls, however, from the next overhang put paid to the entire endeavour. No small tug on the rope worked; no helpful pull on the rope sufficed; no desperate heaving upon the rope, as if dragging home the great whale Moby Dick, got him going. The hulking Kiwi remained stuck, wriggling upon his ropes like Hemmingway's giant blue marlin upon the line. Bitter, bitter retreat was our only option.

'Don't worry, there, mate,' said Gary the Kiwi. 'We'll be back. It's just I'm not feeling so good today. Must be the flu.'

(A euphemism, I was sure, for a heavy hand with the tipple the night before).

'We'll get it next time.'

A miserly bit of bootlace was therefore knotted and jammed in a crack, and sacrificed to the first part of a grudged descent.

As it turned out, there was to be no 'next time' that winter. The cold, dark days of early January already were giving way to longer, lighter, warmer mid-winter days. The faint ice smears were melting away. The powder snow was being stripped from the slabs. A couple of months later, while climbing with Bob Barton, I was able to look out over a frozen Loch A'an at the Longbow Slabs from *Red Guard Winter Direct*, and they were indeed completely bare even though the surrounding hillsides and cliffs, including Hell's Lum, were still deep under snow and ice. They looked dry enough for rockboots. Almost. That day below Longbow Crag, however, we put off our mummery and beat a sad, dare I say nettled, withdrawal up the deep, soft snow in Diagonal Gully. And that winter was my last winter at the game. Life moved on.

> How dull it is to pause, to make an end,
> To rust unburnished, not to shine in use!
> As though to breathe were life![6]

So, you may ask, whatever happened to those long distant Longbow Days and their ilk? Those days when we were very young and filled with the strength and the vitality of our youth, a strength and vitality so ardent for some desperate glory that we dared strive with gods and reach out to touch the Happy Isles lying somewhere beyond the sunset and the baths of all the Western Stars; always keen, of course, to show the world that we had known the Great Achilles and that he was one of us! Those days have retreated, with the years, into the auld lang syne; vanished with the passing of youth and of innocence, touched by growing up and by life's tragedies. Gary the Kiwi and I parted ways after Longbow Crag for I got a new job and then went on to pursue other interests. And I never saw him again. It happened, or so I heard, that he became tied to bigger mountains than these little Scottish hills, and died, as also I heard, some years later on a high Himalayan peak.

Thus it is that desire, and circumstance, and people pass on. Much had remained to do; remained undone. And only regret and memory now remain;

> The memory of what has been,
> And never more will be.[7]

---

6   Alfred Lord Tennyson, 'Ulysses'.
7   William Wordsworth, 'Lucy'.

MUSIC AND MEMORIES

By Brian Davison

'OK, SO IS THERE anything else we need to bring other than tomato plants?' I was finalising the plans for a week's climbing on the Isle of Mull with fish farmer and resident climber Colin Moody (aka Cog). Apparently the plants were difficult to find on Mull in May so with the car loaded Andy Smith and I drove out of Cambridge after work on Friday just in time to see sunrise over Rannoch Moor the following morning. The advantage of being a climber living in Cambridge was that it was miles from anywhere, so wherever you decided to climb you had to be prepared to travel for hours every weekend, and distances become irrelevant once you accept that you'll be driving most of the night.

The weekend on Mull was spent letting the weather improve while we were introduced to various pleasant dolerite outcrops dotted around the island. Cog had been developing these with a variety of partners he had enticed over to his island. We were there with the promise of a bigger cliff. With the working week in full swing and the weather improving Cog gave directions to The Big Cliff on the south side of Loch Buie. There was a two-hour walk, and a nice flat grassy bit for camping as you passed the headland – with a water trickle nearby and a view of the cliff. Information about bouldering walls, dykes and headless ridges eventually lead to information overload.

After a few hours of staggering along the coast we rounded the headland but still couldn't see any cliff and I began to wonder if we'd ever reach the promised land. The flat grass in front looked good for camping though. Then I took another step and rearing up above me was a massive cliff. We pitched tent and set off to investigate, trying to remember the information Cog had told us. Passing under a smaller wall, we scrambled up to a dyke to the right of an impressive compact wall capped by a large roof in the centre of the cliff. A tree poked out at half-height and I recalled Cog talking about 300ft so I suggested Andy head for that on the first pitch. We then realised we'd left our helmets so would have to be careful. Deciding to leave the smaller protection he headed off.

Three full rope lengths later we reached the tree. I forgot to collect the other half of the climbing rack when I left the ground, so with no helmets and half the usual leading protection we had little excuse for slow progress. Sunsets in the islands can be beautiful, but I decided I'd rather get to the top in the remaining daylight so appreciation of its finer points was missed as I led onwards. As the rope ran out the angle eased but the compact nature of the rhyolite offered little in the way of protection or a belay, so tugging on the rope, I continued upwards. A 200ft+ pitch

allowed me to reach the top where I could appreciate the dying embers of the day.

To the left of the dyke line the cliff reaches its full height, the featureless wall topped by a large fearsome overhang. With yesterday's lesson learned we opted for a corner crack-line to its left, which at least should offer some protection. A less traumatic climb was enjoyed, boldly going where no one had wanted to go before, and as we ventured back to camp for lunch we found Cog had knocked off work and come to join us. Asking about the crag heights he explained, the 300ft I remembered had belonged to the small wall we'd passed under which Cog affectionately called the bouldering wall. We climbed on it for an afternoon's sport.

The next day with the local expert to guide us we headed further along the cliff and found another wall with a loose but enjoyable flake system at its top. With no belay to be found I applied the principles of the deadman belay and buried myself to the waist in a peat bog. Sadly the top few pitches fell down a few years later.

'It was 20 years ago today, Sergeant Pepper taught the band to play.' It's not often you hear music on Radio 4 but it was indeed 20 years since the release and all the facts were being regurgitated out of the radio as we waited to board the ferry. We'd survived our week on Mull and so had the central wall.

The next year a Spring visit to Mull and The Big Cliff along with Cog had us sitting at the bottom of the cliff in the rain trying to pick a line up the compact main wall, capped by the massive overhangs several hundred feet above. The wall below the overhang offered an easier-angled scoop and the possibility of skirting the overhang on the right. The alternative was a horizontal traverse to the left from below the scoop; this would allow the corner system to be reached but offered a less aesthetically-pleasing line.

A week in the summer saw me ricocheting around Scotland looking for dry rock. I told climbing partner Andy Nisbet of The Big Cliff and we headed off to Mull. More time was spent sitting in the rain trying to pick a line up the main face.

Another two years were to pass before I could get back to Mull. We walked in along the coast in light drizzle but with a weatherman's promise of fine weather. Late in the day as the walls dried in a gentle wind I set off up the wall below the overhangs on an experimental probe. After a rope length of probing up the brittle wall, I reached a ledge. Being late in the day, Andy was reluctant to follow but I was unable to retreat due to the lack of a belay. Bracing myself on the ledge, I belayed as Andy climbed to join me, bringing the peg runners that might offer a safe retreat. We abseiled, knowing that at least the first pitch was possible even if sparsely protected.

Camping below An Garradh, Mull (1990). Knocking on Heaven's Door (E5, 5c) climbs the main cliff. Photo: Andy Nisbet.

The high point of the previous day was soon reached and I continued on. Keeping your contact points as dispersed as possible reduces the chances of coming off if the rock fails. This doesn't lend itself to easy climbing. Eventually a hard move gained easier-angled rock in the scoop a pitch below the overhangs. With no ledges in sight I had to take a semi-hanging belay from the RP runners which I'd fiddled into incipient cracks. Andy cautiously followed and thankfully spotted a ledge below the scoop, which I had missed. Climbing back to our new improved belay we decided it was time to get off the cliff, so we opted for the easier left-hand exit. A traverse left led to sounder rock and the well-protected corners I knew from my previous visits. Stress free, we soon reached the cliff top.

The following day we re-gained the ledge from where we'd escaped to the left of the overhangs. Now it was time to see if we could do the harder-looking finish to the right of the overhangs.

I set off moving diagonally rightwards across the smooth rock of the scoop. A cautious sparsely-protected pitch lead to a perfect footledge with a crack at its side. The ledge was the size of one foot and the crack, which offered one runner, was sadly just below the ledge. So how to belay? Hang on one runner 500ft above the ground or stand on the ledge on one leg with a length of rope looping down to the belay, oh decisions, decisions.

I decided on a compromise and squatted with one leg hanging down the wall below and the shortest possible length of rope attaching me to the belay. Andy carefully edged his way up the scoop and stopped at a suitable point below me. There was no way we could swap on the belay or he could pass me, so runners were tied to the rope and I racked up. A few feet of climbing allowed me to stop and, while I hung on, Andy moved to the comfort of the belay ledge. With the smell of heather close by I moved over steeper ground and into the top section of the previous dyke climb and the comfort of known territory.

We packed up and walked out in the tense silence resulting from several days of stressful climbing. I thought about the climbing, none of it that difficult, 5c or a bit more, but how to grade the serious nature of the route, the poor protection and brittle holds? In the old shale grades, the leader could probably hope to survive a fall on a mild extremely severe, not so on an extremely severe, and it would be terminal for all parties on a hard extremely severe, so that was the grade sorted. Back at the car I turned on the radio and a voice like sand and glue was singing

I can't use it any more.
It's getting' dark, too dark to see
I feel I'm knockin' on heaven's door.

MIKE O'HARA AND THE DRAGON OF CARNMORE

By Dave Atkinson

THE DISTANT North-West location of Carnmore and a twelve-mile walk-in combine to deter all but the dedicated. There is room (if not permission) for camping in the area around Carnmore Lodge, and a small open barn. The site is dominated by Beinn a' Chaisgein Mòr, a hill that would merit little attention but for the towering buttresses of the 900-foot-high Carnmore Crag, the centre-piece of an area described by Mike O'Hara as the 'most wonderful place in Britain'.[1] Over a few years in the 1950s, in an area where there had been virtually no recorded climbing at all, quality climbs at every grade from the easiest to the highest standards of the day appeared. In the early years of the decade, the crags of Ben Lair were explored by Glasgow University Mountaineering Club teams. But it was Cambridge University Mountaineering Club who developed the great gneiss crags at the head of Fionn Loch in the late 1950s, with the name M.J. O'Hara particularly prominent in the first ascents. It was, perhaps, a last 'hurrah' for the public school/Oxbridge elite which had been pre-eminent in the development of mountaineering in Britain before the Second World War: the classless revolution was well under way elsewhere. It is difficult today to imagine what it must have been like to discover such vast untapped potential at a time when most other mountain crags in Britain were already covered with numerous lines.

I have long thought how magical to have all that unclimbed rock to go at and in a wondrously beautiful place – and of course to be young! I wondered whatever became of M.J. O'Hara. Even my friend and former BMC President Derek Walker who seems to be a personal friend of most of the top names in climbing – of a certain age or deceased – was not able to help though he did lend me a copy of the 1958 Climbers' Club Journal which had an account of the first ascent of *Dragon*, one of Mike's climbs – so called because it was fierce and the final section was solved by George (Fraser)! A bit of Googling combining Mike's name with 'Carnmore' and various climb names did not get much more than I already knew – just walk-on parts in the drama of other lives. But I did know that Mike went to Cambridge University and searching with that found an eminent geologist of his name who was a Cambridge graduate. The geology link proved to be fruitful and eventually I came across a 2007 prize acceptance speech given by a Mike O'Hara who referred to being a member of the Cambridge University Mountaineering Club – that was when I knew I had found my man. A 2004-dated academic paper

---

1 O'Hara, M.J. and Fraser, G., 'Highland Dragon', *Climbers' Club Journal* (1958), pp. 140-7.

turned up: it was called 'New Moon From An Old Hand', and I discovered that Mike was a Principal Investigator in Experimental Petrology for all six Apollo missions which returned samples from the Moon's surface between 1969 and 1974. Now I know that Petrology is a branch of geology studying rocks and the conditions in which rocks form. Evidently the Moon rocks were formed in situ and not projected from earthly volcanoes! A university e-mail address was given – Mike was a Professor but I thought may be retired and the e-mail address dormant – I tried it without stating the nature of my interest and same day got a reply saying that the email address works well but Mike less so – he has Parkinson's Disease. Then I told Mike why I wanted to contact him, and there followed three e-mails each with attachments about his climbs – riches beyond expectation! It turns out he lives not far from Cardiff and as we were trekking there on family business the next weekend I thought *carpe diem* and had an invite to visit. That was how I came to shake the hand that in a youthful idyll slew the Dragon of Carnmore.

Mike lives with his wife Sue – herself a fine walker – Mike told me that at Carnmore once, Sue, on discovering she had left her toothbrush in the car (parked at Kernsary), walked there and back in a day, a 16-mile round trip for a toothbrush! Now aged 78, Mike is also living with Parkinson's Disease, but his intellect and recollection remain sharp, and his interest in my quest was generous. He speaks in the cultured tones of upper middle England, betraying neither the Irish ancestry of his name nor the fact that he was born in Australia. *'My father'* said Mike *'was a lot of everything – illegitimate son of East End Irish via orphanage into trenches early in '14–18 war, gold miner, crossword compiler, outback share salesman in Australia, Cherry Blossom boot polish travelling rep in mid '30s, labourer on cement mixer gang at outbreak of war, construction manager for building of Pwllheli, Ayr, Filey camps for Navy/Billy Butlin and an airfield, entrepreneur converting old buildings to caravan camp in Pwllheli, general manager of construction and operation of Festival Gardens 1948–53, director of Forte's mid 1950s... he walked with me Ullapool-Sheneval-Carnmore-Poolewe in summer 1955 and was still talking about it 25 years later'*. His mother, Mike says, thought that the boy would do better for himself in Britain than in Australia, and at just six months he moved to England, but home from 1941 onwards was Pwllheli, Wales.

Each of the educational establishments that Mike attended turned out to be a significant stepping stone on the road to Carnmore. He attended Dulwich College in south London, but during the Second World War the College evacuated to a large hotel in Betws-y-Coed. It was at this time that he became interested in mountains and the climbing of them (in common, he says, with others at the evacuated school). Mike then won a scholarship (in the Sciences) to go to Cranleigh School in Surrey. At

Cranleigh, Mike won a further scholarship (in Divinity), but more significant was receiving J.H.B. Bell's *A Progress in Mountaineering* (1950), as a school prize, and being inspired to make the first of many visits to Carnmore through its comment '... *the head of the Fionn Loch would be a veritable paradise for the enthusiastic rock climber, for I do not know any other corner in the Scottish Highlands with so much opportunity for exploration in grand and imposing surroundings. It was ... the grandeur and the beauty of the scene that held me spellbound.* '[2]

Admitted to Peterhouse College, Cambridge, Mike studied geology and joined the Cambridge University Mountaineering Club (CUMC). His College room-mate was Eric Langmuir, who through his later work for the Mountain Leadership Training Board and others was to contribute much to making mountaineering a safe and accessible pastime, and who was a lifelong friend (until Eric's death in 2005). Mike's obituary of Eric for the Royal Society of Edinburgh is both appreciative and moving, a testament of friendship indeed.[3]

The CUMC exploration adventure in Carnmore began with Wrangham and Clegg's *Diagonal* (Severe) on Carnmore Crag in 1952. Chris Bonington was there with an R.A.F. party in 1954 for *Poacher's Route* (V. Diff). Mike did not let me get away with observing that these were mere skirmishes compared to what was to come: 'I bet it didn't seem like that to them at the time' he said. Mike remembers a New Year 1955 walk from Kinlochewe by Loch Fada to Poolewe with Peter Evans, Jo Scarr and Bob Downes, when they overnighted at the barn beneath Carnmore Crag. 'That's the line!' Bob said, staring up at that vaulting prow of rock that was to become Fionn Buttress – but Mike and Bob never had the chance to try it together. A return the following Easter marked the start of a prolific campaign of discovery that saw Mike on 39 recorded first ascents over the next three years. He began with a modest haul of seven in 1955, mainly focusing on Maiden Buttress, 300 feet of impeccable gneiss and with routes from V. Diff to VS. Bob Kendell enthused: '*no patches of moss or slime, or dirty cracks full of mud and bramble; none of that crawling through undergrowth and mantelshelfing onto wet grass ledges with your fingers clawing anxiously for holds among the roots – nothing but clean, warm, grey rock*'.[4] In 1956, there were six more climbs, notably the first route on Fionn Buttress (with George Fraser), now unoriginally known as *Original Route* (VS). Kendell, and

2   Bell, J.H.B., *A Progress in Mountaineering* (Oliver and Boyd, 1950).

3   O'Hara, M.J. 2005 Royal Society of Edinburgh (accessed 01.01.11) <http://www.royalsoced.org.uk/fellowship/obits/obits_alpha/Langmuir_eric.pdf>

4   Kendell, R. 'Torridonian', *Cambridge University Mountaineering Club Journal* (1956), p. 32.

*Carnmore 1956. (L to R) Peter Steele, Marjorie Langmuir, George Fraser and (above) Mike O'Hara.
Photo: Mike O'Hara collection.*

Langmuir's sister Marjorie featured on other first ascents, including, on Maiden Buttress, the three-star *Ecstasy* (Severe) with Bob and the intriguingly named *Dishonour* (V. Diff) with Marjorie. In all there were 11 first ascents with Marjorie, and whether she and Mike were ever attached by more than a rope we can but wonder. But there is romance enough in Mike's description of the pair of them standing outside the Carnmore Barn in their duvets, 'shivering slightly' watching the northern lights – 'wide curtains of fluid greenish light writhing, striking across the sky' – in the 'bitter cold wonder of that night'.[5]

Then to Easter 1957, and Mike's fears that Easter 1956 might have been 'more memorable than anything yet to come,' were unfounded. In the Climber's Club Journal of 1958 ('Highland Dragon', written jointly with George Fraser), he records that Easter 1957 was even better than the Easter before.[6] On 7 April, the improved line of *Fionn Buttress* was climbed. I, and others, who have found this to be quite bold for VS, can

5   O'Hara, M. J., 'Carnmore', *CUMCJ* (1957), p. 32.

6   O'Hara and Fraser 1958, op. cit.

George Fraser on the morning of 22 April 1957 prior to the first ascent of 'Dragon'. Photo: Mike O'Hara.

only imagine the challenge facing Mike and Bill Blackwood, climbing in plimsolls, and without nuts and friends. On the crux pitch, *'excellent pocket holds and friction sustained progress up to the left, then back to the right to a pocket handkerchief of a ledge and a marked steepening of the slab... a line of diminishing pockets for fingers and toes beckoned towards an overhung ledge and one hoped a resting place. A runner would have been comforting...* '[7] Higher up, they joined the line of the *Original Route*, giving a 750-foot climb widely regarded as one of the finest in Scotland.

After a trip south to Glasgow, towards the end of April, Mike was back at Carnmore again, and on the final day (22 April) *'George Fraser and I had a date. Sitting there on the grass, and craning our necks to stare up at the wall we had dated, I could not help thinking that it might well be an appointment with fear...* '[8] The first pitch of what was to become *Dragon* had been climbed, and the last section investigated from above, with Bob Kendell the previous year. On the crux, a traverse under the great roof that caps the crag here: *'the leaf piton had to be inserted diagonally upward into the overhang just above my forehead – I could not afford to lose it, I could not afford a hand to steady it because I was barely holding my position with forearm friction on a slanting narrow shelf, and the job had to be undertaken left-handed, and above all I could not afford to fall off. It took a long, long time.'* In response to George Fraser's very understandable enquiry *'If I come off, is there enough rope to lower me to rock?',* Mike *'put in a second piton a few feet further out under the overhang... then rigged a stance from several line slings under thighs and round back so that I could vacate the postage stamp holds and belay George from a few feet above and no*

7   O'Hara, M.J. 'Fionn Buttress First Ascent, complete'. Private papers, unpublished.

8   O' Hara and Fraser 1958 op. cit. (and rest of paragraph).

more than ten feet to the side of the crux move... didn't need anything more than the memory for laxative in the next decades'. Finally finding a way past the great capping roof, George writes: *'below was 800 feet of space, exhilarating and no longer terrifying. With a heave I was over the top... we embraced and shrieked with joy... we lay prone on the soft, flat turf and worshipped horizontally.'* At Hard VS and 5a many people have been impressed and I noted that three UK Climbing Log contributors thought E1, 5b the appropriate grade.

Dragon, Pitch 3, Drooping Flake to The Perch. Mick Goad leads 1973. Photo: Mike O'Hara.

Mike's pioneering activity was not limited to Carnmore. He was involved in early exploration of the Etive Slabs and was with the team led by room-mate Eric Langmuir on the first ascent of *Spartan Slab* (VS), in 1954. But on *Hammer's* notorious Scoop, a three-person ladder (Langmuir on top, Downes in the middle and O'Hara at the bottom) was 'the wrong technique'. Mike was active on Ben Nevis, completing the first route (*North-Eastern Grooves*) that in its subsequent straightened-out version became *Minus One Direct*, said to be one of the finest routes in Britain. On Càrn Dearg Buttress, with Bob Downes, he did the second ascent of Joe Brown's *Sassenach* in 1956 ('desperate' Mike told me) and but for worthy dedication to his academic work could well have been on the first ascent of *Centurion*: in late August of that year Downes and Don Whillans travelled to O'Hara's lodgings in Cambridge to try to persuade him to take up an empty place on Whillans's motorcycle combination. When we met, Mike reflected a little ruefully on his decision not to go with them: *Centurion* was climbed on that trip. In June 1957, Mike and Dragon-partner George Fraser recorded a first ascent in North Wales: *Nunc Dimmittis*, a VS on Crib y Ddrysgl. Mike also made several early British ascents in the Alps, including in 1956 a first British ascent of the North-North-West Ridge of the Piz Gimelli in the Bregaglia.[9] As well as the climbing, there were other adventures including, in 1953, with Ted Wrangham, Roger Chorley (the two drivers of Ted's Jaguar), Dave Fisher, Geoff Sutton, and Eric, the first inside-24-hour Three Peaks outing (Ben Nevis, Scafell Pike, Snowdon). (My friend Mavis Burden was a member of first all-female team to do it, in 1961 – on motorbikes!) But it was the Carnmore

9   O'Hara, M.J. and Fraser, G.J., *CUMCJ* (1957), p. 59.

adventure that caught my imagination, and there is no doubt that this was wondrous beyond the mere statistics. In Mike's words – written and spoken – what comes over is not just the excitement of the climbs, but also the wonder of adventure and companionship in stunningly beautiful surroundings – and being young. Mike's article about Easter 1956 in the 1957 CUMC Journal is lyrical to the equal of Bill Murray:

> Months of drought had burned the moors into a riot of golden browns interlaced with purple, an infinite variety of shades, from which rose crag upon crag of green flecked warm grey rock, sound as the proverbial bell. And the lochs: secret beaches of the finest sand, blue waters, sunlight rippling across scalloped surfaces in a crisp morning breeze; not least of many memories, that first evening when the sun set across the Fionn Loch, a dull red sun that sank slowly towards its own reflection in the great sheet of still black water, leaving us chilled in the enveloping silence of the cirque of Carnmore.[10]

I can but hope that Mike was rewarded by the chance to talk about events chronologically a long time ago but so intense in experience as to seem like only yesterday. He has been in full support of my telling what is, after all, his story, not mine. There was a little melancholy in the background of our conversation: most of the people who shared his youthful adventures are now dead – some, such as Bob Downes and George Fraser, dying in the mountains whilst still young, and others of natural causes but nevertheless taken before their rightful time. From his obituary of Eric Langmuir, I was left in no doubt that for Mike the measure of a person is not just their accomplishments (in whatever field), but in the quality of their relationships (of friends, of family) and their contribution to the betterment of their community, be that climbing, academic or otherwise. It was sobering to be reminded that the trials of later life do not discriminate according to our achievements or the roads we have taken. For Mike, life is significantly restricted by Parkinson's Disease, but he is well served by friends and family, and by the personal qualities of tenacity, optimism and invention which once yielded so many magnificent climbs in a most beautiful part of our land.

The 2007 Prize Acceptance speech which helped me find Mike was upon receipt of the Hess Medal marking 'outstanding achievements in research in the constitution and evolution of Earth and other planets'. It is awarded annually by the American Geophysical Union. In climbing we don't do lifetime achievement awards, but if we did I think Mike O'Hara would be due one around now, don't you? In the absence of that, we can but say that he is one of us and wish him well.

With thanks to Mike O'Hara for sharing the memories, written material and photographs on which this article is based.

---

10 O'Hara, *CUMCJ* (1957) op. cit. p. 28.

STEPPING WEARILY AND BACK WE GO

By Phil Gribbon

SHE WAS GOING slower and slower. She should never have come with us. We had been silly boys to think she was fit enough for a trip to the Faindouran bothy that lurks far away at the back of beyond.

We were going back now and struggling up towards the Moine Bhealaidh, the moss of the bealach, that creates a featureless high plateau between the twin Munros of Beinn a' Chaorainn and Beinn Bhreac to the west and below the long slope of Beinn a' Bhùird that formed a broad barrier to the east.

Our return journey from the bothy in the desolate eastern Cairngorms was proving more demanding than we had anticipated. The isolated snow patches, bleached of brightness, that we were crossing had begun to merge into a more continuous slope. The snow was deepening and the higher we climbed away from the shelter of the valley floor the more effort we needed. The surface was not bearing our weight and a keen strengthening south-west wind was blowing into our faces.

Bill Led made the footsteps that were punched down into the underlying softer snow. Our lassie had difficulty in stepping into his tracks. Was it, or was it not, her fault that she had to wear oversized boots? The decision to go to the distant bothy had been made in the swirling and hazy comfort of singing the night away in the Castle Tavern back in the ould grey toun. It was only a day later that we had parked at the roadside by the Linn of Dee and found that she had not brought her boots. However all was not lost for Cludge generously offered her his spare pair. They were three sizes too large. It was them ones or nothing.

In the morning Bill and the lassie gamely walked by Derry Lodge, through the narrow pass beyond Glen Derry, and dropping down to the Avon followed the rough path to the bothy. There was little snow on this path but pack-burdened and foot flip-flopping along for 20km was a testing trial for her. We who had walked in by the high route over Beinn a' Chaorainn were cooking dinner in the gathering gloom when they came through the bothy door; they looked shattered, quite knackered, glad to be there.

Next day the A team, Cludge and Ross, left early for a traverse over Beinn a' Bhuird and down into Glen Quoich on their way back to Linn of Dee, while we three of the B team necessarily chose an easier but not the easiest route back to the cars. When we eventually got outside a faint sun was still glinting off the snow and outlining the heather stalks protruding through the snow but the wind was rising and fast-shredding clouds were creeping in from the south-west. Our route choice was the shortcut over the Moine bealach but once up from the valley floor we were finding the going hard.

Uneasiness was creeping in; there was the question not only of how long it would take to reach the shelter of the ancient pinewoods in Glen Quoich but whether in deteriorating conditions she would make it in one piece. She was following our example, we were the experienced experts who knew all about mountains and that sort of stuff, and she was prepared to blindly follow wherever we went. The sensible decisions lay with us, the ones who were responsible for our lesser brethren. That was Led and myself. Nonetheless for the moment we kept going, watching the runes and feeling on edge.

She stopped, bent and hunched over her axe. We continued but soon she halted again and we had to wait until she was ready to go on. Her rests grew more frequent and longer and we all began to cool down. We went on but then she staggered and stumbled and fell into the snow and lay there. Our big problem had started. We helped her up and moved slowly on but she soon was down again. With these stops and starts we were rapidly getting chilled. Was she succumbing to hypothermia accentuated by physical weakness? We faced a dangerous situation but realised what had to be done. It was to retreat quickly to the lowest ground, and so turning round we headed back into the Avon valley to escape, recover and think again.

Once we began to descend a huge worry vanished from my mind. Unbelievably we were all flitting down easily but erratically in giant steps with our big-booted lassie managing to go downhill without undue difficulty. It seemed quite crazy to see this recovery and to know what had been happening a short time before. Isn't gravity a wonderful thing, I thought. Had I been kidding myself?

We soon reached the river and, finding a suitable crossing place, got onto the path on the far side. I recall how winter in those distant days was often colder, harsher and more reliable and had a more genuine feel with little snowmelt and deep sub-zero temperatures persisting for weeks on end. Consequently, the river Avon with its jammed platelet sheets and stacked rafts building up into ice dams had been trickling along quietly through a maze of glazed boulders anchored by ice shelves to the river bank. It was crossable; we were getting lucky.

We discussed a plan of campaign. There was a long way to go to the Linn of Dee and it would be dark well before we reached the cars. We might not even make the trip in one go. Someone had to go on alone because our absence at the cars would cause unwelcome worry and even a drastic consequence like warning the mountain rescue about the lost walkers on the high route home. It was Bill who decided to volunteer and promptly set off and now at least he had the chance of a warm bed back in St Andrews.

What options were open to the stragglers? We could return to the Faindouran bothy but that was going the wrong way. Besides we had a negligible amount of food and next day the weather could deteriorate further and make travel uncertain. However upstream there was one redeeming feature, and that was the primitive shelter close to the Fords of Avon where the long overland rough route through the Lairig an Laoigh from Glenmore to Derry Lodge and beyond crossed the river. Such a shelter would be an emergency godsend for hill folk in our situation. It could be our home for the night, if we could find it before it was too dark.

Luckily it wasn't that far, nor was it too hard to see in the gloom. We saw a strange hump like an bulging peat hag squatting fair and square on the valley floor, and getting closer we found it had been covered with heathery sods, lumps of turf and boulders from the river.

In no time we had opened the solid iron door and were standing inside under a curved metal shell on a floor of dry heather twigs. A skimpy meal of leftover scraps would be our hot dinner if we had sufficient paraffin remaining in the wee Primus stove. It didn't take long to rummage about the floor for any goodies left behind by an army trio that passed through a few days before, and somehow they must have known we were coming because neatly placed in a dark corner was a sizable package of bacon slices. We fried our dinner and crawled into our bags knowing we would fry again for breakfast.

We spent a long night in deep darkness in the iron box. Boy, it was unforgettably cold, an experience unique and memorable, our spontaneously unpremeditated night off the bare mountain. What would have happened if we had tried to continue over the high bealach?

In the middle of the night I had inevitably to go outside for a call of nature. I got up, mind dulled and senses asleep. I can still hear to this day the scraping bolt sliding back with a metallic clang as if a great prison door was being opened to another world.

Where was this place before me? Was it a magical frozen wasteland at the start of the route to the South Pole? One of the eerie trackless empty spaces of outer Siberia?

It was sparkling without being seen, all was clear yet wreathed in a mystery of indistinctness, its outermost distance was indefinable even if it was mere metres away, and away up infinitely high the stars lurked as faint pinpricks of beckoning glimmer. Pervading everything was the tangible presence of nothing except utter silence. Just complete peace. I must have gone deaf.

I closed the great door and slunk back into the inadequacy of my sleeping bag. I must buy a new one. My strange visionary moment had gone. Now small chance to sleep, perchance to dream. Tomorrow, the car, the tarred road, the other world.

IN PRAISE OF BEN WYVIS

By John Mackenzie

Oft slandered, rarely praised, compared (most unkindly) to 'a stranded whale north of the Moray Firth'. Okay, it's large and it's long and yes, it even rings a bell with modern youth in having a massive girth. Thus we have a large, long, massively girthed mountain. Not exactly your neat little Sgùrr or slender Aonach and even the name is obscure. The North-West district guide gives 'Majestic hill'; *The Munros* gives 'Hill of Terror' (perhaps) from the Gaelic 'Fuathas' but *Place Names of Ross and Cromarty* by W.J. Watson (1904) gives the following: 'Beinn Uais (but prosthetic 'f' seen in Cabar Fuais); High hill; 'uais' from the root seen in 'uas-al', high, noble; Gaulish ux-ellos; Gaulish 'x' becomes 's' in Gaelic, but in Welsh 'uch-el' high, whence Ochil, Oykel, Achilty.' So far crystal clear but even here it ends apologetically, 'The height of Wyvis is perhaps best appreciated from the higher parts of Inverness and neighbourhood'. So we end up with Beinn Uais ('f' being silent) and pronounced either 'Ben Weevis' (old local) or 'Ben Wivis' (young local) or more correctly 'Byann Ooish.' Incidentally calling a mountain 'Ben' is in fact to call it 'wife' (now there's a quandary) as wife in Gaelic is 'bean' pronounced 'ben'. I leave it to the psychologists and cartoonists amongst you to sort that one out.

All this topographical and nomenclatural obfuscation hides the facts of a fine hill with its best parts well hidden. A bit like a lot of Club Members really. At least 90% and possibly more of walkers and climbers start and end their ascent and descent at Garbat. According to the 'Munros' book this gives 6.5km and 920m of ascent to the summit and to give the book credit suggests a different descent down by the Allt a' Gharbh Bhaid though most go up and down the same way.

The standard route follows the new FC and SNH track that allows a dry-shod ascent to the summit of An Cabar. The initial section overlooks the Allt a' Bhealaich Mhoir with the snout of An Cabar to the left and the lesser butt end of Little Wyvis, Tom na Caillich to the right with the classic U-shaped trench of the Bealach Mòr in between, the line of an old drove road from the West to the greener pastures of the East. Forestry trees do not add much to this bit of the walk but it improves when the path meets the burn which has some good pools. A big welcome sign in Gaelic and English marks the start of SNH property and explains why the hill has an SSSI status. The Woolly hair-moss (*Racomitrium lanuginosum*) is what makes walking on the summit ridges of the Ben and beyond such a pleasure but more of that later.

From the sign upwards the path begins to zigzag its way upwards on the ever steepening flanks of An Cabar. Now, having been up this slope more times than I can remember, I did a very nerdish thing and counted the stone steps ahead. There are over 550 superbly laid setts, some small, some big and these 'Giants Steps' lead past a massive schist boulder. This rest spot is sheltered and gives (in bendy boots) a few problems around 4c on the gentle side and lots harder on the steep side. It lies at around 600m and marks the start of the steepest section up An Cabar, a 300m-plus grind for some and a change down in gear for all the fell runners who whizz past you. The path bobs and weaves a little, overlooking broken crags and an increasingly big drop down into the bealach.

The west end of the summit ridge, An Cabar, is a classic dome. This is not at all apparent from below when the ridge seems to end in an elegant spire. There are two cairns, the southernmost being the summit at 946 (or 950) metres. This at last gets you into the realm of the Woolly hair-moss and the almost level ridge of 2km to the main summit. In mist some unfortunates think that An Cabar is the main summit, presumably a case of wishful thinking though not as bad as mistaking Stob Ban for Ben Nevis as a group did recently.

The gently undulating ridge is scarred by at least two tracks and some braids as well and there has been recent talk of encouraging folk to use just one. A minor bump ahead is Càrn a' Chaiptein and beyond that the ridge narrows. On the left or north-west side the hill presents a remarkably steep unbroken slope, Glas Leathad Mòr, the 'big grey-green slope'. From a distance the hill appears to be one big broad plateau but this is not so. To the north and east where the real interest lies are several big spurs enclosing two big corries that cut deeply into the hill, Coire na Feola (corrie of the flesh) to the east and Coire Mòr (big corrie) to the north east. Navigation to where the summit ridge narrows near the main top at 1046m is totally straightforward in clear visibility but a subtle trap in a winter white-out as I (and a much more famous guide) know to our respective costs. The 'leg' from Càrn a' Chaiptein is long and the ridge does a slight twist so that a straight bearing takes you clean over the edge of the cornice overhanging the headwall of the aptly named Coire na Feola.

Having lightheartedly taken my dog, a black Lab (now deceased from age) for a walk up the Ben in a blizzard (I know this hill, I'll be fine etc. etc.), my ice axe firmly strapped to my sack, we both were immersed in a perfect white-out (the dog seemingly to float in mid-air) when the 'seemingly' turned into 'actually' as we both fell through the cornice and whizzed down the Grade 1 slope below. Walking poles don't make brilliant substitutes for an axe but we stopped quite unharmed 100m or so down, fortunately with no avalanches to contend with. I cut steps back up towards the twin holes, one dog-shaped, the other me-shaped and stepped into a furious wind, a maelstrom, on the ridge. Having lost my

Ben Wyvis – heading east to Glas Leathad Beag.   Photo: John Mackenzie

compass in the slide, I reckoned on facing into the wind (from the south-west) and re-tracing steps. However the wind direction had changed to south-east and so we ended (after a while) back in Coire na Feola again which I only recognised when ending up at the foot of the crags and a route I had done the previous winter. So much for 'knowing the hill'. A long walk out towards Strathpeffer followed and a lift back to Garbat to collect the car.

Of course in summer or winter in clear visibility the summit makes for a good view spot where you can have fun playing 'I–Spy' spotting the wind-farms and oil rigs. By the time you read this there will probably be another wind-farm or two to 'spy'. A much more interesting expedition is to continue east from the summit and down to the Bealach Tom a' Choinnich. Either plod up Tom a' Choinnich (953m) or contour this following the ridge at the head of Coire Mòr. If intent on descending from Tom a' Choinnich then the track on the right side of the burn is as wet and boggy as the ascent up An Cabar is dry and firm. A gate marks the forestry ride where the burn flows west and where this ride ends the track then follows the crest to the left and down to the FC road which then leads left to join the usual route for its last section.

Coire Mòr is not just one corrie but at least three. The greenish grey scoop below the ridge is the aptly named Glas Choire whilst the hanging

Coire Mòr from Glas Leathad Beag. Photo: John Mackenzie.

side corrie leading back towards the summit and ending below abruptly at the Wyvis Waterfall is Coire nan Con, or corrie of the dogs. The main scoop of Coire Mòr lies below this with Loch a' Choire Mhòir at the confluence of the Glas Choire and Coire nan Con and beyond, heading rather drearily south-eastwards, lies many hectares of peat-hagged ground bordering the main burn, Allt a' Choire Mhòir, which changes name downstream to the 'sheepily' named Allt nan Caorach which in turn joins the bigger River Glass. Back in the main Coire Mòr a minor corrie, Coire an t-Socaich, abuts the south-east end of the well named An t-Socach ('The Snout', 1006m) a spur running in the same direction from the Ben's main summit. The other large corrie, the previously mentioned Coire na Feola, runs in a U-shape from below An Socach back up north-west to the summit and is essentially an arm of Coire Mòr.

Back on the ridge overlooking the Glas Choire you enter a wonderful mossy world, overlooking the great corrie and its numerous hanging crags that show marked folding and schistosity. This seems a far cry from the oft-busy summit, a lonely deserted place and one where the true nature of Wyvis really makes itself felt. Here we have seemingly, a northern extension of the Cairngorms, the deeply-incised corrie and the plateau beyond very reminiscent of those hills. To the east the ridge rises to another domed summit at 910m which has a small cairn. The long south-easterly spur from this unfortunately shows clear signs of ATV tracks which actually run over these eastern tops. The fragility of the moss though a delight to walk on is rapidly eroded by vehicles.

A perfectly shaped but quite shallow corrie with broken mossy crags – Coire Lochain – lies just to the north, and beyond the isolated but apparently comfortable Wyvis Lodge at the head of Loch Glass. In the distance, about a half mile away, is the summit of Glas Leathad Beag, the 'small grey-green slope' which at 928m is hotly contended to be a 'Munro', though whether this is a good idea or not remains to be seen. From this 'top' even better views of the turbines, FC conifers and oil rigs in the Cromarty Firth can be had and contrast strangely with the very wild and rather remote feel of the place.

The view back towards the main summit of Wyvis looks quite distant but the walking is easy and once on the ridge at the head of the Glas Choire and overlooking it there is a splendidly round peat tussock with a comfortable top that makes a fine seat. Nearby are a couple of peat 'glaciers' or solifluction lobes that do look very much like black ice, so all in all this is definitely a special spot, isolated, remote and one which has a feel of the north about it.

Yet another 'long walk in' and a very fine if rather boggy approach from the south is to follow the 'Heights' road between Strathpeffer and Dingwall and park at the far eastern end of this where a short spur road near the Heights of Dochcarty ends near a good track. An immediate problem is crossing the Abhainn Sgitheach by (often submerged) stepping stones but if this is okay then a good track leads gently up and past a fine isolated stand of Caledonian pines where a lone standing stone lies which is a modern but touching memorial. The track continues to the bealach between two small but prominent hills, the higher the Pap of Tulloch or Cioch Mhòr at 482m being on the left and worth the short detour and having extensive views, is a pleasant objective on a short day.

Northwards, a descent into trees and a re-ascent over the top or sides of Meall na Speireig leads all too obviously into the mighty bogs and hags of Coire Mòr. This is fine in dry weather but best avoided in wet. Here a choice of lines await; the first is a shorter, drier ascent of the spur leading west then north-west from Meall na Speireig overlooking Coire na Feola and then a round trip over the main summit of Wyvis and down the ATV track from the 910m top on the eastern side of Coire Mòr. The other is the 'Hero's Way', a plunge through the bogs and up into the drier upper reaches of Coire Mòr with grand views of the crags en route and then up via Coire nan Con for a bit of sport or else the more obvious Glas Choire with a choice of including or not the eastern tops. Equally, if a surfeit of bogs is not your thing then a less boggy alternative misses out Coire Mòr and heads up north-east from Meall na Speireig to the long spur from the 910m top and continues the horseshoe round and down via the spur overlooking Coire na Feola. All these possible ways over the hill add something different and show how basically

Coire Mòr, main crag, December 2007. Photo John Mackenzie

uninteresting the 'normal' way via Garbat actually is. If the Garbat approach is 3/10 for interest then the other ways are more like 7/10 depending on the route. A round of all the tops and Little Wyvis (a Corbett at 764m) via Tom an Caillich, makes for an even longer day.

Little Wyvis is best approached from any direction save that from the west where good tracks are unfortunately unwelcoming. A scenic if not too long round can be done from the south via bikes past Contin and through the FC tracks to near Glensgaich and up through FC plantations (if not cut by now leaving impenetrable brash) and then via the spur of Càrn Gorm (556m) and so to the main summit, then over Tom na Caillich and back either by the Bealach Mòr and Garbat if a lift can be arranged or back along the heathery banks of the main burn of the Allt Gleann Sgaithaich. Just remember to check for ticks later. Geologically, both Bens are composed of Moine schists with the added attraction of pegmatite veins in certain areas that contain almandine garnets, schorl, apatite and large 'books' of muscovite and biotite mica.

Climbing-wise Coire Mòr has the only summer rock climbs. Adventurous 1950s pioneers added a couple of Difficult climbs on either side of Fox Gully on the Main Crag which is the highest situated of the several crags and most extensive whilst lower down and left of the waterfall is the cleanest bit of schist on the hill, a long slanting slab with a couple of Severe pads that are quite interesting if you don't mind a long walk in.

In winter the hill takes on the guise of a true mountain, both the corries being remote and a bit of an effort to get to. The nearer of the two, Coire na Feola is now best reached from the Garbat track over An Cabar and then the south-east spur reached from just beyond Càrn a' Chaiptein. Several descents are possible and are also an excellent way to test snow stability as Coire na Feola does avalanche in places. This is not a crag to go on after heavy snowfall as the slopes above the cliffs are topped by large cornices. However in icy conditions there are several fine choices as unlike Coire Mòr, these crags can form long continuous icefalls, the best being *Walking on Air* which when at its best is a run of blue ice at around Grade V, easiest when fat. More mixed lines from Grade III to Grade V also exist, all of which are described in 'Northern Highlands Central' but probably the best mixed route is *Laird of the Rings* (V,5) or the similarly-graded line just to its left, as well as the easier original route *Discovery Buttress* (IV,4).

Coire Mòr's Main Crag is more often in condition being a little higher and tucked away from the sun. To reach it requires a definite effort as you have to go firstly over the summit via the Garbat approach and then do a descending traverse near the top of Coire nan Con contouring towards an easy exit into the main corrie at around 900m, very tricky in mist and where a GPS becomes really useful! The base of the crags is then followed south-eastwards to arrive below a well-sculptured crag ideally suited for mixed climbing and with no cornice problems at the top. All this approach can take up to four hours depending on conditions.

Undoubtedly the three best routes here are *The Last Resort* (IV,4), *Temptress* (V,6) and on the frontal face of the lower crag to the left of *Fox Gully* (I/II) is *Earls Before Swine* (V,6). The name of the latter has a history as does the line. It took four visits before the line was in the right condition and in the intervening time another party, (friends fortunately) sneaked on in hoping for the prize but, like us previously, were confronted with soggy turf and instead opted for an easier line well to the left on another part of this extensive crag, calling it *Swine Before Earls*. So it was a matter of honour not to mention effort to finally find it in perfect condition and climb it and give it the obvious name. *Fox Gully* was first climbed in the 1950s and gives a normally straightforward ascent on steep snow but can often sport a short ice pitch which makes it more entertaining but more awkward in descent. The routes on this crag all have good turf and often incut rock as well as delightful belvederes to view the windfarm opposite and the oil rigs in the Firth which make an uneasy juxtaposition of scale and distance with the remoteness of the crag.

On the lower crags of Coire Mòr, the *Wyvis Waterfall* gives, by the

Simon Nadin on pitch 3 of 'Earls Before Swine' (V,6).   Photo: John Mackenzie.

easiest line, a Grade IV and above the summer slab is a fine and probably unrepeated Grade V ice line. Almost certainly other routes, probably in winter, will appear sporadically over the years. Finally, a Grade III lies in the smaller Coire Lochan, very distant unless an approach from Wyvis Lodge is taken which requires permission to drive up the private road. Like Coire na Feola, most of these routes are described in the current guidebook.

Weather-wise, the hill has a more easterly climate and thus is a little drier than the West but equally can be cloud covered when other hills are clear and this apparently is due to its own special low-pressure cell. In winter it holds snow well though possibly not so copiously as in the Fannaichs but the turf freezes readily in the corries and much of the mixed climbing is best when under thin cover. The big gentle south-western corrie of Coire na Feithe Riabhaich was mooted to become a skiing centre in the 1990s but nothing has come of it though there are infrequent rumbles of interest from time to time. If you can be bothered to carry skis then some pleasant and long easier descents can be had.

So there we have it, Beinn Uais, truly noble if often underrated and well worth exploring outside the comfort zone of the Garbat approach. It is a hill that takes more than one visit to explore and together with its botanical and geological interests has something for everyone.

THE GREAT GAME

By Roger Webb

THERE ARE FEW times in our lives when we experience not the sudden triumph of the race won or the difficulty overcome but the deep satisfaction of fulfilling a long-held dream or ambition. Whether sporting, personal or professional, wild and dangerous, stuffy and dry, public or private the feeling is the same personal peace, tempered with sadness that the dream is gone forever.

At 1 a.m. on 20 January 2008 I was at the peak of that feeling, the sadness hadn't kicked in, total fulfilment had. The cramps in my forearms were gone and I had just found a belay about 10 easy metres from A' Mhaighdean's summit. A dream was in the bag. I tied myself off, took in the slack, gave three tugs to say climb and took in the view.

How had I got there?

On a cold November day in 1991 I stood under the cliffs of Slioch's north-west face. Awe-struck by the potential and the situation, I felt I had found the promised land. I turned to look at the view and ran out of adjectives. A' Mhaighdean floated above a bank of cloud, gleaming in the thin autumnal light, its south-west ridge dropping sheer. It was the best-looking winter line I had ever seen. It became my personal winter grail.

I had to do it.

It took 17 years.

The crag turned out to be Pillar Buttress and there were perhaps four routes on it, all summer, none winter.

The first problem was a partner. Neil Wilson was interested but not enthused. I suspected the prospect was not arduous enough for him. Simon Richardson was interested and enthused but discovered mixed climbing on Ben Nevis. Seduced by the sirens of technical excellence he drifted away from the true faith (and completely transformed winter climbing on Ben Nevis but that is a different story).

Many a climber was approached and all had excuses until I found the answer was right before me all along in the person of Martin Hind, he of the outrageous talent but relaxed attitude. He is so well known for his aversion to early starts that it had not occurred to me that he might be interested. I had forgotten his old nickname, 'Harpic' for 'clean round the bend'. He doesn't like early starts, but in this case he would make an exception.

In January 2000 it all clicked, Martin was free, I was free and the weather appeared to be cold and settled. Our plan was the obvious one, walk in on the Saturday, sleep at Carnmore bothy, get up early on the Sunday and do the route. There were two big flaws in this, in the days before accurate Internet forecasts we couldn't be sure of the weather holding and we had to find the crag in the dark. Blissfully unaware that we would be caught out by both, we set off on the long walk-in mid-morning on the Saturday. These days you can bike from Poolewe at least half the distance, but this was before attitudes changed, and bikes were forbidden and likely to be disposed of if found.

It was a gorgeous day, the hills were frozen solid and white under a blanket of snow, perfect conditions full of promise. Even so, despite the inspiring surroundings, when we arrived at the bothy ready for a rest and looking forward to a pleasant night we were soon disillusioned. Carnmore bothy may be in a superb location, but as a bothy it ranks amongst the worst. Dank, cold and dirty, it is a morale destroyer.

In inadequate sleeping bags we dozed uncomfortably. At 3.30 a.m., aware something wasn't right, I looked outside, the stars and frost were gone to be replaced by ominous cloud, a freshening westerly and the threat of snow. Breakfast was a dour soulless affair, poured down too fast, its joy destroyed by the need to race the weather. Realising that we had no chance of finding the crag from above we set off back across the causeway and east around Dubh Loch to take our chances from below.

Three or more hours of dark stumbling led to a morose dawn of low clag, damp snow and only a rough idea of our location. On a hunch we turned north up steepening slopes. After an interminable slog through glutinous ex-névé we came to a tongue of rock which brought us to a blunt ridge. It wasn't quite what I had expected but in the absence of any other options we started up it. The weather and conditions became disgusting. Ice that the day before was perfect, dripped and rotted, crampons balled up, my glasses steamed up, and as it warmed up we soaked up. The climbing was average and easy. With a sinking heart, I knew we were in the wrong place. The weather got worse, the wind strengthened and our will weakened. After four or five pitches there was a brief clearing. Away to our left there was a brief glimpse of an elegant buttress and then all was grey, damp clag again. In all clag there is a silver lining and ours now revealed itself. The hitherto unremarkable ridge now reared up in a final bastion and the soaked certainty of being in the wrong place was forgotten in a final two-pitch physical battle that warmed hearts and limbs.

At dusk we popped out onto the summit ridge of A' Mhaighdean and struggled up to the cairn. Huddling in its shelter I got out the map, on the front of the map in clear unmistakable lettering it said 'Beinn Dearg and surrounding area'. Casually I asked Martin if he had a map. 'No you've got it' he said. I explained that I had a map but not *the* map. Given that it was dark, we were on top of the most remote Munro in Scotland in a westerly gale that was now full of sleet he took it remarkably well. These days we would phone a friend, but then it wasn't an option. Pooling our memories, we decided to follow the cliff edge into the wind until we came to a large, square-shaped tower which we had noticed the day before. From that a gully descended back to Dubh Loch. If we followed that we could get out of the wind. It is surprising how vulnerable one feels navigating purely on memory, distances are magnified and uncertainty is constantly on your shoulder. We battled along the ridge. The minutes seemed like hours and convinced us that our memories were wrong and if there was a tower we must have long passed it. The lack of an alternative kept us going and at last our torches picked out the flat sandstone pinnacle we had spied the day before. As expected, a gully ran west of south. We set off down into a welcome calm and at last luck ran with us, there was only one abseil and within the hour we came again to the gloomy Dubh Loch. Here our problems, except for a very long walk through the night, were over but out of the shelter of the gully the discomfort was not. Dumping our gear at the causeway we returned to the bothy to collect our bivvy kit and found that the 'morale destroyer' of the night before was now a welcome refuge that was hard to leave, but leave we must for although it was nearly midnight we both had work the next morning. It is hard to describe the misery of the trudge back to the car. Chastened by failure, heading into horizontal sleet with over-heavy, water-soaked rucksacks chafing our shoulders it was a weary party that trooped back into Poolewe at 3 a.m. almost exactly 10 hours after leaving the summit. Humans are strange however; back in the car, exultation at the ridiculousness of the whole enterprise took over. Martin, never one to miss a good line, looked at me saying 'I always said we went a ridge too far'. I could not think of a better name for both the day (or days) and the route.

It was a good route but not *the* route. I had to go back.

Years passed, life got in the way of climbing. I could no longer take a weekend at will. Sometimes the weather was perfect and I lived in fear that others would do 'my' climb. The problems remained the same, partner, time and weather. Martin acquired horses and drifted away for a while. Neil discovered bikes and broke his arms for a while. There was an international meet when the weather was stable and overcast, the hills were frosted white and full of super-fit, super-keen heroes. I was working, distracted by jealous worry, but curiously, no one else seemed to want to do what, to me, was the best line in Scotland.

I waited, and waited, and then came the return of the prodigal partner. Richardson, jaded by technical excellence, returned to the esoteric. Remembering the view from an epic time on Slioch in 1994 he brought a new wave of enthusiasm to the project.

The plan was revised. We both had to work on Mondays so we had to get back to the car at a sensible time. One of the major difficulties was going to be finding the start of the route. From below the ground was too complex for a night approach, from above too dangerous (unless conditions were perfect). If the weather was perfect, as the climb has a southerly aspect, it wouldn't be in condition. The answer was clear, climb at night. We would have all day to find the route, and all day to get home.

Other factors had combined to make life easier. New thinking in the management of the Letterewe Estate meant that bikes were welcome, gear had got massively lighter, Internet weather forecasts had become reliable and there was a step change in headtorch quality. In addition I had a secret weapon, a 'night into day' bike torch with which the second could floodlight a pitch.

The new plan was to leave Poolewe just before dawn with overnight gear, bike as far as possible then walk to Carnmore bothy where we would have a quick meal and leave sleeping bags and stove. We would then walk to the summit of A' Mhaighdean, descend to the foot of the route, abseiling if necessary, and start climbing just before dusk. Allowing seven or eight hours for the climb, that would allow us to return to the bothy before dawn and get some food and sleep before walking out in daylight.

So all we had to do was wait: for the weather, at a weekend, when we were both free.

More years passed. Sometimes the weather was right but in midweek, sometimes right but one of us couldn't make it. I began to doubt it would happen until, in the third week of January 2008, everything came together. Overcast skies, freezing level 600m, clear approach paths and both of us able to go – rarely has a decision on venue been less difficult.

We left the road at 6.30 a.m. on 19 January, packs piled high. No lightweight venture this, we went armed with a full rack, and with Simon in the party that is a very full rack, sleeping bags and food for two days. The reasoning here is simple. Scotland isn't the Alps. You don't have to take it all on the route. Food and sleep reduce your chances of failure through exhaustion and ample gear lessens the prospect of sudden death. Speed has little influence on either.

Until just past Kernsary it was a bike trip, a steady uphill grind in the dark. I huffed and panted whilst Simon breathed and chatted. Occasionally a bit of my bike would fail which Simon would amicably fix. I longed to get to the walk, I have never liked bikes and while I was on one I couldn't quite appreciate the day. Dawn found us at Kernsary, relief from my misery soon after when we left the bikes at the watershed below Beinn Airigh Charr. For me the worst of the day was over. I began to take an interest in my surroundings.

Dawn was grey with no sun which was good. There was no snow on the path which was very good but whether or not the route was in we wouldn't know until we were beneath it. We ambled on lost in thought

The South Face of A' Mhaighdeaan. *Pillar Buttress is on the left skyline immediately below the summit with Trident Gully to its right. Right again is Goats' Ridge with Pinnacle Gully to its right. Photo: Roger Webb.*

and talk steadily covering ground, our heavy packs not yet too heavy, and came to Carnmore well before midday. Here we had a brew and a meal.

Just after noon having left our sleeping bags, stove and food we set off again. Planning to ascend A' Mhaighdean by its north-west ridge, which involves a river crossing, we were saved from a mistake by serendipity when we could find no way over. This committed us to a far better and, though longer, quicker way, via the well-built path that runs across to Shenevall, leaving that track to continue by another built path that, after a relatively trivial river crossing, takes you to the col between Ruadh Stac Mòr and A' Mhaighdean. This was much easier work than expected and hopes began to rise as it became clear that we would reach the summit with time to find the descent in daylight. Our optimism increased when as predicted, at around 600m, we passed the freezing level and more as the last 200m to the summit was on well-frozen névé. 2.30 p.m. saw us on top. To our delight we quickly identified the top of the gully between *A Ridge Too Far* and *Pillar Buttress*, but delight was rapidly tempered by the quick discovery that this would be an abseil not a walk down. Conscious of the limited daylight we geared up and down climbed as far as we could before setting up the first anchor.

Three abseils down what looked to be a very pleasant icy grade II/III gully took us to easier ground at the apex of a basin. On the left was Pillar Buttress. We had done it, reached the bottom in daylight. All we had to do now was find a route. Hurriedly I traversed beneath, looking for a line whilst Simon dealt with the ropes. About 50m up I could see a line of chimney-like weakness running up the buttress crest. The problem was how to reach it. There was an obvious way which involved an evil-looking overhanging chimney, but we were looking for the best way, the easiest way up the hardest feature. We had found the hardest feature but needed the easiest way. Traversing further left, I finally found what I was looking for, a groove system that cut diagonally right and looked as if it ought to connect with the chimneys. I hunted for a belay and Simon joined me, handing me one of my axes. Such had been my eagerness that I hadn't noticed it fall from my pack on the last abseil. For the second time that day luck was with us and Simon had spotted it go. I thanked him and peremptorily told him I was doing the first pitch. Seventeen years of anticipation gives you certain rights in these matters! I was rushing to go when he stopped me, pointing out it was going to get dark anyway, we had found the best line and so were in no hurry. It was time to eat and appreciate our surroundings which were spectacular. The air was now clear and our view extended across to Slioch and over Beinn Lair, white against a steel sky.

We took a break.

The first pitch was a pleasant introduction. A very enjoyable grade IV cracked ramp line ending in a spectacular but safe belay off a block that jammed and overhung the steep chimney we had spotted from below. By the time Simon joined me it was fully dark. I got out the bike torch. We were not disappointed, night was rather alarmingly overpowered. The pitch above looked harder but not desperate, a chimney of about a man's width lying the right side of vertical, running up the spine of the ridge. Simon dispatched this with heart-warming efficiency and I almost began to worry that the great project might end up slightly too straightforward, but when I joined him at the next stance I worried for a different reason. The belay was upon a substantial almost semi-circular ledge. The wall at the back was vertical. It was as if a giant had taken a bite out of our ridge, leaving us with a pleasing ledge but with a less pleasing undercut chimney at its back. I dumped the sacks, took the rack and examined the options. The chimney was now just too wide to span with my arms, and at about head height was blocked by an enormous chockstone. This resulted in an overhang with off-width cracks on either side, still contained however within the now shallower chimney. This was going to be struggle, I looked at Simon, who was putting on our rather thin belay jacket. Clearly, he had reached the same conclusion and was settling in.

Pillar Buttress.
Looking down to the author on the stance at the top of Pitch 1 of The Great Game (VII,7).

Photo:
Simon Richardson.

Illuminated from below I started scratching, the right-hand off-width had a chockstone above the overhang. I aimed for that. It was a full fat grunt, no swearing, because unlike some I rope to, I don't, but a lot of muttered Anglo-Saxon and overdone cries of 'watch me'. Half a lifetime, one warthog and a dodgy nut later I pulled up to the happily solid chock and laced it with runners. Fighting hard, I passed it by a layaway on the left. Unfortunately that was it for features in that crack. Above it rose smoothly and closed at an overhang. I retreated to the runners. I could hear Simon beginning to freeze. I requested light out left, Simon obliged and revealed that the left-hand crack whilst steeper at the bottom continued all the way to what appeared to be a good ledge with a hint of turf dripping over. The decision was made. Hooking my right axe over the chockstone I got my feet high on the right and swung my left axe across. I was rewarded by a semi-solid 'thunk'. Now in a near crucifix and wearing leashes, I had to make a quick decision, forward or back? I went forward in one of those 'I really hope this doesn't pop but at least my gear is good' kind of moves which is much preferred to its cousin the 'I really hope this doesn't pop or I'm dead move'. Throwing my right foot across I got some kind of purchase in the crack and looked up. It was no place to wait (although I'm sure that these days it would constitute a rest!). My wrist was pumping, I swung with my right for a seam of turf running parallel to the main crack, got a something, scrabbled through some more somethings before swinging for the turf that I hoped was at the top. This gave solidity but I pulled up to the inevitable disappointment of seeing I still had three metres to go. Uncomfortably aware that with height each move was getting more like its unwelcome cousin, I wasted time and strength looking for gear. I worried some in. Magically, everything got easier and a good ledge quickly arrived. Smugly satisfied that I had cracked the route I looked about. My headtorch beam flicked to the rock above me and punctured my pride. I had merely finished the prelude. The main act was yet to be played.

Half a head shorter and carrying two rucksacks, Simon showed a disturbing lack of respect for my struggle and merely commented 'nice pitch'.

The next pitch was a frosted, near-vertical wall, bounded on its right side with a curving overhang that got bigger with height, with further overhangs on the left at about twenty metres. A steep groove threaded between the two. The initial wall was complicated by what looked to be a large detached flake, about fifteen metres high and one-and-a-half broad that occupied its centre. There was a thin crack on the left. We agreed to avoid the flake. I nestled down out of the fall line and Simon started the crack. All did not go well. The crack was not as good as it looked and within minutes Simon was in a holdless battle, crampons sparking on smoothness. In extremis he grunted for the flake. I cowered, but the flake unlike the crack wasn't false and quickly he swung up to its apex, where again the holds ran out, and he disappeared from view. I froze in the dark, whilst the rope inched out and scattered shouts and curses echoed from the unseen battle. My shivering turned to shuddering while Simon fought on and his cries faded into the night.

The rope stopped. I contemplated it. Was he safe on a belay, stuck beneath some impasse, frozen with horror at the giant fall he was about to take? I didn't know, so I sat in ignorance waiting. Then the imperious tug, the unmistakable pull of someone who has done their bit and now wants you to do yours. I struggled to undo my belay plate, desperately dismantled my stance as the impatient pull became irresistible, and started the pitch. I didn't bother with the crack, just yarded on the flake, which in my deep-frozen state was all I could do. Even allowing for the added weight of the rucksacks, it was hard. I spent most of the pitch shouting, 'watch me' and ended with that giveaway of the struggling second, all the runners on the rope at my waist. This time though we had cracked the crux.

Next was a turfy corner with an overhung right wall. I could get axes in and occasionally my right foot, but despite being off-vertical the pressure on the arms was great. There was little gear but solid placements until at ten metres there was little of either. Salvation lay out left where I could see a wide turf-filled crack leading to a chimney. The problem was getting across the eight-foot gap between me and it. Halfway across was a blob of turf. I placed my left axe in the blob, slipped the right over its top and pulled across to hang beneath it. A hopeful stab with my left foot found the crack. A fumble later I had switched leashes and sunk a placement in the most perfect turf. I followed that with a warthog and, happier than I had been for a while, romped up to the chimney. It had an overhanging base but was only about five metres long. Confident that it was the last major difficulty, I relaxed, gathering myself for the final effort. At this point my body failed me. I had been feeling the odd cramp in my forearms but quite suddenly both went into spasm forcing my hands into fists. Beating my right hand on the rock gave back control of it, but the left was locked solid, with an ice axe I forced the fist open, and before it shut again, put the axe shaft in it. Down to one hand there would be no more runners but in a chimney less need. I thrutched upwards and forced my fading body on. The chimney closed off but aware of a sense of space to my right I flung out my axe and found something solid, pulled through and found myself on easy ground. A snowy ridge led to the summit.

The cramps went as fast as they had come and as I belayed, I enjoyed my solitary peace. There was no wind and the sky was clear. A bank of cloud had invaded in the night but I was above that, indeed the cloud flowed like a glacier between the peaks. Slioch, scene of so many adventures, was glistening in the moonlight; Beinn Lair beckoned with epics to come. Then came Simon, preceded, as always, by his grin. We shook hands in the traditional manner and continued to the top.

The journey home was not grim as with Martin but arduous all the same. We stopped for a meal, two hours' sleep, and another meal at Carnmore and then staggered home in daylight with our far-too-heavy rucksacks, reaching the car thirty hours after we had left. Elated, but completely exhausted and, for the moment, satisfied. Game over.

BASHER – AN INTRODUCTION
TO THE HIGHLANDS

By Geoff Cohen

MR G.I.S. 'BASHER' Bailey, an expatriate Scot, was a teacher of History and English. A spare man in middle age, with a kindly face and thinning grey hair carefully combed, he had left his native Glasgow at the age of six months and been educated at Manchester Grammar School (MGS) between the wars. He had returned to the school as a master after taking a degree at Oxford which seemed to have involved a great deal of football as well as some history. His approach to teaching his subject was highly idiosyncratic. We listened to long discussions of the merits of public schools, during which he tried to convince us that MGS was as good or better than its more famous rivals, and to extensive disquisitions on the merits of games, particularly association football (as he liked to call it), for forming boys' characters. Whole lessons might go by with no mention of history, and when he turned to his subject it was with a very selective slant. Our first year seemed to be devoted almost entirely to Joan of Arc. History then jumped to the campaigns of Montrose, followed by the Jacobite campaigns of 1715 and 1745, which occupied most of our second year's study. Of Tudor England, the English Civil War and so on little was said. It was only Scottish history that really inspired him.

A possible reason for the concentration on Bonnie Prince Charlie was Basher's passion for the Highlands. Through the winter of each school year he would plan the school's 'Scottish trek' for the following summer, writing to estate factors for permission to camp in remote glens and to grocers all over the Highlands with arrangements for food dumps to be made at judiciously selected points. Then in July a band of thirty-odd boys and half a dozen masters would set out to follow his minutely-planned itinerary. Returning to school in the autumn, the next year's classes would be treated to long reminiscences about the camps and hills of the previous summer (with short intervals to do the history of the Jacobites).

So it was that early one morning just after my 15th birthday I stepped off a train at Blair Atholl after a long night journey from Manchester to see the Highlands for the first time. My kit, bought recently from the ex-army stores, was rudimentary: a shapeless rucksack with thin straps that bit into my inexperienced shoulders, some cheap boots, sleeping bag and groundsheet. More impressive was the standard equipment that the school provided for Basher's expeditions. Each tent held about six people and was supported by heavy wooden poles, including a ridge pole. While on the march the tent would be wrapped around one of the poles which was carried by two boys walking in file. Another pole, also carried by two boys in file had a large Dixie slung from its centre, in which were packed the tins of corned beef that provided the daily lunch. Other poles, about five feet long, were carried vertically, like survey poles, by individual boys.

Our first stop – an easy introductory day – was at Bruar Lodge. Though I had camped in the Lake District before, this corner of Perthshire felt much wilder and more remote. Here we were introduced to the camp routines. No Primus stoves in those days, and camping gas hadn't been heard of; instead wood had to collected, and fires laid while the tents were erected, pits dug for latrines and boys gathered around other pits to peel the potatoes. Next day we had to cross the hills to get to Glenfeshie; I suppose it was via the Minigaig, though I understood too little of the topography to know. This gave me my first introduction to Scottish rain. My vague memory is of the party strung out in the mist on featureless grassy ground near the col with a feeling that the masters were not quite sure which way to go. I was utterly soaked and very envious of more experienced boys who somehow had the ability to keep themselves dry in the face of the penetrating rain. The Feshie camp was very pretty, well supplied with wood and our home for the next two nights as the weather aborted the projected first mountain, Mullach Clach a' Bhlair. Then, in improving weather, the party marched up the Feshie, crossed to the Geldie and so to the ruined Bynack Lodge. Here the afternoon was absorbed not only by the usual camp games but also a run up a hill – the first time I had come across this strange concept! Not that I tried it myself, but there was an nice-looking hill opposite, possibly Meall Tionail, which attracted the attention of one of the school's cross-country runners. To my eyes it looked improbably far away. He assured me he could run up it in half an hour, which I flatly disbelieved. Bets were arranged and I duly lost!

The next day brought us, with a bit of road march, to Braemar, allowing Basher to expound on the Highland Games, Royal Deeside and suchlike – all cultural novelties for me. Early next morning a local boy aged only about eight was engaged to row us across the river in small groups, thus enabling us to walk via Linn of Quoich to Derry Lodge. Here we had another fabulous campsite with plenty of shelter among the Scots pines, in a place full of history. There followed my first Scottish mountain, Ben Macdui, of which after nearly fifty years only a few memories remain – the acres of scree near the summit, my first ptarmigan, and the heady joy of careering downhill on Macdui's southern slopes.

Basher had been talking all that week of the Lairig Ghru, which was to be our big test. All went well, with forbearing weather, and a tired party climbed through the Chalamain gap and descended triumphantly to the Glenmore campsite, having vanquished what we thought of as the crux of the trek. A rest day was ordered, with an option to climb Cairngorm. The road and ski station had not long been opened in 1962, so it was not going to be a difficult day. But at that time I had never heard of Munros and preferred to rest my feet in camp – even to my slowly awakening mountaineer's eyes a trudge up the north side of Cairngorm looked a tad boring.

The crocodile road-marched to a sleepy Aviemore (virtually no developments) and took the train to Inverness, a veritable fleshpot. From here Basher was to take us across country to the mysterious west. A bus dropped us the next day near Muir of Ord and we proceeded up Glen Orrin to camp somewhere that I cannot now place on the map. Be that as it may, the next day we crossed the hills southwest to Loch Monar and walked along the north shore to camp near its west end. The arrangement was for stores to have been delivered by boat to this remote campsite, but we arrived to find nothing there! It was mid-afternoon and the teachers had thirty hungry, tired boys to worry about. Amid much dramatic talk of what might be done to save us, I have a vivid memory of folk going repeatedly down to the loch shore to see if a boat was on its way. Finally, after an agonising wait, the vessel was spied in the far distance, chugging towards us. We were saved a hungry night, and were soon happily peeling spuds around the cooking pit!

Needless to say, Basher wore a kilt for these marches over the hills. I do not recall headgear or gaiters though I suppose he must have carried some kind of windproof jacket. He certainly had a stick and he liked to be in front with the boys following in a reasonably orderly fashion. I am not sure whether a master was deputed to bring up the rear – my memory is rather of a straggly tail. However, if we fanned out across the hillside and got ahead of Basher, we were rapidly reprimanded.

From Loch Monar our trek continued over the Bealach Bearnais and down to Achnashellach – where the rhododendrons somehow lent an air of civilisation after the rigorous emptiness of Glen Orrin and the Loch Monar shores. Then on over the Coulin hills to Annat by Loch Torridon and another rain-swept camp, with the ascent of Liathach cancelled due to continuous rain. The road to Shieldaig was just being built and we walked among the generators next day for the short trek to Shieldaig, arriving early enough for an optional afternoon ascent of Beinn Shieldaig. Earlier that summer I had had my first introduction to rock climbing thanks to a very helpful physics teacher. So as we set off up the mountain I soon veered off on my own to try and climb the rock on its west side. Though the sandstone tiers were small I was, of course, way out of my depth. The main party could be glimpsed far ahead towards the summit ridge as I was still grappling with an initial, steep, grassy corner. I have no idea where or how I scrambled up, only that I was way behind the rest of the party – not that they bothered in those health-and-safety-free days.

Shieldaig seemed unbelievably charming, a kind of village I had not seen before. It was somehow arranged that for our next day we would be rowed over to the Applecross shore, in order to avoid walking around the head of Loch Shieldaig (hardly a long way). This led to our last bit of hillwalking as we crossed the Applecross peninsula directly to the west coast, and, finally, views of the open sea. There followed quite a few miles of dusty walking down the coast to Toscaig, right at the southern tip. It was a wonderful place to spend our last day, revelling in the green turf and the ocean air. A boat took us to Kyle next day, then another to Mallaig where we had a chance to take a horribly cold swim and to sample the delights of a tiny cinema.

It had been an unforgettable three weeks, during which I had been shown some of the finest of Scottish hills, both east and west. A seed had been planted which would last me a lifetime. Basher must have led such treks for over a score of years, introducing hundreds of boys to the land that he loved so much. Looking back it is humbling to think how much our teachers do for us, and how, so often, they are little appreciated. As Frank Richards used to say in the Bunter books that I devoured at the age of eight, 'the ungrateful child is worse than the serpent's tooth'. Yet the wise teacher knows that however little he is appreciated at the time, the memory of good works has been stamped on the mind and will probably remain with his pupils all their lives.

OPEN TO INTERPRETATION

By Mike Dixon

1979 WAS MEMORABLE for four significant events. It was my final year at secondary school, *Apocalypse Now* was released, the Tories won the general election, and for me and a group of contemporaries, it was our first trip to the Scottish mountains. Only one of these had negative connotations.

We piled into a fetid compartment on the overnight train from Crewe, and were subjected to the bigoted comments of two young builders from London, off to Loch Eil Outward Bound for some personal development programme. They wore white ankle socks and slagged off our cheap trainers and jeans. For the first time I heard the contraction 'loadsamoney,' several years before the Harry Enfield character immortalised it. It was the dawn of Thatcherism, the celebration of the 'me society' and this pair personified it. The British Rail buffet was beyond our budget while they returned with mountains of beer and sandwiches, more for show than for any real need. They threw the food they didn't want out of the window with a sneering leer in our direction. 'Fackin gypsies,' they called us when we brought out the stove to brew up. The only upper hand we had was when football was mentioned. Back then, north of England teams like Liverpool ruled Britain if not Europe.

We had to suffer their chippiness from Crewe to Fort William. Shortly after leaving Glasgow I escaped them to investigate the view. And there it was, my first-sighted Scottish mountain, The Cobbler. It was only on show for about five seconds but I could name it instantly as Poucher's *Scottish Peaks* had been pored over at length prior to the trip.

'Be lucky,' they chirped as we said goodbye to this pair of Cockney bankers. And lucky we got as we crossed over the sea to Skye.

Pinnacle Ridge on our first full day led to what was for all of us our first Munro, though the term was not then in common currency and we wouldn't have known what one was anyway. It was impressively longer than Bristly Ridge. From this aptly named Peak of the Young Men, ambitions were fired by the kaleidoscopic 360° view. It was an epiphany. Later we went into Portree in search of an ice cream. The shop just had a type of cheap, flavoured, cylindrical ice bar which back home we knew as Tip Tops. The attractive female assistant looked puzzled when we asked for one. They obviously had a different name for it up here. The penny dropped when we pointed to them. 'So you want a fruity lick do you ?' she asked in complete innocence.

We were still laughing about that as we crammed into the public bar at Sligachan later that evening. Not that we had much money to spend on beer; it became the only refuge from the midges. Any prior scepticism about these vicious natives had been eradicated within twenty seconds of attempting to pitch the tents. Breakfast that morning had to be eaten on the move; we were learning fast. The day ended with us huddled round a crackly, dying transistor radio in a canvas Force Ten tent, listening to Led Zeppelin tracks played back to back. Despite the sunburn, the gritty scalps caused by the dead midges in our hair, the gabbro-scoured fingers and the diet of Springlow dehydrated meals, we were mellow and content.

The next day we connected Bruach na Frithe with Am Basteir. Naismith's Route felt bold for us at the time. David soon progressed from routes first climbed by old timers in ties and tweeds to climbs of a whole different genre. In a couple of years he was involved in the first ascents of routes with names like Margins of the Mind and Cystitis by Proxy, earning a promotion straight to Olympus or in other words the top table in Pete's Eats. While others were heading off to the Falklands, he and his peers were taking climbing degrees at Bangor then graduating to joining a leisure class on the dole, a fully paid-up member of Maggie's climbing army. The rest of us bumbled around, not progressing beyond VS, while Mur y Niwl and A Dream of White Horses were the only routes we did with names which were not prosaic.

During that trip we all talked about doing the main ridge one day but it was a while before I had it seriously in my sights. For several years, technicalities became more important than the bigger picture and anyway, I thought, I could always still do it when I was past it as a climber.

But there were some salutary lessons about leaving it too late. Two older friends on separate attempts had got as far as Basteir Tooth, tantalisingly close to the end. One abandoned because of lack of daylight. The other's companions were too tired to continue whereas he had enough juice to get to Gillean. However he was unwilling to solo Naismith's Route. To bypass the Tooth on the Coire a' Basteir side and double back for Am Basteir then on to Gillean would only have meant one thing for him: he hadn't really done it. But failure can be painful; neither had been back to reattempt it and now never would. Others, perfectly competent, had been thwarted by the weather, often heat. Some had underestimated the whole undertaking; the sight of the long side of the TD Gap put paid to several dreams. The lowly grade of the individual pitches tells you nothing about the nature of the whole day. Others who claimed a traverse, had avoided key pitches or didn't start at the true end, starting for instance at Coire a' Ghrunnda. Read some websites or blogs and you'd think everyone is skipping across it in a six hour breeze. In reality it has humbled more than a few suitors.

It's open to interpretation what a true traverse entails, so here is my own fairly conservative definition. To summarise: you really should begin at Gars-bheinn, a peak not in any tickers' list yet surely one of the finest situated peaks in these isles. It's one of the few British peaks where you can make believe you're in the Lofoten Islands with its slopes running right into the sea. Grunt up the TD Gap, divert for Sgùrr Alasdair, romp up one of the unlikeliest looking Diffs around in the form of King's Chimney, tread air on the In Pinn's East Ridge, tightrope across between Sgùrr a' Ghreadaidh's tops, pad down the rooftops in cat burglar style on Bidein Druim nan Ràmh's central peak, play at fly-on-a-wall on Naismith's Route on Basteir Tooth. One well-known mountain guide reckons Sgùrr Dubh Mòr has to be included as well (thus collecting all the Munros) while a minority would put the case for finishing on Sgùrr na h-Uamha. These have never bothered me. I've dodged An Caisteal each time too. On the first traverse in 1911, Shadbolt and Maclaren had to climb the latter to satisfy their own ideals. Missing this particular top would have meant straying from what Shadbolt described as the 'path of virtue'. Use of a rope at any stage is permitted. For purity you should complete from Gars-bheinn to Gillean without a bivvy but one the night before is fine and a splendid preliminary to contemplate what is ahead of you. Stashed water or being supplied with provisions en route isn't an issue with me. Prolonging it over two full days means extra gear but a more relaxed pace. However a weighty rucksack can detract from the enjoyment and traversing in one push always felt more elegant and satisfying. Shadbolt and Maclaren's style is one to aim for, completing in a very respectable 12¼ hours. And the best bit of all… the East Ridge of An Stac, historically a loose non-recommendation, in essence, the epitome of the Cuillin: improbable looking, friendly on closer acquaintance. Flutter around its barrel-shaped prow, enjoy its glorious situation, but don't make a mistake. The In Pinn that follows is just the icing on top.

And that's how I did it on my first traverse in 1994; three of us, a solid effort but unspectacular time in a perfect, cool temperature. Donald was the least fit but with a good head he could handle the extended concentration required. Neil had failed on an attempt with his wife on a scorching day two years before. He described the whole experience of a successful completion as like gorging on a sumptuous meal. In future he'd prefer to sample and savour it in shorter bites. I was pleased but thought I could have gone much quicker and at least twice waited an hour for the others to catch up. But it was 14 years before I tried it again. I still had something to satisfy, basically my ego.

So off I set on a solo attempt in June 2008. All went well despite prior worries about tackling the TD Gap. King's Chimney was sobering due to the fall of a friend soloing it the previous year. Geoff decided to test if the mountain gods still favoured him when he departed from the rock high up the corner. The gods were still fond of him but gave him a broken femur which was quite a fortunate let-off. I'd have put serious money on him bouncing off Collie's Ledge and ending his days in the Alasdair Stone Chute. Naismith's Route was a long way off but by the time I got there I was dehydrated and not feeling at all bold. I retreated a short way along the initial traverse and tried to recruit someone to hold my rope. No such luck. I sat and brooded then decided to take the Lota Corrie route. I consoled myself with the fact that even Alison Hargreaves elected not to solo Naismith's behind us back in 1994. No qualms for the guides who often dodge the Tooth with clients. Future bookings, bonuses, free drinks at the Sligachan and the well-being of their clients must all take precedence. I wouldn't argue with that. There are many possible variations between Gars-bheinn and Gillean.

For avoiding Naismith's and taking the Lota Corrie option you certainly get punished with the subsequent height loss and re ascent. But I finished satisfied. I was even piped to the cairn by a chap from Ardersier on a personal odyssey to play the pipes on the summit of every Munro. If you don't like the instrument be warned; he still hasn't completed.

Then when I was in the pub a few evenings later I was told I hadn't done it for dodging Naismith's, admittedly by someone who had never done the ridge and probably never would. But I had to agree he had a point. By missing the Tooth completely you also dodge the hardest technical move (despite the lack of exposure) on the whole ridge on the step up to Am Basteir. At least I'd done that. A weary Shadbolt had to step on Maclaren's shoulders to overcome this obstacle on the first traverse. He makes no mention of straying from the 'path of virtue' in using this direct aid.

The following year I fancied doing it again but this time as training for the Greater Traverse. Bob was fit having completed various long runs and cycles. Eyeing up his gleaming, bald head I could have sworn he'd polished it to make him go faster. We took a bivvy at the top of the Stone Chute and finished after a long, hot, close day. On the final ridge of Gillean we passed my prospective partner for the Greater Traverse guiding some less experienced folk around and dumping water for our attempt. Each time I've done it has felt tougher than the previous even though I slashed my time on the solo attempt. You make excuses about the heat and partners but eventually the finger points at you. The Greater Cuillin Traverse still remains a dream.

Compared to that first trip, I look on the Cuillin differently now. I'm amazed by how much loose rock is up there. But since then I've been to the Stiperstones and Yosemite. The aura has waned, the anticipation about a visit is not as fervent. The sacrosanct has become the familiar; still a special place though. Looking at that jagged skyline can be as rewarding as grappling with it. I've watched others get more out of just absorbing the view from Elgol, Torrin, The Storr, Drynoch etc. without needing to set foot on the peaks. In the past I thought they were missing something, now I understand. To maintain the mystique you should probably never set foot on them. Paradoxically, it was always going to be downhill in a sense after that first day out on Sgùrr nan Gillean.

Some of my best memories of the Cuillin are nothing to do with achievement or views. Like Willie romping over Clach Glas in flip flops, passing several earnest mountaineers all with mouths agape.

The time at the Coruisk hut where we'd all had a great Saturday regardless of what we'd done. The next day the Mad Burn was raging, fed by the incessant rain and we turned to a stash of old climbing and Scots Magazines to pass the time. Now, Tommy Weir enthusing about dotterels or Perthshire never did anything for me but then someone discovered two Top Shelf Glossies at the bottom of the pile. It was enlightening to see the whole cross section of the hut (no women), a range of ages, jobs and backgrounds united in bawdiness and great unselfconscious belly laughs. The late Norman Mailer thought political correctness was the greatest affront to free speech in these modern times. In places like Coruisk, we can enthuse about lofty ideals, the setting, the Dubhs, John Muir, alpine plants, Sea Eagles, routes like King Cobra, but there's always another side to man lurking beneath the surface. Growing older helps you strip back the pretensions or makes you less tolerant of them. The Cuillin experience would be highly diluted without the company of others.

Certain bits away from the ridge stick in the memory as much as the main spine. Like lying on the top of the intriguing peak of Sgùrr Coire an Lochain, the last Cuillin summit to be climbed. From this angle the In Pinn looks like the Leaning Tower of Pisa and I was almost willing it to keel over on the Coruisk side. Or Druim nan Ràmh, a rare place for the Cuillin, where you stride out for most of it on a wide highway with no sign of wear. With your mind unencumbered by technical ground you can savour the great close ups of the wild Coruisk side of the ridge. Or the NE Ridge of Sgùrr a' Choire Bhig, a retiring, boiler-plated gem with some tricky moves and interesting route finding, completely neglected compared to the Dubhs.

Skye wasn't even the Cuillin any more; the Duirinish coastal walk sealed that, with its stacks, waterfalls and great bothy. We had it all to ourselves despite it being a May Bank Holiday weekend.

As time has passed prospective ridge partners have become fewer and fatter with the ridge fading off the radar for most. However Chris and I talked about it and despite being on the wrong side of 50 he was keen, lean and fit, an Oxford chemistry graduate who made his pile in the unusual but ubiquitous field of tampons. His Christ Church confidence did not endear him to everyone but I always found him good company. I hadn't known him long but days on Tryfan, Cadair Idris and an alpine

Helvellyn in January 2010 laid the foundations for the future good times I was anticipating. A month later his 11-year-old daughter was reading a poem about him to a large, gathered audience. Reaching the top of Stob Coir' an Albannaich in a white-out he strayed a couple of steps too far from the safety of the summit cairn and had climbed his final mountain. The ridge had some darker associations now and I felt a chapter was closing.

May 2010 heralded the return of the Tories and the introduction of the concept of the 'big society'. November saw an early dump of snow and me and a Guardian-reading, cosmic caperer over in Kintail enjoying a pad over Beinn Fhada and its splendidly situated south-west ridge over Sgùrr a' Choire Ghairbh. One minute we're together then there's no sign of Willie. No reply to my shouts caused me to retrace my footsteps. He was disoriented, his legs barely able to support him and clearly unable to continue. Initially he headed off 180° in the wrong direction on the tracks we had already made. Putting on his gloves stretched his cognitive capacity to the full. Stroke? Heart attack? A spliff too many? (One shared with Kirriemuir and AC/DC's Bon Scott.) Luckily nothing serious was later diagnosed but a ride home in the chopper ensued, my greatest relief being that it wasn't my car left parked at the Morvich Centre as we took the quick way over to Raigmore.

Waiting for the Sea King, it was a cold but windless night. From our perch I watched the sun die behind the Cuillin Ridge. A band of acid orange framed that jagged skyline, above it a layer of lemon then eggshell blue. In the canopy were brooding, whorled clouds while at sea level lay a silvery, viscous Loch Duich. Some like to attach a deeper, metaphysical interpretation to such scenes; I just like to stare. When the cold kicked in and I needed a distraction, I killed time scanning each section of the now starkly black crest, naming every jink and spike to myself. It looked just too fantastical to be of this world. My biggest regret was that I'd done the ridge, but in that instant I knew I had to do it just one more time. I don't really know why or what I was expecting to get out of it. It just felt the right thing to do.

> Can I ever express all the beauties of Skye.
> Can I tell of its distant, but sharp outlined peaks:
> Tell of sounds for the ear and sights for the eye,
> With the peace and the calm that your tired spirit seeks.

> C.M. Dixon, *Glenbrittle House Log Book* 1951.

THE ICE CLIMBS OF THE MERRICK

By Stephen Reid

IF FEW CLIMBERS are aware of the wonderful granite climbing in the Galloway Hills, even fewer have any idea of the potential of this neglected area for winter climbing. The ice climbs of Cairnsmore of Fleet and those of Craignaw, in particular the classic Dow Spout (II/III), have made it into print in the past[1], but it is the Black Gairy of the Merrick that provides the biggest concentration of winter climbs in the area, and probably the most reliable conditions.

As a winter climbing venue, the Black Gairy should be ideal, sitting, as it does, at around 600m and being, as it is, composed of dank, vegetated, north-facing, metamorphic rock. However the traditional steady accumulation of snow with winter routes building up gradually over a period of weeks is hampered somewhat by the crag's open aspect westwards to the sea some 20 miles away where lurk the warming Gulf Stream currents responsible for the sub-tropical paradise that is Logan Botanic Gardens on the nearby Stranraer Peninsula. Thankfully though the Black Gairy is essentially an ice crag, similar to Beinn Udlaidh, and the routes are icefalls fed by summit springs. Thus it only needs a hard freeze to bring it into condition and a hovering freeze/thaw cycle to fatten it up nicely – the icing on the ice so to speak. And in winters such as that of 2009/10 the icing can be exceptional. Snow, while adding to the picturesque atmosphere (and possibly the difficulty) is not really essential except in so much as it improves the photography. The crag's major routes are around four pitches long and over 150 metres in length and many of its classic climbs are IIIs and IVs. However, before this all begins to sound too idyllic it should be remembered that this is Galloway and the approach therefore makes Knoydart seem like a stroll in a very well manicured park, though it has to be said that the approach is actually a bit of a doddle for Galloway.

Despite all this winter iciness, the first recorded route was a summer ascent of its one deeply cut gully, the attractively named *Black Gutter*, by G Girdwood at some time in the 1920s, though legend has it that it was first climbed in Victorian times by the farmer from Shalloch on Minnoch in the course of rescuing a sheep, the ascent being accomplished at night in a thunderstorm with the added complications of rockfall and the unwanted attentions of an aggressive eagle. One feels that, like many climbing stories, this is a tale that may have grown in the telling. The first winter ascent seems likely to have gone unrecorded but it is known that the right branch was climbed by Davie Sproat and Alan Kelso in the

---

1   The Spout of Clints and Smear Test, *FRCC Journal,* 1998
      Dow Spout, *SMC Journal*, 2003

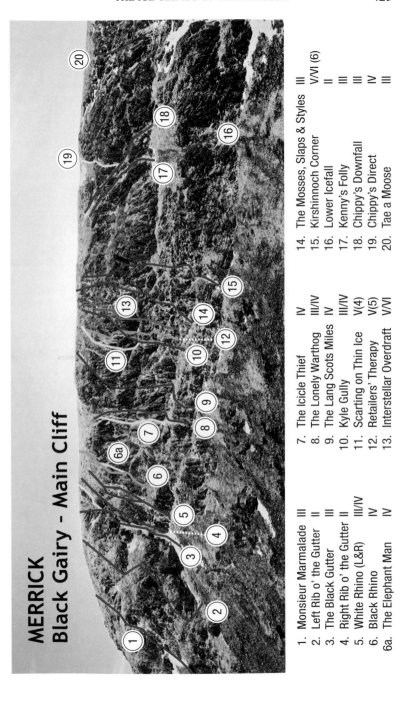

MERRICK
Black Gairy - Main Cliff

1. Monsieur Marmalade — III
2. Left Rib o' the Gutter — II
3. The Black Gutter — III
4. Right Rib o' the Gutter — II
5. White Rhino (L&R) — III/IV
6. Black Rhino — IV
6a. The Elephant Man — IV
7. The Icicle Thief — IV
8. The Lonely Warthog — III/IV
9. The Lang Scots Miles — IV
10. Kyle Gully — III/IV
11. Scarting on Thin Ice — V(4)
12. Retailers' Therapy — V(5)
13. Interstellar Overdraft — V/VI
14. The Mosses, Slaps & Styles — III
15. Kirshinnoch Corner — V/VI (6)
16. Lower Icefall — II
17. Kenny's Folly — III
18. Chippy's Downfall — III
19. Chippy's Direct — IV
20. Tae a Moose — III

1970s and the left branch by Eric Christison, Jim Wilson, Kenny George, Alastair Watson and Merv Atkinson in 1985. Whatever its history, it is a fine grade III gully with rock scenery reminiscent of *SC Gully* in Glen Coe and it often retains névé late in the season.

In the 1970s and 1980s various routes between grade II and IV were climbed but not fully recorded by Sproat and other Kyle Mountaineering Club members such as Christison, Wilson, George, Watson, Atkinson, Alec Dowers, M Pashke and C Murray. These included *Left Rib o' the Gutter* (II) by Sproat, *Right Rib o' the Gutter* (II/III), Dave McGimpsey and Sproat, the excellent *Kyle Gully* (IV) (one of the great lines of the crag), Christison and Atkinson, and culminated in the impressive and unrepeated vertical icicle of *Interstellar Overdraft* (V, though it does a very good imitation of a VI) by Robin McAllister and Stuart Mearns in 1993 – the tale is that it was thawing and Rob was concerned that he was going to fall off the mush at the top of it and that none of his screws would hold in the soft ice. All in all a sporting near-death experience!

In 1996 two inveterate Galloway pioneers, John Biggar and Colin Hossack, and someone whose surname they can't remember (though his Christian name was Stewart), chipped in with three shorter icefalls on the right-hand side of the main crag, including *Kenny's Folly* (III) and *Chippy's Downfall* (III), named in honour of the Livingston brothers, antique restorers to the gentry of Castle Douglas, who had turned down an invitation to participate on the grounds that the conditions would be rubbish.

Seven years passed before the next new route and the first recording here of names that were already famed in the history of Gallwegian exploration, Andrew Fraser and Ian Magill. Their *Lang Scots Miles* (IV), albeit possibly climbed before by the Kyle MC, is one of the best routes on the crag, with steep icefalls leading to an easier but very scenic upper gully. Andrew writes:

> The name came from the two and three-quarter hour slog in knee deep snow from the road. We were surprised to find such good conditions and such was the depth of snow that we did not realise for another six years that this was an ice venue which didn't need any snow.

In 2006, good conditions in March enticed John and Linda Biggar to explore the left-hand end of the crag (until 2010 they were accustomed to approach over the Merrick from the south, so the left end was the first reached). The first obvious icefall right of the Black Gutter gave them, Dave McNicol and Adam Brooke-Mee the fine *White Rhino* (III/IV) with two variation finishes. Just over a week later the Biggars returned with myself and Colin Wells in tow and we climbed the next two major parallel lines to the right. While the Biggars' *The Lonely Warthog* (III/IV) is, as its name implies, renowned for the paucity of its protection, our

MERRICK - Black Gairy
Right-hand Cliff

20. Tae a Moose	III
21. Fat Triplet	II
22. Skinny Triplet	III
23. Thick Triplet	II

24. A Fridge Too Far	III
25. Path to the Sun	III
26. Headtorch Gully	I/II
27. Nice Finish	I/II

28. No Time for Lunch	II/III
29. Kirriemore Gully	II
30. The Right Rib o' the Gairy	II/III

James Kinnaird leads the crux pitch of Retailers' Therapy (V) during the first ascent.

Photo: Stephen Reid.

The Icicle Thief (IV) provides the most reliable ice on the crag – though it too seems likely to have been climbed by Kyle MC judging from some old gear found near the top of the third pitch recently.

The next few winters were poor and the new routes record shows this with only two climbs added, *Monsieur Marmalade* (III) by John Biggar and James Kinnaird (James is a grocer, which might explain the route's name) and *The Mosses, Slaps and Styles* (III) from Fraser and Magill. However in early 2010 superb conditions, with the icefalls in magnificent form, little snow and generally fine weather, allowed a thorough exploration of the crag. First on the scene were Fraser and Magill (who else?!) who contributed *Black Rhino* (IV), a short two pitch line adjacent to *White Rhino*. A month later James Kinnaird and myself stared up at the crag in amazement – with ice spilling in all directions, it looked more like Rjukan than Galloway. Spoilt for choice, we climbed an excellent series of icefalls just to the right of *Kyle Gully* to give what James christened (on the basis that we are both shopkeepers) *Retailers' Therapy* (V) and then abbed back down to do a similar job up the thin gangway on its left, which proved to be *Scarting on Thin Ice* (V). A few days later we were back for more and managed to claw our way up *Kirshinnoch*

James Kinnaird follows the crux pitch of Kirshinnoch Corner (V/VI) during the first ascent. Photo:Stephen Reid.

Corner (V/VI), the longest and possibly the hardest route on the crag. The first three pitches are straightforward but the fourth is 40 metres long and very steep and sustained with thin 'spray on' ice and turf. Fortunately it is amazingly well protected as long as you have a full set of cams which for some odd reason I did – strange as it's about the only place on the crag you can place them. Above, two further pitches lead to the top; these are easy – and a good thing too.

In early March, John Biggar and I checked out the far right end of the crag and came away with four short routes, all very enjoyable, and including the three gullies known as *The Triplets* (II, III and III), and John was back the next day with Linda, Ian Brown and Sandy Currie and added another four, the best of which is *Path to the Sun* (III), whilst James and I (who had spent the day checking some of the existing lines) pitched in at dusk with the aptly named *Headtorch Gully* (II). I returned with Colin Wells a week later in the hope that *Interstellar Overdraft* might have fattened up sufficiently to be justifiable only to find that it had in fact fallen down but came away with *Elephant Man* (IV), a companion route to *Black Rhino*, and that was the final new climb of an amazing winter, one that saw a doubling in the number of recorded lines.

With a good start to the 2010/11 winter it was hoped that more of the same would follow but in the end it was only Fraser and Magill who got anything new done with two additions to the shorter right-hand end, including the aptly named *A Fridge Too Far* (III) – and that brings the Merrick up to date.

As a venue for those living south of the Highlands and north of the Lake District, it is well worth considering in a long cold spell. Until recently it was possible to drive (probably illegally) up various forest tracks from Kirriereoch to the west and the walk in was then a not too difficult (for Galloway) 50 minutes. However I understand that now a locked gate bars the way so for the next guide the approach will be...

From the public car park and picnic spot (NX 358 866), follow the track, branching left at a fork, to Kirriereoch Farm gate. Don't enter the farmyard, but take the track which passes in front of it and turn right almost immediately. Follow this track for about one kilometre to the next junction, just before a bridge over Kirriemore Burn. Turn right, cross the bridge and turn left immediately along a track that is not marked on the map for about one and a half kilometres until it doglegs sharply back on itself (NX 388 869). A firebreak drops down from here to the Kirshinnoch Burn. Follow the south bank of the burn to the crag which lies on the right shortly after the second stone wall is crossed (1 hour 45 minutes – but can be shortened by using bicycles). There is an excellent gearing up point under a 5m high prow-like buttress at the base of the right bounding rib of the crag, adjacent to the descent path, whilst a third stone wall higher up the valley leads directly to the foot of the *Black Gutter*. The crag can be also be approached from Glen Trool to the south but this takes a lot longer.

Needless to say, as with any approach in Galloway, a set of walking poles will help you avoid tripping over the worst of the tussocks and it is also worth remembering that if over optimism or a sudden thaw has meant that none of the routes on the Black Gairy are actually 'in' when you arrive, you may yet salvage the trip by carrying on up the glen and round into the east-facing corrie of the Howe of the Caldron where resides the Merrick's only other winter climb, *North-East Couloir* (II), which is more of an icefall than a couloir and which provides the highest and most reliable ice in the Galloway Hills, with a return by way of a fine summit to complete the day.

My thanks to John Biggar, Andrew Fraser and James Kinnaird for their assistance with this article.

EILDE EXPLORATION

Two New Venues in Glen Coe

By Simon Yearsley

MALCOLM BASS AND I, along with a variety of friends, have been busy exploring the beautiful Coire Eilde in Glen Coe. Most climbers who travel up the Lairig Eilde are aiming for the classic ridge of Sròn na Lairig on the south east ridge of Stob Coire Sgreamhach. Malcolm and I wandered slowly up this fine ridge on 12 December 2010, after several beers and vodkas too many in the Clachaig the night before to celebrate Malcolm and Paul Figg's ascent of the West Face of Vasuki Parbat.

The guidebook mentions 'an easy grade I gully which leads up to join the main route' on the summit buttress to the right of the ridge, but we were taken by the short but steep buttress immediately right of the gully. The base of this summit buttress is at 900m, faces due north, and the steep central wall provides an obvious challenge, with other interesting lines to each side. We vowed to return when our heads were slightly clearer.

Whilst descending back into Coire Eilde, we stumbled (almost literally!) on a second reason to return to the corrie: in the bottom of the corrie, the Allt Coir' Eilde tumbles into a long, steep-sided canyon which is almost invisible until you are standing on the very edge. We were amazed to see about a half a dozen superb icefalls dropping into the deep canyon. The recent thaw was making some of them run with water, but there was no doubt that the early December freeze had created lots of ice in this superb and unusual feature, and it was ripe for exploration. It was too late in the day to even find an easy way down into the canyon, and it also needed a wee bit more of a freeze.

I returned on 22 December with Dan Peach, and we headed up first to the 'Sròn na Lairig Summit Buttress'. We climbed *The Promise,* 110m III which takes a nice line up the left edge of the main summit buttress, before moving right into a pleasant, hidden, twisting gully line to the top of the buttress.

Dan and I then scurried down to the canyon and abseiled in from a convenient boulder. The canyon was like no place either of us had ever been in Scotland. The main canyon felt like a hidden world, and was about 250m long, 10–15m wide with superb steep walls dripping with incredible icefalls, most of which were 30–40m long pure ice routes. Rather than the half a dozen we had expected, as we walked up the canyon, we were amazed to find at least 16 compelling ice lines including an awesome feature of three vertical pillars of beautiful blue ice. We chose a line of steep ice above an obvious frozen pool towards the top of the canyon, and climbed *Primero Pool*, IV,4.

I returned again two days later on 24 December, this time with Neil Silver and Simon Davidson. Neil and Simon loved the venue, and likened it more to a Mexican desert canyon than a Glen Coe ice venue… hence the Mexican vibe to the naming of the subsequent routes! Christmas Eve gave two lines: the two tiered *Andale Andale!* – a solid V,5 with a superb initial ice pillar and steep finishing section – and *Jumble Left-Hand* again at V,5 up a large area of ice with at least three potential lines. Neil led the initial vertical and thinly iced wall of Jumble LH before moving to the centre of the icefall to finish.

Simon Davidson then returned on Boxing Day with Tom Broadbent and came away with three fine lines: the short but sweet *El Mini* at IV,4, which lies about 100m downstream of the main canyon; and *Aye Carumba*, V,5, the right-hand of the two obvious lines opposite the abseil point. They finished the day with *Jumble Right-Hand*, again at V,5.

Malcolm was keen to get amongst the action in what was now called 'Eilde Canyon', and made the regular long trip up from North Yorkshire on 28 December. He led the beautiful ice formation, *Zapatista* V,5, which gave possibly the most aesthetic route so far in the Canyon. I was

Malcolm Bass on Zapatista (V,5), Eilde Canyon.

Photo: Simon Yearsley.

Simon Yearsley on Central Amigo (V,6), Eilde Canyon.

Photo: Malcolm Bass.

determined to have a go at one of the three vertical pillars, which had already been named *The 3 Amigos*. Setting off up *Central Amigo*, I was glad I'd borrowed Malcolm's axes with their brand new picks, and the fantastic blue pillar gave the steepest line (so far!) in Eilde Canyon at V,6. We finished a great day with Malcolm leading *El Mixi!* – an excellent icy corner opposite *Primero Pool* with a fine mixed section at mid height which proved surprisingly tricky to protect.

The 'Sròn na Lairig Summit Buttress' was proving too much of a draw for our more usual mixed climbing tastes, so on 8 January Malcolm and I headed past the Eilde Canyon, and higher up into Coire Eilde with Paul Figg and Neil Silver. Both teams were successful, with Malcolm and Paul climbing the most obvious weakness in the steep central wall – a fine grey pillar which petered out into a steeper barrier before the angle relented a little before rearing up again at the very top. *The Grey Pillar* VI,7 gave a superb, if short, two pitch route, probably deserving of two stars, and finishing via a steep corner crack. Neil and I found another fine line starting right of the steep central section via an awkward chimney, before heading back left on the main buttress to a conspicuous slot on the skyline… *The Slot* V,6 is again an excellent route which pulls through the eponymous final obstacle to belay on the summit on the

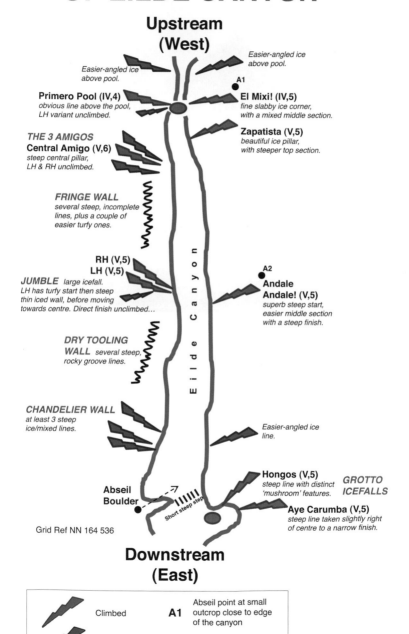

PLAN VIEW 'TOPO' OF EILDE CANYON

Upstream (West)

Easier-angled ice above pool.

A1

Easier-angled ice above pool.

Primero Pool (IV,4)
obvious line above the pool,
LH variant unclimbed.

El Mixi! (IV,5)
fine slabby ice corner,
with a mixed middle section.

THE 3 AMIGOS
Central Amigo (V,6)
steep central pillar,
LH & RH unclimbed.

Zapatista (V,5)
beautiful ice pillar,
with steeper top section.

FRINGE WALL
several steep, incomplete
lines, plus a couple of
easier turfy ones.

Eilde Canyon

RH (V,5)
LH (V,5)

A2
Andale
Andale! (V,5)
superb steep start,
easier middle section
with a steep finish.

JUMBLE large icefall.
LH has turfy start then steep
thin iced wall, before moving
towards centre. Direct finish unclimbed...

DRY TOOLING
WALL several steep,
rocky groove lines.

CHANDELIER WALL
at least 3 steep
ice/mixed lines.

Easier-angled ice
line.

Hongos (V,5)
steep line with distinct
'mushroom' features.

GROTTO
ICEFALLS

Abseil
Boulder

Short steep step

Aye Carumba (V,5)
steep line taken slightly right
of centre to a narrow finish.

Grid Ref NN 164 536

Downstream (East)

| | Climbed | **A1** | Abseil point at small outcrop close to edge of the canyon |
| | Unclimbed | **A2** | Abseil point 15m back from edge |

Diagram: Simon Yearsley
(Labels amended slightly)

same large block as *The Grey Pillar*, making for a very sociable finish as one by one the climbers arrived on the summit gabbling excitedly about their routes and taking in the glorious prospect down Loch Etive. Thin turf was a feature of both routes, and neither was particularly easy to protect.

The most recent visit to Eilde Canyon was on 11 January 2011 by Simon Davidson, this time accompanied by Neil Carnegie. The pair climbed *Hongos* V,5 – the left-hand of what were now known as the *Grotto Icefalls*, which gave a fine pitch on chandeliered and mushroom-featured ice. They finished the day with a second ascent of *Central Amigo*, confirming its quality and steepness.

It's not often that two 'new' venues are found in such a popular area as Glen Coe. The 'Sròn na Lairig Summit Buttress' is a fine wee crag which is reminiscent of Lost Valley Minor Buttress, and at 900m and facing due north should be in condition pretty frequently with a trio of fine routes and more still to do. Eilde Canyon is really like nothing else in Scotland – very sheltered from wind on a wild day, and at an altitude of 500m is only 100m lower that Beinn Udlaidh, which is probably a good indicator of good conditions in Eilde Canyon. Ten of the most obvious ice lines have been done, but there are plenty more gems still to fall. Wait for a good freeze, check if Beinn Udlaidh is 'in', put your sombrero on, adopt a faux Mexican bandit accent, and … 'vamos muchachos'.

A bigger version of this topo guide (with many photos of both Eilde Canyon and the Sròn na Lairig Summit Buttress) can be downloaded from <www.bigtreecampervans.com>.

NEW CLIMBS SECTION

OUTER ISLES

LEWIS SEA-CLIFFS, GREAT BERNERA, Creag Liam:
Bridge Builder   20m   E5 6b **. Dave MacLeod, Tim Emmett. 2 Jun 2010.
The arete left of *The Prow*, gained from a logical approach from the right
(especially in high seas). Start right of the crack of *The Prow*. Move leftwards
across the wall on big holds and up to a bulge on the arete. Climb over this, just
right of the arete (crux) to better holds above.

SEANNA CHNOC:
Seanna Chnoc or Old Hill (NB 116 434) is one of a small group of islands lying
wonderfully at the head of Loch Roag, approx 4.5km NNW of Campus Bostadh.
A large number of routes have been climbed by Paul Headland, Keith Archer,
Tom Oaks and Paul Bradbeer and a guide written by them. It is on the website at
http://www.smc.org.uk/NewClimbs.php.

LEWIS SEA-CLIFFS, Air Mor Mangurstadh, Buaile Chuide, Screaming Geo:
Exit Point   40m   E7 6c ***. Tim Emmett, Dave MacLeod. 1 Jun 2010.
Follow *Paranoid Slippers* to just beyond its crux. Step up, then make a rising
traverse left at the edge of the vertical wall until it is possible to access an
undercut groove in the spectacular hanging arete (just above the flake of *The
Shadow Dancer*). Follow this to a good rest below a roof. Make a long reach
through the roof and hard moves above onto the hanging upper arete. Once a few
moves up the arete the climbing eases off rapidly.

Roadside Crag:
Descriptions were sent from a crag on a corner of the road just north of Dail Beag
(NB 234 456). They have been climbed many times before.

Port Stoth (NB 524 659):
At the back of Port Stoth Bay is a small cliff on the north side.

Picnic Bay Arete   10m   Severe. Gwilym Lynn. 5 Aug 2010.
The bounding left-hand arete clearly visible from the approach.

Bouldering Mat Umbrella   10m   VS 4c. Gwilym Lynn. 5 Aug 2010.
The bounding right-hand arete, with awkward moves low down leading to a
loose finish.

Sandy Sandwiches   10m   Severe. Gwilym Lynn. 5 Aug 2010.
The crack to the left of the right-hand arete joining the arete near the top. Some
loose rock.

MANGERSTA, Rubh' an Taroin:
Neighbourhood Watch   30m   E3 6a ***. Ian Taylor, Tess Fryer. 3 Jul 2011.

Start 10m right of *12 Years On* at a groove. Go up the groove to a pink/yellow ledge. Continue through the bulge above and follow a superb grey ramp-line up and left.

Rubh' an Taroin, Black Wall:
Black Cat Direct   E4 5c. Ian Taylor, Tess Fryer. 3 Jul 2011.
Follow the groove direct past the dubious blocks.

LEWIS HILLS, Creag Mo:
The Realm   80m   E8 6c ***. Tim Emmett, Dave MacLeod. 31 May 2010.
Start below the curving flake feature in the huge horizontal roof.
1. 30m 6c   Move easily up to the roof and carefully arrange various cams in the roof, taking care with soft flaky rock. The rock improves immediately you begin the flake. Launch out across this on big holds until they run out at halfway. A sustained bouldery sequence leads out to and around the lip to gain a standing position on a good foothold above the roof. Step right and belay.
2. 50m 6b   Move up the wall a couple of metres and make a delicate traverse left on poor sloping edges to gain a very welcome runner in a thin crack. Make a hard move to get established in the crack. Continue up this with excellent climbing, moving left below the stepped overlaps to successive wall cracks leading to the top.

Creag Dubh Dibadale:
Note: *Big Licks* E3 5c *** is very sustained, high in the grade (Ian Taylor). A better description for pitch 6:
Above are three groove lines. Gain a ledge in the middle groove by coming in from the right-hand groove. Move into the left-hand groove etc.

HARRIS, Sron Ulladale:
Note: *Stone* is very easy for the grade, probably E4 (Ian Taylor).

HARRIS, Clisham:
Incarnation   100m   III,4. Andrew Latham, Antony Latham. 22 Dec 2010.
This is a very obvious frozen waterfall. The route takes the left side of this (NB 154 079). Scramble for 10m up a left-trending ramp to the first belay stance. Make your way up interesting ground for 10m, followed by an easy snow-slope to a belay below the corner on the left (40m). Move left to a blocky corner. Climb the corner and then up mixed rock and ice up the obvious weakness (40m). Move up and left to a roof and from a large flake, step out right round the arete. Finish up the pleasant icefall, trending left at the top.

BARRA, Breaker Wall:
Old Codger   25m   E3 5c **. Jason Walker, Graham Tyldesley. 9 Jun 2011.
Climb the flake in the centre of the wall left of *Classic Corner*, starting from a tidal island in the middle of a rock pool. Climb the groove above exiting right onto a ledge at the top. Make steep moves up and slightly left to a sloping rail. Traverse left along the rail before finishing slightly right (common with *Rock Dance*?). A more direct and independent finish could be possible before traversing left along the rail but may be a grade harder.

Missing Musketeers 35m E3 6a **. Ian Taylor, Tess Fryer. 9 Jun 2011.
Start up *Classic Corner* for 5m, then traverse left and go up a thin flake in the middle of the wall, to good holds. Go up, then left until able to pull rightwards through the capping bulge.

Barra Wall:
Snake Charmer 35m E4 5c ***. Tess Fryer, Ian Taylor 11 Jun 2011.
A fine sustained pitch that slithers up the wall right of *Cobra*. Start on a ledge up and right from *Cobra*. Go up a shallow left-slanting groove to a flake, then move up and right to a good ledge. Break through the roof above on monster undercuts and jugs to gain a very shallow groove. Follow this until it peters out and an awkward move leads to better holds. Trend left to finish.

MINGULAY, Trundle Geo (NL 550 819):
Eagle Gravy 60m E1 *. Peter Graham, Franco Cookson (alt). 25 Jun 2010.
An adventurous route taking the obvious line up the main wall at the top of the geo. Loose snappy rock. Start at the lowest point of the main wall on the south side of the geo. Approach by abseil. Topo provided.
1. 25m 4c Climb straight up the wall (no gear) to reach a ledge and gear behind a large dubious flake. Traverse right into a short corner, which is climbed to a ledge.
2. 35m 4c Move across right and slightly downwards into the bottom of the obvious ramp/corner line, which is climbed to the top.

Geirum Walls, Platform Wall:
Not-so-Butch Cassidy and the Stanley Kid 19m HVS 5a. Craig McMahon, Adam Cassidy. 30 May 2010.
1. 10m 4a From the large platform, start 1m left from the corner of the platform and climb directly to a spire beneath the roof on the left-hand end of the main overhang.
2. 9m 5a Traverse the overhang and finish up the crux of *Seriously Twitching*. Topo provided.

ST KILDA, Hirta:
Boat Race 90m E6 ****. Dave MacLeod, Tim Emmett. 3 Jun 2010.
Climbs the superb gabbro cliff below the Maiden's Stone. Approach by passing under the stone and following a grassy rake to the top of the route (a big open easy angled slab). Continue walking down and left (facing out) until it is possible to abseil to small platforms just above the sea. A large horizontal break marks the way, running leftwards into the heart of the cliff, below the impressive vertical central wall.
1. 20m 5c Traverse the big break leftwards past a hard section (wet on the first ascent) to gain an obvious ledge. Belay at the left end of this.
2. 25m 6a Pull steeply onto the immaculate vertical wall and follow a crack-line and continuation moving left on perfect gabbro to big ledges and a belay at the basalt dyke.
3. 45m 6a Work up and rightwards following the line of a thin seam in the steep slab above (poor gear). Committing moves lead to a good ledge. Move left on

this and climb an easier big groove over bulges to eventually gain the easy finishing slab.

THE SHIANTS, Galta Mor:
This is the highest cliff, with an arch shaped roof in the lower half.

The Puffin Diaries 50m E7 6c *. Tim Emmett, Dave MacLeod. 30 May 2010.
Just left of the arch-shaped roof feature dominating the cliff is a tapering groove that runs out on the left arete of the arch.
1. 20m 6c Abseil or access the base of the groove by boat. Climb the groove to good nuts as it runs out on the left arete of the arch. Swing around the arete wildly using a hanging block to crucial gear in a break. Make bouldery moves to a good crack leading through the left side of the arch. Continue directly in a faint groove on tiny holds to gain a standing position on the headwall (crux). Move up to stand on a block.
2. 30m 6b Climb the well protected but sustained and technical finger crack in the slab to easier angled rock below the final roof. Traverse boldy rightwards on easier ground but increasingly suspect rock to the left-hand of two final grooves right of the roof. Climb the groove taking care with the rock and belay well back.

COLONSAY, Duntealtaig, The Corners (NR 385 982):
Above a non-tidal boulder beach at Duntealtaig lies an impressive series of corners, aretes and cracks, facing north-east. Approach via the track through Uragaig and go left near the end of the track through a gate signposted to the beach (as for Arch Crag). Walk diagonally rightwards up through the field round the bottom of a mound and continue up to the cliff-side fence. Hop over this and descend a steep grass slope to the bottom of the crag.

Gardener's Question Time 25m HVS 5a. Ellis Ash, Dave Sykes. 24 May 2011.
The right-hand corner line is mostly pleasant but has some loose holds near the top. Fence belay 60m back (pull through a rope or use a spare).

Squall Wall 22m E3 5c **. Ellis Ash, Dave Sykes, Tom Bridgeland. 24 May 2011.
A classic crack climb. Takes the steep crack in the left wall of the corner left of *Gardener's Question Time*. Preplace a 60m belay rope from the fence to a sloping ledge at the top and left of the crack. Follow the crack direct, with a welcome change in angle at 10m. Pull left at the top to belay on the sloping ledge. Pull out using the belay rope or abseil off this. Extra medium cams useful.

MULL, ERRAID, IONA:
Many routes climbed by Colin Moody and partners are on http://www.smc.org.uk/NewClimbs.php.

EILEAN DUBH, EILEAN NAM MUC:
These islands lie west of Erraid and many routes have been climbed by Chris Dickinson and partners. See http://www.smc.org.uk/NewClimbs.php.

SKYE

The following routes were too late to make the new *Skye Sea-cliffs* guidebook.

NEIST, The Green Lady:
Gruagach   25m   HVS 5a **. Danny Laing, Matt Munro. 1 May 2011.
Climbs the south wall of the Green Lady by a wandering line that may take in some ground already covered by other routes. Start at the south arete, climb to a flake with a sprig of heather on top, step up on this and climb a thin crack thinly up and right to two blocks at a point where the subsidiary ridge abuts the Green Lady. Surmount blocks and climb directly to the top.

Shimmering Area:
This area lies north of Tower Gully.

Wobble   35m   HVS 5b. N.Bassnett, R.Brown, M.Hudson. 9 Aug 2010.
One hundred metres south of *Two Faced* is a long clean narrow buttress, best identified as starting lower than its often wetter neighbours. Start up a left-facing corner on the left side of the buttress before moving onto the front face. Climb up the left-hand side, easily avoiding a small wobbly hold, to a slight cracked recess on the left, with the crux immediately above. Alternatively here, a series of moves on the right reduces the overall route to VS 4b. Belays can be found at the top of the buttress. A grassy slope gains the top.

Rogue Reporter   35m   VS 4c. Willie Jeffrey, Noel Williams. 30 Jul 2011.
Weaves a way up the buttress to the right of *Wobble*. Start in the centre of the buttress and slant up rightwards to a good flake. Climb back leftwards until it is possible to traverse right and then gain a ledge by a semi-mantelshelf move. Continue to a shallow right-facing corner. Make some moves up the arete of the corner before stepping right onto the face. Slant rightwards and gain an earthy ledge. Step left and climb up before moving right to an awkward exit onto a ledge. Continue up a short wall to the top. There are two stakes in the grass slope above the buttress.

Financial Sector:
The Big Money   30m   E3 6a **. Gary Latter. 30 May 2010.
Good well protected climbing up the hanging finger-crack just right of the sharp arete left of *A Fistful of Dollarite*. Climb the easier lower wall past ledges to gain thin crack. Go up this with difficult moves to gain good finger-crack leading to a ledge. Finish up a tricky thin curving crack, struggling to avoid stepping into the gully. Parts of this route are already climbed by *All the Small Things*.

Gritstone Reminiscence Bay:
The wall south of *Nothing Special* has diagonal striations running downwards from the left. Two vertical cracks cleave the face.

Hook Man   18m   VS 4b. N.Bassnett, Clare Aspinall, R.Brown. 22 Apr 2011
Gain the base of the right-hand crack. The crack features worthwhile climbing and a friendly pocket.

Mimic Bay:
Unnamed 15m HVS 5b ***. Mick Tighe & party. Oct 2010.
South of *Mimic Corner* is this excellent crack in the upper wall above the crevasse.

Unnamed 15m E4. Mick Tighe & party. Oct 2010.
Another crack 5m south again, possibly E4 but climbed with some aid.

Esoteric Sector:
The pathway south of the Mimic section goes through a cairned boulder field. Twenty five metres south of the emergence of the path, the cliffs establish a more continuous nature. The next three routes have belays just below the top.

Closing the Book 33m E1 5b *. N.Bassnett, R.Brown. 15 Apr 2011.
Seventy five metres north of *Neist Police* is a buttress with a mid-height pinnacle opposite a lonesome boulder featuring a jagged cliff-facing crack, some 50m downslope. Immediately right, the cleaner buttress with a left-facing irregular corner to mid-height offers this varied outing. Climb a short wall and the open book corner with its closing chapter to mid-height. Committing moves to the arete permit an awkward access rightwards to the mirrored J crack.

Sea Boots 33m VS 4c. R.Brown, N.Bassnett. 17 Apr 2011.
Two buttresses to the right and level with the reversed J section of *Closing the Book* is a right-facing layaway corner which starts with a tilt. Start up rock left of a grassy ramp. Above a perched block move up and right to a pocket in the sidewall. Step back left and up to skirt the juniper ledge to the base of the arete from which height can be gained, before a traverse left to the corner and the meat of the route.

Splot 33m VS 4c. N.Bassnett, R.Brown. 19 Apr 2011.
Right of the grassy ramp of *SS* is a massive semi-attached block creating an overhang at mid-height with a similar blocky overhang further right. Right again is floor to ceiling continuous rock with a rhomboidal roof at two-thirds height and an mosaic of cracks left of the overhang. Start in a short corner with a heather ledge top and then climb fairly directly to the cracks moving left to avoid the odd hollow sounding one.

Destitution Point:
Dunhallin 16m Severe. Ian Sykes, R. Brown. 1 Jul 2011.
Immediately right of *L'Americano* and in line with the slab of *Man of Straw* is a black cracked and stepped pleasant slab, which is climbed first on the left before moving to its right arete. Care should be taken at the central exit.

Portrait Area:
Twenteen 25m Hard Severe 4b *. Mark Hudson, N.Bassnett. 24 Apr 2011.
Start 2m right of *Portrait Pillar* at a straight crack. Climb this, and good black flakes above (sometimes damp – stepping leftwards across the wall raises the grade to VS 4c) to the platform above the *Portrait Pillar* wall. Finish up a rib on the right.

Golden Leaf 25m   Severe *. N.Bassnett, R.Brown. 5 Jun 2011.
Adjacent to two green baize topped blocks, and 5m right of *Portrait Pillar*, is narrow irregular square rib which supports a crack. Above the crack, move right to follow the groove direct. Stepping left at the very top reduces the overall grade to Very Difficult *.

NORTHERN HIGHLANDS NORTH

BEINN DEARG, Glensquaib Cliffs:
Note: *Finlay's Buttress* (2007) and *Sidewinder* (1999) share a first pitch but are largely separate afterwards, *Sidewinder* being nearer *Fenian Gully*.

Pearl Buttress   260m   IV,5. Andy Nisbet, Duncan Tunstall. 23 Feb 2011.
A line based on an icefall on the right side of the lower tier of the buttress with *Wall of Retribution*. The lower section was too thin so was started at the right corner of the lower tier. Climb a groove until possible to traverse left across the top of the icefall and up to reach a wall left of thicker ice in a chimney (55m). Climb the chimney (20m) and continue easily up to below a turfy line just right of the steepest area of the upper tier (50m). Climb the turfy line (55m). Pass a rock outcrop on the left and climb steep ground (the right edge of the steepest section) to easier ground (30m). Going further right here would have reduced the grade to III,4. Finish easily (50m).

West Buttress:
Peace Process   350m   IV,3. Andy Nisbet, Duncan Tunstall. 23 Feb 2011.
An ice line on the face between *Gastronomes' Gully* and *Silken Ladder*. There are two large areas of ice and linked by lower angled ice or snow. Climb to the first ice patch, about 100m up and right of the start of *Silken Ladder*, then head leftwards to the second. This was climbed initially on the right, then diagonally left across it. Finish trending left.

BEINN DEARG, Waterslide Slabs:
(NH 253 797)   Alt 630m
A long slide of narrow slabs lies west of the waterslide of the Allt Beinn Dearg, about 700m north-west of the Silver Slabs (SMCJ 2009). Park at the west end of Loch Droma and follow the track north from Lochdrum house over the col between Meallan Mhurchaidh and Meall Feith Dhiongaig and down to Gleann Mucarnaich, crossing the Allt Mhucarnaich (easy save in spate), 1.5 to 2hrs.
   The slabs are composed of calcareous schist which gives limestone-like features of pockets on very clean sound rock but devoid of protection save at the overlaps which take Friends but not nuts. These need not be carried apart from one Rock 9. The rock dries in a day after rain.

Textured Slab   160m   Very Difficult **. John Mackenzie, Eve Austin. 23 Jul 2011.
A delightful outing best climbed with sacks to combine an ascent of Beinn Dearg. Descents are to the east or right towards the waterslide. The climb starts halfway

up the slabs where the rock becomes continuous. Start by a long thin block on the east bank of the slabs. The climb takes a central line up the slabs and finishes by a pointed block seen from below.

1. 50m Walk and pad easily to an overlap by a heather clump. Step over this and go up to a short horizontal crack.

2. 25m Continue in the same line to a terrace.

3. 30m Go up easy but more interesting slabs to the large main overlap, belaying near the centre below a left-slanting ramp.

4. 30m Move up the left-slanting ramp and step right onto the upper slab. Continue over a short overlap, crux, to below the top overlap by a shallow corner near a curious orange stone; a good pitch.

5. 25m Climb the shallow corner and final slab to broken ground but continue to the pointed block.

Silver Slabs:

Boom Time Direct Finish 25m Hard Severe 4b *. John Mackenzie, Eve Austin. 2 Aug 2011.
From the juniper ledge and big block above the start of the third pitch, continue straight up the front face of the flake buttress with an overhang near the top. Very quick drying and an alternative finish easily traversed into from the grassy ledge from either *Meridian* or *Lost in Translation* if those are wet.

Meridian 125m HVS 5a **. John Mackenzie, Eve Austin. 2 Aug 2011.
A direct line up the middle of the slabs, bold in places but with good climbing. Small to medium Friends essential.

1. 25m 5a Start midway between the jutting block of *Boom Time* on the left and a wet corner to the right at the bottom overlap. Climb up to a thin left-slanting crack and surmount the well protected overlap to an initially steep slab. Climb this direct to an overlap just right of a clean cut corner.

2. 55m 4c Climb the overlap to a steep slab. Go up this in the centre via hidden holds and continue with minimal protection up the clean slabs and small overlaps to the terrace that cuts across the slabs below the final overlapping headwall slabs. Belay on the right at a big cracked block.

3. and 4. 4b or 4c. Finish either on the left as for *Lost in Translation* and *Boom Time* or to the right as for *Slideshow*.

LOCH BROOM, Creag Mhor:

Note: John Mackenzie & Eve Austin climbed an 80m Grade III icefall on the lower tier of crags about 150m above the main road (NH 180 873) on 3 Jan 2010. This lower tier was a mass of ice, mostly too thin but some was good and wove a line in two pitches up the best of it. Above is the bigger Upper Tier with two good potential lines, but too thin on the day.

Beinn Eilideach, The Eilideach Boulder:

(NH 16943 92322) Alt approx. 520m
This is the craglet which has a longer south face and a shorter west face. Though limited to four mini routes, they have a delightfully insecure feel.
Approach via a track from Leckmelm ('viewpoint 1 mile'). Follow the track to the viewpoint and strike up the hillside. There are two climbing areas; a sunny

south facing craglet offering excellent bouldering on clean rippled schist and an equally clean north facing crag overlooking a lochan down from the summit. A delightful hill and viewpoint with the option of bouldering or crag or both. Routes by John Mackenzie; picture included:

1. West Face; Diff. Climb anywhere left of the SW arete.
2. South-West Arete; 4c. A pleasant climb up the arete to a rather more awkward finish.
3. Ripples and Jugs; 5b *. Start up the ramp then the right-facing corner to a thinner finish.
4. Momentum and Inertia; 6a *. The overhanging wall just right of the last route finishing with a wicked mantel. A splendid problem!

AN SOCACH, Lochan Pollaig Crag:
Radius Gully, Index Finish – Broken Finger Variation   35m   IV,4. Steven Andrews, Dave Allen. 7 Jan 2011.
Follow *Radius Gully, Index Finish* until the upper icy, rightward-slanting ramp is reached. Continue to the furthest prominent icefall. Climb this directly until a steep turfy break is reached. Traverse rightward to continuation ice. Follow it to the top.

SEANA BHRAIGH, Luchd Coire:
Note: Penny Clay & Colin Wells made a direct start to *Query Cleft* up a big ice pitch (avoided on the left by the normal route) at Grade IV,4.

ARDMAIR, Big Roof Buttress:
Zealous Zygote   10m   VS 4c. John Lyall, Jonathan Preston. 18 May 2010.
Start just left of *A Bit on the Side* and gain a big flake, then step right and go up a left-slanting ramp to a ledge. Take a wide slanting crack on the right and a slab to finish.

Jammy Dodger   10m   VS 4c. John Lyall, Jonathan Preston. 18 May 2010.
The jam crack to the left and the groove above.

Last Laugh   10m   VS 4c. John Lyall, Jonathan Preston. 18 May 2010.
The next crack to the left, past a small holly to an off-width crack in a corner.

CUL MOR, Coire Gorm:
By Appointment   215m   VII,7. Iain Small, Ross Hewitt. 3 Feb 2010.
Climbs the left side of the steep buttress on the far right of the corrie and finishes up the open face above. Start at a big right-facing corner directly under the left end of the band of roofs.
1. 45m Climb the big turfy corner, then transfer left into a smaller hanging corner that leads to a ledge. From its left end take a steep fault, pulling onto slabs and a belay.
2. 60m Step down and right into a big groove and follow it to an easier snowslope. At a cul-de-sac, head directly up take a right-facing corner in a steep wall. Exit from the top onto an easier snowslope.
3. 50m Go directly up the snowslope and a short ice smear to belay by a chimney on the left.

4. 60m Follow the short chimney and turfy ground above to an obvious fault in a steeper rock band. Climb this and easier open ground above.
A further 80m of easy ground leads to the top.

STAC POLLAIDH, West Buttress:

Enigma Variations 80m V,8. James Edwards, Roger Webb. 28 Nov 2010.
On this ascent the final crack of *Enigma Grooves* was dry and not justifiable as a winter route. The grade assumes possession of large gear which allows overhead protection at the crux (pitch 2).
1. and 2. As for *Enigma Grooves*.
3. As for *Enigma Grooves* until below the final crack, then move left to join *Party on the Patio* at the through route.

Jack the Ripper - Killer Finish 25m E2 5b. Graham Tyldesley, Adrian Crofton. 12 Jun 2011.
Halfway up the final pitch of *Jack the Ripper*, step around the arete to the right to gain the base of a crack. Climb the crack to the top. Gets a bit close to *Felo de Se* but is an exposed, sustained and worthwhile finish.

North-West Corner Left-Hand IV,7. James Edwards, Roger Webb. 22 Dec 2010.
Climb the first two pitches of *North-West Corner*. From the second belay the original route is an obvious turfy line slanting slightly right. On the left there are three corners in a row starting from a ledge about 15m above. Climb the centre one which gives a sharp lesson in bridging.

REIFF, Pinnacle Cliff:
Note: *Pool Wall* (SMCJ 2009) is left of (rather than right of) *Chimney Corner*.

Rockers Cliff:
An Easy Day for Damocles 15m E4 5c **. Ian Taylor, Tess Fryer. 30 Aug 2010.
On the west-facing wall, under the left end of the Damoclean block, is a line of stepped corners. After an awkward undercut start, climb a thin crack and gain the upper corners with a difficult mantelshelf move leftwards onto a ledge. Continue to the top of the corners and finish ungracefully round the left end of the block.

Stinking Geo:
Blindside 10m E4 6a/b **. Tess Fryer, Ian Taylor. 30 Aug 2010.
Right of *Pooh, Pong, McPlop* is a steep wall with a permanent water streak. Climb the left edge of this wall, starting by swinging in from the left along a good break. From a good ledge move left and continue up the edge via a hard move to the top.

Leaning Block:
Note: Ian Taylor thought *Crossfire* (SMCJ 2009) to be E3 6a * rather than E2 5c **.

Amphitheatre Bay:
Relatively Free   25m   E4 6a **. Ian Taylor, Tess Fryer. 23 Jul 2011.
Start a little to the right of *Lost at Sea* and climb a snaking flake and crack to
reach a big break. Go right along the break and pull into a corner, which is
followed to the big roof. Move left and go steeply through the roof at a weakness,
then finish up a tricky thin crack. Well protected.

Jigsaw Wall:
There is a vertical but undercut wall to the right of *Jigsaw Wall*.

Dirty Little Gritstone Pleasures   10m   E5 6a **. Dave Brown, Andy Reeve. 29
Jun 2011.
From the right end of the starting slab of *Jigsaw Wall*, gain and climb a fragile
flake until the break. Small cams. Move right to a blind vertical crack and climb
this to further horizontals and the top. Microcams essential.

The Ultimate Sandstone Experience   10m   E4 6a **. Andy Reeve, Dave Brown.
29 Jun 2011.
Start on a flat boulder below the right-hand rib of the wall (6m left of *Dirty Little
Gritstone Pleasures*). Hang slopers and campus to gain a standing position
above the lip. Teeter upwards to a challenging finish on sloping holds.
Microcams essential.

Rubha Ploytach:
Clay Pigeon   12m   E3 6a *. Tess Fryer, Sheila van Lieshout, Ian Taylor. 25 Jun
2011.
Follow *Claymore* to the first break, traverse right along the break, then go
steeply up to finish at the top right corner of the wall.

Plaid on the Rox   15m   E3 5c. Ian Taylor, Sheila van Lieshout, Tess Fryer. 25
Jun 2011.
The arete right of *Maid in a Box*, gained by starting up that route, then hand
traversing along the first break.

ACHMELVICH, Clean Cut Crag:
Faithless   15m   E3 6a **. Tess Fryer, Ian Taylor. 30 Apr 2011.
The groove line right of *Flightless*. Needs low tide.

Note: *Calypso* was thought E4. *Flightless* – the grade and quality confirmed.

OLD MAN OF STOER:
Tall Stoeries   60m   E4 ****. Dave Brown, Andy Reeve. 27 Jun 2011.
The seaward face has a large overhang breached by a crack, and a flake-line
above. Start on a slab below this.
1. 30m 5c Gain the left-facing corner in the centre of the seaward face, from the
left. Climb this to exit rightwards onto a green coloured slab. Move up and belay
on the left.
2. 30m 6a Traverse a hanging slab rightwards to make bold moves to the

overhanging crack. Crank up this to a well positioned flake and easy slabs (possible fulmar) which lead to the top.

QUINAG, Western Cliffs:
Rickets 200m V,6 **. Andy Nisbet, Jonathan Preston. 22 Dec 2010.
A deep gully curving right behind *Ricketty Ridge*. Start up a steep ice pitch (or mixed) to an easing (25m). Continue up a shallow groove, including another short steep section of ice, leading towards the gully and belay at its base (50m). Climb the gully past a steep section of back and foot (50m). Continue up the gully to a ridge on the right (50m). Climb more easily to a snow gully on the right (25m). Another 50m leads to the top (not included in length).

Ramshackle Gully 200m IV,4. Andy Nisbet, Jonathan Preston. 23 Dec 2010.
A gully right of *Ricketty Ridge*. Start as for *Ricketty Ridge* up the broad scoop, actually the logical start to the gully (80m). The initial section of the gully looks difficult, so climb turfy ground on the left before moving right into the gully (40m). Climb the gully up and right, then move left into its shallow upper section (40m). Continue up this leading onto snow (40m) and joining *Rickets* to finish.

TARBET SEA-CLIFFS, Balmy Slabs, Western Sector:
Gravity Grave 20m E1 5a *. Michael Barnard. 1 Jul 2011.
The imposing right arete of *Black Tidings* has little protection until the last few moves.

Note: *Barmy Slab* (SMCJ 2009) seems to share sections with *Violator*. The following description has been suggested.
Barmy Slab 15m VS 5a **. James Duthie, Michael Barnard. 25 Jul 2009.
Belay on ledges 4m right of the huge cleft. Start up a crack in the initial steep wall (as for *Violator*); where this gets difficult a move right gains the slab above. Step back left on the edge of the slab to finish up the crack immediately left of the large open corner of *Cornucopia*.

FAR NORTH-WEST CRAGS, Ridgeway View Crag:
Another Perspective 20m HVS 4c *. Ross & Clare Jones. 10 Apr 2011.
Climb the slab right of *Oars Aft* to cracks and a right-facing corner under the headwall. Pull up right and up the overhanging right-slanting niche to the top.

Creag an Fhithich, Back Stage:
The following routes are located on the on the small isolated slab to the right of the main crag containing the immaculate hanging finger crack referred to on page 258 of the existing guidebook. The crack is named *Trident* (Severe 4a ***).

Rain Dance 9m Very Difficult *. Steve Kennedy. 19 Sep 2010.
The left-slanting crack-line left of *Trident*.

Solitary Existence 9m E1 5b/c **. Steve Kennedy. 19 Sep 2010.
Climb the thin slab between Rain Dance and the crack of *Trident* without straying into either crack-line. Bold.

Screamer   9m   Very Difficult *. Steve Kennedy. 19 Sep 2010.
The groove/crack right of *Trident*.

Creag Garbh Mhor, Red Slab:
Precambrian Rose   30m   VS 4c *. John Mackenzie, Eve Austin. 5 Jun 2011.
Between *Beauties Edge* and *The Crack* is a steep wall. Climb this direct starting
just right of *Beauties Edge's* alcove, climbing up a red wall en route and exiting
onto the red slab close to where *Beauties Edge* joins it. Good clean steep rock
easier than it looks.

Sandwood Bay, Crag 2:
Note: Andrew Moles found that some of the routes had become fairly
inaccessible since the previous year, because shifting sands had left deep pools
at their base.

BEINN CEANABEINNE:
See the Arctic Bear – Variation   35m   4c. Ben Sparham, Steve Perry, Katie
Long. 25 Jul 2011.
This opens up the fantastic 4c top pitch to anyone who doesn't fancy the 5b pitch
beneath it. Overall grade HVS 4c. Start 8m left of the curving arch, where red
gneiss meets grey. Follow pockets up and then left to a prominent ledge. Move
out rightwards along the ledge to the base of the left-slanting crack of pitch 2.
Topo provided.

SKERRAY SEA-CLIFFS, Clashaidy Buttress:
(NC 667 636)   Partially Tidal   North-East facing
From the parking place at Achtoty, instead of walking north-east as for the other
cliffs, walk downhill directly to a small rocky inlet. The climbs are on a small
buttress to the left. On the right is a prominent spur that looks like a crocodile's
head (Crocodile Rock), which gives an entertaining deep-water traverse from
the tip of the nose inwards near high tide.

Swashbuckling Superheroes   9m   VS 4c. EUMC party. May 2007.
The crack-line on the left side of the buttress, passing an obvious square slot.

Pervy Seal   9m   Hard Severe 4b. EUMC party. May 2007.
The tapering groove feature near the right-hand side of the buttress, using good
holds on the right.

CAITHNESS SEA-CLIFFS, AUCKENGILL:
Slippery Bug   6m   Hard Severe 4b. Leonard Mckinney, Karen Clarke. 2009.
Walk towards the sea from the back of the quarry, then turn right around the base
of the first stack and continue up onto a small flat slab about 1m higher. Here is
the route, a 6m right-facing corner.

SARCLET, Silver Surfer Buttress:
There is lichen on the upper part of the routes on the wall around and right of
Silver Surfer (SMCJ 2005), but it makes little or no difference to the quality of
the routes. Mick Tighe thought *Silver Surfer* was HVS but excellent.

Bhouy Zone 35m E2 5b *. Mick Tighe, John McClenaghan. 24 Apr 2010.
A few metres right/north of Silver Surfer on the main wall is an 8m crack come groove line. Climb this and the continuation wall above with a deviation right at half-height to avoid a loose block. Excellent, exposed climbing overlooking *Silver Surfer*.

Cubby Roo 35m HVS 5a ***. Mick Tighe, John McClenaghan. 24 Apr 2010.
A few metres right again a shallow depression runs up to the headwall which is defined by a horizontal crack at two-thirds height. Climb the depression on immaculate rock and continue up the hidden crack in the headwall.

Pension Day 35m VS 4c **. Mick Tighe, Doug Lee. 6 May 2010.
Right again there are some small overhangs at around 6m. Climb the excellent little wall to pass the overhangs on the right. Step back left into a shallow depression and follow this and the wall above on pockets, fractures and cracks.

Big Buttress NE Face:
Edge Over the Sea 35m E1 5b **. Dan Moore, Ian Jones. 8 Jun 2011.
Climb the initial crack of *Walking on Water* to the easing below the roof, then break out left from the good ledge across the wall towards the left arete to the base of a shallow corner. Climb this and the continuation groove and cracks above just right of the arete to the top.

Heithe Buttress:
Kenneth 35m HVS 5a *. Dan Moore, Ian Jones. 10 Jun 2011.
From a sea-level ledge just below and right of *Lithium Fry-Up*, traverse across the slabby wall and climb easily up its right side via the obvious cracked fault on good jugs to a good ledge and optional belay below a leaning right-facing corner adjacent to *Lithium Fry-Up*. Climb the well protected corner to a small spike at the top and pull steeply left around the arete at the top.

Wee Buttress (ND 343 421)
This is the smaller buttress directly north from Big Buttress across the geo and although titled Wee Buttress, it is 25m high. A deep chimney bisects it and the following routes lie on the left-hand section which has a large non-tidal ledge running along the front, and a pillar formation in the middle. The top is a bit scrambly.

Mini Mii 25m VS 4c *. Raymond Wallace, Rob Christie. 25 Sep 2010.
From the left side of the ledge, step left around the pillar into the base of an open groove. Climb the groove to a small roof that is turned to the right then follow the crack above.

Crib Robber 25m E1 5a *. Raymond Wallace, Rob Christie. 25 Sep 2010.
Climbs the thin, left-trending crack in the middle of the slab with a couple of difficult moves to reach a ledge. Step off the ledge to mount and climb the blunt arete on the right.

Wii Play 25m HVS 5a *. Raymond Wallace, Rob Christie. 25 Sep 2010.

Climb the left-facing corner until forced to make some awkward moves through the corner of the roof then follow the crack through the prow above.

There may be Dolphins 25m VS 4c *. Rob Christie, Raymond Wallace. 25 Sep 2010.
To the right of the big ledge, climb the slabby pillar to an open groove passing a block.

OCCUMSTER, Main Area:
So It Goes 20m HVS 4c **. Ross Jones, Matt Dent, Clare Jones. 22 Aug 2010.
Climb the wall right of *Tralfamadorian* and left of the arete on excellent rock and spaced protection. The best route in the main area.

Cave Area
Ten metres south of an arch in the north-east tip of the headland to the north of the Cave Area is a large hanging corner.

Mada-chuain 20m VS 4c. Ross Jones, Matt Dent, Clare Jones. 22 Aug 2010.
Climb easy ledges to the corner at 10m and climb this to the top. Mada-chuain is gaelic for Killer Whale.

LATHERONWHEEL – Notes from Ross Jones:
The largest stack was climbed by John Sanders in 1998 prior to Simon Richardson and Mark Robson. John also found abseil tat on his ascent.

Don't Think Twice (1998). Rab Anderson suggests 2 stars (SMCJ 2006) as the final easy bit is not good and invariably will have a fulmar. However as a route it remains an absolute classic with fine pumpy climbing through a daunting overhang.

Big Flat Wall Area – *Personalized Dwarf* (2005): The line of the original ascent isn't logical and the line has been climbed direct which is better and does not change the grade of the route. We thought the grade was Hard Severe 4b. A better description would be: 12m Climb the wall left of *Looking for the Line* and right of the arete. A picture and a topo provided.

The line for *Looking for the Line* (2002) is also incorrectly shown in the 2004 guide topo on p383. The topo shows the route going into the right-facing corner at one-third height. The route goes straight up the middle of the wall left of the corner.

ORKNEY, Yesnaby:
Many new routes have climbed by Neil Morrison & Tim Rankin, while others have been deep water soloed by Julian Lines and friends. The exact details have yet to be sorted.

Roseness:
Neil Morrison & Tim Rankin climbed four new routes in July 2011.
1. E6 arete right of *Paul's Stall* starting just right of that route and forging straight over the prow.
2. E1/2 on the right side of the arete right of the above and *Paul's Stall*.
3. E1/2 right again up a cracked wall.
4. E1 squeezed in right of the cracked wall.

HOY:

Longhope Direct 455m E10/11 ***. Dave MacLeod, Andy Turner. 21 Jun 2011.

A free ascent of the original aided crack in the headwall of Drummond and Hill's *Longhope Route*. This straightens out the A2 crack pitch with a more direct entry to the crack and finish through the final roofs. A sparing approach to protection with long slings is required to make the long weaving pitches possible. But this is important to save energy for the crux pitch and to make it feasible as a one-day ascent. The grade is for a one-day ascent without falls. The route follows that taken by the Arran/Turnbull free version as far as the Guillotine. Start at a boulder platform near the right end of a clean red wall.

1. 55m 5c Climb up trending left, then back up right to a big detached block. Climb boldly over the bulge to an easier section working up right on good rock, then back left and up a corner to a belay beneath the centre of a large roof.
2. 50m 6a Hard moves just right of a thin crack in the roof lead to good gear. Climb the right-slanting corner to a good ledge. Move right and continue in the same line, then traverse left along an enormous concave break to belay at the edge of the grass.
3. 110m 5b Move up and left on steep grass. At the left edge of a barrier, follow a rock slab and continue up, and then leftwards on bulging grass and slabs to the foot of the left-facing corner system in the upper wall (belay possible here at 70m). Move together up the slab, corner and pleasant walls above to a belay below steep left-facing chimneys.
4. 50m 6a Climb the chimneys, then swing left for 5m and climb the 'vile crack' via two chockstones (Camalot 5 useful). Swing 3m left at its top to a nut belay on a large flake.
5. 60m 5c Go up the flake and right around a roof, then up to a second roof and traverse left to sandy red bulges. Move up a series of steps and climb a green crack to the huge break. Walk left along the break over big boulders to belay below the left-facing corner.
6. 65m 5c Climb the corner, step right and continue direct over steps, then move 10m left to a niche. Move right up the 'giant steps' then stomach traverse left to a short corner. Climb the corner, and flakes above to the Guillotine. Bold.
7. 65m 6c Traverse left along the break, then climb the overhanging wall boldly to the base of the headwall crack. Climb this past several cruxes to a small ledge below the capping roofs. Move up to these, step right and then climb leftwards through two roofs. Move right to fulmar ledges and climb grassy ledges to the summit. F8b+ climbing.

Rora Head, Gully 3:

Slick John 40m E4 6a **. Dave MacLeod, Andy Turner. 20 Jun 2011.

An attractive finger crack in the centre of the wall, left of *Rosamund's Birthday*. Abseil to a footledge on *Rosamund's Birthday* about 8m above the grassy start of that route. Climb *Rosamund's Birthday* for a few metres to its normal belay. Traverse left along a ledge to a prominent right-slanting wide crack. Climb this for a few metres, then break out left to gain the striking thin finger crack. Climb this on great rock and protection to the top.

Rubblehouse Wall 40m E2 5b. Andy Turner, Dave MacLeod. 20 Jun 2011.

The right-hand of two cracks in the wall directly opposite *Rosamund's Birthday*.

Abseil to a footledge at the foot of the cracks. Climb rightwards on dubious rock to gain the line of the right-hand crack. Follow this with slightly less difficulty but sustained climbing with some loose holds remaining.

SOUTH RONALDSAY:
Note: Mick Tighe and friends have climbed many routes at Halcro Head which is about 1km north of Tomb of the Eagles – no details yet.

SHETLAND:
Ross Jones has collected a large number of new route descriptions, as climbed by himself and local climbers. See http://www.smc.org.uk/NewClimbs.php.

NORTHERN HIGHLANDS CENTRAL

SLIOCH:
Katabasis 300m VI,6. Simon Richardson, Roger Webb. 15 Feb 2011.
A sustained mountaineering line up the left edge of Main Buttress. Start just left of the lower tier and climb easy turfy ground (to the right of *The Slioch Slim Plan*) to the first terrace. Move right along the terrace for 40m and climb a series of corners until they merge with the broad left crest. Continue up this, then traverse right below the final headwall to join the final cracks of *Xenophen* and gain the Neck. Another 150m of scrambling up the connecting ridge leads to the summit.

STONE VALLEY CRAGS, The Valley Walls:
Windy Cracks 15m Severe. Stuart Macfarlane, Jeannie Northover. 2 Jun 2011.
In the bay beyond *Three Stepped Slab* is a short steep crack. Climb this and move slightly left to another hidden crack that continues to the top. The bottom crack is Severe and the upper crack Difficult.

Flowerdale Beag:
(NG 868 719) Alt 270m South-West facing
Approach: As for Flowerdale Wall. This crag is just below and slightly to the left of Flowerdale Wall. It provides short routes suitable for novices.
Descent: Walk off to the right.

Too Windy for Blood Suckers 10m Severe. Jeannie Northover, Stuart Macfarlane. 2 Jun 2011.
An eliminate up the wall between *Cracking On* and *Central Crack*. Use of either crack is not permitted for holds. *Central Crack* may be required for gear by the less bold.

Rowan Wall 10m Severe. Stuart Macfarlane, Jeannie Northover. 2 Jun 2011.
An eliminate up the wall to the right of *Central Crack*. The use of *Central Crack* and the crack-line to the right is not permitted for holds or gear.

Cracking On 10m Very Difficult. Jeannie Northover, Stuart Macfarlane. 2 Jun 2011.

The first crack-line left of *Central Crack*.

Central Crack 10m Very Difficult. Stuart Macfarlane, Jeannie Northover. 2 Jun 2011.
The most obvious and central crack-line.

Caterpillar Crag:
Chrysalis 12m VS 4c. Rod Mackenzie, Elke Braun. 1 May 2011.
Start about 2m right of the bottom of the third crack. Climb up to a slabby bulge, pull up rightwards through middle of the bulge, then trend right over a sloping ledge to finish.

Rum Doodle Crag:
Rum Doodle Arete – Variation Finish VS 4c. Jeannie Northover, Stuart Macfarlane. 1 May 2011.
Rather than walk off or climb a straightforward groove on the left, a better finish is to climb the steep crack on the back wall.

Red Barn Crag:
Dogfight 20m VS 4c. Jonathan Preston, John Lyall. 27 Sep 2010.
Climb the cracked wall left of *A Load of Old Bosche* to a wide heather ledge. Cross the ledge and make a few moves up the wide corner-crack on the right, then follow the obvious crack in the wall on the left to finish at the top of *Curse you Red Barn*.

Stone Valley Crag:
Arete Direct 25m VS 4c. Jeannie Northover, Rod Mackenzie, Stuart Macfarlane. 3 Jun 2011.
To the right of the prominent corner of *Updraught* is an arete. Climb the arete direct and continue to the top. This route joins onto *Updraught* but is a more direct start.

AZTEC TOWER:
The Inca Trail 15m VS 4c. Stuart Macfarlane, Jeannie Northover. 5 Jun 2011.
Start at the base of *Warrior God* and follow the left-diagonal crack out to the arete of *Conquistador* and then continue up the arete.

LETH CHREAG:
Lethargy 25m VS 4c. Bob Brown, John Mackenzie. 28 Apr 2011.
Immediately to the left of *Spider Corner* is an overlapped slab (well right of the corner of the *Direct Start* to *Spiral Staircase*). Climb the overlap and slab leftwards to a ledge. Step across left and finish up *Spiral Staircase*. A good start but a poor finish.

GRUINARD CRAGS, Gruinard Beach:
Willie Crackit 7m VS 4c **. Jonathan de Leyser, Ruaridh Forbes. 30 May 2011.
A route on a rock about 40m west of Beach Crag. On the map it looks like a small island but it is joined to land even at high tide. Access is same for Beach

Crag, a walk along the beach at low tide. The line on the rock is south facing and not accessible at high tide. It is an obvious 7m vertical hand-jam crack slanting slightly leftwards and overhanging slightly at the top.

Carn Goraig:

Pure Deid Brilliant 15m E1 5b **. Jonathan Preston (unsec). 30 Apr 2011.
The left-slanting crack-line immediately left of *The Wicked*. Climb the crack passing three triangular holes to finish rightwards via a fine flake-crack.

The Not So Bad 12m VS 4c *. Jonathan Preston (unsec). 30 Apr 2011.
The corner at the left end of the wall. Bridge up the corner, stepping up and left at a small roof to stand on a large block. Finish up the crack above passing a small tree.

Faerie Crags, Corner Crag:

On the north-west face is a scooped area with a skull face right of the most overhanging section of wall. Three routes gain the scoop by the same line of weakness, then take different exits.

Golgotha 15m HVS 5a. John Lyall, Andy Nisbet. 22 Apr 2011.
Gain the scoop by slanting left on good holds, then continue working left in an exposed position to finish up a corner which gains the top of the left arete of the scoop.

Nose Direct 15m HVS 5a. John Lyall, Andy Nisbet. 22 Apr 2011.
Gain the scoop and climb straight up to finish up a short overhanging crack.

Eyebright 15m E2 5b. John Lyall, Andy Nisbet. 22 Apr 2011.
Gain the scoop and move right to climb a steep groove, finishing out left at a capping roof (one rest). The pro is fiddley initially but very good on the steep section so the grade is because it's tiring placing it.

Elphin Crack 12m VS 4c. John Lyall, Andy Nisbet. 22 Apr 2011.
Right of *Wild Goose Chase* is a heathery corner. This route takes a left-slanting crack system just to the right. Continue in the same line to the top.

The Sidhe 15m Hard Severe 4b. John Lyall, Andy Nisbet. 22 Apr 2011.
Climb a right-slanting crack in brown rock right of *Elphin Crack*. Keep trending right to finish by a short left-slanting corner.

Faerie Crags, Mystic Wall:

At the right end of the long wall which is the main section of Mystic Wall is a south-west facing wall of clean red rock.

Alysium 20m Hard Severe 4c. John Lyall, Andy Nisbet. 22 Apr 2011.
At the right end of this red wall, follow a right-slanting corner, finishing up a ramp out right.

AN TEALLACH AREA, Mullach Coire Mhic Fearchair:

Slaying the Ghost 120m VI,6. Simon Richardson, Roger Webb. 2 Jan 2011.
The prominent corner-line in the centre of the crag.
1. 20m Start 5m right of the line of the corner and climb a stepped chimney-slot to a prominent ledge cutting across the face.
2. 50m Move up and left across steep mixed ground to gain the foot of the upper corner.
3. 20m Traverse up and right into the bulging corner and climb it (thin ice on the first ascent) to a terrace.
4. 30m Surmount a large chokestone above and continue up easier ice and snow to the top.

Junction Buttress:

Injunction 130m HVS *. Andy Nisbet, Duncan Tunstall, Simon Yearsley. 3 May 2011.
Immediately left of the main change of aspect of the cliff (which forms a blunt arete leading to the biggest forest on the crag) is a pocketed wall, cleaner and steeper on its left side.
1. 35m 5a Climb this wall, starting on the right and trending left to its left arete. Belay on a tree on its left side.
2. 35m 4b Continue up the arete to the left end of the forest.
3. 25m 4c Go up a wall behind to reach a diagonal fault. Follow this diagonally right and go up to a ledge.
4. 35m 4b Climb a slabby wall above to the top.

Clapham 100m HVS **. Andy Nisbet, Duncan Tunstall, Simon Yearsley. 3 May 2011.
The right end of clean slabs at the right end of the cliff.
1. 15m 4a Start by climbing broken but tricky ground to an area of slightly lower angled slab.
2. 45m 4c Climb this diagonally right to a break, then straight up via an obvious crack in an upper slab to a ledge. Poorly protected initially.
3. 25m 4b Climb a slab above, cross *Rightward Slant* and climb another slab on the left to reach a smooth upper wall.
4. 15m 5b Climb the wall by a thin seam slanting right (5b) or an easier line of pockets to its right (4b).

AN TEALLACH, Ghlas Tholl, Hayfork Wall:

The Wailing Wall 90m IX,9 ***. Murdoch Jamieson, Martin Moran. 23 Dec 2010.
Takes the left side of the upper Hayfork Wall which presents a superb fissured face 70m high, potentially one of the finest mixed climbing venues in the country. With a high altitude (900-970m) the wall gathers snow readily and is often in condition. Start up right of the chimney of *Haystack* at a turfy promontory directly under the centre of the wall and 6m left of the corner of *Silver Fox*.
1. 45m Climb the turfy wall to reach a narrow terrace, traverse 8m left and make hard committing moves up a leftward diagonal break through the overhang to a small wedged block. Make thin moves leftwards to gain the base of a slim

corner-crack which is followed to a ledge and belay at a huge block. A magnificent pitch.
2. 45m Climb on to the block and go left up a steep flakey wall, continuing for 12m to a break under a compact section. Move left to a huge flake (optional hanging belay) and traverse sensationally left to gain a bottomless chimney which is climbed to the top (block belay 8m up and right).

Note: Martin Hind & Owen Samuels climbed a direct start to *Crashed Out* (SMCJ 2007) on 19 Jan 2011, named *Hay Heck*, graded VII,6. They climbed directly up a nose left of the start of *Crashed Out*, crossed it at its ledge and continued straight up to the top of its corner. After this the routes coincided.

Hay Bale 30m III,5. Roger Webb, James Edwards. 19 Jan 2011.
A route on the buttress between the forks. Climb up mixed ground avoiding easier ground on left, left of an obvious corner on left side of the buttress and taking in a big slab higher up to top.

Toll an Lochain, Gobhlach Buttress:
Gobhlach Ramp 350m II **. Andy Nisbet. 19 Mar 2011.
A big grooved ramp-line which lies on the left side of the buttress. Initially snow with short ice steps, it leads into a recessed section with a steeper exit on ice at its very back. Immediately above this, take a groove leading out right. This leads to a snow trough with a short step to enter, then the easy upper crest. Probably Grade III when leaner.

Loch Broom:
Note: John Mackenzie and Neil Wilson climbed *Bonar* in Jan 2010 and thought the first pitch Grade IV,4, also the approach 15mins.

STRATHFARRAR, Sgurr na Muice:
Flying Pigs 170m III,4 *. Neil Wilson, John Mackenzie. 12 Dec 2010.
Takes the chimney and buttress that forms the left branch of *If Pigs Could Fly*.
1. 30m Climb the initial ice step of *If Pigs Could Fly*, then move up left to a good belay crack below the wide chimney.
2. 50m. Climb ice on the left side of the chimney before moving up right, following the chimney past a narrow section to good belays on a ledge on the left. A good interesting pitch, very well protected.
3. 40m. Step left and climb a wide crack to turf then continue to another wide chimney. Climb this and over an overhang higher to step left above and climb a groove which leads to a big flake belay on the right. Another good pitch, which is also well protected.
4. 50m. Straightforward turfy climbing now leads to walking ground with the summit a short distance off to the left.

Makin' Bacon 300m III,4 *. Mike & Pippa Cocker, John Mackenzie, Eve Austin. 28 Jan 2011.
This interesting route lies between *Pigsty Gully* and *Three Little Piggies* but closer to the former. A small initial tier with an inset turf groove leads to an easy snowfield. Above this is the first of the bigger tiers, cut by a narrow ice and turf

Jason Walker grapples with the very steep King of the Swingers (F7a), Creag nan Luch.
Photo: Andy Tibbs.

runnel, steep at the top, giving a long pitch of 55m. The climb continues up the next snowfield to a prominent slanting corner on the left which has a narrow turf strip up the back. Climb this excellent and quite technical pitch to a small rock spike above, 55m. Move up and left towards the buttress that lies right of *Pigsty Gully's* exit and is split centrally by a runnel. Climb the fine narrow runnel to where it splits into two grooves. Both were climbed, the left having a tricky chockstone near the top.

Snatched From the Jaws of Thaw 100m III. John Mackenzie, Eve Austin. 23 Jan 2011.
To the left of *A Wee Cracker* is the overhung groove and to the left again is a prominent corner capped by a roof and a near vertical ice pillar to its left. Brief fun up the ice, pleasant above and often in condition.
1. 30m Climb the snowy corner line to the only crack on the corners right wall well below the roof.
2. 30m Up to the roof, step left and climb the ice pillar to easier ice or snow to belay above on rock.
3. 40m Step right and go up a shallow groove to move left and up to the cornice. This can usually be avoided on the left by a traverse.

STRATHCONON, Scatwell River Slabs:
The Lance 20m E2 5c. Raymond Wilby, Claire Hayden, Andrew Wilby. 3 Jul 2010.
Start 4m left of the river level start of *Northern Line* at a small pine tree with a bulbous base. This is 3m right of the direct start of *Circle Line*. Climb the rib for 8m, with a crux move at 6m (peg runner). This gains a thin crack on the slab (micro wires). Step right onto the slab and climb straight up to the bottom of the crack of *Circle Line*. Traverse 2m right along a small overlap and go centrally up the slab to climb the wall crossing *Northern Line* at the double overlap. Gain the slab above and go straight up to finish.

The Shield 55m E1 5a. Raymond Wilby, Andrew Wilby. 28 Jul 2010.
A traverse of the slabs from right to left.
1. 35m 5a Start at the direct start of *Circle Line* (the bottom of the rib). At 8m follow the overlap leftwards across the slab above a holly tree on an upwards trending line of cracks and flakes, to belay on *Grand Central* at a small rowan tree. The central section is run out.
2. 20m 5a Follow double increasingly faint cracks to gain the flake on *The Joust* and follow this to the jammed block on *The Tilting Yard*. Follow this route to finish.

Creag Ruadh, North-East Face:
(NH 273 543) Alt 670m
A broken face that has tiers of rock but forms ice in the right conditions. Nothing special but worthwhile if nearby. Descend from the col (or approach from below) between the top of Creag Ruadh and the 740m top to the NW. Contour below the crag to a huge boulder. A broken face with icefalls lies up and right, several possible lines but this appeared the most interesting. All lines are escapable between the tiers.

Creag Ruadh Corner   75m   II/III. John Mackenzie. 20 Feb 2011.
A discontinuous ice-filled corner lies left of a shallow gully. Climb the three corners separated by easy ground. Some short steep ice sections and good turf leading to the 740m top.

NORTHERN HIGHLANDS SOUTH

DRUIM SHIONNACH, West Face:
Argentine Chimney   100m   V,6 *. Sandy Allan, John Lyall. 3 Jan 2010.
1. 50m   Start as for *Silver Corner* up the right-hand chimney to a snow terrace; cross this leftwards to join *Silver Slab* for a short way. Break diagonally left, heading for a large block and ledge just right of a narrow chimney in a corner. Bold.
2. 50m   Climb the excellent chimney, then the rocks left of the easy trough of *Silver Edge*.

Lemon Groove   90m   V,6 **. Mark Davidson, Rosie Goolden, Andy Nisbet. 27 Nov 2010.
An improbable line past the right side of the bigger right cave, giving an exciting and very helpful pitch. Climb steep snow to reach the start, on the wall below and left of the left and lower cave.
1. 20m   Climb to the cave, then traverse its right wall to a short groove which leads to turf and the right cave.
2. 30m   Move right and climb turf steps leading back left to a groove which overlooks the cave and leads up its right edge into a shallow chimney. From its apex, step left on to a turfy slab and go diagonally left up this into a wide turf gully. Follow this to a good crack on the left.
3. 40m   Climb the gully and its continuation on the right to the top.
Note: Continuing up the fault on pitch 2 would join *Argentine Chimney* and would be a better line.

Macavity   90m   V,6 *. Andy Nisbet, Jonathan Preston. 21 Dec 2010.
The fault-line leading past the left side of the bigger right cave.
1. 20m   As for *Lemon Groove* to the big cave, although a groove was climbed up the initial awkward wall, which had less ice.
2. 40m   Climb turf up the left wall of the cave to gain a smaller cave above. Move up left, then pull out right to gain the chimney above the cave. Climb this to the wide turf gully where *Lemon Groove* joins. Go up this to its top.
3. 30m   Finish as for *Lemon Groove*, up a groove on the right, then easy ground.

Magpie Groove   80m   VII,8 *. Pete Macpherson, Martin Moran. 19 Jan 2011.
Above the big ramp on the right side of the cliff is a big overhung recess with an appealing smooth corner on its left side. Start as for *Bowling Alley*.
1. 20m   Climb the easy icy groove and move right to the start of the big snow ramp; block belay below the corner.
2. 35m   The corner gives sustained bridging until just under the roof. Place high runners, then swing boldly up left into a shallow chimney which deepens into a

cleft. Belay on the higher ramp of *Cross-Bow* at a flake.
3. 30m Climb the turfy walls directly above to the top of the cliff.

CREAG COIRE AN T-SLUGAIN:
Note: Mike Lates climbed three routes on the lower cliff in January 2009. Above and left of the lower section of *Double Gully* is a ramp which has been climbed when *Double Gully* was deep in powder but is not worth a grade. Starting at the base of this ramp and climbing straight up to a higher ramp is 40m Grade III. Climbing out left from *Double Gully* about one-third up to the ramp by a steep enclosed chimney is 15m IV. Similar but two-thirds up *Double Gully* by a steep ice boss is also Grade IV. Topo provided.

THE SADDLE, Carn Mor Coire Mhalagain, Faraway Buttress:
(NG 928 124) Alt 820m South-East facing
This buttress lies on a ridge named Carn Mor Coire Mhalagain on the 1:25000 map. The approach over Bealach Coire Mhalagain and traversing the hillside under The Saddle summit is very rough and consolidated snow is recommended. The return along a fine ridge eastwards towards The Saddle summit is perhaps the highlight.

Faraway Groove 100m II. Andy Nisbet. 28 Nov 2010.
The buttress has a twin central groove system and the route takes the right groove. Climbed in lean frozen conditions, there were three tricky steps. The last was harder than Grade II but could easily bank up.

FIVE SISTERS, Sgurr na Carnach:
Rodent Ridge 200m II/III. Andy Moles, Malcolm Reid. 13 Dec 2010.
The ridge line on the right-hand side of *Dog's Leg Gully*. The lower part, which starts up grooves behind a large block and continues to a knife-edge crest, was not white enough on the day of first ascent and bypassed, but looks good. Above this the line meets the top of the right branch of *Dog's Leg Gully* at a crest. Trend up left from here on mixed ground to emerge next to the left branch of *Dog's Leg Gully*, and continue up the broken turfy crest on its right side to the summit. It is often easy to escape into the gully but the crest is more fun.

BEINN FHADA, Coire an Sgairne:
Rumbling Ridge 120m III,4. Andy Nisbet. 18 Mar 2011.
The second buttress from the left end and separated from the buttress at the left end by an easy gully. It has a sharp rocky crest when seen from the left but most of the difficulties are actually escapable to the right. Follow turfy grooves on the lower crest, which is right of the lower continuation of the sharp crest. These lead into a snow runnel. Take a left branch which leads on to the rocky crest above its difficulties.

BEINN LIATH MHOR, South Face:
The followings routes are situated on the large slabby buttress well left of *South-East Rib* (Highland Scrambles North, p183), roughly mid-way along the South Face, which contains a prominent roof in the centre. The routes ascend either side of the roof. Follow the path from Achnashellach until just short of Loch

Coire Lair then climb fairly directly up to the buttress. Descent was by a single abseil from a convenient block (60m ropes).

Doll Restoration 70m Very Difficult. Steve Kennedy, Cynthia Grindley. 22 Apr 2011.
The left-hand line. Start close to the shallow gully on the left and climb the slabby rib defining the left side of the buttress in two pitches.

The Walking Dead 50m VS 4c *. Steve Kennedy, Cynthia Grindley. 22 Apr 2011.
The right-hand line. Start about 10m above the right edge, avoiding the lower broken section by traversing left a short distance along a narrow grassy ledge until below a corner with some pale coloured rock. Take a line close to the corner to reach a ledge on the left below the clean upper slabs and a left-facing corner containing some large blocks (35m). Climb the corner, then move left and finish up the thin slabby wall above the right end of the roof - crux (15m).

SGORR RUADH, Central Couloir:
Note: Below and left of the start to *Mayfair* (SMCJ 2008) is a long shallow chimney which leads up right to the same big groove finish. Start up the chimney to reach a high ledge (40m). Traverse right along this to join the normal route and climb up this to the slab-ramp. This was climbed direct to reach the upper groove (30m) and finish up this as for the normal route (50m). Poorly protected and maybe VII,6. Ben O'Connor Croft, Helen Rennard, Duncan Tunstall. 5 Dec 2010.

Crimson Buttress 130m VI,7. David Bell, Andy Nisbet. 20 Feb 2011.
The crest of the buttress right of *Brown Gully*, on the right of the Central Couloir. Start at the top right side of the first bay on the right below where Central Couloir widens out.
1. 45m Climb left up a chimney to a chockstone with a possible through route. Pass this on the left and step back right over its top. Traverse a small turf ledge right, then go up to follow a ramp leading up left to the crest of the buttress.
2. 25m The steep crest is cut by a groove with bulging steps. Enter the groove from the left over the first step. Climb the second, then traverse right (crux) and go back left to pass the third. Finish up the groove to a big terrace.
3. 45m On the left is a gully which is on *Parallel Lines*. Start up it but soon climb diagonally left to the crest of a buttress (between *Brown Gully* and *Parallel Lines*). Climb this to a terrace.
4. 15m Finish over a step.

Woundwort 160m V,6. John Lyall, Andy Nisbet, Jonathan Preston. 2 Dec 2010.
A ramp system on the front face of the buttress with *Crimson Buttress*. Start right of *Crimson Buttress* at the top right side of the first bay on the right below where Central Couloir widens out. Here the ramp leads out right but is only seen from further back as the start is steep. Climb up through a bulge to the easier angled main ramp. Follow this with minor variations possible to a good ledge (40m). Head out right to the crest and go round this to reach a small bay at the end of easier ground (20m). Go up to a steep groove which leads up slightly left to the

big terrace (15m). Head left to the gully which is on *Parallel Lines*. Follow it to a crest formed by a big pinnacle (50m). Go up to the top (35m).

MAOL CHEAN-DEARG:
East Ridge   120m   II. Andy Nisbet. 6 Feb 2011.
As seen from Bealach na Lice, the north side of the east ridge is a steep sandstone face and at its left end is a line up the vague crest of the east ridge. Start round on the north side from the toe of the ridge and find a way up left to the crest. A left-slanting groove gains the easier upper crest which soon becomes walking and leads towards the summit.

North Face:
Baldrick   100m   Severe 4a. Andy Nisbet. 22 Jun 2011.
A direct line up a central rib on the face, starting just right of a small but distinct bay at the cliff base. The rib has pale rock up to the halfway ledge, then darker rock initially on the steepest section just above the ledge. It may be the rib between the two ramps but only one ramp (the right?) was obvious and this route finished up its very top. Good clean rock with positive holds but there were signs it might be slow to dry (climbed in dry conditions).

Note: A prominent waterfall on the north side of the road from Lochcarron to Kishorn was climbed in winter 1982/83 by David Whalley, Mark Sinclair & Al McLeod at Grade III. It was accidentally missed out of Northern Highlands South.

BEINN BHAN, Coire nan Fhamair:
Note: Two large holes on the plateau near the top of *Gully of the Gods* are now a hazard in winter. The larger hole is at NG 80220 45480, 863m, 10m from the cliff edge.

Godzilla   200m   IX,8 ****. Guy Robertson, Pete Benson. Jan 2011.
An obvious direct version of *The Godfather*, with four new pitches gives a magnificent line with some serious climbing. Start beneath the obvious corner-crack more or less directly beneath the upper corner of *The Godfather*.
1. 45m Climb into and up the corner-crack, then move right up a ledge to belay by an enormous flake.
2. 25m Stand on the flake, then go right into a up shallow grooves with little protection to an uncomfortable ledge.
3. 20m Go horizontally right into another bottomless groove and climb this to easier ground which leads past one short bulge to below a steep smooth corner.
4. 30m Climb the corner to join *The Godfather* and go left to its belay.
5. etc. Finish up the top two pitches of *The Godfather*.

APPLECROSS CRAGS, Loch na Creige Crag:
Little Ellie   20m   HVS 5a *. Graham Iles. Summer 2008.
Start about 10m right of *Little Plum*. Take a line just left of the black streak in the centre of the crag climbing directly through three overlaps.

Ardheslaig, Left Half:
Fire in the Glens 35m Very Difficult *. Mark Bull, Gillian Duncan. 7 May 2011.
Start just left of the central fault at a small tree. Climb a slim groove, and then cracks just left of the grassy fault to a small ledge at two-thirds height. Finish up the slab above, keeping right of a prominent quartz vein.

Creag Ob Mheallaidh:
(NG 837 537) West facing
This short steep gneiss outcrop is located on the rocky hillside east of the Ob Mheallaidh bay and is best seen ahead on the skyline when passing the bay on the drive east from Shieldaig. Park near the bend in the road and start up the hillside left of a small birch wood, moving up and left below smaller outcrops to the foot of the crag (10–15mins). At the far left end of the crag is a steep smooth wall; immediately right of this is a left-facing corner-groove.

Deceitful Groove 10m VS 4c *. Michael Barnard. 5 Mar 2011.
The corner-groove is surprisingly sustained.

Cut It 12m VS 5a **. John MacLeod, Michael Barnard. 10 Apr 2011.
Right of the corner-groove, the obvious left-right diagonal crack gives the best outing on the crag.

Dictator Ship 15m Hard Severe 4b. Michael Barnard. 5 Mar 2011.
Halfway up the wall right of the diagonal crack is a small slanting overlap. Start below and just right of this and climb directly up to a large flake. Continue up past the right end of the overlap to the top.

On the right-hand side of the crag is an obvious left-slanting slabby corner. The following route climbs the rib to its left:

Cross Winds 20m Hard Severe 4a. Michael Barnard. 5 Mar 2011.
Start 6m left of the slabby corner at a miniature crack with a small pocket beside it. Climb directly up the wall to the mid-height break (cams useful). Move up through a steeper section and continue up the rib to the top.

Friendly Fire 20m Severe. Michael Barnard. 5 Mar 2011.
Follow the left-slanting slabby corner to the mid-height break. Climb through an awkward step (crux) to finish up the easier top corner.

The Moorings 15m VS 4c *. Michael Barnard, John MacLeod. 10 Apr 2011.
Climb up to and follow the shallow left-trending groove overlooking the slabby corner. Step left to avoid a steeper bit before moving up and right to the top.

BEINN NA-H-EAGLAISE, East Face:
Tinker's Gully 130m II. Peter Biggar. 8 Jan 2011.
A shorter gully between two sharp buttresses well to the right of *Hogmanay Buttress* where the summit ridge of the hill bends round into the north. Well seen from the turn off from the A896 for Fasaig and Alligin (NG 906 528). Snow and

icy steps lead to a choice of finishes – both good – the turfy ramp to the right is easier.
Note: This short route is actually enhanced by making a devious zigzag approach by stream beds and along attractive sandstone terraces from the Annat path. The other routes on the hill are much easier of access.
Hogmanay Buttress (SMCJ 2010) was climbed by Peter Biggar & Roger Robb, not Ronnie Robb.

Forsaken Gully   120m   I. Peter Biggar, Roger Robb, Pete MacDonald. 25 Mar 2011.
This lies about 200m left of *Tinker's Gully*; it is well defined and may be corniced. The arete on the left of the gully bed is an alternative. There is a steep line of crags below the gully with several breaks in it which would give a much harder start if iced.

Descent from any route:
It is best to follow the declining summit ridge north-west, then descend west to the path up Coire Roill between Beinn Damh and Beinn na-h-Eaglaise; follow this path down to the clump of pines by the river, cross over and follow the Beinn Damh track on the left bank of the river through the woods to the road. Any other descent is either steep, rough and problematic, or much longer.

SEANA MHEALLAN:
Up and 25m left from *Neville the Hedgehog* is a grassy area with a wall running left for some distance. *Hind* climbs the flake-crack opposite a large flat boulder, about 2m right of a grotty left-facing corner.

Hind   10m   Very Difficult. Daniel Sutherland, Sean Watt. 12 Oct 2010.
Climb direct to a break and layback the flake-crack.

Stag   26m   VS 4b. Daniel Sutherland, Sean Watt. 12 Oct 2010.
This lies about 15m left of *Hind* and takes a slab with a right-trending crack. Climb the left crack to a break, then step right onto the right-trending crack. Climb the crack until it becomes full of grass. Strike boldly upwards left to finish on a large ledge. Step 2m left and climb twin cracks in the slab above.

DIABAIG, Upper Slabs:
The Mancunian Question   40m   Hard Severe 4b. Nick Dominelli-Whiteley, Jon de Leyser. 2 Jun 2011.
Start on a wrinkled wall above a step in the gully approx 30m up from the top of the Main Wall. Head up a right-facing ramp to a large block before stepping left into a finger crack. Continue to the top, across a large ledge and up an easy crack to a second ledge. Climb twin finger cracks (direct is better but 4c or 5a. A pleasant and enjoyable route with some good climbing although care should be taken with the holds on the lower section. Splitting into two pitches is suggested.
Note: This is thought to be different to *The Gooseberry*; a topo and pictures were sent.

Terrier Trauma Wall:

Collie's Corner   25m   HVS 5a *. Michael Barnard, John MacLeod. 30 Apr 2011.
The central corner gives a sustained pitch. Start directly below the corner and climb up to a steep wall. Traverse left beneath this wall before moving back up right to climb the corner.

Charlie's Dome:

Broons' Wall   80m   HVS **. Michael Barnard, John MacLeod. 30 Apr 2011.
Right of *Charlie's Tower* is a fine slab. Start at the bottom left of this slab below a thin right-trending crack which peters out after a few metres.
1. 40m 4c Move up the crack before stepping right to gain a right-slanting ramp. Follow this for a few metres until able to move back up to gain the left-hand continuation crack. Climb this up to and through a short steeper section to reach easier ground leading to a good ledge.
2. 40m 5b Go up to climb the small steep dome on the left (runners in the crack on the right) to gain and follow easier ground to the top.

DIABAIG, Little Pillar:

Tidal   South facing
Looking south along the coast from Diabaig village, one can make out a couple of short steep walls just above the sea. The most visible is a small promontory with an obvious triangular red wall overlying a small stony beach. This is Red Slab and can be gained by a scramble along the shoreline from the village at low-mid tide. About halfway there one passes the foot of a narrow gully (this is down and left of *Diabaig Pillar* – see photodiagram p244 Northern Highlands South). The steep sidewall of this gully is a fine feature composed of good sound rock.

Proud Arete   15m   Hard Severe 4a ***. Michael Barnard. 5 Mar 2011.
The imposing left arete gives some brilliant positions for the grade. Start up a flake-crack to gain the blunt arete which is climbed direct to the top.

Feel Euphoria   15m   E1 5b **. Michael Barnard, John MacLeod. 10 Apr 2011.
Excellent wall climbing. Start up the second thin crack right of the arete, continuing directly to finish up the obvious short top crack.

Periwinkle   20m   VS 4c **. John MacLeod, Michael Barnard. 10 Apr 2011.
Juggy climbing in a great position. Start 5m right of the arete. Climb thin cracks to gain the main fault-line which splits near the top. Take the right-hand finish through a small steepening (crux).

Red Slab:

Tidal   North-West facing
The obvious triangular red wall on the small promontory a few minutes further along the shoreline is home to a couple of routes.

Gneiss Jugs   12m   VS 4c. Michael Barnard. 9 Apr 2011.
Start below the right end of a small overlap on the left side of the wall. Climb up

to and follow a right-slanting crack. Where this runs out, step left and move up on small holds to mantelshelf onto a grassy ledge.

The Red Slab   12m   VS 4c *. Michael Barnard. 9 Apr 2011.
The central line on the wall. Reach up for and climb a shallow left-facing corner to a slanting break. Move leftwards up this to gain and follow a vertical crack to another break. Hand-traverse this to a problematic finish up around the left arete.

BEINN EIGHE, Eastern Ramparts:
Feast of the East   VIII,9 *** Francis Blunt, Murdoch Jamieson, Martin Moran. 19 Dec 2010.
The first pitch climbs a short bold groove then moves left and back right to the Girdle Ledge (7). The cracked corner through the double roofs proves very strenuous (9). The crack-line of pitch 3 gives a superb sustained pitch (8). The winter ascent finished up a short corner on the right (5).

Pale Rider, Eastwood Variation   100m   E3. Geoff Cohen, Andy Nisbet, Des Rubens. 30 Apr 2011.
1. 40m 4c Follow the normal route to the Upper Girdle but belay at the point of arrival below a left-facing corner.
2. 20m 5c Gain and climb the corner to the belay ledge of *Paleface Wall*. A fine pitch.
3. 25m 5c Climb pitches 3 & 4 of *Paleface Wall* (run together on this occasion).
4. 15m 5b Climb a right-slanting crack-line right of the finish of *Paleface Wall*.

Note: *Simpleton* was climbed free by Gordon Macnair & Andy Nisbet at E2 5c on 1 May 2011.

West Central Wall:
West Central Gully Variation   VII,8. Nick Bullock, Pete Benson. 2010.
Climb the icy corner on the right of the normal route to reach an icicle, then follow this on thin ice to the summit snowslopes.

Far West Buttress:
Mullein   40m   VS 4c. Andy Nisbet, Jonathan Preston. 3 Jul 2011.
Right of *Fuselage Gully* left branch (with the wreckage) is a buttress with the VI,7 corner. This is a summer ascent of the corner, climbed to its top, then move left on to the crest to finish. Continuing up the crest would have been about Moderate.

Westlife   60m   IV,5. John Lyall, Andy Nisbet, Jonathan Preston. 15 Nov 2010.
Right of the buttress with the corner is a wide gully leading to overhangs. This route takes grooves on the right wall of the gully. Start on the gully face of a subsidiary buttress. Climb through a steep shallow slot to the top of the buttress. Go slightly left up cracked grooves parallel to the main gully to a ledge (35m). Continue in the same line up a roofed chimney, then go right up a blocky groove to the top (25m).

Wild West 60m V,6. Andy Nisbet, Jonathan Preston, Garry Smith. 16 Mar 2011.
Climbs more directly up the right side of the right wall of the gully. The subsidiary buttress forms a corner between it and the main wall; start up this. There is a much steeper corner just to the right. Climb the corner almost to a ledge, then step right and climb up through a bulge to a ledge. Gain a higher ledge, then move left, up and back right to reach a terrace (35m). Climb a groove, passing under a big chockstone, then move right to gain the crest between the gully wall and the front face. Follow this, finishing on its right (25m).

Occidental 60m VS *. Andy Nisbet, Jonathan Preston. 3 Jul 2011.
The right end of the right wall of the gully has a big right-facing corner with a wide crack in its back and a wider crack in its right wall.
1. 35m 4c Climb the corner, either past three wedged blocks or by bypassing them on the left arete. Move left to a ledge, then up and back right round on to the front face to a ledge with a huge flake forming a pinnacle at its right end. Gain the terrace from the top of the pinnacle (as for *Chalice*). A direct and independent line staying on the right wall of the gully would be better but might be harder.
2. 25m 5a Climb the wall right of the arete above, then another wall and easier walls to the top.

Athame 30m E1 5a **. John Lyall, Andy Nisbet. 18 Apr 2011.
Heading right from *Occidental*, the first feature on the front face of the buttress is a smooth wall with distinctive wine glass shaped twin cracks. This climbs the left crack after soloing up to reach it. Sustained jamming, well protected with Friends 2.5 to 4 and hexes of similar size. Climb two walls above the crack to reach the terrace. Finish up *Occidental* or abseil down to climb *Chalice*.

Chalice 70m V,6 *. John Lyall, Andy Nisbet, Jonathan Preston. 15 Nov 2010.
The right of the distinctive wine glass shaped twin cracks.
Start at the cliff base left of these. Climb a ramp with a bulging start rightwards to a pinnacle below the right crack (10m). Stand on the pinnacle to gain access to the crack. Climb the crack, steep but very helpful, to a ledge with a bigger pinnacle. From the top of this, climb a wall to the terrace (25m).
There are a variety of finishes but an independent one was taken. Walk left on to the gully wall, passing under the chockstone of *Wild West*, to a long groove (10m). Climb this groove (25m).
Summer: Severe 4a. John Lyall, Andy Nisbet. 18 Apr 2011.
Start up the arete right of the bulging start but soon move into it. Follow the crack as for winter to the terrace. A corner left of the winter groove was climbed to the top.

Chock-a-Block 60m V,6 *. James Edwards, Andy Nisbet, Colin Wells. 14 Nov 2010.
This climbs a wide crack in the right wall of a corner which is formed right of the wine glass shaped twin cracks. Start on the front face below the corner. Climb steps to the same pinnacle as on *Chalice*. Step right from the pinnacle to a ledge below the corner. Pull up into the wide crack, which is very steep but full of chockstones. It widens into a squeeze chimney, from which the top of a big

pinnacle can be gained. Climb up left to a ledge (35m). Finish up the steep fault above, including a through route (25m).
Summer: Severe 4a. Andy Nisbet, Jonathan Preston. 3 Jul 2011.
Start right of the winter route and climb a crack in the front face direct to the big pinnacle. Continue as for winter except a wall right of the through route was climbed.

No Fly Zone   70m   V,6 *. Andy Nisbet, Chris Pasteur, Duncan Tunstall. 28 Feb 2011.
Right of the corner of *Chock-a-Block* is another wall with a big left-facing corner forming its right end and a smaller left-facing corner facing it. The original route *Far West Buttress* starts up the big corner and moves left into the smaller corner. This route climbs the smaller corner throughout but then takes a wide fault right of *Far West Buttress*. Climb the corner, sustained but with continuous cracks and joined by *Far West Buttress* halfway up, to a ledge (30m). Traverse easily right along the ledge (10m). Climb a short wall into a wide fault. Exit the fault by two short awkward chimneys on its left side to reach blocks at the top (30m).

Far West Direct   70m   HVS 5b *. Andy Nisbet, Jonathan Preston. 3 Jul 2011.
Start up a crack just left of the original *Far West Buttress* to join it. From where the original route traverses left, climb on up over overhanging blocks to a roof. Move left under the roof and make a difficult move up into a crack (3.5 Friend). Go up the crack to the halfway ledge. Walk 10m right to finish as for *No Fly Zone* (but slightly more direct).

Raptor   70m   VI,7 **. Steve Ashworth, Brian Davison, Andy Nisbet. 12 Mar 2011.
Just right of the right arete of the initial left-facing corner of *Far West Buttress* is a big groove which leads to very steep ground. Climb the groove through a difficult bulge with a prominent chockstone and continue up the groove to a roof. Pull left round the roof to a ledge below another roof. Move left from the ledge to the top of a groove and climb out the top of this to the halfway ledge (40m). The fault of *No Fly Zone* would be the obvious finish, but this ascent climbed up a wall into a roofed groove just left of the rib which forms the left side of the fault. Move up the groove, then make a long step right on to the rib and climb it to a ledge which leads right to join the finish of *No Fly Zone* (30m).
Summer: VS 5a *. John Lyall, Andy Nisbet. 18 Apr 2011.
1. 40m 4c As for winter.
2. 30m 5a A more direct line than in winter. Climb the wall right of the winter line to reach a steep wall forming the base of the rib. Climb this by a steep finger crack just right of the crest and continue directly up walls.

Crackhead   70m   V,6 **. Sandy Allan, Andy Nisbet, Jonathan Preston. 25 Nov 2010.
Start up the same groove as *Raptor*. Climb the groove through the difficult bulge with the chockstone but take its right fork to the steep ground. Traverse right round a corner on to a flake-ledge which leads to a ledge below a vertical leaning corner (30m). Climb the corner, hard but very safe, and subsequent corners and flakes trending slightly right to below a roofed corner (30m). This corner is right

of a steep wide crack with a distinctive jutting block. Finish up the roofed corner (10m).

Summer: VS 4c *. John Lyall, Andy Nisbet. 18 Apr 2011.
A line independent to Raptor was climbed. Start right of the winter route and climb a wall and crack direct to the ledge below the vertical leaning corner. Climb the corner (crux) and continue as for winter.

Flake City 60m Hard Severe 4b *. Andy Nisbet. 5 Sep 2010.
Short but surprisingly good rock. Start up a big left-facing corner in a steep clean area of rock near the right end of the buttress. Climb the corner to a large wedged flake. Swing out to the arete and move right round a flake. Go up and left to walk behind a huge flake, then climb short walls to a steep wide crack with a distinctive jutting block. The belay here is as for *Crackhead* and the route then crosses it. Climb up to a bulge at the base of the crack, then swing out left and climb a vertical wall on excellent holds to the top.
Winter: V,7. Andy Nisbet, Jonathan Preston. 8 Feb 2011.
By the summer route except that the steep wide crack with the distinctive jutting block was gained by stepping in from the right via a small ledge on the arete to grab the block. The wide crack was then climbed to the top.

Avro 60m VS 4c. John Lyall, Andy Nisbet. 18 Apr 2011.
Right of the big corner of *Flake City* is a huge chimney-flake. Climb the slabby wall left of this to reach a right-slanting crack which leads to a steep wall. Climb this by a flake-crack to reach the terrace. Above the terrace, climb steps to finish up a groove right of the finish of *Crackhead*.

Pineapple Cliff:
Pina Colada VS *. Dave McGimpsey, Andy Nisbet, Sue Wood. 24 Jul 2011.
By the winter line in two pitches (4c 4b).

CAIRNGORMS

COIRE AN T-SNEACHDA, Mess of Pottage:
Beeline 90m HVS/E1 *. Allen Fyffe, John Lyall. 3 Sep 2010.
The edge right of the *Honeypot* chimney.
1. 25m 4a Follow the right-slanting crack right of *Honeypot* (*Wachacha* winter variation).
2. 25m 4a Climb the slabby rib on the right of the gully and belay to the right of the upper chimney.
3. 40m 5b Take the wide crack on the right, then traverse steeply left to gain the edge and follow this to the top.

The Firefighter 80m VS *. John Lyall, Andy Nisbet. 12 Oct 2010.
Start up a wide crack just right of the winter direct, then move left into the winter route and climb to the ledge above the tapering slot. Move up left to another ledge (35m 4c). Climb the wide crack above and continue up clean short walls to the top (45m 4a).

Note: Warm summer weather. AN climbed *Savage Slit* in full winter nick 8 days later.

Fintastic 50m   VS. Allen Fyffe, John Lyall. 3 Sep 2010.
Start as for *Sharks Fin Soup*.
1. 30m 4c Slant up left to gain the sharp edge left of the fin. Climb this and the wall on the left. Continue up a crack, then through a bulge to a belay on the left edge.
2. 20m 4b Climb the slab by a right-slanting crack to easy ground.

Black Sheep   III. John Lyall, Jonathan Preston. 19 Jan 2010.
Followed the summer line on the lower tier.

Aladdin's Buttress:
Note: Andy Nisbet climbed the groove left of *Tom Thumb* at 50m Grade III (17 Jan 2011) but is unlikely to be the first.

Fluted Buttress:
Facet Hunters   140m   IV,6. Sandy Allan, Andy Nisbet. 30 Dec 2010.
The rib right of *Spiral Gully*. Start where *Wavelength* leaves *Spiral Gully*.
1. 50m Climb straight up on icy slabs to a block in a big snow corner.
2. 25m Climb the corner until 10m below its top (and where it meets *Spiral Gully*). Head out right across the sidewall on ledges to a ramp above and follow this until just below the crest above *Spiral Gully*.
3. 20m Climb the wall above rightwards to stand on a pinnacle. Make an awkward move over a bulge on the left to reach a groove which leads up right (also joining *Lambda*).
4. 45m Gain and follow the crest to the top.

Rosslyn Chapel 50m V,7. Alex Kelly, Andy Nisbet. 25 Oct 2010.
Between the grooves of the V,7 and IV,6 finishes to *Spiral Gully* is a shallow groove leading into a crack above a small roof. Climb this to a ledge (10m, crux). Climb a roofed corner which leads into a big finishing gully (40m).

Fiacaill Buttress:
Trampled Underfoot, True Finish   30m   IV,6. Rupert Rosedale, Mark Walker. Winter 2008.
Above the short corner take the roof-capped chimney directly above, and finish directly.

Cap in Hand, Freedom Finish   45m   IV,5. John Lyall, Andy Nisbet, Jonathan Preston. 23 Nov 2010.
Belay beneath the roof-capped chimney. Move left and pull out right to ledges, climb past a flake and up a short corner, then easily to the top.

Omerta 60m VIII,9. Pete Macpherson, Martin Moran. 13 Nov 2010.
Start at the bottom of *Belhaven* at a short wall. Go about 10m further up *Fiacaill Couloir* to the left end of a ledge. Climb up to this and traverse back right to the foot of a tapering pillar.

1. 10m Climb a right-slanting crack with a small roofed niche at its bottom left and pull onto a ledge below a steep wall.

2. 25m Step left onto a block, then pull right onto the wall and climb a right-slanting crack. Very strenuous and difficult to protect due to crack being turf filled (one rest). At the top of the wall, mantel into a small niche and pull over. Climb up a ramp to below the upper wall.

3. 25m Go further up the ramp over a block to below a steep crack. Climb the crack (well protected) to the right end of a horizontal break. Move left along the break to turf. Pull over on turf and go up a groove to the top.

COIRE AN LOCHAIN:

The Gathering 60m IX,9 **. Guy Robertson, Pete Macpherson. Feb 2011.

A counter-diagonal to *Pic n' Mix*. The first pitch is brilliant, but the second disappointing as it avoids the challenge of the final tower direct. Start up *The Head-hunter* but at a huge flake-crack step left into the obvious groove in the arete. Climb this, then steeply up right across a leaning wall then into the obvious capped groove. Follow this over the overhang and up to the first belay on *Never Mind* (30m). Go left and climb the wide crack (as for *Never Mind*) then pull delicately out left onto a smooth wall. Climb diagonally leftwards up across this into the final chimney of *Grumbling Groove* and follow this to the top (30m).

No. 4 Buttress:

Sarcophagus 60m III *. Michael Barnard. 23 Jan 2011.

To the left of *Oesophagus* is a steep arete; immediately left again and overlying the lower section of *Right Branch Y Gully* is a snowy corner-groove with a steep wall at its base and leading up to finish between two towers. Start up another groove up and left of the initial wall and climb this to the base of another steep wall. Traverse right below this wall, crossing a snow arete, to gain the left-hand groove. Climb this to easier ground before taking the final open groove above to a steep finish.

Tracheotomy 80m VS 4b. John Lyall, Andy Nisbet, Jonathan Preston. 4 Jul 2011.

Start up a groove on the right side of the rib between *Oesophagus* and *Tracheotomy* winter. Climb this until it get mucky, then move left and climb the rib to its top. Climb the crest of a sharp rib on the right, then traverse right on to the winter route. Follow this to below the final tower (50m). Climb this and the upper crest as for winter (30m).

CREAGAN COIRE A' CHA-NO:

This attractive little granite cliff lies tucked under the east flank of the Sròn a' Cha-no spur on Cairngorm. The crag faces east and overlooks Strath Nethy. It lies less than 2km away from the Coire na Ciste car park and the approach to the descent (*Recovery Gully* NJ 017 063) takes just over an hour. The descent is even quicker at about 45min.

The crag is up to 70m high and sports 15 routes, ranging from Grade II to VII. Most of the major features have been climbed, but there is potential for many shorter lines. With a cliff base of 950m, the routes come into condition early.

Later in the season the cliff catches the sun, and some routes may bank out and have cornice difficulties.

The Cairngorm pioneers investigated the climbing potential of the crag way back in the 1950s (it is mentioned in Mac Smith's 1960 Cairngorms guidebook) but it was felt to be too short for worthwhile winter climbing. Times change and winter routes no longer need to be longer than 150m to be acceptable! Cha-no provides a welcome alternative to the Northern Corries, with the benefit of turfy cracks, a beautiful view and a secluded feel away from the hustle and bustle of the ski area.

Cutty Sark   35m   IV,5. John Lyall, Andy Nisbet. 18 Jan 2011.
A line on the left buttress, some 60m left of the one with *Anvil Corner*. On its south side is a triangular feature with a steep chimney-crack forming its left side and a corner forming its right. Climb the corner to the top of the triangle and a continuation fault to the top.

Quiet Corner   40m   V,7. John Lyall, Scott Frazer, Mick Twomey. 7 Feb 2011.
A left leaning corner tucked in on the left side of *Chimney Rib*.

Chimney Rib   60m   IV,4. Roger Webb, Simon Richardson. 21 Nov 2010.
The prominent pinnacled rib guarding the left flank of *Recovery Gully* is cut by a deep chimney on its front face.
1. 35m   Climb the chimney over a chokestone, pass through 'the jaws' in the chasm above and climb to the top of the pinnacle.
2. 25m   Descend the pinnacle and climb easy mixed ground to the right of *Recovery Gully* to the plateau.

Recovery Gully   50m   I
The broad gully provides the easiest ascent and descent to the crag. The cornice should normally be passable at the top of the buttress to the right.

Flaked Out   50m   VI,7. Simon Richardson, Sandy Simpson. 14 Nov 2010.
The attractive stepped flake on the front buttress of the buttress immediately right of *Recovery Gully*. Start by scrambling up 20m of easy ground to the foot of the flake.
1. 30m   Climb the two-stepped flake to reach a ledge beneath a bulging offwidth corner. Climb this (crux, one fall on first ascent) to a platform.
2. 20m   Finish up the wide crack in the centre of the bulging headwall.

Anvil Corner   60m   VI,6. Sandy Simpson, Simon Richardson. 14 Nov 2010.
The classic of the crag, taking the prominent clean-cut corner on the left wall of the sharp arete of Anvil Buttress (defined by a prominent anvil-shaped block at its top).
1. 40m   Climb a series of three steep steps to enter the corner and follow this to a deep notch in the ridge. An excellent pitch.
2. 20m   Continue up the crest of the buttress to the top.

Anvil Gully   45m   IV,4. John Lyall, Andy Nisbet. 18 Jan 2011.
A wide fault left of *Anvil Corner* has an easier left side and a longer steeper right

side. Start just left of *Anvil Corner* and climb to a V-groove. Go up this to the narrower upper fault. This has a steep finish; move out on to its left wall and climb this to the top.

Duke's Rib 60m II. Roger Webb, Simon Richardson. 21 Nov 2010.
The shallow angled rib between *Anvil Corner* and *Jenga Buttress*. Easy climbing up the lower rib leads to a window and a steep left-facing corner on the final tower to finish. Moderate in summer.

Jenga Buttress 70m III,4. Sandy Simpson, Simon Richardson. 14 Nov 2010.
The longest feature on the cliff.
1. 40m Start left of the steep lower wall and climb a gully to gain the rib. Continue up this over a steep step to a good platform.
2. 30m Continue up the buttress crest, over a series of steep technical sections to gain the plateau. Excellent well protected climbing.

Daylight Robbery 60m V,6. James Edwards, Simon Richardson, Roger Webb. 8 Jan 2011.
Good climbing up the initial wall and right flank of *Jenga Buttress*.
1. 30m Start 10m right of the initial gully of *Jenga Buttress* and climb a steep right-facing turfy corner to reach a broad ledge.
2. 30m Continue up the steep bulging right-facing corner above the left end of the ledge and make a steep exit onto *Jenga Buttress*. Finish up this.

Smooth as Silk 70m VII,7. Simon Richardson, Iain Small. 12 Dec 2010.
The vertical wall left between *Jenga Buttress* and *Arch Wall* is cut by a hanging offwidth crack at half-height.
1. 35m Start 5m right of *Daylight Robbery* and climb the prominent right-facing turfy groove to gain the broad ledge of *Daylight Robbery*. Move right along this to belay directly below the offwidth.
2. 35m Climb a left-facing groove then a step crack to below a roof. Move right through this to enter the bulging offwidth. Climb this to its top where progress is barred by another roof. Step onto the steep wall on the left and move up to some welcome turf. Continue up the groove above, and where it trends right to join the upper groove of *Arch Wall*, step left to gain the continuation groove and follow this to the top.

Arch Wall 50m VII,7. Roger Webb, Simon Richardson. 21 Nov 2010.
A serious route through the prominent arched roof to the right of *Jenga Buttress*.
1. 20m Climb a series of turfy grooves passing by a chokestone and V-groove low down, to reach a good platform on the left.
2. 30m The arched roof looms above. Climb up then left then make a series of steep moves leading up to a flake on the left side of the roof lip (bold). Pull into the groove above, and follow it to the top.

Arch Enemy 45m V,5. John Lyall, Andy Nisbet. 18 Jan 2011.
A right diagonal line starting below *Arch Wall*. Start at a big spike. Climb to a narrow chimney and over its chokestone. Continue up the line over two steep

steps to steep snow which leads in the same line to a short snow arete and a potential cornice.

Fingers and Thumbs   50m   IV,5. Simon Richardson, Iain Small. 12 Dec 2010.
The prominent right-slanting gully bounding the right side of *Arch Wall*.
1. 30m Climb the easy lower gully and belay below the steep headwall by a pinnacle on the right.
2. 20m Climb up the right side of the headwall, step left at its top, and finish up the continuation groove above.

Tower Chimney   50m   V,5. Simon Richardson, Iain Small. 12 Dec 2010.
1. 40m Start directly below the steep bulging tower to the right of *Arch Wall*. Climb a right-trending ramp and pull into a niche. Move up to a vertical vegetated groove, step left onto its left wall and make a steep exit onto a turf ledge. Move up to the hidden squeeze chimney on the right and follow this to the right side of the tower.
2. 10m Finish easily on the right side of the tower.

COIRE AN SPREIDHE:
Central Couloir   300m   II. Simon Richardson, Roger Webb. 16 Jan 2011.
The slabby cliffs of Coire an Spreidhe are cut by a vegetated fault starting at NJ 017 047. Climb the fault, passing a steep step after 50m to emerge on the upper snowfields. Break through the mixed ground above to a corniced exit. A worthwhile mountaineering excursion climbed under conditions of heavy snow; the route will have more interest in leaner conditions.

CARN ETCHACHAN:
The Sword Independent Finish   60m   IV,5. John Lyall, Andy Nisbet, Jonathan Preston. 13 Dec 2010.
The Sword climbs the ramp of *Red Guard* (summer), then leaves it to finish as for *Red Guard* (winter). Instead, continue up the ramp to its top and take the summer line of *Red Guard* out right. Perhaps easier than the original finish.

SHELTERSTONE CRAG:
Stone Temple Pilots   250m   X,9 ****. Pete Macpherson, Guy Robertson. 28 Jan 2011.
One fall taken on the crux.
1. to 3. 100m As for *The Steeple*. Belay below the crux fault of *Steeple/Haystack*.
4. 25m Climb the very steep and pumpy fault of *Haystack* (crux), passing an in-situ peg over the bulge. Belay up and left at a small ledge (cramped)
5. 12m Follow the ramp as for *Haystack* for about 9m to a left-slanting fault/ groove. Climb this to a good ledge. Belay at left end of ledge below a steep tapering corner-crack.
6. 45m Climb the crack steeply until it is possible to step left onto a foot hold on the arete. Move left (bold and delicate), stepping across to below a steep wide crack. Arrange gear and pull through steeply onto turf and follow a turfy left-facing corner (common with *Citadel*) until it is possible to move up and right to the belay below the overhanging crack/groove of *Haystack*.

7. A pitch of *Spire*. Move up and right following the steep right-trending weakness. Belay below top pitch of *The Steeple*. A sensational, pumpy and outrageously exposed pitch.
8. Climb the final pitch of *The Steeple*.

HELL'S LUM CRAG:
Anonymouse 100m HVS 5a. John Lyall, Andy Nisbet. 11 October 2010.
Based on the rib between *Deep Cut Chimney* and *Nobody's Fault*. Start at the base of the *Deep Cut* chimney itself.
1. 40m 5a Climb the chimney for about 8m before moving right on to the rib. Climb the rib but with most of the runners at either edge to a ledge just below and 5m left of the main chimney of *Nobody's Fault*.
2. 40m 4c Move right into and climb the chimney of *Nobody's Fault*. Near its top, step back left on to the rib and climb it to a steep band. Go up left on a ramp which leads to a ledge overlooking *Deep Cut Chimney*.
3. 20m 4b Climb a steep crack, then two more short walls to the top.

The following route is on a crag down to the left of the Lower Slab of Hell's Lum (NH 995 015), and just left of the Feith Bhuidhe (the next tier above Waterfall Wall).

Purgatory Wall 55m Severe 4a. Harry Holmes, Alastair Clarke. 12 Sep 2010.
1. 25m Start at the right of the crag. Follow a left-slanting vegetated fault up to a ledge. Exit the ledge on its right side and follow groove to a foot ledge. Belay at the left side of the ledge.
2. 30m Return right along the foot ledge. Start up the centre of the slab and trend leftwards at the top. Easier ground leads to the top.
Variation Start: Hard Severe 5a.
Start at the right of the crag left of a pink streak (drainage line). Bridge across the drainage line until the left-slanting fault and the normal start can be gained.

STAG ROCKS:
Truly Accidental 130m III,4. Martin Holland, Ali Cashman. 17 Feb 2011.
Starts from the initial snow bay of *The Accidental Tourist*, but climbs directly up the buttress rather than up and left, with a good first pitch.
1. 30m From the snow bay, two grooves head straight up separated by a thin rib. Climb the left-hand and wider groove, steeper than it looks, and finish up a shallow right-trending and narrowing chimney to reach the rib on the right (10m left and down from the chimney of *Truly, Madly, Chimbley*).
2. 50m Move up and left to an inverted V-notch. Climb through this and go up slabs and overlaps direct to a small prow.
3. 50m Easy snowslopes lead to the top.

Thumper 80m III. John Lyall, Andy Nisbet, Simon Yearsley. 10 Nov 2010.
The ridge between *The Cardinal* and *Diagonal Gully* gives a minor but pleasant climb, less affected by sun than other routes. Start at the same place as *The Cardinal*. Climb up to a wall, move right and up a corner, step right again and go up a rough corner line until moves left lead to the crest above its steep lower section. Follow the crest to a large block (50m). Continue to a turfy groove

which leads up the crest to a slight pinnacle. After this the going gets much easier (30m) and turns to walking.

CHALAMAIN GAP:
Note: Two routes were climbed by Gwilym & Caroline Lynn on 19 Dec 2009. Routes have been climbed here in the past but not recorded, and the crag thought too minor to start now.

SGÒR GAOITH, A' Phocaid:
Spymaster 150m III **. David & John Lyall. 10 Mar 2010.
Starts up the next corner on the right wall of *Deep Pockets*, above the start of *Mixed Spice*. Climb the short corner and ramp to gain an ice filled gully, which is followed direct over a vertical step to the top. Ice screws were required for runners and a belay at the end of the first pitch.

Note: Tom Evans, Paul Wells, Alastair Cochran & Vincent Jack, in Feb 2011, climbed the second gully from the right on the right side of the corrie (topo provided). Grade II on the day but it banks out.

COIRE GARBHLACH, Lower Corrie:
Spice Boys 150m III. Sandy Allan, Andy Nisbet. 16 Dec 2010.
A ridge left of *Garlic Gully*. Start left of the rocky crest left of *Garlic Gully*. After a steep start, climb easier heathery shelves to a steep band. Go left up a ramp to the crest. Climb a flakey pinnacle and a sharp crest to another short wall. Above this is another crest leading to a steeper band. Climb this by a shallow groove (crux). A final buttress leads to easy ground.
Note: The shallow gully left of this ridge is Grade I and has been climbed several times. There is an optional ice pitch, which can be up to 15m and Grade II/III, but can also bank out. It can be bypassed on the left.

Gael Force Ridge 100m IV,6. John Lyall, Andy Nisbet. 10 Jan 2011.
By the summer route. Approach by the start of *Garlic Gully* and start left of the toe of the buttress.

Upper Corrie:
Bertie's Gully 140m I *. Martin Middleton, John Swinden. 12 Dec 2010.
The fine central gully on the buttress on the north side of the Upper Corrie (NN 8855 9445).

CAIRN TOUL, Corrie of the Chokestone Gully:
Foxy Woxy 130m IV,5. Simon Richardson, Helen Rennard. 27 Mar 2011.
A mixed line up the right flank of *The Flying Fox* buttress.
1. 35m Start in the mouth of *Chokestone Gully* about 20m up and right of the toe of the buttress. Climb a gully leading into a left-trending groove. Climb this over several bulges until underneath a smooth groove. Step left and climb a bulge to a small ledge. (This last section is common with *The Flying Fox*).
2. 25m Traverse 3m right to a large ledge, then step right into a square-cut gully. Climb the left side of the gully to easy ground.

Steve Elliott on Northumberland Wall (E2,5c), Diabaig.
Photo: Graeme Gatherer.

3. and 4. 70m   Climb the crest of the buttress joining *The Shroud*. The large cornice was surmounted via a steep break about 20m to the left

COIRE SPUTAN DEARG, Flake Buttress Area:

Penguin   85m   V,7. John Lyall, Andy Nisbet. 29 Jan 2011.
A winter ascent based on the summer route. Start below the summer start. Climb out left on to the buttress on turf, then go right up a turfy corner to the ledge below the flake-crack (15m). Climb the flake-crack as for summer, with a technical start (25m). Finish up varied ground right of *Flake Buttress* (45m).

CREAGAN A' CHOIRE ETCHACHAN:

Gaddzooks!   140m   VI,6. Helen Rennard, John Lyall, Andy Nisbet. 21 Jan 2011.
An ascent of the original summer line of *Avalanche Gully* taken by Mr. and Mrs. Gadd in 1955, as judged by two steel pitons in situ. It follows a groove system left of the main gully line. Start up the ice of *Avalanche Gully* until 5m below its overhang. Climb a crack leading up the left wall to a ledge on the left (30m). Climb the turfy groove above until the steel pegs are seen on the right. Move up and step right above the pegs (or climb past them) to gain a big slab-ramp. Step right, then down to move into its corner. Climb this (initially serious) to an easier section and a final bulge to easier ground (40m). Continue up the easier groove to the crest of Pioneer Buttress. Follow a groove on the right to a step (40m). Go over the step and finish on snow (30m).

Kukri   120m   V,6. Andy Nisbet, Helen Rennard. 19 Jan 2011.
Based on the grassy fault which bounds the arete of *Delicatessen* on the right.
1. 40m   Climb the 'steep terrace' which is the common descent for summer routes until level with an inset slab which is formed right of the arete of *Delicatessen*.
2. 30m   Climb a wide crack in a lower slab, or gain it from the right, to reach the inset slab. Climb turfy blocks up left to the corner which bounds the inset slab on the left. *Enigma* probably continues up the corner. Instead, traverse right with a thin move to gain a crack near the right side of the slab. Climb the crack to the top of the slab.
3. 30m   Move right into the main fault and climb this steeply to a capping rock. Pass this on the left.
4. 20m   Finish up steep snow (20m).

Machete   100m   V,5. Andy Nisbet, Duncan Tunstall. 3 Mar 2011.
A companion route to *Kukri*, climbing the lower section of the grassy fault but finishing on the right. Thawing, maybe IV,5 in better conditions. A complete ascent of the fault would be logical but the lower section is slow to ice up. Start right of the 'steep terrace'.
1. 30m   Climb to the base of the fault on snow and turf.
2. 30m   Continue to an obvious steep barrier. Go up right below this until possible to step left on to it. Climb a shallow groove on turf and ice to the easing where *Kukri* joins the fault.
3. 30m   Leave the fault and follow a cracked ramp up right, then return left to easy ground.
4. 10m   Finish easily.

LOCH ETCHACHAN CRAG

This area of cliff on the south side of the loch has a number of ice lines as well as one rock route. The winter routes are good if rather short-lived though an easy descent on either side of the cliff allows a few to be climbed in a day. A little ice is helpful on the mixed lines. The climbs have easier upper sections – route lengths are given to where the ground starts to level off. In the centre and forming the lowest point of the cliff is the main buttress, a large and imposing area of rock home to the summer route *Bacchus*. Immediately left of this is an easy gully, *Central Couloir*; left again is a smaller more broken buttress.

Wintertime Winds 60m II. Michael Barnard. 26 Feb 2011.
A right-slanting ramp-line in the left-hand buttress. Climb a short step and move up the ramp to another step solved by a short awkward chimney (crux). Continue up the ramp and climb an icy groove to easier ground.

Etched in Blue 50m III *. Michael Barnard. 26 Feb 2011.
The obvious corner of water ice immediately right of the left-hand buttress.

Central Couloir 70m I. Michael Barnard. 26 Feb 2011.
The gully immediately left of the main buttress has a couple of icy bits low down but soon becomes straightforward. Move back left and up through the upper rocks.

Four Seasons in a Day 100m III. Michael Barnard. 26 Feb 2011.
An icy line of weakness runs down the left-hand side of the front face of the main buttress, terminating in a steep wall. This route gains the foot of this line of weakness by a traverse in from the left. Start just below the obvious traverse ledge.
1. 50m Climb up and right to reach the ledge and move along this easily to where it peters out. Step down and right to gain the line of ice which is followed up to below the upper corners.
2. 50m Climb the upper corners to easier ground, finishing as for *Central Couloir*.

Up and right from the main buttress are a series of fine vertical icy grooves. A cornice can sometimes form above this section but this is easily outflanked.

The Choker 50m III,5. Michael Barnard. 26 Feb 2011.
The chimney on the left has a large chockstone within it. Climb up to the chockstone, pass this on the outside with difficulty (inside may also be possible) and continue up the icy groove above to easier ground.

Ice Man 50m II. Michael Barnard. 26 Feb 2011.
The next icy groove right.

Make like Shepherds 50m II *. Michael Barnard. 26 Feb 2011.
Slightly steeper and more sustained than its neighbour.

Get the Flock Outta Here 50m IV,4. Michael Barnard. 26 Feb 2011.
The right-hand line has a short steep section at half-height.

BEINN MHEADHOIN:

Demerara 10m E6 6c *. Julian Lines. 24 Apr 2010.

This technical route climbs the topless crack to the right of *Classic Crack* on the summit tor of Beinn Mheadhoin. Climb the flake-crack for 5m to a horizontal break, then climb the bulging wall on flakes and a pocket via gritstone style moves. Low in the grade; the first ascent was pre-practiced before a solo above some snow, but graded for a lead as there is protection. At 1182m it is perhaps the highest extreme in the country?

BEINN A' BHÙIRD, Coire an Dubh Lochain:

Crystal 200m VI,7. Roger Webb, Simon Richardson. 28 Feb 2011.

A direct line up the right side of Glaucous Buttress based on the groove system right of *Tearaway*. Named in memory of Chris Dale.

1. and 2. 70m Climb easily up the lower slabs on banked up snow and ice to reach the foot of the groove.

3. 50m Climb the right-facing corner over a couple of steep steps to reach the terrace below the headwall. Belay to the right of the depression taken by *Tearaway*.

4. 30m Move right and climb the right side of the headwall by a series of short corners and grooves to reach an easing.

5. 20m Continue in the same line up a shallow left-facing groove to the cornice.

Garbh Choire:

Genghis Can 200m IV,4. Andy Nisbet, Duncan Tunstall. 5 March 2011.

A line up the left side of Mandarin Buttress, crossing *Salamander* which finishes up the shallow gully between the two halves. Climbed entirely on ice and snow. Start low in *The Flume*, before it narrows, and where an icy ramp leads out right on to the lower buttress. Follow the ramp and a groove above, leading to the mid-height snowslope where *Salamander* crosses. Head leftwards towards a large inset slab area which lies high up and left of the steepest ground. Gain the slab via an icy crack-line and climb it to the cornice. This was climbed some 10m right of the finish to *The Flume* but if bigger, then *The Flume* finish could be reached.

LOCHNAGAR, Southern Sector, Perseverance Wall:

Ideal 70m III,4. Craig Lamb, Stephen Gaunt. 25 Oct 2010.

Start in a small groove just left of *Perseverance Groove*. Climb the groove up to a steep step (crux); pull through to good turf. Continue to easier ground heading to the crest of the rib on the right. Climb through the shallow groove above towards *Perseverance Rib* but stay left pulling through a second steep step which again leads to good turf and easier ground. Stay to the left of the rib and continue to the plateau, finishing through a low angled chimney.

Shadow Buttress A:

Chasing Shadows 170m VI,7. Simon Richardson, Helen Rennard. 2 Mar 2011.

The icy groove system between the Feathered Arete and *Multiple Chimneys*. Start 20m left of *Polyphemus Gully*.

1. 50m Climb a diagonal crack/ramp rightwards to reach a bulging roof. Pass this in its right side to enter a short hanging groove. Climb this and exit past a

chokestone on the right onto an icy ramp. Follow this more easily up and right to a belay about 5m below the first stance of *Polyphemus Gully*.

2. 50m Follow the square-cut fault on the left for 20m. Where it ends, bear right and climb the left-facing corner formed by the lower section of the tower cut by *Multiple Chimneys*.

3. 50m Continue up the groove above (between the Feathered Arete and *Multiple Chimneys*) and follow it up and right.

4. 20m Exit the top of the groove and climb the short snowslope above to a steep cornice exit.

Eagle Buttress:

Eagle-Eye 280m VII,6. Sandy Simpson, Simon Richardson. 6 Feb 2011.
The corners on the left side of the *Where Eagles Dare* headwall.

1. to 3. 150m Climb *Eagle Buttress* to the central depression (as for *Where Eagles Dare*).

4. 40m Climb the grooved rib trending left until above the prominent corner taken by *Eagle Groove*. Step up and right over a steep wall to belay below a steep right-facing corner.

5. 30m Climb the corner (strenuous) to gain a terrace. Continue up a slabby wall until level with the base of the *Where Eagles Dare* headwall.

6. 60m Continue up the steep wall directly above, gain a depression and then an exposed ramp leading up and right to the top.

Smear Fear 280m VII,7 or VI,6. Simon Richardson, Iain Small. 6 Mar 2011.
An icy mixed line based on the hanging icy groove bounding the right side of the *Where Eagles Dare* headwall. The grade depends on the thickness of the ice on pitch 6.

1. to 3. 150m Climb *Eagle Buttress* to the central depression (as for *Where Eagles Dare*).

4. to 5. 80m Continue up and right following the upper ramp-line above *Eagle Buttress*, to gain the foot of the smear via a series of icy steps and steep cracks.

6. 20m Climb the smear. Bold and steep, or just steep, depending in the thickness of the ice.

7. 30m Continue up the gully to the right of the headwall to the top.

Tough-Brown Face:

Crazy Sorrow IX,10 **. Guy Robertson, Pete Benson. Jan 2011.
Superb climbing with the crux pitch on the second pitch as in summer. Strenuous and well-protected over the roof, then sustained and bold up the crack-line above. Ice may help (as on the first ascent) but will reduce the protection opportunities. A total of six pieces of in-situ gear were found above the roof, half of which were removed, the remainder having been hammered in irretrievably. None of it appears trustworthy. For pitches 1 and 2 follow the summer route, but belay on the ledge at the end of the crack system. For pitch 3 go right to the end of the ledge, then join the horizontal traverse on *Rolling Thunder* (very thin, but more ice will help). For pitch 4 etc. take the escape rake out right.

The Stack:

Heliopolis and *Ultramontane* have been repeated by Pete Benson & Neil

Morrison, then Daniel Laing & Wilson Moir. *Heliopolis* is easy for the grade and is probably E2 with some rather flaky rock so worth 1 star rather than the original 2. *Ultramontane* is worth its E4 6a grade and 2 stars, but the ominous sounding mantel is straightforward and not really a mantel.

Both routes start at the junction of the *Left Branch* and *Crumbling Cranny*. For access, 50m ropes easily reach the bottom but it is straightforward to walk to the base by ascending or descending the *Left Branch*.

West Buttress:

Apophis   35m   E7 6b. Alastair Robertson, Will Harris. 31 Aug 2010.

The Radar Wall is the smooth square east facing wall just below the plateau between *Black Spout Right Branch* and *West Gully*. The route takes a line up the slabby face near the left arete of the wall, and though not technically desperate the crux is unprotected and very insecure. It is best accessed by a 40m abseil from the plateau to belay on steep grass below the wall. Climb broken ground to below a good square ledge near the centre of the wall. Mantel the ledge and follow an obvious ramp system delicately up and leftwards (bold) to gain the arete, and a ledge just round the other side (the only gear on the route here, sling on the hollow flake out left, and a small wire just above – too low for the crux). Step immediately back right onto the face and make a hard move up the vague scoop, continuing upwards to a rest at a pinch above. Step right and climb the thin seams above, trending rightwards (harrowing), to finally gain a good hold just to the right of the projecting roof above. Finish direct more easily, passing the roof on the right, to gain the plateau.

CREAG AN DUBH LOCH, Broad Terrace Wall:

Culloden   IX,9. Gordon Lennox, Tony Stone, Iain Small. 22 Dec 2010.
By the summer route.

Central Gully Wall:

Vertigo Wall, Left-Hand Finish   90m   VII,8. Andrew Melvin, Robbie Miller, Henning Wackerhage. 12 Mar 2011.

Climb the first three pitches of *Vertigo Wall* and belay above the ice.

4. 30m Climb thin ice up and left. Traverse left on a narrow ledge below a gently overhanging wall and move into a shallow corner. Climb up steeply on good turf to a belay.

5. 30m Follow turfy ramps left and upwards and then some ice to below a left-leaning offwidth crack.

6. 30m Climb the offwidth crack until you can sit on it. Lean out left, then swing left. Pull up and climb to a spike. Step up from the spike and boldly climb the steep slab above on thinner and thinner hooks to the top.

Note: *Black Diamond* (SMCJ 2010) was repeated by Pete Benson, Ali Coull & Neil Morrison. The consensus was E4 4c, 6a, 5c, 5b **, with two good and surprisingly independent pitches. Pitch one is essentially an approach pitch as per *King Rat* or *Mousetrap/Kraken*, then two good pitches, then you fight to stay off *King Rat*. For more sustained climbing, a scoot across onto the upper section of *Waterkelpie Wall* would be good, or two abseils reaches the ground from the top of pitch 3.

False Gully Wall:

Ludwig 60m E3 *. Julian Lines, Danny Laing (snr). 22 Apr 2011.
A pleasant climb that climbs the thinner curving groove to the left of *Masque* and the wall above.
1. 20m 5b Climb the curving bow shaped groove to a ledge on the right (common with *Masque*).
2. 20m 6a Climb *Masque* for 3m before making a thin traverse left onto a slab. Continue up into a corner system and belay on a sloping ledge (a purer way to climb this pitch is by stepping left from the belay to pull through an overlap into the line – 6b? but with a direct fall onto the belay).
3. 20m 4a Step right and follow the obvious line to finish.

EAGLES ROCK, Mid-East Buttress:

Note: John Lyall notes that *Whisper* (winter) takes the groove right of *Gibber* whereas the summer *Whisper* takes the next groove right.

Plateau Buttress:

Fairytale 200m III,4. Andy Nisbet. 5 Jan 2011.
An icefall which starts immediately right of A Likely Story Slab and continues up left of Plateau Buttress. There were four icy sections separated by snow. The third was steep and climbed direct by the steepest route.

Vanguard 60m III. Andy Nisbet. 5 Jan 2011.
A line entirely on ice through the steep rock taken by *Vanguard*, although certainly not the same line. Start at the top right corner of the bay with *The Drool*. Take a line leading out right immediately under the steep wall. Traverse right into an iced ramp followed to a ledge. Move left to ice and climb this to the top. A groove straight up is also possible but less dramatic.

Flanker's Route 140m IV,5. Andy Nisbet, Duncan Tunstall. 2 Jan 2011.
The line might fit with the summer route although climbed in very icy conditions and much of the route was on ice. Start at the left end of the lowest rocks. Climb a ramp right of the snow gully leading up to *The Drool*. At an overlap, move right and continue upwards (50m). Climb easily up into a large recess, then take a V-groove leading out right to a platform (40m). Climb a short off-width crack with a chokestone, then choose a line through extensive ice to the top (50m).

GLEN CALLATER, Coire Kander:

Kandy Bar 55m V,5 *. Paul Mather, Rachel Mather, Nick Bailey. 9 Jan 2011.
Climb the parallel icefall to the right of *Tuircish Delight*.

CANNES GLEN:

The Red Carpet 150m IV,4. John Higham, Iain Young. 2 Jan 2011.
A well-defined, narrow and straight gully cuts through the crags before the obvious icefall of *Where Eagles Dare* is reached. Climb this in three pitches to the plateau. A classic gully, though needs a very hard freeze.

GLEN CLOVA, Coire Brandy:

Space Pirates 70m VIII,8 **. Gordon Lennox, Tim Rankin. 30 Jan 2010.

1. 40m *Smuggler* pitch 1.

2. 15m From the stance by the blocks, step round right and climb a turfy corner stepping right at its top onto a terrace below the final headwall.

3. 15m Climb up into a right-facing corner below an overhanging shattered fault-line. Climb the strenuous fault to a slight niche (bulldog), and move up to a stopping place on the left. From here a flying ramp leads out left. Tenuous and powerful moves in a spectacular position lead across this to an icicle hanging over the lip and leading to easy ground.

The Scorrie:

Deer Tracks 250m II. Martin Cooper, Jenny Cooper. Jan 2011.
Climbs the shallow curving gully right of *Y Gully*. Climb the initial icefall 20m. The gully opens out moving easily to a final narrow section leading to the top.

Craig Maud Area:

The Night Watchman 230m III. George Allan, John Thomas. 7 Jan 2011.
The sprawling buttress to the right of *Pinnacle Ridge* and *North Gully* of Craig Maud contains two obvious parallel slots at half-height. Start beneath the right-hand slot and climb a depression to reach it. Enter the slot (crux) and exit up leftwards. Easy ground with short steps leads to the plateau. A good freeze is needed.

GLEN ESK, Unich Buttress:

Esk-ape 200m IV,5. Brian Duthie, Henning Wackerhage. 4 Dec 2010.
A climb with good situations but too much heather for stars. It crosses *North Ridge* (SMCJ 2010).

1. 25m Start some 50m up the gully and climb broken ground to reach a diagonal heathery ramp parallel to the gully. Belay in a niche with a crack-line above.

2. 25m Traverse right and regain the ramp to reach a small tree.

3. 25m Follow the diagonal line and belay in a niche.

4. Traverse left to a tree. Climb right and up to reach the easier ground. Aim for the steeper section below a larger tree near the crest.

5. Climb the steeper section to reach the tree and then the crest. Easy ground to the end of the ridge remains.

Climb broken ground to reach a ramp with much heather.

Earn Craig:

Dschubba 160m V,7. Andy Nisbet, Duncan Tunstall. 28 Dec 2010.
The easiest line in the area of *Rock and Two Veg* (SMCJ 2009). Start just left of centre on the crag base, where a ramp leads up left to a forest.

1. 40m Go right and back left to gain the ramp. Follow it over a step to the biggest tree in the forest.

2. 30m Go rightwards up a small turf ramp in the steeper ground above, then make a rising traverse right to a groove line which leads though overhangs above.

3. 25m Climb the groove and a short chimney with bushes (*Rock and Two Veg* avoids these on the right) to reach the 'large vegetated area', which is the biggest ledge on the crag.

4. 45m From the left end of this ledge, go up turfy ground leftwards to reach another ledge. Traverse this left to its end.

5. 20m Go up and right to a bush on a ledge. Step past this, then up and make thin moves left to gain a smooth slab above (distinct sting in the tail). The route unexpectedly finishes.

Golden Buttress 215m E2/3 **. Simon Richardson, Duncan Tunstall. 24 May 2009.
A route in the centre of the crag, starting from a grass ledge where the crag base starts to rise significantly up right. Start at the left end of a grass rake that finishes just to the right of a short clean-cut rock arete and below a small roof.
1. 45m 5a Use the central crack to pull over the overhang and climb the slab above. As it steepens, follow a leftwards curving ramp to gain a grass ledge above with interest.
2. 40m 4b Starting from the left end of the grass, follow a clear line up the left edge of the slab to reach the first break. Follow this rightwards to the centre of the face.
3. 25m 5c Continue up the groove line which steepens up the face. As it ends step up and right to gain the continuation line on the right. Follow this to an excellent pedestal.
4. 30m 5a Traverse down and right to reach the corner 15m to the right (wet), so continue traversing where a steep move gets above the overhangs and a traverse left returns to a large grassy belay ledge 20m above and just right of the previous belay.
5. 45m 5a Climb up above the belay, then follow the obvious ramp-line up and right. At its end it steepens; climb directly up past a tree to reach the ledge belay (as for *Right-Hand Route*).
6. 30m Traverse left on the lower break before following the grassy ramp up on the left to regain the rock and follow a nice triangular slab to the top.

Right-Hand Route 180m HVS. Simon Richardson, Duncan Tunstall. 3 May 2009.
Start at the right corner of the buttress below the rightmost clean wall. Follow easy angled grass ramps backwards and forwards for about 50m to the left side of the slabby wall.
1. 40m 4c Climb the cracks in clean slab on the right. At the top traverse left and climb the cracks above to the large break.
2. 40m 4b Follow a grassy ramp right, then up and back left below the steep wall in the centre of the cliff.
3. 30m 5b Climb up and left to a roof. Traverse left under the roof to its narrowest point, then go straight up a clean crack for 20m.
4. 40m 4b Follow the break up and diagonally left.
5. 30m 4b Take the easiest line up and left.
Topo provided.

Raging Bull 170m V,6. Andy Nisbet, Duncan Tunstall. 26 Dec 2010.
Start at the right side of the cliff, to the left of the foot of *Earn Gully*. The first objective is an icefall in the middle of the buttress. Climb easily for 20m to a short wide crack where the cliff steepens.
1. 50m Climb to the right of a wide crack to a tree. Continue up a short way to reach a ledge on the left. Follow this to its left end and then climb up steeply for

15m. Continue on easier ground to a ledge.

2. 30m Continue up on the right of a rock wall. This can be reached by a short wide crack. Above follow the line up diagonally left to the first steep ice.

3. 40m Climb the short ice step. Traverse left to the larger icefall which is climbed direct. Continue up until a final steep buttress is reached.

4. 30m Climb a short corner directly above the belay for 5m to a ledge. Follow the ledge right to the first icefall. Climb this direct to a tree on the left.

5. 20m Finish up an easy snow ramp above.

Bruntwood Craig:

Gro'lryc Gully 150m V,5 **. Andy Nisbet, Duncan Tunstall. 8 Jan 2011.
This is the steeper and better defined left branch of a Y-shaped gully in the centre of the crag. Start up the gully base until it is possible to traverse left to below trees. Climb through the trees and right to the base of the main gully (60m). Climb to an impressive chimney and climb it as fits the route name (25m). Continue up the gully, on this occasion on steep and fragile ice (VI,5 on the day) to easier ground (45m). Finish past the cornice (20m).

Avatar 160m III **. Andy Nisbet, Duncan Tunstall. 8 Jan 2011.
A well defined gully on the right side of the crag. Climbed on continuous thin ice, it could be a grade easier in the best conditions but maybe always serious. An initial pitch is avoidable by heathery ground on the left. The main gully gives sustained climbing to a cornice passed on the left.

Craig Maskeldie:

Logue's Direct 230m V,6. Duncan Tunstall, Stephen Venables 15 Feb 2011.
This climbs the first two thirds of *Shaula Ridge* (SMCJ 2010) direct, giving an additional three pitches that match the short top section of *Shaula* in difficulty and quality. Start where the ridge begins just to the right of the start of *Dochty Gully*. Climb a short step to easier ground to belay below the distinct rock step. Climb this direct in its centre for 40m to where the angle eases. Continue for two long pitches to join *Shaula Ridge* below its steep step. Climb this to the summit.

WATER OF SAUGHS, Corrie na Berran:

Saughs Ridge 100m II. Simon Richardson. 30 Dec 2010.
The right-hand ridge bounding the corrie, which can be seen in profile when walking up the Water of Saughs. Start just right of the crest and climb a wide gully to its end. Move left on to the broad crest and follow this to its end at a prominent cairn at NO 442 729.

S Gully 100m III. Simon Richardson. 30 Dec 2010.
The main cliff at the head of the corrie is defined by a steep triangular wall in its centre. Start 50m to its left and climb a 30m icefall leading the shallow 'S'-shaped gully above.

Isosceles 150m II. Simon Richardson. 30 Dec 2010.
Climb the broad ramp defining the left side of the triangular wall. From near its top, break left through mixed ground to reach an open gully (the next feature right of *S Gully*).

Pythagoras 150m II. Simon Richardson. 30 Dec 2010.
The gully that slants up and left, defining the right edge of the triangular wall.

GLEN PROSEN, Bawhelps:
Divine Providence 150m III,4. Simon Richardson. 4 Jan 2011.
The S-shaped gully on the left side of the crag. Climb mixed ground for 50m to a steep ice pitch. Surmount this and continue up the steep step above to gain the meandering gully above.
Zigzag 150m III. Simon Richardson. 4 Jan 2011.
Start 40m right of *Divine Providence* and climb up to an ice step. Continue up the easiest zigzag line above to finish up the buttress between *Divine Providence* and *Break Left*.

Break Left 150m II. Simon Richardson. 4 Jan 2011.
From halfway up the ramp running left to right under the right side of the cliff, a well-defined left-slanting gully cuts the left wall. Follow this to a terrace and continue in the same line to the top.

SIDLAW HILLS, Lundie Crags (NO 277 377):
Provide short climbs for those living in the area who fancy something more adventurous than a walk and have a couple of hours to spare. The climbs are turfy requiring a few days hard freeze followed by snowfall. Probably in condition for a few days every winter but being SE facing, they do strip readily in the sun. Martin Cooper has climbed a few routes here, the most notable being:

New Year 15m II. Martin Cooper. 2 Jan 2010.
Climb the centre of a broad tongue of rock extending from the top of the escarpment. The top of the route is located 140m west from the mast clearly visible at the top end of the escarpment. Approach from below.

NORTH EAST OUTCROPS

LONG HAVEN QUARRIES, Hawks Nest:
Overarching Imperative 15m E4 6b ***. Graham Tyldesley. 19 Mar 2011.
The corner line left of *Pumping Velvet*. Initial hard bridging up the undercut start leads to a bridging rest at mid-height. Burly laybacks and undercuts around the roof land you on a ledge at the top.

Kaboom 25m E4 6a **. Graham Tyldesley. 5 Feb 2011.
Left of *The Winds of War* is an overhanging wall split by a crack. This route climbs the crack. Abseil directly from the block at the end of the plateau down an obvious corner line. After clearing the corner, kick off the wall and gain a good ledge at the mouth of the tunnel passing back through the headland. Traverse right to gain the crack and climb it until moves out left on the wall gain a diagonal ledge. Follow this back into the widening crack before gaining the easy corner above.

The Winds of War – Arete Finish   15m   E2 5b. Graham Tyldesley, Dave Ogden. 19 Mar 2011.
After exiting the *Winds of War* chimney, step left and climb the arete to the top. A bit eliminate on poor rock without much gear – nice line though.

South Face of Scimitar Ridge:
Jinx   15m   E8 6c ****. Gordon Lennox. 25 Aug 2010.
This route climbs the crack-line emanating from the ledges down right of *Comfortably Numb* to jugs at the first thin horizontal break. The initial crack is technical bold and committing, protected by a small offset wire, then a Friend 1 after the difficulties and a Rock 3 by the jugs. From here traverse right to gain the crack near the arete (two DMM 3 nuts). This is followed by some desperate moves to small crimps on the right (5 nut placed with difficulty near the top of the crack). Move right to gain the arete and finish up this in a fantastic position.

RED TOWER:
Jacala   16m   E8 6c F7c+ S3 ***. Julian Lines. 19 May 2011.
This is an absolutely immaculate piece of granite wall climbing, which is very dangerous to solo (spring tides only). Start on a thin ledge beneath the diagonal crack. Follow the crack for 3m until beneath a left-hand flake, then use this to reach the break and make a hard move to reach 'the ear' (*Wasted Years* moves right here). Continue directly up the wall on layaways past some undercuts to gain a left-hand boss. Continue to the break using opposing layaways. Finish direct up the granite shield more easily.

CUMMINGSTON:
Pomme de Terre   15m   HVS 5a *. Martin Collins, Dave Binney. 29 Jun 2011.
Start up *Appletiser* and traverse round right to join *Le Crunch*. From here step right into the right-trending crack-line on the headwall above the arch. Stunning position. Take care at the top. Quite a logical line,with that nice position above the arch, great for all those jaded HVS climbers!

PORTNOCKIE:
Desperate Fish Wives   42m   HVS A2. Liam Johnson, Jim Leahy. 6 Jul 2011.
A route on the sea arch come through cave just east around the headland from Bow Fiddle Rock. Also it can also be reached by walking to the far west end of Cullen Beach and following the path along the cliff base for a few minutes. It climbs the obvious square-cut blocky looking flying roof crack.
1. 12m   Hand-traverse leftwards into the cave at low tide along big incut hand holds sometimes with feet on the barnacles until a hanging belay on Friends before the line takes a definite step up and left.
2. 30m   Free climb up and left on a good incut edge. Fix a Friend, then start aiding up the prominent line with a move at half-height to gain a slightly higher break at a particularly blocky looking section. Belay on a pre-placed abseil rope from two stakes above.

REDHYTHE POINT, Plateau Face, North-East side:
Badger Ramp   10m   Very Difficult. Iain Powell, Katie Munro. 10 Jun 2011.
Head over the grassy col to the north-east side of Plateau Face towards the

jumble of broken rocks. At the very north end there is a rock island just a few metres out to sea. There is a stagnant pool and the descent is down the ramp via abseil on the right to a small uneven ledge 1.5m above the high-tide line. Climb the ramp using the 'floating' corner-crack.

Diajamelly 15m Severe 4b. Iain Powell, Katie Munro. 11 Jun 2011.
Start as for *Badger Ramp* and after 3m step right onto the north face and traverse a ledge to the start of a right-rising crack. Climb the crack to the top.
Don't Lose Your Nuts! 12m VS 4b. Iain Powell, Katie Munro. 12 Jun 2011.
Climb onto the ramp 1m above *Badger Ramp* and follow this rightwards to the roof. Traverse left following the crack and then over the roof at its narrowest point on good holds to the top.

Don't Lose Your Nuts Direct 12m VS 4c. Iain Powell, Katie Munro. 15 Jun 2011.
Climb straight up the face from below the narrowest point of the roof, over this and to the top.

The Tea Cleft:
Under Pressure 16m E1 5a. Iain Powell, Katie Munro. 20 May 2011.
The slab on the left-hand side as you look into The Tea Cleft from the grassy col. Start at the corner-crack under the small roof at low tide.

CLACH NA BEINN:
Note: *Giardia Groove* (SMCJ 2010) is actually a winter ascent of *Cave Crack*.

HIGHLAND OUTCROPS

BEINN BHEAG, Lochailort:
This is an isolated slab under the summit of Beinn Bheag with several routes developed by Donald King and Mike Pescod in 2001. Descriptions for these are too late for this volume, but hopefully will make the SMC web-site.

Die By the Drop 12m E10 7a **. Dave MacLeod. 31 Oct 2010.
The extremely smooth left-hand side of the slab. Start up the E4 crack for a move but head off rightwards and climb up a very hollow patina flake. From a standing position on this, reach right and place a dubious microwire. Step left and climb the blank slab through a desperate bouldery sequence to gain a couple of slightly better quartz knobs. Place a small cam on the right and continue with more ease to the top.

Apophenia 12m E8 7a **. Dave MacLeod. 25 Nov 2010.
Very precarious climbing up the centre of the slab. Climb direct to the twin seams (one microwire in each, the left one common to *Die By the Drop*). Step right and move up until forced to traverse precariously leftwards with a very worrying foot change (crux). Press on through a serious of tiny crimps to reach a good nut and easy ground in the small groove.

DRUIM FIACLACH:

Located on the south side of this rocky hill at the head of Loch nan Uamh is a fine arete (NM 733 848) with a steep left wall and a grassy corner-gully on its left. Park near the bend in the road (NM 726 845) and start eastwards along a grassy track near a burn. Cross the railway and strike up the hillside; the arete becomes more obvious as height is gained, 25mins.

Arisaig Arete 55m VS **. Michael Barnard. 28 Jun 2011.
An exhilarating climb with two contrasting pitches. At the base of the arete is a steep wall; start below this at the foot of an obvious shallow corner-groove.
1. 20m 5a Climb the corner-groove, exiting right. Step right past heather and move up to the base of the clean arete.
2. 35m 4b Follow the arete with little protection all the way to the top.

LOCH MOIDART, Castle Tioram:

The Craic of the Clanranalds 8m E2 5c *. Seb Rider. 23 Jun 2011.
The route is situated just above a small rocky beach on the westerly side of the rock of Castle Tioram. Road access is from Cul Doirlinn. Follow the steep overhanging crack exiting to the right avoiding the ivy at the top. Rock schist, aspect westerly, well protected.

POLLDUBH, Sheep Fank Wall:

Mint Sauce 30m E1 5c *. Ken Applegate, Alex Wheeldon. 29 Mar 2011.
Start as for *Sheep Fank Direct* and climb the same initial groove, then its corner for 5m to the first roof. Make a delicate traverse left across a hanging slab to gain the arete of *Fence Edge* and finish up this.

Black's Buttress:

Note: *Poème à Loup* (SMCJ 2010, p 147) was repeated by Steve Kennedy, Bob Hamilton & Cynthia Grindley and thought to be E2 5b and worth the two stars given.

Upper Scimitar:

Bad Life Choices 10m E7 6b. Johann Urbano. 9 Apr 2011.
Go straight up the centre of the slab on smears and small edges between *Where the Mood Takes Me* and the obvious big crack on the left. Easier for the tall, protected by pads.

BRIN ROCK, Crag One:

Austrocelt Sound System 40m E6. Guy Robertson, Phil Ebert. 5 Sep 2010.
An outstanding route up the overhanging wall and hanging slab left of *Treasure Island*. Start down and left of that route at a small stack of flakes.
1. 20m 6b Step off the flakes and climb directly on good holds to a left-rising break. Move several metres left along this to the first protection (Friend 0, crucial), then step back right and use layaways to gain the top of a triangular feature. Make a move straight up, then step left on slopers before making long moves back up and right to a good shake-out. Hand-traverse the ledge left to a thin crack and use this to stand up and gain holds over the lip which lead to a belay in a niche.

2. 20m 5c Climb the crack on the right, then step left into another crack which is followed to a bulging black streak. Climb boldly up the streak to gain a standing position in the base of the obvious right-trending ramp. Ignore this (tempting) and continue up bearing slightly left across the headwall to the top.

ASHIE FORT:

Peat Tong 10m Very Difficult. Davy Moy, Andy Tibbs. 31 May 2011.
Start halfway between *Web Astair* and the left end of the crag. Climb a straight crack-line with small ledges; it has a steep start.

Brain Damage 10m E3 6a **. Andy Tibbs, Davy Moy. 11 Oct 2010.
The very steep line between *Firecracker* and *Points of Departure* is well protected.

Moss Shoe Shuffle 10m HVS 5a. Davy Moy, Peter Langlands. 2 May 2011.
Climb a faint crack 4m right of *Kenny's Revenge* and continue up a slab to the top.

After Quark 10m HVS 5a. Davy Moy, Dave Allan. 26 Apr 2011.
Climb a right-facing corner 6m right of *Kenny's Revenge*, then go straight up a slab.

Doubt Corner 10m HVS 5a *. Davy Moy, Dave Allan. 26 Apr 2011.
Two metres right of the last route. Cross an overlap into a shallow right-facing stepped corner and then directly over an overlap at the top.

Ruby Tuesday 10m E2 5b *. Andy Tibbs, Davy Moy. 12 Oct 2010.
A wall and overlap right of *Quark Strangers*.

Clavicle Attack 10m HVS 5a. Davy Moy, Peter Langlands. 2 May 2011.
Right of the last route is a right-facing corner capped with a wee overhang. Climb the corner and over onto a ledge. Go slightly right and up the headwall via a scoop.

BEN NEVIS, AONACHS, CREAG MEAGAIDH

BEN NEVIS, The Little Brenva Face:

Right Major 320m IV,6. Ewan Lyons, Ewan Olivarius. 29 Jan 2011.
Start about a third of the way along the approach ramp to *NE Buttress*, where an in-situ sling 5m up marks the start.
1. 50m Go up to the sling, traverse left along a narrow ledge, then go up an open gully to its end. Traverse up and right to a shelf under a steep wall to below a short groove.
2. 50m Go up the groove, then trend up and right across snowslopes to belay at the left end of a large terrace under a deep groove.
3. 60m Follow the groove up left, then back right until underneath a large steep wall on the left; belay below a short rock barrier.

4. 40m Surmount the rock step with difficulty (crux) and gain a steep ramp up and right to an improbable traverse along a ledge below the steep wall. Belay down and right of a short icy corner on the top pitch of *The Lime Green Gaiter*.
5. 60m Climb a corner and easier snow, then over an icy bulge to a rock rib in the middle of open snowslopes.
6. 60m Go up and left on easy snow to join *Route Major* at the intersection with *Frost Bite*.

Tower Ridge East Flank:
Triple X   150m   VIII, 8 *. Ines Papert, Charly Fritzer, Dave MacLeod. 28 Jan 2011.
A thin icy mixed climb starting up the summer line of *Rolling Stones* but following thin icy slabs to its left and then a difficult mixed chimney to reach the Eastern Traverse.
1. 40m As for *Rolling Stones*. Follow the left-slanting ramp easily leftwards to its termination. Arrange gear and then gain and follow the traverse line going back right with difficulty to eventually gain ledges. Bold for leader and second, a little ice/neve very useful.
2. 55m Climb the left-slanting corner for a few metres, then traverse left across the slab on very thin ice. Surmount a steepening to gain intermittent cracks leading leftwards up the slabs to a sentry box. A steep pull over this leads to large ledges.
3. 55m Move leftwards along the ledges to below the steep V shaped chimney (common to *Faith Healer*). Climb this to the Eastern Traverse; move up this a short way to belay.

The Pretender   55m   VII,9. Nick Bullock, Andy Turner, Bruce Poll. 17 Feb 2011.
A direct line up the previously unclimbed buttress to the right of the *Great Chimney* area. The main pitch is very well protected by a good rack of cams up to number 4 and a good selection of wires. One fall taken on pitch 2.
1. 30m Climb the icy buttress via steep ice steps, leading to a large shelf and the very steep wall above.
2. 25m The wall is split by a wide crack/chimney somewhat reminiscent of *Darth Vader* low down and goes into a very steep wide crack direct with a thinner crack/recess/overhang running right into an overhang finish. The right version was taken. Knee bar rests, head jams and shoulder jams are advisable and available for the weak or not needed for the strong.

Douglas Boulder:
Feckless   170m   VI,7 **. Pete Benson, Nick Bullock. 27 Nov 2010.
1. 30m Start up the massive overhanging flake in the line of the deep chimney of *Gutless*. Climb the corner of *Gutless* passing a smaller overhang to a ledge beneath the deep chimney of *Gutless*.
2. 40m Reverse a few moves down from the belay until level with an icy groove on the right wall. Climb the groove through the bulge and continue in the same line above passing overhangs until the angle eases and a large ledge beneath a steep wall is reached.
3. 50m Climb a dark icy corner to the right of where the last pitch topped out.

Initial steep climbing through a bulge leads into a corner of perfect hooks and torques. Belay on a ledge/nose, to the right of the top of the corner.

4. 50m Climb an overhang, corner-line and wide crack on the left of the belay until the climbing gets easier. Turf and snowy ledges are climbed direct until just beneath the top of the Douglas Boulder.

Rutless 20m VII,8 **. Nick Bullock, Matt Helliker. 30 Nov 2010.
A direct finish to the deep chimney cleft of *Gutless*. A short test of fitness that feels a whole lot longer than it is. The climbing is brilliant, the crux is placing gear.
1. 20m Directly above the deep fault-line of *Gutless* and beneath a seriously steep wall is a wide ledge. From the left of this ledge and directly above the finish of *Gutless*, climb an overhanging icy crack for approximately 5m until a small ledge is reached. Traverse the ledge, right to left to reach a good rest pedestal in a corner. From the ledge, climb the very steep corner above to exit on the left.

Nutless 145m VI,7 **. Matt Helliker, Nick Bullock. 29 Nov 2010.
The first winter ascent with a direct start. Start approximately 10m left of the obvious corner chimney/fault-line of *Gutless* and beneath a slabby wall which leads to a short overhanging right-facing corner at approximately 15m.
1. 20m Climb the slabby wall beneath the overhanging corner with a delicate move left before reaching the base of an overhanging corner. Climb the corner and pull the steep exit to belay directly above and beneath a short overhang/roof.
2. 10m Pull over the roof directly above the belay and traverse the ledge left until beneath the groove/corner of *Nutless*.
3. 50m Climb the groove, difficult for a few moves until turf in abundance speeds up proceedings. Moving slightly left following a groove until beneath a big off-width overhanging flake system. Climb this direct until pulling onto a large ledge beneath a beautiful overhanging bow-shaped corner-crack.
4. 15m Climb the bow-shaped overhanging crack with a slab on the right.
5. etc. Climb direct to the top of the Douglas Boulder.

Secondary Tower Ridge:

Rogue's Rib Direct 210m VII,7. Iain Small, Simon Richardson. 19 Mar 2011.
A direct ascent of the summer line. The winter version (Clough-Grandison) climbed the top section of the buttress after starting up *Italian Climb*.
1. 35m From the foot of *Italian Climb*, move left along a narrow ledge for 3m then climb straight up to a steep wall cut by twin cracks. Climb the wall to easier ground leading to a steep slabby section. Turn this via a steep groove on the right to reach a ledge.
2. 50m Continue up an open groove leading to an open chimney that cuts through the steep headwall above. Surmount a steep slab at its top to reach a good platform and block belay.
3. 60m Climb the undercut right-facing groove at the back of the platform to reach easy ground leading to a neck. Cross this and move up to the foot of the second tier. Belay below an undercut chimney cutting through the centre of the second tier.
4. 25m Climb the chimney by cracks on the right, followed by a delicate traverse

to gain the gully bed. Climb the gully to where it ends below a bulging wall and step right to belay by stacked blocks. This pitch is common with the Clough-Grandison line.

5. 40m Move left to below the bulging wall and climb this to the continuation gully above. Climb this to near its top then trend right to a shallow corner. Follow this to the crest of Secondary Tower Ridge.

Garadh na Ciste:
Note: *Broad Gully Variation* 100m III. Christian Minett, Paul Cubbins, Tom Williams. 12 Mar 2011.
A thin ice runnel on the right about 25m past the traverse for *Pinnacle Buttress of the Tower*. Finish by a traverse left for 60m at the snowfield to join *Tower Ridge* just on the Great Tower and the Eastern Traverse.

Pinnacle Buttress of the Tower:
Goodfellas 230m VII,8. Simon Richardson, Iain Small. 21 Jan 2011.
The impressive front prow of Pinnacle Buttress of the Tower between *Face Dancer* and *Stringfellow*.
1. 60m Start up and left of the lower tier and climb icy grooves raking up and right (as for *Fatal Error*) to the terrace.
2. 20m From the foot of the ramp taken by *Stringfellow,* climb a line of grooves parallel to *Fatal Error* until directly below the hanging groove.
3. 30m Gain the groove by crossing a steep slab from the left and then climb it (sustained and technical) to gain a well-defined triangular niche.
4. 20m Pull steeply out of the niche and follow the vague fault-line up the rounded crest of the buttress to gain the large ledge at the end of pitch 3 of *Stringfellow*.
5. 40m *Stringfellow* climbs the slab and right-hand of twin grooves above. Instead, make a steep pull onto the crack system left of the *Stringfellow* slab and follow the ramp to the steeper left-hand groove. Continue up *Stringfellow* to the platform below the crux headwall of *Stringfellow*.
6. and 7. 80m Climb the headwall as for *Stringfellow* (20m), then follow the easy crest to the foot of The Great Tower.

Number Three Gully Buttress:
Apache 110m VIII,9. Steve Ashworth, Paddy Cave. 13 Nov 2010.
1. 40m From the foot of *Thompson's Route* climb a series of short walls and sloping ledges to gain a narrow gangway at the foot of the cracked wall.
2. 30m Make a committing sequence of moves up the blank gently overhanging wall to gain the steep crack follow this to a good ledge.
3. 40m Follow the continuing crack-line above the ledge as the angle eases to gain a ledge under a triangular recess. Pull through the roof and climb easy ground to the summit of the buttress.

Creag Coire na Ciste:
Catriona 65m VIII,8. Peter Davies, Tim Marsh. 21 Nov 2010
Climbs the short but striking arete to the left of *Cornucopia*. A superb second pitch. Protection is excellent once the crack at one-third height is reached. Start as for *Cornucopia*.

1. 10m Climb easy angled snow and mixed ground leading to a short groove formed by the left side of the slabs beneath *Cornucopia*. Belay beneath the arete.
2. 30m Begin by climbing the left side of the arete past a ledge and an obvious flake. From a standing position atop the flake, swing round on to the right side of the arete. Move up a small corner, then make commiting moves to get stood on a sloping ledge. From the ledge, climb a steep crack a little to the right of the arete until level with a small corner that cuts into the upper third of the arete. A tenuous step left leads to a good rest at the base of the corner. Climb the steep corner to reach a sloping terrace. Continue to a belay beneath a corner at the right-hand side of the wall taken by pitch 2 of *The Secret*.
3. 25m Climb the steep turfy corner and then easier angled ground leading to a short snowslope and the cornice.

To Those who Wait 55m IX,9. Greg Boswell, Will Sim. 4 Jan 2011.
The steep crack-line up the overhanging wall which is round the arete to the left of *The Secret*.
1. 30m Climb an icy right-facing corner until it steepens, then traverse a rock shield on the right to enter a hanging chimney with difficulty. Continue up the stepped turfy ground above to below the steep wall.
2. 25m Climb the steep crack and wall with increasing difficulty until below the three-quarters way ledge. Gain this, take a deep breath then launch up the overhanging wall above.

Note: Iain Small & Tony Stone on 12 Feb 2011 climbed a line of corners and offwidths in line with *Avenging Angel*, named *Angels with Dirty Faces* (VIII,8). Above, the route follows a steep crack and corners left of the finish of *Archangel*.

South Trident Buttress:
Note: *Pinnacle Arete Variation* 35m IV,6. Andy Huntington, Robin Clothier. 23 Oct 2010.
On pitch two at the big ledge instead of heading right, take the direct line up a steep crack come narrow chimney which exited beside the top of *The Clanger*.

Moonlight Gully Buttress:
Flying Saucer Attack 75m III. Anne Le Coant, Alex Kelly. 5 Feb 2011.
Start 20m up *Moonlight Gully*. Climb the left-hand edge of Moonlight Gully Buttress overlooking *Moonlight Gully* for 15m. Make a rising traverse across the buttress to meet *Diagonal Route*, just left of large cave in centre of the face (30m). Traverse across the cave leading to *Right-Hand Chimney* and easy ground to the top (30m).

Number Five Gully Buttress:
Lysystrata VI,8. Rich Cross, Andy Benson. 30 Nov 2010.
Two pitches of steep and technical climbing with excellent protection, by the summer line.

Free Range 145m VII,7 ***. Malcolm Bass, Jim Higgins, Simon Yearsley. 12 Feb 2011.
This fine route is based around the summer route *Chicken Run*. It gives excellent

mixed climbing, of similar character and quality to *Tower Face of The Comb*. Start as for *Chicken Run*.

1. 25m Climb the steep crack to a ledge.

2. 25m Move up and right for 3m, then head straight up the steep flaky wall to the traverse line of *Chicken Run*. Follow this to the 'great flake belay'.

3. 40m Four metres right is an obvious steep left-facing right-angle corner. Gain the base of the corner and climb it strenuously to a very hard move onto the sloping ledge on the right. Peg runner high on the right. Move back left to pull over the bulge. Above and slightly right is a line of steep chimneys and grooves, hidden from below. Climb these in a superb position to an exit right onto a good ledge.

3. 30m Move right along the ledge to where it is possible to break through the short steep barrier wall. Continue up a short V-groove to easier ground. Trend rightwards to belay at the base of a wide open corner system.

4. 25m Climb the fine corner system to the top where *Ledge Route* comes in from the right.

North Wall Carn Dearg:

Brave New World 125m IX,8. Iain Small, Simon Richardson. 20 Feb 2011.

A direct line up the wall between *Kellett's North Wall Route* and *The Past is Close Behind*. Very sustained with a bold and committing final pitch.

1. 25m Start 15m right of the initial chimney of *Kellett's North Wall Route* and climb a short wall to crack. Climb this to a left-trending ramp to a steep exit onto Broad Terrace.

2. 25m Move up and right across the terrace and climb the right-facing chimney-gully (down climbed by *MacPhee's Route*) to Flake Terrace.

3. 35m Reverse back down the chimney for 5m and step right onto a narrow dwindling ledge cutting across a vertical wall. Follow this to a right-facing groove, climb this over a bulge to a roof, step delicately right then continue up steep cracks to Diagonal Terrace.

4. 40m The vertical headwall above is breached by a steep corner leading up to an apparent featureless wall. Climb the corner, pull over a bulge and continue to a roof. Surmount this (bold) and climb the impending headwall above on discontinuous cracks to reach the top of the wall. Either descend left to reach *Waterfall Gully*, or abseil the line of the route.

Raeburn's Buttress:

The Great Flake Start 130m VII,7. Nick Bullock, Rich Cross. 8 Feb 2011.

A direct start to *The Great Corner*.

1. 60m Start below the centre of Raeburn's Buttress and trend up and right to below the first steep corner and the obvious mini-cenotaph.

2. 40m Turn the corner on the right on steep turf steps and belay beneath a steep chimney.

3. 30m Climb the chimney and then descend the Girdle Traverse ledge to beneath the first pitch of *The Great Corner*.

MAMORES, Stob Ban, South Buttress:

Tippy Toe 200m IV,5. John Lyall, Andy Nisbet, Jonathan Preston. 1 Dec 2010.

A route based on the groove right of *Groove Rider*. Start at the base of *South*

Gully where the base of the buttress on the right leaves the gully wall. Head up left on easy turfy ground to a short wall (35m). Climb this and traverse left along a ledge to the groove. Climb this to a steep corner (40m). Start up the corner, then traverse right along the lip of a bulge to reach turf near its right arete. Climb to an easier section, then take a continuation line to an easing (45m). Continue to the crest and follow it to the summit (80m).

SGÙRR A' MHAIM:

Devil's Rib 200m III. Ewan Olivarius, Ewan Lyons. 4 Dec 2010.
The most prominent rib in the hanging corrie, halfway along the west side of the Devil's Ridge between Stob Choire a' Mhail and Sgurr a' Mhaim. Alt 820m, start point NN 163 663. Approach from Glen Nevis. The route finishes on the ridge just north of Bealach a' Chip. Start at the toe of the buttress.
1. 50m Go up left and then back right underneath an overhang by a steep step. Find the line of least resistance between small outcrops until an easy snowslope leads to a belay on the crest below the next steepening.
2. 50m Move up and left to gain a short rock step just left of the spiky crest of the ridge. Carry on up until the angle eases to reach steeper ground. Turf belay.
3. 60m Climb the middle of the steep ground past a block on the right, then across a short neck.
4. 40m Easy ground leads to the top.

AM BODACH:

Central Buttress 400m II. Andy Nisbet. 4 Dec 2010.
This is the best defined buttress (*Solstice Gully* is to its right), starting above the flat area in the corrie floor and leading directly to the south cairn of Am Bodach summit area (the north and probably higher cairn is 60m away). Start at the base and climb steep turf to an easier section. Continue up just left of a sharp rock crest to reach easier slopes leading to the cornice.

CÀRN DEARG MEADHONACH:

Note: The route *Family Affair* (SMCJ 2010 p155) is the same route as *Chevron* described in SMCJ 2008 p172. The description from 2008 but with the name *Family Affair* should be used.

AONACH MÒR, An Cul Choire:

Inverted Ridge 120m III 4 *. Pete Harrop, Steve Kennedy. 18 Apr 2010.
The next short buttress beyond (north of) *Infinite Ridge*. The buttress resembles an inverted V and the right leg was climbed. At the point where the ridges converge a short icefall was climbed leading to a finish up easy snowslopes.

AONACH BEAG, Central West Face:

Cryogenic Corner 150m IV,4. Sandy Allan, Andy Nisbet. 1 Jan 2011.
An iced right-facing corner about 60m right of *The Navigator*. Climb steep snow to the base of the corner (40m). Climb the corner to an overlap (20m). Climb the overlap on ice 5m right of the corner, then continue on iced slabs to rejoin the corner and continue to an easing (40m). Move up left to an arete and climb snow and easy-angled ice up , then right to snowslopes (50m).

Glycerol Gully   200m   II. Andy Nisbet. 6 Mar 2011.
An icefall which forms in the vague rib right of *Cryogenic Corner*. Start where snow leads up left to *Cryogenic Corner*. Climb ice pitches separated by snow, with the steepest section passed by easier ice on the right, to reach a left-slanting snow trough. Go up this for about 30m to where another icefall in a slight gully leads up right. Follow this up and then left into a corner (direct would be steeper ice) which leads to the big upper snowslopes.

STOB A' CHOIRE MHEADHOIN, Coire Shomhairle (NN 326 745):
Àite Cruinnichidh   55m,   II/III. John Proctor, Chris Banks. 1 Jan 2011.
An icefall at the left end of a lower tier of steep ground at the top of the corrie. Clearly visible in the topo provided.

One One Eleven   70m   I. John Proctor, Chris Banks. 1 Jan 2011.
A straightforward snow gully in the upper tier, directly above the icefall and with small patches of ice.

CREAG MEAGAIDH:
Special Delivery   220m   VI,6 ***. Donnie O'Sullivan, Peter Davies, Mike Gardner. 12 Feb 2011
An excellent ice climb in a stunning position. To the left of *South Pipe Direct* and overlooking *Staghorn Gully*, there is a hanging slab topped by a steep wall. A prominent line of snow drains down to the top of the steep wall and in good conditions a cascade of ice forms. A long pitch of ice leads in a direct line up to the base of the main cascade. The cascade is unlikely to completely touch down but icy mixed climbing, which may not be visible from the corrie floor allows the icefall to be gained with surprising ease.
1. 55m Start from *Staghorn Gully* directly beneath the cascade (30m right of *Postal Strike*). Climb 70 degree ice for 25m to an icicle fringe. Climb the icicles (90 degrees for 3m) to reach the easier angled slab. Climb this to a belay on the right side of the cascade.
2. 45m Climb an icy corner for 10m to where good rock gear protects a delicate leftwards traverse to gain the main icefall. Climb the icefall for 30m and continue to a rock belay on the right.
3. 60m Regain the easier angled gully and continue in a direct line towards the upper snowfield.
4. 60m Snowslopes lead to the cornice.

CENTRAL HIGHLANDS, Fort Augustus Area:
Return of Nedi the Jedi   40m   III. Michael Carrol, David Whalley, Ian Kelly. 8 Dec 2010.
Leave Fort Augustus for 3.5km on the A82 heading to Spean Bridge. Park at a forestry track by the road (NH 356 054). Walk up the track for 10mins, climb through the forestry to a waterfall, 10mins. NH 360 055. Climb the falls direct or the left-hand side to a tree belay. Great for a short day and can be included with Culachy Falls, NH 373 059, but a longer walk in!

CREAG DUBH:
Paper Trail   130m   IV,5. John Lyall, Andy Nisbet. 11 Jan 2011.

The big fault immediately left of Great Wall. Start up a diagonal crack (the start of *Men Only*) – this is often bare of snow – and climb the fault to a tree (25m). Continue up the fault over an icy bulge and a second bulge with a tree, to reach its top (35m). Traverse a ledge left, then climb turfy ground left then right to trees (35m). Climb a diagonal crack to a bulge, then traverse right to easier ground, followed to the top (35m).

CENTRAL HIGHLANDS, GEAL CHARN, Creag Dhubh:

Wee Softie   45m   II/III. Martin Holland, Pamela Millar. 2 Dec 2008.
This route is on a crag high on left of the crag shown NE of the main crag. It is on the left/upper tier of this crag at approx. NN 596 799. The lower level of this crag may be the one where the routes *Flight of the Navigator* and *Map and Compass* are described in SMCJ 2004, although the map ref is wrong (it's in the loch).
1. 18m   Start 5m right of the cave and climb turf and ice steps to the higher of two bent over trees.
2. 25m   Continue up turf and ice to two saplings at the base of an iced slab. Climb the slab leftwards to pass a triangular overhanging nose on its left.

Narwhal   50m   III,4. David & John Lyall. 4 Feb 2009.
The buttress between *Wafer Me* and *Ice Cream*. Steep ice to start and in the middle, followed by a line left of the final headwall to eventually break out right to finish.

Merlin   100m   IV,4 *. John Lyall, Jonathan Preston. 7 Jan 2011.
Starts about 200m right of *The Hex Factor*, where a shallow gully runs into an amphitheatre. Climb the easy gully and steep icefall above.

Hidden Gem   120m   IV,4 *. John Lyall, Jonathan Preston. 7 Jan 2011.
Just right of *Merlin* is a steep buttress with a right-slanting easy gully on the right flank. Follow the easy gully, and the minor left branch cutting behind the buttress, to belay beneath an ice chocked chimney. Follow the chimney, then the steepest ice on the left side of the next wall to the top (50m).

Both the routes described in SMCJ 2004 with an incorrect map ref were repeated in 2010. John Hall, Alan Hunt & John Swift repeated *Flight of the Navigator* but graded it IV,5 (admittedly conservative) and reported a map ref of NN 595 799. Mark Bannan repeated *Map and Compass*, giving III,4 as before.

GLEN COE

BUACHAILLE ETIVE MOR:
Line Up   VIII,8. Andy Nelson, Kenny Grant, Andy Sharp. 21 Dec 2009.
Start up the vegetated chimney of *Route 1*, then work up and left past an obvious small block, then up the short wall to the *Line Up* stance. From here follow the

summer route. The climbing is superb, intricate and quite bold in the first two pitches, sustained throughout, with sensational, well protected climbing on the last pitch up the corner and through the roof.

Great Gully Upper Buttress:

Weasily Recognised   15m   VS 4c *. Gary & Karen Latter, Alex Thomson. 9 Jul 2011.
The obvious crack towards the left end of the crag, halfway along the wall left of *Happy Valley*, gained from the right.

Stoatily Different   15m   E1 5a *. Alex Thomson, Gary & Karen Latter. 9 Jul 2011.
Climb direct line up the wall starting just right of the crack. Poorly protected.

World Class   45m   HVS 5a *. Michael Barnard, John MacLeod. 23 Jul 2011.
A fine outing. To the right of the initial wall of *Facade* is a crack with an obvious leftward kink. Go up to climb the crack, following it out left before moving up to the ledge below the upper wall. Step left below the top groove of *Facade* and climb steep cracks to the top.

Barbeque Rib   50m   HVS 4c. Michael Barnard, John MacLeod. 23 Jul 2011.
The rib left of *Bent Crack*, finishing up the steep top groove of *Facade*.

Notes: *Happy Valley* itself will be more like 20m than the given 30m, and *Yam* 30m (not 40m).
  Jamay was climbed free by Ben Darvill & Gary Latter on 11 Jul 2009, at no change to the original (E3 5c **) grade.
  The top groove of *Facade* was the physical crux (and possibly the overall crux!) of *Barbeque Rib*, suggesting an upgrade to VS 4c. *Bent Crack* and *Bent Crack Rib* will both be more like 50m than 40m.

STOB COIRE SGREAMHACH EAST, Sron na Lairig Summit Buttress:

All three routes lie on the steepest and highest buttress just right of the 'easy grade I gully' mentioned in the current Glen Coe guidebook. Alt 900m, North-facing.

The Promise   110m   III *. Simon Yearsley, Dan Peach. 22 Dec 2010.
A nice route taking the left-hand edge of the buttress. Starts at the foot of the easy gully.
1. 55m Climb the rib right of the gully in a pleasant position to just below a col with a small tree.
2. 55m Follow the obvious turfy line trending up and right. This becomes more enclosed as it twists left then right, before easier angled ground leads to the top.

The Grey Pillar   60m   VI,7 **. Paul Figg, Malcolm Bass. 8 Jan 2011.
Slightly left of the centre of the steep, stepped lower walls of the summit buttress is a grey pillar with a groove on its left side. This is the line.
1. 30m Climb blocky turfy ground up and right to enter the groove. Climb this over a bulge (crux, thin turf) to a small ledge on the right.

2. 30m Climb up and right over another bulge to a right-trending ramp. Follow this to a snow bay. Finish up a deep crack in an open corner.

The Slot 60m V,6 *. Neil Silver, Simon Yearsley. 8 Jan 2011.
Start on the right-hand side of the buttress in a bay which has a short pillar on its top left.
1. 25m Climb a steep grove to the right of the pillar, and continue up and slightly right to a fine belay.
2. 35m Follow the gully for 15m to where a steep wall bars the way. High up left

on the skyline is an obvious beckoning slot. Climb up steep turfy ground to the base of the slot, and climb it in a fine position to the top.

COIRE EILDE, Eilde Canyon:
Simon Yearsley and friends have explored the canyon formed by the Allt Lairig Eilde and climbed several icefalls on its walls. The routes have been described on a topo.

AONACH DUBH, Far Eastern Buttress:
Japseye Variation to Yen 35m VI,6. Adam Hughes, Colm Burke, Dave Burke. 10 Mar 2011.
Follow *Yen* to the ledge and belay below the steep crack between *Yen* and the obvious chimney. Climb the steep crack, crux, to join the chimney at its top and belay (25m). A short pitch leads to a bay and easy ground.

AONACH DUBH, North Face:
Note: The second peg on *The Clearances* is no longer there. Ian Taylor thought E4 5c, 6a.

AONACH DUBH, West Face, No.2 Gully Buttress:
Rose Late 75m IV,6. Sandy Allan, John Lyall, Andy Nisbet. 7 Dec 2010.
A winter ascent based on what was assumed to be the summer line (but the descriptions in the current guide are poor). Start near the base of *The God Daughter* (SMCJ 2009). Take a ramp leading up left, then its continuation to reach the halfway terrace near its left end (35m). Climb over bulging blocks to gain and climb a wide crack to reach a good ledge (10m). Move left and climb steep turfy steps to the top (30m).

Oz 65m VII,7. Sandy Allan, John Lyall, Andy Nisbet. 8 Dec 2010.
A winter ascent close to the summer line. The first pitch is steep and sustained but the second pitch (common to *Steptoe* – SMCJ 2009) is serious and several peg runners were used. Climb a turfy groove immediately right of *Rose Innominate*, then step right into the main groove. Climb this to the wedge shaped crack, then move left to gain the terrace (30m). Climb pitches 2 and 3 of *Oz* (35m). These are the same as the pitches on *Steptoe* summer; the descriptions even fit.

The Wonderful Wizard 75m V,6 *. John Lyall, Jonathan Preston. 4 Dec 2010.
Start at the right end of the ledge, below the pinnacle of *The Verger*.

1. 45m Climb a wide crack on the right, then up a snow bay and short chimney. Follow a gully to a big left-leaning corner in the next tier, then move right to belay beneath a steep groove.
2. 30m Follow the groove to the top.

Shrike Ridge 85m IV,4 **. Steve Kennedy, Andy MacDonald. 27 Nov 2010.
An excellent short winter route (see SMCJ 2010) which is very accommodating and well protected. Start just right of the short steep wall at the foot of the knife-edged arete. Climb the cracked slabby wall right of the edge then move left onto the arete. Continue up the broad ridge finishing up a short corner on the right. Ideal when higher conditions are doubtful. Abseil descent possible to avoid the open slopes above the West Face.

Killing Time 90m III *. Bob Hamilton, Steve Kennedy. 4 Dec 2010.
The groove immediately right of *Shrike Ridge*. Finish directly up a slim groove.

No.5 Gully:
Guidelines 90m IV,4 *. Steve Kennedy, Andy MacDonald. 18 Dec 2010.
No.5 Gully divides into two branches in the upper third just above The Rake. The right branch forms a narrow gully. This route climbs the broad buttress lying between the two branches. It may correspond with the upper section of *E4F5 Route*. Start at the foot of the right branch where it narrows, move left and climb a short groove to a steep wall at 10m. Traverse horizontally left on turf ledges to the middle of the buttress then up to a block belay (50m). A short wall and arete leads to the top of the right branch (40m). Finish up No.5 Gully.

The Amphitheatre:
Winifred's Pinnacle, East Face 20m II/III *. Steve Kennedy, Andy MacDonald. 27 Nov 2010.
Winifred's Pinnacle sits in the upper right corner of the Amphitheatre. This is the first recorded winter ascent, the pinnacle having first been climbed in October 1900 by Mr and Mrs Abraham on their honeymoon! The exposed summit provides a magnificent outlook over the west face and beyond. Access either via No.4 Gully or from The Rake (can conveniently be combined with an ascent of *Dubh Chasm* as on this occasion).
Start at the neck in the deep chasm behind the pinnacle (*Dubh Chasm*). A stiff pull up the initial short wall leads to a ledge which is traversed left to a large block. Step left from the block then follow a groove up and right to the top. Abseil descent.

Winifred's Seduction 40m IV,6 **. Steve Kennedy, Andy MacDonald. 9 Jan 2011.
An excellent route located on the north flank of the pinnacle. The difficulties are short lived and well protected. Start about 10m below the neck and climb a short chimney. Move right via ledges passing below a small projecting block aiming for a steep wall and crack near the right edge. Climb the steep crack to a small pedestal. Step right into a chimney which is followed to the top. Abseil descent.

Dubh Chasm 130m III **. Steve Kennedy, Andy MacDonald. 27 Nov 2010.

Andy Nisbet on the first pitch of Oz (VII,7), Aonach Dubh, during the first ascent.
Photo: John Lyall.

An entertaining outing with impressive rock scenery. The upper face of The Amphitheatre contains a remarkable chasm which runs almost horizontally leftwards from the top right corner of the Amphitheatre to near the top of *North Ridge*. The only difficulties are found in the final 8m. Enter the deep confines of the chasm from The Amphitheatre (near the base of the south edge of Winifred's Pinnacle) and climb the first easy section to a neck behind the large pinnacle (Winifred's Pinnacle). Descend slightly from the neck and enter the final section finishing up a short mixed wall. Easily reached from the Rake. Not to be confused with *The Slot* which lies on the lower left side of The Amphitheatre.

BIDEAN NAM BIAN, Church Door Buttress:

Temple of Dumb 45m E4 5c *. Ian Taylor, Tess Fryer. 29 Jul 2011.
Follow the second pitch of *Temple of Doom* for 6m and where it moves left, move right until below a large corner. Gain the base of the corner by a circular move out right to avoid a loose looking flake, then continue up the sustained corner, pulling left onto a ledge at the top. Finish easily.
Note: The peg on *The Lost Ark* is no more and the route is nearer E5 in its current state.

BIDEAN NAM BIAN, West Top:

Stramash 120m IV,4. John Lyall, Andy Nisbet, Jonathan Preston. 22 Nov 2010.
This climbs the right edge of the buttress, right of *The Hash*. Start at the base of the buttress and climb a shallow groove to a ledge right of *The Hash* (60m) – various starts to *The Gash* may cross this. Go up right via a wide flake-crack (crux) to a ridge which forms the right edge of the buttress. Follow the ridge to a thread (40m). Finish up the ridge (20m).

Odyssey 80m II/III *. Bob Hamilton, Steve Kennedy. 29 Jan 2011.
An icefall forms on the right side of the steep buttress right of *Minute Man*, just before the buttress peters out into easier ground. Climb the icefall in two steps to reach a large snow bay. Mixed ground leads fairly directly to the top. The lower section can largely bank out in a heavy build up.

The following routes are situated on the small isolated buttress right of the main buttress containing *Minute Man*. Although the routes are short, they provide excellent, sustained mixed pitches.

Westie 90m II. John Lyall, Andy Nisbet, Jonathan Preston. 22 Nov 2010.
Start left of the base of the buttress. Climb a groove to a terrace below steep ground. Move left and climb a second groove, then a third which both lie just left of steep ground. Finish up a short groove on the right. The third groove has a steep finish and might make the route Grade III.

Puppet on a String 50m V,6 **. Bob Hamilton, Steve Kennedy, Andy MacDonald. 23 Jan 2011.
The main central groove provides a sustained and absorbing long pitch. Climb the left-facing corner, then move left around the lower roof into the main corner. Follow the corner to a further small roof which splits the corner/groove. Move

left and climb an awkward wall (crux) which leads into the upper left-hand groove which is followed to the top.

Tiger Feet   50m   IV,5 *. Steve Kennedy, Andy MacDonald, Bob Hamilton. 23 Jan 2011.
Right of *Puppet on a String* is a further corner/groove. Climb the lower section until the corner steepens and becomes better defined. Leave the corner and follow an easier line out right below a projecting buttress to reach a ledge overlooking the gully on the right (20m). Make an exposed step out left onto a slabby wall which is climbed using a groove on the right (crux). Follow the groove then step left and finish up a cracked wall on the left (30m).

Pirouette   45m   VI,7 **. Lewis Harrop, Steve Kennedy, Bob Hamilton. 19 Mar 2011.
A fine sustained pitch up the attractive looking slabby wall immediately left of the groove of *Tiger Feet*. Start at the foot of the groove and climb a system of cracks leading up the left wall. Finish by moving out left below the bulging upper wall via a groove leading to the left edge. Step left from the edge and finish up a short groove. The difficulties increase with height.

BEINN A' CHRULAISTE:
Note: In the Glen Coe guide p371, the first ascentionists of *Highest Gully* and *Candlemass Gully* should be P.W.F. Gribbon & P.J. Biggar. Both routes were climbed in winter.

GLEN ETIVE, STOB COIR' AN ALBANNAICH, North Corrie:
Tomb Raider   70m   III *. Steve Kennedy, Andy MacDonald. 12 Dec 2010.
The groove/gully on the right of the buttress containing *Air of Detachment*. Climbed in lean conditions. Probably easier later in the season.

Croft Original   50m   III *. Andy MacDonald, Steve Kennedy. 12 Dec 2010.
This route climbs the obvious short gully on the right side of the coire where the buttresses start to peter out. The cornice formed the crux and was outflanked by a tricky leftward traverse.

GARBH BHEINN (ARDGOUR), Pinnacle Buttress:
Contortion   220m   VII,7. Simon Richardson, Roger Webb. 5 Dec 2010.
The well defined corner system on the right side of the front face of the Upper Pinnacle. The route may approximate to the summer line *Iubhair Grooves*.
1. 30m Start near the right side of the buttress below an overhanging chimney. Climb the chimney (strenuous with unusual positions) and exit into a ledge below a steep bulging wall.
2. 40m Step right to bypass the wall and follow a line of steep turfy steps (poorly

protected) to gain the upper left-facing corner system. Climb this to where it funnels into a blank slab on the left.
3. 50m Climb the slab, and then continue up the left-facing corner above. Continue in the same line, passing several steep steps, to a good ledge.
4. to 6. 100m Continue up the crest of the buttress to where it become as

horizontal crest. Finish along this for a further two pitches joining *Pinnacle Ridge* for its final ropelength.

SGURR NA H-EANCHAINNE, Lower South-East Face:
(NN 005 653)   Alt 120m   South-East facing
The Strand   110m   III *. Henry Methold, Davy Austin. 24 Dec 2010.
The prominent waterfall forming the lower reaches of the Allt Tairbh (Bull Burn) very occasionally forms an icefall. The metagabbro rock band and the route are visible from Nether Lochaber and located not far above the A861. The route only comes into condition during prolonged and exceptionally cold conditions. From the west side of Corran Ferry proceed 1.5 km north along the road to Keil Farm. Cross a road bridge over the stream and follow the foot path sign through a field and up beside the farm. A short walk up a steep slope leads to the obvious gully.
1. 60m A steep start. Climb up the gully and trend right to a narrow corner.
2. 50m Climb a short wall on the left to a platform. Continue to another short gully and climb on the left. Walk off right.

GLEN GOUR, Indian Slab Crag:
Arrowhead   190m   VS 4b *. Bob Hamilton, Steve Kennedy. 12 Jun 2010.
Left of the start of *Indian Slab* is a slightly lower tier of slabs. Climb cracks up the centre of the lower tier left of a heather ledge to a wide grass rake (30m). Walk a few metres right and climb the narrow slab left of a vertical grassy crack (left of *Time Lord*) to a grass ledge (30m). Continue by *Time Lord* or *Indian Slab* (130m). Mild VS.

Outlaw   70m   Severe *. Bob Hamilton, Steve Kennedy. 12 Jun 2010.
Climbs the rib left of the prominent corner of *Outrider*. The route shares the same start as *Outrider* but closely follows the left edge of the initial slab throughout instead of moving right towards the tree and corner.

The following route is located on the upper section of the crag up and well right of the finish of *Indian Slab*. The upper rocks are steeper and run diagonally leftwards up the slope. From the lower slabs they look bow shaped with a vague central grassy bay. A small black cave will be seen in the main mass of rock left of the bay.

Crazy Horse   75m   HVS 5a **. Steve Kennedy, Bob Hamilton. 12 Jun 2010.
Climbs the slabby wall left of the cave. Start directly below the cave and follow a leftward trending line to the left edge of the cave. From the cave make an exposed traverse horizontally left for a few metres (crux) then follow cracks directly above to a heather ledge at the top of the wall (45m). Finish easily by rocks on the right of a grassy gully (30m). Descend by slopes on the left or abseil the route from the top of the initial wall.

ARDNAMURCHAN, Creag an Fhir-eoin:
Fuji   20m   E1 5a. Colin Moody, Cynthia Grindley, Andy Hyslop. 24 Jul 2011.
Climb the unprotected scoop right of *Stromboli*. Pull over on the easy flake, then climb the rounded rib.

Unnamed 14m Severe. Colin Moody, Cynthia Grindley. 24 Jul 2011.
Bridge up the shallow chimney right of *Fuji*, then move out right above the steep lower wall to a slanting crack, runners. Step right and climb chickenheads to the top.

SOUTHERN HIGHLANDS

MEALL BUIDHE:
Note: Martin Holland notes a descent of the obvious gully to the left of *Eldritch* (topo provided) at 125m Grade I with the odd steepish section and some good rock scenery and would make a great easy approach to the summit. Perhaps climbed before, but the name *Search Party Gully* suggested.

BEINN AN DOTHAIDH, North-East Corrie:
Emstead Grooves 105m III. Martin Holland, Pamela Millar. 25 Nov 2010.
Start about 150m up right from the base of *Emel Ridge* at a turfy slab. This is up and left of a seperate 5m buttress with a square-cut chimney below the main crag.
1. 55m Climb the left corner of the slab on turf ledges. Move diagonally right underneath a wall to a platform on the right edge and a belay in a small triangular niche with a roof crack.
2. 50m From the niche traverse left on flakes to gain and climb a stepped groove. Easy ground is reached after 25m and followed up and left to a large block belay on *Emel Ridge*.

BEINN DORAIN, Creag an Socach:
Note: *The Sting* received two repeats and was thought VI,6.

Second Coming, Contented Rat Start 45m V,7. Viv Scott, Sam Loveday, Andy Hein. 18 Dec 2010.
Takes a system of grooves in the arete left of the ramp of *Second Coming*. Not a great line but fun turfy mixed climbing similar to other routes on the crag. Start 5m left of entry ramp to *Second Coming* under a square groove with a crack in the left wall.
1. 20m Climb the well protected groove to a steep exit (crux) to a large turf ledge.
2. 25m A slim groove (with a wide crack on the left) runs up the arete. Climb this moving rightwards at the top, then go straight up on turf to belay just left of chimney on *Second Coming*.
3. Follow *Second Coming* to finish. A possible independent exit could trend rightwards up ledge/wall systems but these were black.

BEN UDLAIDH, West Sector:
The Crooked Smile 65m VII,7 ***. Greg Boswell, Neil Carnegie. 8 Dec 2010.
Start just left of *The Smirk* below a steep bulge. There is an obvious icy fan hanging down from the lip of the big roof (when in condition).
1. 25m Climb the short bulge up and left to a turfy band/break in the steep wall.

Traverse the steep wall leftwards (bold) to the thin ice fan. Gain the ice with difficulty (tenuous) and climb the hanging pillar to the cave/ledge.
2. 40m Step right out of the cave and delicately climb the steep ice to a large snowy ledge. At the back of the ledge there is another steep ice wall; climb this to its top and finish up the easy ground as for *The Smirk*.

BEINN LAOIGH, Stob Garbh, North Face:
Tarsus 340m III. Sonya McCallum, Andy Nisbet. 19 Dec 2010.
The crest of the buttress right of *Garbh Couloir* (SMCJ 2008). A mixture of some good tricky sections and much easier ground, but better than it looks from below. Start immediately right of *Garbh Couloir* and follow an icy groove and its snaking shallow continuation to below the steepest section of the buttress. Climb up underneath its left side, then traverse left before pulling through a bulge and breaking back up right on a hanging ramp. Climb the final steep tier by a right-slanting line.

BEINN NARNAIN, Yawning Crag (NN 267 064):
This is the crag named as such on O/S Explorer 364, whereas the crag with this name in the guidebook is further east.

Hidden Gangway 140m III,4 **. Andy Bain, Jake Thackrey. 13 Mar 2011.
Start at the toe in the centre of the main crag.
1. 35m Start up a right-slanting slab and go up to the start of a chimney, then trend right to a cave.
2. 35m Climb right and around the corner to a hidden gangway over an obvious gully to a chockstone cave.
3. 10m Climb to the top of the cave roof and out right (crux) into an open snowfield to reach a small outcrop wall.
4. and 5. 60m Traverse left over the cave roof and up a blocky ridge to the top.

Slanting Slabs 110m II. Andy Bain, Jake Thackrey. 13 Mar 2011.
Start 10m left of the main crag at an obvious chockstone cave.
1. 55m Start by going through the large chockstone and up rightwards over a slab to a recess.
2. 55m Finish up over the recess and out onto an open slope above with small outcrops to the top.

THE BRACK:
Mammoth IX,9 ****. Guy Robertson, Greg Boswell. Dec 2010.
Strenuous and sustained with perfect protection; a top quality winter route (much better than in summer!). Follow the summer line for two pitches, with the second probably the crux. For pitch 3, go horizontally left for a few metres from the belay and climb a turfy crack, overhanging at its top, to belay below a wide right-trending crack (20m). Follow the crack back into the summer line and follow this to the top.
Elephant Train 125m V,6. Donnie O'Sullivan, Tim Marsh, Peter Davies. 9 Jan 2011.
A link of the start of *Elephant Gully* with the finish of *Hogwart's Express* gives a worthwhile expedition. Commodious ledges at every belay.
1. 20m Climb *Elephant Gully* and belay on the right wall above the first cave.

2. 20m   Cross the gully and gain a horizontal ledge leading easily leftwards beneath a large roof. Belay at its end.

3. 50m   Climb up and left to reach the base of a hanging groove. Make one hard move to get established in the groove and then follow a rising right to left line of weakness for 40m to reach the base of a prominent tapering corner. This corner is pitch 5 of *Mainline* and where the route joins *Hogwart's Express*.

4. 25m   Climb the corner (crux) and belay beneath the final short wall.

5. 10m   Climb a diagonal crack through the final wall.

BEINN AN LOCHAIN:

Cat's Gully   350m   II. Graeme Kemp, Catherine Zancanaro. 9 Jan 2010.

The gully is towards the left end of the east face of Beinn an Lochan, and is easily seen from the A83, especially when heading north. From the summit of the Rest and be Thankful, go past the South end of Loch Restil and aim for the large gully that falls from the southern shoulder of Beinn an Lochan.

In its lower section the gully is essentially a steep water course; however, as height is gained, it becomes steeper and numerous short ice steps are encountered. Escape to either side is straightforward at this stage. Higher, the gully becomes steeper and more enclosed. At a narrowing, approximately 50m below the top, an awkward chimney is bypassed by a traverse right then back left on ice and frozen turf. The route then continues, without difficulty, up the gully which opens out as it reaches the broad south ridge of the mountain.

Riding the Storm   70m   VII,7. Iain Small, Simon Richardson. 9 Jan 2011.

The left-hand of two prominent crack systems cutting the front face of the *Heart of Darkness* buttress.

1. 25m   Climb the easy first 10m of *Heart of Darkness* to the niche. From its bottom left side, climb an awkward hanging chimney-slot to a sloping ledge, then continue over a chokestone and up a steep left-facing corner to exit onto a broad turfy ledge.

2. 45m   Continue in the same line up a left-facing corner-ramp to reach a narrow ledge. Traverse left along this above *Saxifrage Gully* until it is possible to break out right up a steep crack. This leads to easier turfy ground and the top of the buttress.

BEN LOMOND, A Buttress:

Flake Dance   90m   IV,5 *. Sonya McCallum, Andy Nisbet. 18 Dec 2010.

A line up the left side of A Buttress. Start below the easiest line leading up left to a first terrace. Follow this, then move up right and back left to break through a steep wall (easier further left). Take a ramp leading up right (50m). Continue up the ramp and return left to below a steep unavoidable band. Climb this via a flake system, then continue left and right on turf to the top, joining *Pole Dance* at the very top (40m).

Note: Although this route and two recent ones are described as being on A Buttress, by the original nomenclature they are probably on the right side of B Buttress. But from a climbing point of view, it makes sense to rename this area as A Buttress.

C Buttress:

Lomond Buttress   100m   III,4. Ewan Olivarius, Fraser Hughes. 27 Nov 2010.
Approximately 15m left of *Lomond Corner* is a short narrow chimney.
1. 50m Climb this to reach a small cave (possible belay). Traverse rightwards
until a delicate move gains a right-facing corner. Climb this with interest, then
move up and left to belay.
2. 50m Follow a ramp up and left to easier ground.

Coille Ramp   80m   II. Sonya McCallum, Andy Nisbet. 18 Dec 2010.
A prominent left-slanting ramp, starting about 25m left of *Lomond Corner*, was
climbed in two pitches and leads to the cliff-top.

BEINN EUNAICH:
Black Shock   170m   V,5. Roger Everett, Simon Richardson. 28 Nov 2010.
The prominent fault-line running up left and diverging from *The Black Shoot*.
1. 50m Start 20m left of *The Black Shoot* and climb steep vegetation interspersed
with a couple of rock steps, to the start of the fault. Belay on small trees.
2. 30m Traverse under the fault and enter it from the left. Climb up to a small
cave and exit steeply left to a ledge.
3. 40m Continue up the line of the fault via a couple of steep walls and continue
up easier ground to a terrace.
4. 50m Finish up the dwindling fault-line over a series of steep steps to reach the
broad terrace at the top of the buttress.

Eas Eunaich   80m   IV,4. Jim Graham, Iain MacCallum. 21 Dec 2010.
At NN 140 307. A line on the left-hand side which was pretty thin but reasonably
solid (tied-off ice screws) – 30m, 50m. The right-hand side of the fall was steeper
and would give a good climb with less water running behind it. Named *No
Country for Old Men*.

GLEN OGLE:
Better As a Fry Up   40m   III. Craig Smith, Alan Gray. 9-Jan 2011.
Ascend an open icy gully approx 100m south of a boulder field on the west side
of Glen Ogle above Glenogle Farm. NN 57545 25382.

Direct Finish   20m   V,5. Craig Smith, Andrew Fulton. 9 Jan 2011.
Halfway up *Better As a Fry Up*, climb the icicle formed on the left wall direct.

BEN LAWERS, Creag an Fhithich:
Note: John Proctor & Chris Banks climbed an icefall set apart at the left-hand
side of the crag on 5 Feb 2011 – *Consolation Prize* 7m IV,4.

MEALL GHAORDAIDH, Creag Laoghain:
Note: The big gully left of *No Pain Laoghain* (SMCJ 2010) was climbed by
Iain Thow on 9 Apr 1982 at Grade I.

MEALL NAN TARMACHAN, Cam Chreag:
Banshee Gully   100m   I/II. Martin Holland, Martin Campbell. 20 Feb 2011.
Follows a left to right-trending gully/ramp line across the buttress immediately
right of Carlin's Buttress, with one narrow steepening on the first pitch and a

ramp-line before joining the exit slopes of the right-bounding gully. Warthogs required for belays.

ARRAN

COIRE NAM FUARAN:
Lies at the head of Glen Sannox to the south-west of the saddle. Approach either from Glen Sannox, or from the ridge above via an easy gully 300m north-east of North Goatfell. Descent from either route is easiest down Coire Lan to Corrie.

Naanaarpoq 450m II/III. Robin Barnden. 5 Dec 2010.
A bastion at the left end of the corrie wall is split by a deep cleft. The route starts at an icefall that emerges over rocky slabs beneath the cleft. Climb the ice to enter the cleft and follow a series of snow and ice steps. At the back of the cleft trend right over icy ramps and a further short pitch to emerge on open snowslopes above. Climb snow and turf to the ridge and emerge about 200m SW of Mullach Buidhe summit. The name is an Inuit word meaning 'taking extravagant pleasure in being alive'.

Note: About 100m to the north of this route is a pleasant gully (initially another cleft) that maintains a direct line at a steady angle right to the ridge. It is about 400m Grade II, with potentially deep snow and a few small ice steps. Robin Barnden, 2010.

LOWLAND OUTCROPS

GLASGOW AREA, Auchinstarry:
Plumline Arete 7m E3 6a. Brendan Croft. 11 Jul 2011.
An eliminate. Climb the clean arete between the start of *Promontory Direct* and *Plumline Crack*, avoiding the adjacent routes. Protected by side-runners in *Promontory Direct*. The crux is getting your left foot on to a large hold on the arete.

Neilston Quarry:
There is a new write-up of all the routes by Malcolm Nicolson on http://www.smc.org.uk/NewClimbs.php.

GALLOWAY HILLS, THE MERRICK, Black Gairy:
Tae a Moose 75m III. Andrew Fraser, Ian Magill. 5 Dec 2010.
About 100m down and left of the main icefall of *Fat Triplet* is a wider icefall. Climb this to easier ground (45m). On the tier above is a steep boss of ice, which is turned on the left, then continue up shallow gully to finish (30m).

A Fridge Too Far 60m III,4. A.Fraser, Ian Magill. 5 Dec 2010.
This is the buttress right of the *Triplets*, climbed on frozen turf. Start at the left toe of the buttress, just left of some ice. Climb turf, moving up left into a shallow chimney on the left edge of the buttress. Up this, and steep ground above to

easier ground then traverse 6m left into the wide snowy gully in the centre of the buttress (30m). Take the left branch of this and continue up easy ground to the top (30m).

MULLWARCHAR, Yellow Tomach:
(NX 462 883)   Alt 375m   East facing
A rarely visited and very broken crag, one for lovers of Gallwegian esoterica! However the rock is clean and quick to dry where it isn't seeping and the outlook is delightful. It lies on the east face of Hoodens Hill.

Russet Wall:
This small brown square wall lies at the bottom left corner of the cliffs. Descent is tricky.

Tomach or not Tomach?   18m   Severe 4b. Stephen Reid, Andrew Fraser. 11 Oct 2010.
The rather grassy left arete and slabs above.

Gala Performance   18m   HVS 5a. Stephen Reid, Andrew Fraser. 11 Oct 2010.
The major crack from the left to a ledge. Follow the crack above, just right of a corner, to easy slabs.

White Slab:
The obvious white slab in the centre of the crag and some way above a large tree is best gained by a rising traverse from the foot of Russet Wall.

Yellow Belly   36m   VS. Andrew Fraser, Stephen Reid. 11 Oct 2010.
1. 26m 4c Climb cracks up the centre of the slab exiting rightwards.
2. 10m 4b The wide crack just to the right is followed by blocks.

The Main Slab Area:
The most obvious and largest feature lies towards the right side of the crag. Unfortunately much of the Main Slab itself is slow to dry.

The Auld Alliance   45m   HVS 5a. Stephen Reid, Andrew Fraser. 3 Sep 2010.
A pleasant climb with good protection, up the right side of the Main Slab. It starts up the brown streak in the middle of the slabs, then goes right of this at the overlap. Start just right of centre below a small blocky prow. This is about 15m directly blow the prominent diagonal break that the climb takes through the main overlap. Climb up to the prow and step on to it from the left. Make hard moves directly up cracks in the slab above and pull on to a narrow terrace. Follow a diagonal finger crack up leftwards and step back right through the overlap. Climb the right edge of the slab above to an impasse and step up and right to a small grass ledge. Follow the blocky rib on the right to a final small smooth slab and go straight up this.

No Country for Old Men   43m   E1 *. Andrew Fraser, Stephen Reid. 3 Sep 2010.
A good and well protected route aiming for the obvious crack which splits a block high up at the right side of this area. Start 20m right of the Main Slab at a

grassy chimney formed by a large pyramid shaped block.
1. 35m 5a Go easily up the chimney to a terrace (possible belay). Climb the groove in the wall above to an awkward finish and continue up slabs and grass to the foot of a fine crack in the headwall.
2. 8m 5b Climb the crack to a ledge. Continue up the continuation crack with increasing difficulty and exit rightwards to a huge block.

The Top Tier:
The long broken final tier is devoid of obvious lines and can be climbed or not climbed at all just about anywhere. So far one route has been done.

Doonward Bound 27m VS 4c. Andrew Fraser, Stephen Reid. 11 Oct 2011.
Start on the right, on the left edge of some slabs and above a short slab. Climb a slab, then another harder slab lying between a rib on the left and an undercut crack on the right. On reaching easier ground, traverse left for 3m and finish leftward up the juggy headwall.

The Tauchers, Lower Foresters':
This tiny, rather pink, buttress lies low down on the far left of the climbable rock.

Weasley Recognised 12m HVS 5a. James Kinnaird, Stephen Reid. 30 Aug 2010.
On the left side are three thin cracks; start under the right-hand one. Move up to under a bulge and traverse right to a good spike, which enables an awkward pull up onto a ledge. Continue more easily up the buttress above, first left then right, to the top.

Stoatally Different 12m E1 5b. Stephen Reid, James Kinnaird. 30 Aug 2010.
On the right side of the buttress is a vertical crack with a left-slanting crack to its left. Gain and climb the vertical crack.

Upper Foresters':
A similar sized buttress which lies high up on the far left of the climbable rock, some 200m above the lower buttress. Though only short, the climbs are on superb clean granite and are worth doing. It can be reached quite quickly by following goat tracks well to the left of the corrie.

Galloway Chainsaw Massacre 12m HVS 5a *. Stephen Reid, James Kinnaird. 27 Aug 2010.
Fine thought-provoking climbing up the left-hand crack-line on the main wall, with an airy step left to top out. Watch out for the superb hidden wire just when you most need it. At the lower end of the grade.

Harvester 12m HVS 5a *. James Kinnaird, Stephen Reid. 27 Aug 2010.
The crack-line 2m to the right is hard to start but soon eases off.

The Woodlanders 14m VS 5a *. Stephen Reid, James Kinnaird. 27 Aug 2010.
Another crack-line lies 2m right. Make a hard start up this to gain a slim ledge. Move up and rightwards to a sloping gangway and go left up this, then follow

jugs up the wall to the top.

Strip the Conifer   15m   E1 5b *. James Kinnaird, Stephen Reid. 27 Aug 2010.
Yet another crack-line 2m right leads to a shallow scoop. Start just left of this and
climb the wall, making desperate moves up left to gain decent footholds. Climb
the cracked pillar, exiting rightwards to a sloping gangway and step right again
to finish up a wall on good holds.

Shiver Me Timbers   15m   HVS 5a *. Stephen Reid, James Kinnaird. 27 Aug
2010.
On the right side of the main wall is a large scoop system with twin exits. Climb
a short steep wall to heather, then climb the left side of the scoop to gain a
shallow groove, stepping left at its top. Move up and step right to gain easier
ground.

The Tiers:

The Covenanters   35m   HVS 5a *. Stephen Reid, James Kinnaird. 16 Sep 2010.
An enjoyable and well protected route up the slab and cracked headwall up to the
left of the white slab. Climb a rib to reach the base of the slab. Step onto the slab
from the left and reach a left-slanting diagonal crack. Follow this until it is to
where it bends left and climb straight up to the crack splitting the headwall which
is followed to the top.

Above this route is a short wall that is easily climbed via cracks (Difficult) and a
short way above this a wall with an obvious left-slanting groove in it.

Wee Beastie   20m   HVS 5b. James Kinnaird, Stephen Reid. 16 Sep 2010.
A short wall leads to a terrace. Struggle up the left-slanting groove in the buttress
above.

Where the Eagle Soars   45m   VS. Stephen Reid, James Kinnaird. 16 Aug 2010.
Start above the first short wall of *Tiers before Bedtime* and 6m left of the small
perched boulder.
1. 35m 4c Climb up the right side of a large detached block and then a short wall
to a terrace. Continue up the obvious left-facing corner above, which is not
without interest. The wall just left of the corner has also been climbed.
2. 15m 4b On the left side of the headwall is a thin crack, just left of the steps of
Tiers before Bedtime. Climb this direct.

Divine Interference   45m   VS. Stephen Reid, James Kinnaird. 16 Sep 2010.
Start 20m down and right of the huge boulder at a crack with flakes at the left end
of a clean rough barrel shaped wall.
1. 12m 4c Gain the flakes from the left and pull up onto a slab which is climbed
with interest to a huge thread on the left.
2. 18m 4b Step onto the boulder and traverse right over grass to the leftmost of
three cracks. Climb this, and a short wall just left of a grassy groove, to below a
cracked arete.
3. 15m 4c Climb the arete to a ledge and pull over a bulge to gain the final crack,
which is the left side of a huge flake.

DUNGEON HILL, Dungeon of Buchan, Dungeon Buttress:

Dauntless Heart 35m E1. Stephen Venables, Stephen Reid. 14 Jul 2011.
An unbalanced eliminate.
1. 20m 5b Climb the awkward dirty cracks between *Battle Axe* and *Carrick Corner* to a junction with the former. Move up left to a ledge and belay at a large balanced block at its left end.
2. 15m 4a The delightful pink wall above the spike leads straight to the top.

CRAIGNAW, The Point of the Snibe, The Seven Pillars:

Goatee 10m Very Difficult. Stephen Reid, James Kinnaird. 21 Apr 2011.
Follow the rightmost crack in the sixth pillar to a ledge, then the easy angled broken groove.

Wisdom Wall:

The Young Pretender 12m HVS 5b. James Kinnaird, Stephen Reid. 21 Apr 2011.
5m right of *Long Tall Sally* are twin horizontal cracks. Finger traverse the upper one leftwards with difficulty to gain a ledge, pull up and traverse back right on heather to a finger flake that splits the upper buttress – finish up this.

CAIRNSMORE OF FLEET, Clints of the Spout:

Mulled Wine 100m III,3 *. Linda Biggar, John Biggar, C.Hossack. 23 Dec 2010.
A parallel line of less continuous ice smears about 20m right of *Smear Test*. The top ice-fall is quite well hidden and gives a very fine pitch. Scramble up and right from the start of *Smear Test* to start.

RHINNS OF KELLS, Milldown:

Fridge Magnate 125m III. Andrew Fraser, Ian Magill. 11 Jan 2011.
This climbs the buttress right of the lower section of *Better Gully*, then continues to climb the crag high on the right side of the gully. At the bottom of the right side of this buttress is a steep, wide wall which slopes up left. Start at the left end of this and follow a shallow gully over steps (45m). Above, take the central of three grooves to easier ground then continue slightly rightwards for 15m to climb an icefall (50m). A walk of 80m up leftwards leads to the upper tier. This is climbed by following the iciest ramp (bounded by a steep left wall and in the middle of the crag), finishing to the right (30m).

THE BORDERS, Moffat:

Note: An ascent of *Spoon Burn*, as marked on the OS map in Moffat Dale, by Jim Lawrence, Simon Mortlock & Jonathan Mortlock on 27 Dec 2010. Start from the road just beyond Backhope and before Carrifan on the north side of the valley from approx NT 154 105. It provided an interesting gorge with the stream bed frozen well enough to walk on from the road apart from a few weak spots. A series of pitches up to 5m and then a larger 6m pitch with water flowing behind. Grade I/II.

STIRLING AREA, Cambusbarron, Fourth Quarry:

Sticky Willows 20m E2 5c. Keith Alexander, Mark Atkins. 17 Jul 2011.

Left of *The Rock of Crack* and *Confessions of a Speed Freak*, is a short offwidth leading to a striking left-arching crack, which finishes at a slabby ledge on the left. Cut left, then back right across easy but loose terrain to finish. Low in the grade and well protected, but on spooky rock, and with a pretty awkward crux.

North Third, Birds & Bees Buttress:
Rockhopper Rib 20m E3 5c *. Keith Alexander, Mark Atkins. 22 Jul 2011.
The rib immediately left of the corner of *Beeline*. Climb the shallow, slightly flaring crack, stepping round the right-hand corner to a thin ledge about halfway before pulling back left to continue up the rib, finishing to the left at the top.

FIFE, The Hawcraig:
Short Circuit 25m VS 4c/5a **. Charlie Mackie, Sarah Kelly, Charlie Seviour, Kirsty Rowe. Oct 2010.
In between *Saki* and *Slack Alice*. Start up *Saki* for 5m. Then head out right to the arete. The crux is safe moving from the slot on the arete to getting established up into the vertical finger crack. Continue up the crack to the top rejoining the left side of the arete higher up.

Popeye 20m E1 5a *. Sonya Drummond, Melanie Hayes. 21 Aug 2010.
This is between *Brutus* and *Torment*. Climb the corner underneath the roof, then pull through the roof itself and onto a technical slab on the left. Boldly climb the headwall above to the top.

Limekilns:
Scary Doodle 12m E5 6b. Charlie Mackie. 5 Jun 2011.
A line between *The Charleston* and *The Ivy League*. Start about 4m right of the left arete. Make a hard move to a T-shaped slot. Move right along a hand ledge before moving straight up, just left of the pod on *The Ivy League*. Make crux moves through some crimps on the face till the good break at two-thirds height. Follow another hand ramp up and left to the top break, before finishing just right of the arete at the top and as for *The Charleston* for the last 2m.

EDINBURGH AREA, Salisbury Crags:
Cat Nick Arete 30m V,4. Harry Holmes, John Proctor. 29 Nov 2010.
As for the summer route.

Blackford Quarry:
Good Craic 11m Severe 4c. Peter McAuley, Louise Kernaghan. 28 Apr 2011.
An east facing crack on the back of the quarry pinnacle. A small path leads around the back of the pinnacle where two cracks join to form a main right-slanting hand crack. Start up the right-hand side crack (or the left-hand side crack for an easier variation). The insides of the cracks are a little too smooth for even the best of cam placements.

FASTCASTLE AREA, Midden Craig:
Think Twice 10m HVS 4b. Ross Jones, John Sanders. 11 Sep 2010.
Just south of the main crag is a fin of rock which forms a corner, almost a chimney. Climb the large corner on poor rock.

MISCELLANEOUS NOTES

THE W.H. MURRAY LITERARY PRIZE

As a tribute to the late Bill Murray, whose mountain and environment writings have been an inspiration to many a budding mountaineer, the SMC have set up a modest writing prize, to be run through the pages of the Journal. The basic rules are set out below, and will be reprinted each year. The prize is run with a deadline of the end of April each year. So, assuming you are reading this in October, you have six months before next year's deadline in which to set pencil, pen or word processor on fire.

The Rules:

1. There shall be a competition for the best entry on Scottish Mountaineering published in the *Scottish Mountaineering Club Journal*. The competition shall be called the 'W.H. Murray Literary Prize', hereafter called the 'Prize'.

2. The judging panel shall consist of, in the first instance, the following: The current Editor of the *SMC Journal*; The current President of the SMC; and two or three lay members, who may be drawn from the membership of the SMC. The lay members of the panel will sit for three years after which they will be replaced.

3. If, in the view of the panel, there is in any year no entry suitable for the Prize, then there shall be no award that year.

4. Entries shall be writing on the general theme of 'Scottish Mountaineering', and may be prose articles of up to approximately 5000 words in length, or shorter verse. Entries may be fictional.

5. Panel members may not enter for the competition during the period of their membership.

6. Entries must be of original, previously unpublished material. Entries should be submitted to the Editor of the *SMC Journal* before the end of April for consideration that year. Contributions should preferably be word-processed and submitted via e-mail, although double-spaced typewritten hard copies will also be accepted. (See Office Bearers page at end of this Journal for address etc.) Any contributor to the SMC Journal is entitled to exclude their material from consideration for the Prize and should so notify the Editor of this wish in advance.

7. The prize will be a cheque for the amount £250.

8. Contributors may make different submissions in different years.

9. The decision of the panel is final.

10. Any winning entry will be announced in the *SMC Journal,* and will be published in the *SMC Journal* and on the SMC Web Site. Thereafter, authors retain copyright.

THE W.H. MURRAY LITERARY PRIZE 2011

The only guidance given to the judges is that the Prize should be awarded for the best article submitted on the general theme of 'Scottish Mountaineering'. This has been interpreted very loosely in the past and the award has been given for articles about climbing abroad by climbers based in Scotland. There is no firm restriction on length, although a maximum of 5,000 words is suggested. Entries may be fact or fiction, prose or verse. Although the remit appears to be very flexible there was much discussion among the judges this year about whether some of the submissions qualified as 'mountaineering'. However, the judges had no difficulty identifying half a dozen articles which stood out from the rest. In the end it was the quality of the writing that was given the most weight even though in some cases the mountaineering connection is rather tenuous. This still left some difficulty in identifying an outright winner. It was eventually decided to make a joint award for the first time. The award this year is shared between Paddy Buckley (*Strange Happenings at Ben Alder Cottage*) and Robert Richardson (*Night in the Big Bedroom*). Congratulations to them both.

The article about Ben Alder Cottage was described as 'a fascinating historical piece' and 'beautifully presented and sympathetically researched'. It reads very easily and holds the attention. Despite the brevity of the article about bivvying out on Ben Nevis it was judged an outstanding contribution – 'well-written, evocative and alluring' – with a great title. There is a lesson here for future contributors. More does not necessarily mean better.

There were an encouraging number of first time contributors this year. Peter Macpherson's account of his ascent of *Stone Temple Pilots* with Guy Robertson made a big impression and ran the winners close. The intense drama of this momentous first ascent is well described. The brief references to family at home highlight very effectively the inherent conflict between family life and the selfish pull of climbing. One solution of course is to climb with your family, and the submission from Peter Biggar is an extremely worthy piece about climbing with his son. *Following in Father's Footsteps* is described as 'warm, evocative, knowing without ego,' and 'though perhaps a little long, holds together well'.

Another fairly short piece, *Cheating the Reaper* by John Burns, was very well regarded. It has 'lots of smart writing and a satisfactory, sustained approach to its climax'. It wasn't clear if this account was fact or fiction, but there was no mistaking the quality of the writing. The story of the early explorations at Carnmore over fifty years ago is extremely well told by Dave Atkinson. This fascinating piece has some similarities with the Ben Alder article, and describes how one of the key figures from all those years ago was tracked down and interviewed. *Mike O'Hara and the Dragon of Carnmore* is 'a fine historical view of the early adventures on a major crag. A very well-written last page with a gracious conclusion.' *Adventures on Creag Mhòr* and *Naranjo de Bulnes* were both commended by the judges. *The Memory of What Has Been* was also regarded as very noteworthy though it would have benefited from being shorter.

All in all a good standard of submissions. Many thanks to all the contributors. As usual, the winning entries can be downloaded from the club website.

And finally – the judges were amused to note that two separate contributors had fallen foul of the spellchecker and encountered *waste-deep* ground cover.

SCOTTISH WINTER NOTES 2010–11

The 2011 season was a long one, starting early and continuing consistently cold from mid October to late March. There some were superb settled periods during December and January, although conditions were a little more challenging through February and March. Late season classic ice conditions never really materialised, but even so, the 2011 winter was one of the best in recent decades.

What is particularly striking is the high standard of the new routes. In previous seasons the average first ascent would be about Grade IV, but this winter the majority of new routes were V or over. Of note was the number of on sight Grade IX first ascents. Previously, only one Grade IX first ascent had ever been on sighted, (*Defenders of the Faith* (IX,9) on Beinn an Socach by Dave MacLeod and Fiona Murray in 2006), but in 2011 there were nine!

It is difficult to single out specific performances, but Greg Boswell's magnificent run of routes, including the first ascent of *To Those Who Wait* (IX,9), stands out. Guy Robertson had a scintillating season with no less than five new IXs – his finest ascent was undoubtedly *Stone Temple Pilots* (X,9) on The Shelter Stone climbed with Pete Macpherson. Martin Moran also had an exceptional start to the season with three new Grade VIIIs and a Grade IX together with the coveted second ascent of *The God Delusion* on Beinn Bhan.

There were some remarkable repeats such as Andy Turner's forceful ascent of *The Hurting* and the second ascent of the legendary *Extasy* on Creag Meagaidh, together with the development of new crags such as Eilde Canyon in Glen Coe and Creagan Coire Cha-no on Cairngorm. Andy Nisbet continued to range far and wide across the Highlands, amassing dozens of quality new Grade V and VIs.

But rather than specific routes, it was the sheer number of winter climbers operating at a high level that really set this season apart. Routes like *Sioux Wall* on the Ben, have opened the door to Grade VIII for dozens of climbers, and this touchstone grade is now a realistic objective for many. Success breeds success, there was a spirit of constructive competition in the air and everyone took clear encouragement from each other's achievements. Scottish winter climbing has been shining brightly for several years now, and there is no question that the passion and intensity now burns as fiercely as ever.

To Those Who Wait (IX,9)

Ever since the first modern mixed climbs were added to Ben Nevis 15 years ago, the impending crack-line on the right wall of Number Three Gully has been stared at by hundreds of winter climbers as a futuristic objective. It had seen at least one serious attempt, but most have been deterred by its unremitting steepness. Enter nineteen-year old Greg Boswell and twenty-year old Will Sim. Boswell is a relative newcomer to the Scottish winter scene, and made headlines last season with second ascents of *Ship of Fools* (VIII,7) and *Pic'n Mix* (IX,9). Alongside these achievements, Boswell has amassed a career's worth of classic VIIs and VIIIs, many climbed on consecutive days. Will Sim's pedigree is more mountaineering-based with a string of major alpine classics climbed in fast times such as the second ascent of the East Face Route on Cerro Piergiogio in Patagonia.

On 31 December, the pair headed up Number Three Gully to take a look at the crack-line. It was a typically dreich Scottish winter day – the crags were black and dripping wet after the post-Christmas thaw and conditions looked hopeless. The forecast predicted a slow cooling through the day and they had chosen their venue wisely because not only is the Number Three Gully area one of the highest venues in the country, but when winds start funnelling up from Coire na Ciste it hoars up remarkably quickly. 'The rock was riming up before our eyes... it was swiftly getting whiter and whiter,' Greg wrote in his blog. After two hours of patient waiting below the crack, the cliff was transformed with a thin layer of white frost. Sim led the awkward entry pitch, and then Boswell set off up the meat of the route – the impending crack-line. Greg's account of his lead on his blog, and his tussle with a delicately poised television-sized block makes for palm-wetting reading, but eventually he pulled on to the plateau after a remarkable on sight lead. *To Those Who Wait* was graded IX,9 and was particularly noteworthy because it was climbed by such a young team.

Boswell's lead has parallels with Tom Patey's first ascent of Douglas-Gibson Gully on Lochnagar – Scotland's first Grade V gully – at a similar age of nineteen. Throw in Boswell's early repeat of *The Duel* (IX,9) on Stob Coire nan Lochan with Steve Lynch, and his first on sight ascent of the legendary *Happy Tyroleans* (IX,10) in January on Coire an Lochain with Mike Tweedley, and we may have an upcoming talent comparable to the great Robin Smith.

Stone Temple Pilots (X,9)

Guy Robertson and Pete Macpherson pulled off a major coup on 28 January when they climbed a new direct line up the front edge of the Shelter Stone. Their new route, called *Stone Temple Pilots* (named after a '90s rock band), links the first three pitches of *Steeple* with the crux pitch of *Haystack*, followed by a new pitch into *Citadel* and a finish up *Spire*.

'For me, the Shelter Stone is in some ways Scotland's ultimate winter cliff,' Guy told me. 'It's rarely in good wintry condition, it's remote, the routes are very long and arduous, and the climbing is just utterly fantastic, getting progressively harder and more out there the higher up one gets! To climb a directtissima up the front edge has been a long-standing dream for me, and I was very lucky to have Pete on the other end of the rope.'

The pair left the car at 02.30 a.m. and started up the lower Steeple corners at 05.20 a.m,, climbing the first big pitch in the dark and the next two as dawn broke. They then continued up through the crux 5c pitch of Haystack.

'Pete dispatched this very smoothly despite a slip at the start of the difficulties (rather than lower down he just hopped straight back on),' Guy explained. 'We split this pitch (Pete had downloaded all his kit) and then we stepped left before the end of the ramp onto a commodious ledge and belay. We didn't have a guidebook and couldn't remember where Haystack went, and with the clock ticking it all began to get rather exciting! With no choice but to forge on, Pete opened a new hard pitch straight up then slightly left, eventually joining Citadel where this goes right to below the headwall.

Then it was my big lead. Despite cramping biceps and only a couple of hours light left, I managed to drag myself up the penultimate pitch of Spire before Pete dispatched the last 5b crack of Steeple – just in time for the darkness to envelope us.'

The pair graded Stone Temple Pilots X,9, making it the most difficult Scottish new winter route ever climbed on sight, although later Guy commented:

'Whatever the grade, it's kind of irrelevant. The Stone has some of the most inspiring and challenging winter climbing this great country has to offer. For a well-balanced and keen team there's probably nothing anywhere else to compare!'

Ben Nevis

The first major new route of the season was *Apache* (VIII,9), climbed on 13 November by Steve Ashworth and Paddy Cave. The pair were part of a four-man Lakes based team who spent three days staying at the CIC Hut and Ashworth had his sights firmly set on the impressive barrel shaped headwall to the right of Sioux Wall on Number Three Gully Buttress. 'I'd been looking at this line for a long time,' Steve told me. 'From Creag Coire na Ciste, it's on the immediate skyline and in profile it looks amazing.'

The weather that day was not ideal for high standard winter climbing with a strong wind blowing huge amount of spindrift, and all but the steepest routes were buried under deep powder. Ashworth led the first pitch up the steep arête to the left of Thompson's Route and then handed the lead over to Cave for the crucial second pitch up the gently overhanging barrel-shaped wall. 'Paddy had to climb a steep blank section for a few metres to reach a crack,' Steve explained. 'Fortunately, the crack had good hooks, and it turned out to be one of those brilliant pitches that looks harder than it actually is!' The third pitch climbed the continuing crack-line and then pulled through a triangular recess, to reach the top of the buttress.

The following weekend, the spotlight fell once again on Ben Nevis when Pete Davies and Tim Marsh made the first ascent of *Catriona* (VIII,8) on Creag Coire na Ciste. This spectacular and unlikely-looking line follows the left arête of the corner taken by the modern test-piece *Cornucopia*. Davies had made an ascent of Cornucopia the previous weekend (when Ashworth and Cave were climbing Apache) and he had spotted the line. He returned with long-standing partner Marsh, and after starting up the entry slab of Cornucopia, Davies than made a four-hour on sight lead of the arête. Marsh then completed the route, by finishing up the steep vegetated corner to the right of The Secret.

The mixed routes on the Ben saw a lot of traffic in December with multiple ascents of Tower Face of the Comb, Darth Vader, Strident Edge, Slab Route, Cutlass and Gargoyle Wall. Babylon and Sioux Wall were especially popular and had close to a dozen ascents apiece with *Sioux Wall* now established as the most climbed Grade VIII in Scotland. Nick Bullock was active on the front face of The Douglas Boulder, making the first winter ascent of *Nutless* (VI,7) and adding *Rutless* (VII,8), a new direct finish to *Gutless*, with Matt Helliker. Bullock also teamed up with Pete Benson to climb *Feckless* (VI,7), the thinly iced shallow groove right of Gutless.

Later in the season, Iain Small and I climbed the crest of Pinnacle Buttress of the Tower taking a line between Face Dancer and Stringfellow. *Goodfellas* (VII,8) proved to be an excellent expedition with a spectacular hanging groove on the very front face of the buttress. We also made the first ascent of *Brave New World* (IX,8) on the North Wall of Carn Dearg. The highlight of this sustained four-pitch route was the final headwall, which overhangs at the top with no obvious line of cracks, and Iain's on sight lead was the epitome of adventurous Scottish winter climbing. Nearby, Nick Bullock and Rich Cross made the second ascent of *The Great Corner* (VIII,8), the huge feature on the right flank of Raeburn's Buttress, adding a new three-pitch start to the left. Bullock was full of praise for the route, saying after that he 'enjoyed it more than The Needle... brilliant!' Bullock later teamed up with Andy Turner and Bruce Poll to add *The Pretender* (VII,9), a very steep two-pitch crack on the buttress right of *The Great Chimney*.

On Creag Coire na Ciste, Small and Tony Stone linked the cracks and grooves between *Stormtrooper* and *Archangel* to give *Angels with Dirty Faces* (VIII,8), whilst Malcolm Bass, Simon Yearsley and Jim Higgins made the first ascent of *Free Range* (VII,8), which is based on the summer VS *Chicken Run* on Number Five Gully Buttress. Across on the Little Brenva Face, Ewan Lyons and Ewan Olivarius added *Right Major* (IV,6), a new six pitch-long direct start to *Route Major*. Ben Nevis also saw some important repeats. Mike Tweedley and Greg Boswell made the second ascent of *Apache* (VIII,9), and Tim Neill and Keith Ball repeated *Stormtrooper* (VIII,8) and *Archangel* (VII,7).

Later in March, Iain Small and I climbed *Rogue's Rib Direct* (VII,7). This was the first time the 200m-high buttress to the left of *Italian Climb* has been climbed in its entirety in winter. Previous ascents began at two-thirds height after starting up Italian Climb. Across on Creag Meagaidh, Pete Davies, Donnie O'Sullivan and Mike Gardner made a superb addition to the Post Face. *Special Delivery* (VI,6) takes the prominent hanging icefall above Staghorn Gully, approximately 50m to the right of last year's new addition *Postal Strike*.

Glen Coe

Big news from Glen Coe was the first winter ascent of *Satyr* by Donald King and Andy Nelson. King first attempted the route (graded E1 5a in summer) with Mike Pescod in late November. He returned with Nelson on 30 November who climbed the serious first pitch (thought to be worth IX,8 as a stand-alone lead) before finishing up Central Buttress. The pair returned on 5 December, and climbed Central Grooves to reach their high point, and then continued up Satyr for two more ropelengths to the top. The second pitch proved to be another demanding technical lead. King and Nelson returned once again two days later and re-climbed the entire route to record the first winter ascent. *Satyr* was graded IX,9 and ranks alongside *The Duel* as one of the most difficult winter routes in Glen Coe.

Jonathan Preston and John Lyall visited No. 2 Gully Buttress on the West Face of Aonach Dubh and made the first ascent of *The Wonderful Wizard* (V,6). This lies at the right end of the crag and follows a series of cracks, chimneys and grooves. Despite No. 2 Gully Buttress being given an altitude of 520m in the Glen Coe guide, it is higher than this and is quite recessed, so collects snow well. Lyall returned with Andy Nisbet and Sandy Allan three days later and added a new climb approximating to the summer line of *Rose Late* (IV,6). The following day the trio returned to make the first winter ascent of *Oz* (VII,7). This turned out to be a far tougher affair, with Nisbet leading the crucial first pitch. Across in Ardgour on Garbh Bheinn, Roger Webb and I added *Contortion* (VII,7), which climbs the steep front face of the Upper Pinnacle via a series of chimneys, cracks and grooves.

Skye

The Cuillin saw a high level of activity early in the season. On Bealach Buttress on Sgùrr Mhic Choinnich, Guy Robertson and Greg Boswell made the first winter ascent of *Black Cleft* (VI,7) and Mike Lates and Francis Blunt had an exciting time following their noses up *Happy Go Lucky Route* (VII,7), after an attempt on Lost Arrow was thwarted due to lack of ice. The following day the same pair made the second ascent of the magnificent *Storvegan* (VI,8) on The Storr, and Blunt then teamed up with Pete Macpherson and Martin Moran to made the first winter ascent of *Shadbolt's Chimney* (VII,7) on the Basteir Tooth on Skye. This 50m-high fierce slit on the north face of the Tooth, was first climbed by Shadbolt and MacLaren in 1906. The contorted chimney climbing prompted Macpherson to say afterwards that this was 'the weirdest route I have ever climbed'.

Several teams visited Coire Scamadal, last year's new ice venue. Conditions were not as good as last season, although Doug Hawthorn and Ewen Todd added *Greymane Wall* (V,4), the steep ice and mixed ground left of Silverpine. Arguably the most notable achievement on Skye however, was a full traverse of the Cuillin Ridge by Ben O'Connor Croft and Neil Mackay at the end of November. This was an outstanding piece of mountaineering and quite possibly the earliest in the season that the Ridge has ever been traversed. Most teams wait until February or March to take advantage of more daylight and consolidated snow.

Northern Cairngorms

Early in November, Martin Moran and Pete Macpherson climbed the crack system cutting the imposing left wall of the classic V,6 mixed corner of *Belhaven* on Fiacaill Buttress in Coire an t-Sneachda. Moran led the awkward entry pitch and then Macpherson continued up the thin crack cutting through the steep blank wall above. This turned out to be very sustained and the crack was full of ice and frozen dirt making it difficult to protect. Unfortunately Macpherson had to take a rest just one move below easy ground at the top of the pitch.

Moran then led the final steep crack up the final wall, which fortunately was better protected. 'The crux wall is very steep and intimidating,' Pete told me. 'I wasn't sure if it would go or not and struggled from the first move to clear the cracks and place a small wire. Halfway up the wall there is a small narrow ledge, which is good for feet, but you are still hanging on arms. Other than that the holds for the feet are about the size of match sticks! I had to fight to get a cam in an icy crack on the final moves and that finished off my arms so I had to take a rest.' *Omerta* (the unsaid Mafia law of silence and secrecy) was graded VIII,9 and takes its place alongside the likes of *Daddy Longlegs* (VIII,9) and *Demon Direct* (IX,9) as one of the more challenging test-pieces of the Northern Corries.

Later in February, Guy Robertson visited Coire an Lochain with Pete Macpherson and climbed the obvious counter-diagonal to *Pic 'n Mix*, which takes the front face of the steep tower high up Y Gully. Guy had tried the line with Greg Boswell earlier this year, but he was still recovering from flu, so when he reached an impasse he down climbed to save the route for another day. The pair

Guy Robertson on The Gathering (VIII,9).

named their addition *The Gathering* (VIII,9) because they shared the belay with Pete Harrison, Simon Frost and Dave Garry who made the third ascent of Pic'n Mix (IX,9). 'We shared a laugh,' Guy explained, 'and they made Pic'n Mix look about grade III!'

Andy Nisbet made several visits to Creagan a' Choire Etchachan, which had formed its best ice since 1977. Together with Helen Rennard, he added the fine *Kukri* (V,6) which is based on the vegetated corner and hanging slab right of

Photo: Pete Macpherson.

Delicatessen. But the finest discovery was *Gaddzooks* (VI,6), a line of icy grooves to the left of *Avalanche Gully* with Rennard and John Lyall. This icy groove is based on the original summer line of Avalanche Gully (which sports a huge overhang that ices in winter). Rennard led the long crux pitch, passing two substantial steel pegs left from the original summer ascent by Mr. and Mrs. Gadd in 1955, prompting Lyall to come up with the name – 'Gaddzooks! The Gadd pegs are still here!'

Southern Cairngorms

Towards the end of the late December freeze, there was a remarkable addition to Creag an Dubh Loch when Gordon Lennox, Tony Stone and Iain Small made the first winter ascent of *Culloden* on the awe-inspiring Broad Terrace Wall. Their achievement was so understated that it almost passed under the radar screen. This summer E2, which overhangs for much of its 125m-length had been a winter objective for Lennox for a number of years. Small led the 5a summer entry pitch, before Lennox battled with the 5c summer crux. Finally, Stone led the steep finishing cracks to a delicate and serious finish, just reaching the plateau rim as darkness fell. The trio graded their on sight ascent IX,9, and many other steep crack-lines across the country must now be considered potential winter targets.

The big event on Lochnagar was the first winter ascent of *Crazy Sorrow* on the Tough-Brown Face of Lochnagar by Guy Robertson and Pete Benson. This rarely climbed summer route is graded E4 6a and the crux second pitch involves pulling over a big roof. It was first climbed in winter, after summer pre-inspection, by Alan Mullin and Steve Lynch in 2002. Unfortunately Mullin decided to abseil off without climbing the third pitch which leads to easier ground on Tough-Brown Ridge, so as a result, *Frozen Sorrow* as Mullin called his 'route', was considered to be unfinished and therefore classified as an attempt.

When Benson started up the first pitch the weather was wild, but as he belayed under the crux roof of the second pitch the wind relented and the skies cleared. 'I had to give it everything to get over the roof,' Guy told me. 'But the protection was good so I decided there was nothing to lose by giving it a go.' The decision to classify the route as an attempt in the Cairngorms guide appears to be correct, as Benson then had to lead another demanding technical 8 pitch to reach easy ground and the crest of Tough-Brown Ridge. The pair graded the route IX,10 and Guy said afterwards that the moves around the roof was one of the most testing technical sequence he has ever made.

Across on the Eagle Buttress headwall, Sandy Simpson and I climbed *Eagle-Eye* (VII,6) to the left of *Where Eagles Dare*, and Iain Small and I added the thinly iced *Smear Fear* (VII,7) to the right of *State of Independence*. Nearby, Helen Rennard and I had a good find with *Chasing Shadows* (VI,7), an icy mixed line that lies deep in Shadow Couloir and climbs the left wall of Polyphemus Gully. Later in the season, Henning Wackerhage, Robbie Miller and Andrew Melvin added the challenging *More Vertigo Finish* (VII,7) to Vertigo wall on Creag an Dubh Loch.

Away from the hotbed of action on Lochnagar and Dubh Loch, new route activity continued at a more reasonable pace with Andy Nisbet leading the charge with over 15 new routes. Highlights included three routes on Eagle Rocks, such as the first winter ascent of *Flankers Route* (IV,5) with Duncan Tunstall, and four new additions to Glen Esk. The best discovery here was *Gro'lryc Gully* (V,5), which takes a line up the centre of Bruntwood Crag, and was again climbed with Tunstall.

On Beinn a' Bhùird, Roger Webb and I climbed the prominent groove to the right of *Tearaway* in the lower section of Glaucous Buttress to gain the steep groove in the headwall above. *Crystal* (VI,7) was named in memory of Chris Dale who had tragically died a few days before. Chris was one of the quiet men of Scottish mountaineering with a string of outstanding first ascents across the Highlands and the Alps. He was a prodigious talent with routes such as The *Argonaut* (VII,8) on Lochnagar, climbed way back in 1984, to his credit. He will be missed.

Southern Highlands

In December, Guy Robertson and Greg Boswell's made the first winter ascent of *Mammoth* (IX,9) on The Brack. Intrigued by its winter potential, Robertson had climbed Mammoth, a rarely climbed E3, the previous summer. 'On the third pitch I noted that although the summer line would be hopeless in winter (it's a parallel-sided hand-to-fist crack, and the only good clean pitch on the route) about five metres left was an amazing-looking overhanging crack quite literally festooned with turf,' Guy told me. 'I couldn't see where it went in relation to the final pitch of the summer route, but it looked enticing enough to draw me back when the opportunity arose.'

When Robertson returned with Boswell on 7 December they were unsure whether they would be able to climb the route because of its obvious difficulty, and uncertainty around the crack on the third pitch. 'We were totally stoked to nail it on-sight,' Guy explained. 'We led through with me leading the first pitch. I took a fall a couple of feet off the deck, then dispatched it, with Greg leading the summer crux and myself the unknown crack on pitch three. On pitch four the turfy crack continued rightwards to join the summer line about ten metres or so below the top. All in all it gave us three pitches of 9, the middle two very sustained and strenuous, and a final pitch of 7, again very sustained. Despite failsafe protection all the way, we've settled on a grade of soft IX,9. Whatever the grade, it's probably the best short, hard, accessible and well-protected route I've climbed in Scotland – an absolute stunner!'

Robertson and Boswell's ascent of Mammoth prompted several more visits to The Brack. Pete Macpherson and Pete Benson added a new VII,9 finish to *Great Central Groove*, and on the impressive wall to the right, Graham Stein and Andy Lole made an early repeat of *Resolution* (VI,7). Nearby on Beinn an Lochain, Iain Small and I climbed *Riding the Storm* (VII,7), the steep crack-line cutting the steep front face of the Heart of Darkness buttress on the north-east ridge.

The Bridge of Orchy cliffs were popular. Many teams climbed the classics on Beinn an Dothaidh such as Pas de Deux and Menage a Trois, and in December the freezing level was low enough for Creag an Socach to come into good condition. There were many ascents of *Messiah* (probably the season's most popular Grade VII), and Dan Moore and Shauna Clarke made an early repeat of *The Prophet* (VI,7). Nearby on Beinn Udhlaidh, Greg Boswell and Neil Carnegie made a difficult new addition with *The Crooked Smile* (VII,7), which takes the hanging ice smear to the left of *The Smirk*. A little to the west on Beinn Eunaich, Roger Everett and I climbed the prominent Grade V,5 fault-line to the left of *The Black Shoot*.

Northern Highlands

The finest achievement in the North-West was the first ascent of *Godzilla* on the Giant's Wall on Beinn Bhan by Pete Benson, Nick Bullock and Guy Robertson. This new IX,8 takes a direct line into the upper two pitches of *The Godfather.*

Martin Moran on King of The Swingers (VIII,10), Beinn Eighe.
Photo: Pete Macpherson.

'It's a super-direct, true winter-only line with awesome turf-dependent climbing and a really spectacular feel – the stuff of dreams,' Guy Robertson said afterwards.

In December Moran teamed up with Murdo Jamieson and Francis Blunt to make the first winter ascent of *Feast of The East* (VIII,9), a summer E1 5c on the Eastern Ramparts of Beinn Eighe. A few days later he roped up with Jamieson again, to climb *The Wailing Wall* (IX,9) on the awe-inspiring left side of Haystack Gully. Moran returned to Beinn Eighe with Pete Macpherson to make the first winter ascent of *King of the Swingers* (VIII,10). Unfortunately, Macpherson took a small fall before the crux traverse of this summer E3 6b therefore losing the on sight. He was also forced to take a rest higher up the pitch, but the resulting climb is one of the most spectacular on the mountain and the first route to be rated technical 10 in the Northern Highlands. The same pair also added a fine VII,8 up the big left-facing corner which is on the left side of the prominent recess on Druim Shionnach in Glen Shiel.

In the far north on Stac Pollaidh, Roger Webb and James Edwards added *Enigma Variations* (VII,8), a good mixed route based on the summer HVS *Enigma*, and on the West Face of Quinag, Andy Nisbet and Jonathan Preston climbed the gullies either side of Rickety Ridge resulting in *Rickets* (V,6) and *Ramshackle Gully* (IV,4). Further south, Nisbet and Preston teamed up with John Lyall to climb *Woundwort* (V,6) on Sgòrr Ruadh, to the right of the Central Couloir, and in Glen Shiel, Nisbet added *Lemon Groove* (V,6) and *Macavity* (V,6) either side of the big cave on Druim Shionnach. Finally, Rich Cross and Jon Bracey made the third ascent of *The Godfather* (VIII,8) on Beinn Bhan.

Roger Webb and I made the long walk in to Slioch and came away with *Katabasis* (VI,6), which climbs grooves near the left edge, and on Sgorr Ruadh, Nisbet and Dave Bell added *Crimson Buttress* (VI,7), which takes the rib right of Brown Gully. Finally, Roger Webb and I made the six-hour approach to the north side of Mullach Coire Mhic Fearchair, one of Scotland's remotest Munros, and climbed the prominent central corner cutting through the cliff. *Slaying the Ghost* (VI,6) was a little easier than it looked from below and like all the best routes it sprung a welcome surprise – from halfway up a hidden ribbon of ice led all they way to the top.

Repeats

Martin Moran and Pete Macpherson had an excellent start to the season with the fifth ascent of *The Secret* on Ben Nevis (VIII,9) before making the second ascent of *The God Delusion* (IX,9) on Beinn Bhan. This touchstone route was first climbed by Guy Robertson and Pete Benson in December 2008 and is widely regarded as the hardest route in the Northern Highlands. Moran and Macpherson used snowshoes for the approach and were full of praise for the first ascensionists after climbing the route in a 21-hour push.

Big news from late January was the second ascent of *The Hurting* (XI,11) in Coire an t-Sneachda by Andy Turner at the end of January. Turner had attempted the route a few days earlier, but he took a small fall at one-third height so decided to return for a re-match with Phil Dowthwaite. Turner's successful ascent was a gripping battle of hard technical climbing with difficult to protect icy cracks, confirming the route's reputation as one of Scotland's most demanding winter pitches. Turner made the first ground up ascent of *The Hurting*, and the next logical step was to climb it on sight.

This advance was nearly fulfilled remarkably quickly, when 19-year old Greg Boswell made two attempts on the route, falling tantalisingly close to the top. He returned on 18 February with James Dunn to find the route hoared white and a very strong wind hitting the wall. Boswell's gear was poor due to icy cracks, and he reached his previous high point with the wind growing ever stronger. He managed to move quickly past the strenuous moves on smeary foot placements, to arrive on the less steep top section of the headwall.

'After about half an hour trying to figure out where to go,' Greg explained, 'I made the thinnest move I've ever done. I had a Zero cam in an icy crack eight metres below, and the gear below wasn't much better. I felt sick and tired, but falling was definitely not an option. I forged my way up the blind white abyss and reached a good neve ledge. Easy moves led to the top. The pain and Hurting was over...'

At the end of January, well-known German climber Ines Papert visited Scotland with Austrian Charly Fritzer. They warmed up with ascents of *Daddy Longlegs* (VIII,9) and *Ventricle* (VII,8) in Coire an Lochain, before moving to the Ben and making the second ascent of Boswell's *To Those Who Wait* (IX,9). They then teamed up with Dave MacLeod to make the first ascent of *Triple X* (VIII,8), an icy mixed climb based on the summer route *Rolling Stones* on the East Flank of Tower Ridge.

The climax of the trip took place in Coire an Lochain where they both led *Happy Tyroleans* (IX,10) and Fritzer cruised *Demon Direct* (IX,9). The following day the weather was poor, but after climbing *Savage Slit*, the pair spotted an unclimbed line up the steep blocky wall between *Fallout Corner* and *War and Peace*. The result was *Bavarinthia* (IX,9), a superb two-pitch climb up an impressively steep wall. Bavarinthia was an almost unique event in Scottish winter climbing. Very few overseas teams have succeeded in climbing new winter routes in the Scottish mountains – two notable exceptions being Raven's Gully Direct Finish and Happy Tyroleans.

Greg Boswell and Mike Tweedley also made the second ascent of *Omerta* (VIII,9) in Coire an t-Sneachda, (first climbed in November by Martin Moran and Pete Macpherson), and Nick Bullock had a remarkable weekend on The Shelter Stone. He climbed *The Needle* (VIII,8) with Andy Houseman and *Citadel* (VII,8) with Rob Greenwood the following day, and still managed to give a lecture on Saturday night at Glenmore Lodge.

Finally on Creag Meagaidh, Guy Robertson and Pete Benson made the second ascent of *Extasy* (VIII,8) on Creag Meagaidh at the end of February. This landmark route, which takes the awe-inspiring 300m-high wall between *Smith's Gully* and *The Fly*, was first climbed by Dave Hesleden and Bruno Sourzac from France, during 2005 International Winter Meet.

New Venues

On the eastern side of Cairngorm overlooking Strath Nethy, Roger Webb, Iain Small and Sandy Simpson and I explored Creagan Coire Cha-no. Fifteen routes were climbed with pride of place going to *Arch Wall* (VII,7), *Anvil Corner* (VI,6) and *Smooth as Silk* (VII,7). Andy Nisbet also visited the cliff with John Lyall and came away with the first ascent of *Arch Enemy* (V,5). A little later, James Edwards, Roger Webb and I nipped in to make the first ascent of *Daylight Robbery* (V,6) on the right flank of Jenga Buttress. With a 2km approach, this is the most accessible winter cliff in the Cairngorms, and is likely to become popular with teams looking for an alternative to the Northern Corries.

The big event in Glen Coe was the development of a superb new ice venue rivalling the nearby Beinn Udlaidh for the quality and quantity of ice. Eilde Canyon was discovered by Simon Yearsley and Malcolm Bass on their way back from climbing the classic Sròn na Lairig ridge early in the season. The narrow 250m-long canyon now has ten new icefall routes climbed by Yearsley and Bass together with Dan Peach, Neil Silver, Simon Davidson, Tom Broadbent and Neil Carnegie. Pride of place goes to the beautiful ice formation *Zapatista* (V,5 – Bass), the steep *Central Amigo* (V,6 – Yearsley) and the two-tiered *Andale Andale!* (V,5 – Silver/Davidson). Yearsley believes there is room for at least six more routes, so expect the canyon to get busy once it gets cold again!

Finally, Andy Nisbet spent several days of his busy season quietly developing the mixed climbing potential of the Far West Wall on Beinn Eighe with James Edwards, John Lyall, Steve Ashworth and Jonathan Preston. *Chock-a-Block* (V,6), *Westlife* (IV,5), *Chalice* (V,6), *Crackerhead* (V,6), *Raptor* (VI,7) and *Flake City* (V,7) all offer good quartzite mixed climbing similar in quality to the popular routes on the nearby Fuselage Wall.

Simon Richardson

100 YEARS AGO: THE CLUB IN 1911

The 22nd Annual Meeting and Dinner took place on Friday 2 December 1910 in the North British Hotel, Edinburgh, with Gilbert Thomson presiding. Treasurer Nelson announced a balance of £179 2s. 2d., which together with the Life Membership Fund brought the Club's total funds to £477 0s. 2d., a considerable downturn from 1909 – due to unusual Clubroom expenses. Secretary Clark announced 10 new members, the membership thereby increasing to 189. Librarian Russell acknowledged the handsome gift to the new Clubroom of an Electric Lantern and Screen by Dr & Mrs Inglis Clark, and later announced a winter programme of Club Lantern Nights. The Clubroom Rules forbade many things, but promised tea from the caretaker Mrs Gilchrist (including toast, biscuits, butter and jam) for 6d.

The New Year Meet was held at the Loch Awe Hotel with 38 members and 5 guests attending. Early arrivals enjoyed two poor days on the peaks of Cruachan, while an intrepid contingent of young Turks mis-led by the indefatigable Frank Goggs and Arthur Russell, made their way to the Meet by attacking Beinn Bhuidhe from Glen Falloch, and proceeding North to Loch Awe – a gruelling traverse at any time of year. Greetings were received by telegram from the L.S.C.C. (Tyndrum), and from the Dundee Rambling Club (Killin). On New Year's Day, some climbing was achieved on the forgotten crags of Beinn a' Bhùiridh by Goodeve, Ling, Raeburn and Charles Walker.

Bedraggled on Beinn Bhuidhe:
(L to R) Cumming, A White, Goggs, Macalister, Russell, D Menzies, MacRobert.
Photo: SMC Image Archive.

Apart from a short gully on that other forgotten crag, Stùc a' Chroin, recorded by William Garden on 4 March (*SMCJ*, xi, 278–82), there was no reported activity until the Easter Meet in mid-April. The main Meet was spread over Sligachan and Glen Brittle Lodge (lent by Colin Phillip). Although the weather 'had been worse at other Easters', there was much snow and so there was no scope for difficult rock-climbing: the well-iced Pinnacle Ridge and Thuilm Ridge of Mhadaidh were perhaps the best efforts. Only 27 could be accommodated on Skye, so other Meets took place, at Inveroran (8), Fort William (15) and Tyndrum (2), and these enjoyed similarly unhelpful weather.

In May, the only ascent worth noting seems to have been that of Mr Henry Alexander of Edinburgh (not the future author of the Cairngorms guidebook), who employed a gang of labourers to manoeuvre his car to the summit of Ben Nevis, then still under ten feet of snow. The ascent occupied a full week, so the supremacy of the pony remained intact (*SMCJ*, xi, 307).

At the beginning of June, Willie Ling, Mr & Mrs John Bell and Ruth Raeburn went to Sligachan. After warming up with this party on Pinnacle Ridge (2 June), Ling deserted it in favour of two other guests, Alastair McLaren and Leslie Shadbolt, and moved to Glen Brittle via the *Slanting Gully* of Sgùrr a' Mhadaidh. McLaren was a Scottish sheepfarmer and Shadbolt a London cement manufacturer – an odd couple who had met in the Lake District around 1905. On the 4th, believing they were following the normal route to the Cioch, McLaren led Ling and Shadbolt up *Little Gully*, probably its second ascent: it was first climbed by Guy Barlow in 1908 (mentioned in his Application Form). McLaren continued above the terrace, and the party reached the upper ledge by a direct variation of Collie's route (*Ling's Diary*, Book 9, p. 40). Ling was plainly impressed by what he had seen of Shadbolt and McLaren, and immediately recruited them to membership, with Bell as their Seconder. So it was only as members-in-waiting that McLaren and Shadbolt made the first traverse of the Cuillin Ridge on 10 June (*SMCJ*, xi, 326–9). Leaving Gars-bheinn at 6.07 a.m., they reached Sgùrr nan Gillean at 6.25 p.m. Their traverse was an honest one, including the Caisteal, the Theàrlaich-Dubh Gap, Sgùrr Alasdair, and Naismith's route to the Tooth. It is interesting that more time was expended between Sgùrr Theàrlaich and the MhicCoinnich col than on any other obstacle – a section of the ridge disgracefully un- or mis-described in Club publications until Noel Williams' *Skye Scrambles* guide.

Later in June, Ling and Glover continued their exploration of Fisherfield and Letterewe, from a base at Larachantivore, an expedition described by Glover (*SMCJ*, xii, 21–30). On the 22nd, they celebrated the Coronation of King George V with an evening ascent of Beinn Dearg Mhòr – 'a verse of the National Anthem was chanted at the summit'. On the 23rd they visited Tòrr na h-Iolaire above Carnmore, and made the first climb there. No effort seems to have been made to locate this route by later Editors, and now – as so often with routes of the period – it has disappeared from guidebooks.

Coronation Day on Buachaille:
Robert Watson (L) and brother (R).
Photo: SMC Image Archive.

A group of younger climbers had formed in the Club around this time. Centred on Harry MacRobert, it comprised Arnold Brown, William Macalister, James Thomson, Robert Watson, Robert Workman and James Young. It was this group who had attempted to keep up with Goggs and Russell on their New Year tramp across the bogs of Beinn Bhuidhe. Team MacRobert had failed to make a summer ascent of *South Castle Gully* of Ben Nevis in 2010 – an elaborate human pyramid collapsing (*SMCJ*, xi, 237), but on 15 July they succeeded using more orthodox methods – and with the assistance of William and Jane Inglis Clark (*SMCJ*, xi, 366).

The Alps enjoyed a good summer with dry rocks almost to the summits. Edward Backhouse, Robert Corry & Wm. Mounsey, in various combinations and with the help of guides climbed the Droites, the Géant and the Verte as well as several other lesser peaks in the Mont Blanc range. Ling and George Sang had 17 days together in the Pennine Alps, during which they climbed (from Saas Fee) the Weissmies, traversed the Nadelhorn ridges, and the Portjengrat before traversing the Rimpfischhorn to Zermatt. They then climbed the Matterhorn and Dent Blanche before descending to Les Haudères and up again to Arolla, where they met our new President Godfrey Solly's party. After climbing Mont Blanc de Seilon they moved to the Panossière and finished their holiday with the Grand Combin. Sang then went home, but Ling went back to Arolla and did the Bouquetins and Mont Collon with Solly's party. Solly and Lissant Collins climbed the Wildhorn (Western Bernese) before going to Arolla where they joined George K. Edwards, Wm. Haskett-Smith, J.M. Archer Thomson and others. Apart from the climbs with Ling already mentioned, they managed the North Face of the Pigne d'Arolla and the Aiguille de la Za. Finally Henry M.D. Watson, presumably guided, made a traverse of the Pennines similar to Ling and Sang's, but omitting the Matterhorn.

Skye also enjoyed what James Thomson called 'a summer of grace'. However, Thomson's long sojourn through late July and August included a good deal of the usual bad weather, and he left in September just as the good weather returned (*SMCJ*, xii, 129–36). His long article – short on detail – describes various interesting ascents with assorted companions. However, nothing new was accomplished except some exploration of the Coire Ghrunnda Castle, and a scrambling route on the south-west side of Sgùrr nan Eag. Team MacRobert supplied a second article (*SMCJ*, xii, 77–83), written in a similarly vaporous style. It describes a traverse of the Dubhs Ridge, beginning at Sligachan and ending with a forced bivouac on the slabs below Lochan Coire a' Ghrunnda – another under-described obstacle. Information elsewhere identified the bewildered climbers as Macalister, MacRobert and Young.

However, in early September a very strong party arrived at Sligachan (Bronwen Jones, H.O. Jones, McLaren, E.S. Reynolds, Shadbolt and Archer Thomson), and added one or more new climbs per day for a week (*SMCJ*, xii, 31–40; *AJ*, 26, 17ff). McLaren and Shadbolt climbed *McLaren's Chimney* on Sgùrr nan Gillean (probably previously climbed by John Mackenzie), and *Zig-Zag Route* on the West Buttress of Sròn na Cìche, but their most interesting effort was the huge *South Buttress* of the Castles (Harta Corrie). This enigmatic route received a second ascent from Willes Johnson and E.L. Wigham in 1949, and was probably not climbed again until this century. Certainly no guidebook editor can have looked at it until Noel Williams did very recently. There is a long story about the start to this route which should be told elsewhere, but the key passage is a short vertical crack with a large (vibrating) splinter of rock projecting from it. The initial grade of Difficult given to this route was entirely preposterous – Severe and Extremely Dangerous would have been more appropriate. In writing this and the other paragraphs about Skye above, I acknowledge the indispensable assistance of Stuart Pedlar's unpublished monograph about the Cuillin – *Across Unmeasured Space*.

At the end of September, Raeburn and Russell climbed the eponymous *Easy Route* from Coire na Ciste on Ben Nevis (*SMCJ*, xii, 54). This is the first we hear of Raeburn in 1911 after his climb on Beinn a' Bhùiridh on New Year's Day, and we do not hear of him again in 1911 until Hogmanay. *Ling's Diary* records no climb with him, and he was absent from the Alps. For a climber who had been so persistently active in the preceding 15 years, this gap in the record is extraordinary. Finally, on 22 October, James Parker, Henry Alexander, Bruce Miller and W.A. Reid made the first proper rock climb in the Garracorries, the *Black Pinnacle* of Braeriach (*SMCJ*, xii, 84-89).

As well as some of the articles mentioned above, The *Journal* for the year

Sligachan, September 1911: Back: *Amphlett, Tomkinson, Rule, Scoones.* Middle: *Shadbolt, Mrs Amphlett, Miss Tomkinson, Arnold Brown, Prof. Baly.* Front: *McLaren, MacRobert &* 'E.M.'.

Shadbolt & McLaren (the two on the left with pipes) had made the first continuous traverse of the Cuillin Main Ridge on 10 June in 12hr 18min.

Photo: SMC Image Archive.

featured a fine description of the Cowal Hills by Scott Moncrieff Penny (there is still nothing better – xi, 313–25), a thorough description of the climbs on Sgùrr Alasdair by Francis Greig (xi, 344–50), and an entertaining and racy account of the Gaiter Club by Ramsay (xi, 284–91). This was the year when the moribund Gaiter Club – which was more or less a dining and drinking club, with an hereditary President and a fixed membership – gave its remaining funds of £100 to the Club to further its Guidebook project. Perhaps the most interesting snippet, however, was one of Editor Goggs' *Odds and Ends* (xi, 306) in which he reviews John Beddoe's *Memories of Eighty Years*. Beddoe describes a failed ascent of the *Cat Nick* on Salisbury Crags in the 1850s where he falls on his companion, the antiseptic Joseph Lister, bruising Lister severely. But Beddoe notes that 'I had often ascended by it' and that he believed that Walter Scott had also climbed it! I think that this makes the Cat Nick the first recorded rock climb in Scotland, unless we count Forbes' 1836 *Tourist Route* on Sgùrr nan Gillean as such a thing.

Robin N. Campbell

24 October 1911: (L to R) Macalister, Young and Raeburn at the Luncheon Stone, Ben Nevis.
Photo: SMC Image Archive.

SCOTTISH MOUNTAINEERING TRUST – 2010
Scottish Charity SCO09117

The Trustees met on 5 February and 1 October 2010.

During the course of these meetings support was given to Anna Muir for Research Field Work, N Hawkins for the Collie & Mackenzie Sculpture, R McMorran – Centre for Mountain Studies, T J Hunter – Arctic Adventure Expedition 2010, J S Peden – Oban Mountain Rescue Team, D Luther – Edinburgh University Medics, D Baird for the Cairngorm Outdoor Access Trust, R Taylor for an expedition to Torugart-Too (from the Sang award), Amanda Houston – BSES Svalbard, Zoe Sayers – BSES Indian Himalayas, J McBain for the National Library of Scotland, R Maund for Scottish Council for National Parks, Culag Community Woodland Trust, Lochinver, RSPB – Bothy and Montane Wildlife Cairngorms, R Crawford for Dundee Mountain Film Festival, Jonathon Conville Mountaineering Trust for Scottish Winter Course 2010/2011 and to Perth College for Public Engagement Event.

The Trustees until December 2010 were P V Brian (Chairman) (ex officio as immediate past President of the SMC), R Aitken, J T H Allen, R Anderson (ex officio as Convenor of the Publications Sub-Committee), B S Findlay, D W Rubens (ex officio as President of the SMC), A Macdonald, C R Ravey, R J C

Robb and D N Williams (ex officio as Editor of the SMC Journal). J Morton Shaw is the Trust Treasurer and James D Hotchkis is the Trust Secretary.

The present Directors of the Publications Company are R K Bott (Chairman), K Crocket, M G D Shaw, C M Huntley, C R Ravey and T Prentice (Publications Manager). C R Ravey (both a Director of Publications Company and Trustee) provides liaison between the Publications Company and the Trust as does R Anderson in his capacity as Convenor of the Publications Sub-Committee.

The following grants have been committed by the Trustees during 2010:-

Anna Muir – Research Field Work	£300
N Hawkins – Collie & Mackenzie Sculpture	£500
R McMorran – Centre for Mountain Studies	£700
T J Hunter – Arctic Adventure Expedition 2010	£250
J S Peden – Oban Mountain Rescue Team	£3,000
D Luther – Edinburgh University Medics	£250
D Baird – Cairngorm Outdoor Access Trust	£2,500
	(per annum for 4 years)
R Taylor – Expedition Torugart-Too (Sang Award)	£250
Amanda Houston – BSES Svalbard	£200
Zoe Sayers – BSES Indian Himalayas	£300
J McBain – National Library of Scotland	£516
R Maund – Scottish Council for National Parks	£5,000
Culag Community Woodland Trust, Lochinver	£1,000
RSPB – Bothy and Montane Wildlife Cairngorms	£2,000
R Crawford – Dundee Mountain Film Festival	£1,500
JCMT – Scottish Winter Course 2010/2011	£1,508
Perth College – Public Engagement Event	£1,000

The Trustees record their gratitude to Bob Aitken, Roger Robb and Ann Macdonald (who are retiring by rotation) for their services to the Trust. The Trustees also wish to record their gratitude to Paul Brian for so competently chairing the Trustee meetings over the last 2 years.

J D Hotchkis
Secretary

MUNRO MATTERS 2010

By Dave Broadhead (Clerk of the List)

After a few years in the job I am accustomed now to the seasonal ebb and flow of correspondence, which tends to dry up to a trickle after the New Year and gives me the opportunity to go through the old letters a third time in order to compile this report before the start of the Spring surge. Now that the editor has delayed publication of the SMCJ until later in the year, there seems no obvious reason why the Munro List should follow the precedent of the Inland Revenue, so henceforth it will follow the calendar year. The following Compleations were received between 1 April 2010 and 31 December 2010. As ever the five columns give number, name and year of Compleation of Munros, Tops and Furths as appropriate. * SMC member ** LSCC member.

4494	Richard Cross	2010		4534	Howard Bunyan	2010	
4495	Hazel G. Robertson	2008		4535	Dustin Bunyan	2010	
4496	E. Ross Walker	2008		4536	Mark Williams	2010	
4497	Mia Wells	2010		4537	Allan Stevenson	2010	
4498	Andrew Wells	2010		4538	Steven C. P. Cham	2010	
4499	William Corrigan	2009		4539	John Turner	2009	
4500	Shona C. Ballantyne	2010		4540	Paul Leitch	2009	
4501	Stephen F. Tomlinson	2010		4541	Marcus W. Roberts	2010	
4502	Colin H. Wigston	2010		4542	Sheila G. Roberts	2010	
4503	John Roberts	2010		4543	Robert Ian Reive	2010	
4504	Ailith Stewart	2006		4544	Martin Sansby	2010	
4505	Tim Hindle	2010		4545	James Mercer	2010	
4506	Norman Hull	2010		4546	Pete Nienon	2010	
4507	John Parkinson	2010		4547	Martyn Crowder	2010	
4508	Michael Fletcher	2010		4548	Sarah E. Robertson	2010	
4509	Cedric Clemerson	2010		4549	David Robertson	2010	
4510	Stephen J. Martin	2010		4550	Thomas Oswald	2010	
4511	John Johnson	2010		4551	Alistair R. Duncan	2010	
4512	David Mathews	2010		4552	Alastair Murray	2004	
4513	Alastair B. Scott	2010		4553	Bob Langton	2006	
4514	Ken Wiseman	2010		4554	Giles Morris	2010	
4515	Brian Green	2010		4555	Charles A. Exley	2010	
4516	Raphael Bleakley	2010		4556	Andrew Stumpf	2010	
4517	Anne Van Der Wal	2010		4557	Martin Wilson	2010	2010
4518	Jan Vijfhuizen	2010		4558	Donald Wallace	2010	
4519	Mark McKain	2010		4559	David Gibson	2010	
4520	Julia Jackson	2010		4560	Les Reilly	2010	
4521	Geoff L. Davies	2010		4561	Gabrielle Waugh	2010	
4522	K. Michael L. Thurman	2010		4562	Helen Gardener	2010	
4523	Monica M. Rogerson	2010		4563	Andrew Gardner	2006	
4524	John Crascall	2010		4564	James A. Anderson	2010	
4525	Marc Day	2010		4565	Howard Castle-Smith	2010	
4526	Keith Slater	2010		4566	Ruth Ward	2009	
4527	James Millington	2010		4567	Robert Healey	2010	
4528	*Alan Fox	1999		4568	Donald Pow	2010	
4529	John Pope	2010		4569	Valerie E. Sykes	2010	
4530	Gregory P. Lambert	2010		4570	Mervyn Picken	2010	
4531	Howard Beanland	2010		4571	Alan Williams	2006	
4532	Linda Revels	2009		4572	John Spiers	2010	
4533	Donald Jenks	2010		4573	Jennifer Jordan	2010	

4574	Robert Jordan	2010	
4575	Carol Taylor	2010	
4576	Diana Maddison	2010	
4577	Mary C. M. Rogers	1995	
4578	David A. Rogers	2010	
4579	Jill Johnston	2010	
4580	Tom Hartley	2009	
4581	Iain Mackenzie	2010	
4582	Eric J. Brown	2010	
4583	Vince Harrison	2010	
4584	Lionel Bidwell	2010	
4585	Ann F. Carter	2010	
4586	Stewart Wilkinson	2010	
4587	John Lee Marshall	2010	
4588	Roy Stirrat	2010	
4589	Lesley Gregg	2010	
4590	Peter K. Lang	2009	
4591	Paul Webster	2010	
4592	David Morley	2010	
4593	Russell Anderson	2010	
4594	Ian Renwick	2010	
4595	Ian J. Sheppard	2010	
4596	Trudi Sharp	2010	
4597	David Chapman	2010	
4598	Jim Willsher	2010	
4599	Roddy J. Murray	2010	
4600	Deborah Ramage	2010	
4601	Andrew Ramage	2010	
4602	James P. R. MacLaren	2010	
4603	Debbie Richards	2010	
4604	Simon Cornelius	2010	
4605	Colin Stuart	2010	
4606	Fraser Gorman	2010	
4607	Fiona O'Neil	2010	
4608	Michael J. P. Cullen	2010	
4609	Trish Parkin	2010	
4610	Fabian Seymour	2010	
4611	Tom Pattison	2010	
4612	John Paul Smith	2010	
4613	Tom Smith	2010	
4614	Richard J. Cockburn	2010	
4615	Julian Fletcher	2010	
4616	Gerard Thompson	2010	
4617	Adam Forsyth	2010	
4618	Andy Hosking	2010	
4619	A. Dewar	2010	
4620	John Irvine	2010	
4621	Simon Parkes	2010	
4622	Jim Hollman	2010	
4623	Jane Elder	2009	
4624	Michael Howell	2010	
4625	Jim Bull	2010	
4626	John Wagstaff	1998	
4627	Neil Owen	2010	
4628	Adrian Kentleton	2010	
4629	William Barclay Wilson	2010	
4630	David A. Wright	2010	
4631	John Miller	2010	
4632	Nick Williams	2010	
4633	Neale M. Lamond	2010	
4634	Jamie Acutt	2010	
4635	Cedric Wilkins	2009	
4636	Dougie McColl	2010	
4637	David Barraclough	2010	
4638	Diane Michelle Gilroy	2010	
4639	Anthony Gibbison	2010	
4640	J. Gordon Cooper	2010	
4641	Keith Nixon	2010	
4642	Peter Robinson	2010	
4643	Stewart M. Murray	2010	
4644	Alex Mayes	1985	
4645	Graham Forbes	2010	
4646	Joan Noble	2010	
4647	Nicole Borque	2010	
4648	Susan Fowler	2010	
4649	Alan Heaton	2010	
4650	Fiona P. Duncan	2010	
4651	Ali Odds	2010	
4652	Janice Macdonald	2010	
4653	Arthur Greenwood	2010	
4654	Derrick Bowman	2009	
4655	David Bowman	2009	
4656	Dorothy Elliot	2010	
4657	Billy Elliot	2010	
4658	Robert R. Welch	2010	
4659	Trevor Dearnley	2010	
4660	Peta Barber	2010	
4661	John Wintle	2010	
4662	Allan F. Ward	2010	
4663	Janice Thompson	2010	
4664	James M. Thompson	2010	
4665	Charmian Heaton	2010	
4666	Stuart Robertson	2010	
4667	James B. Walker	2010	
4668	Jennifer Banks	2010	
4669	Andrew McLearnon	2010	
4670	Robin Park	2010	
4671	John W. Kay	2010	
4672	Phil Mathews	2010	
4673	William Wilson	2010	
4674	Kenneth Brown	2010	
4675	Keith Dillon	2010	
4676	Larry Foster	2010	
4677	Ann Thorn	2010	2002
4678	Alvar Thorn	2010	2002
4679	Andrew Kaye	2010	
4680	Anthony R. Jack	2010	
4681	Betty Wilson	2010	
4682	Stewart Wilson	2010	
4683	Mike Thornton	2010	
4684	Maureen White	2010	
4685	Jamie McDonald	2010	
4686	Colin D. Smith	1995	
4687	Thomas Beutenmuller	2010	

4688	Helen Thomas	2010
4689	Michael Thomas	2010
4690	Bern Hellier	2010
4691	Frank Baillie	1997
4692	Tim Weller	2007
4693	Jane Toothill	2010
4694	John J. Conaghan	2010
4695	Paul Fitzpatrick	2008
4696	Michael Feliks	1987
4697	Andrew Brown	1987
4698	Richard Allatt	2010
4699	Joseph Richardson	2010

4700	Caroline Evans	2009
4701	Robin Whitworth	2010
4702	Damon Ritchie	2010
4703	Walter Kelly	2010
4704	Kirsten Paterson	2010
4705	Helen Hamilton	2010
4706	Clive D. Williams	2010
4707	Isobel Murdoch	2010
4708	Graham Murdoch	2010
4709	John Jackson	2010
4710	John McGill	2009

Some simple analysis allowing comparison with last year (shown in brackets) shows total registering 217 (239); comprising males 78% (81%); resident in Scotland 59% (63%); with couples 15% (12%); average age 53 (52); size of compleation party 15 (14); and time taken 22 (22) years.

I noticed in a 2010 Himalayan Club newsletter that my Kathmandu equivalent, Elizabeth Hawley, who keeps a list of Everest summiteers, had reported 5070 ascents by 3431 individuals. How long before they overtake the number of Munroists?

Reading through so many interesting letters, it is clear that Compleaters show an abundance of certain personal qualities which have helped them to reach that final summit.

INSPIRATION

Correspondents often identify what first kindled their interest in the Munros. Andrew Wells (4498) remembers 'my interest in the Round was awakened when I met a climber with a copy of the Tables. I recall a happy evening browsing through them with the aid of a dram of Lagavulin.' Roy Stirrat (4588) 'started when a member of the Hillwalking Club at Aberdeen Grammar School, led by Donald Hawksworth (72) and I. T. Stephens (89). As schoolboys we had vaguely heard of Munros, but just knew that this was what our two bachelor teachers did at weekends.' Ian Renwick (4594) 'began with Blaven, at the time not having heard of Munros. A couple of days later while looking around the Tourist Information Centre in Fort William I came across the SMC guide.' He finishes 'realistically I won't aim for a second round, nor will I try to Compleat the Corbetts. I have however stumbled across another book which might well keep me occupied for some time – The 100 Greatest UK Cycling Climbs! The top rated climb is the Bealach na Ba.' Janice (4663) and James M. Thompson (4664) wrote that 'during a week's holiday in Aberfeldy, we were looking for something to fill our day. Whilst browsing around the Tourist Information Centre, I was drawn to a wall mounted map and the name "Schiehallion" caught my eye.' William Wilson (4673) remembered that he 'started walking in 1995 with my brother. Both being big lads at about 20 stones and our occupation being digger operators we took to walking to start getting fit and take more exercise.' Gerard Thompson (4616) reported 'my first Munro was Ben Chonzie, climbed at the tail end of a golfing holiday and wearing golf shoes.' Thomas Beutenmuller (4687), a German citizen, admits 'it actually took me four or five years after my first Munro to realise what a Munro was! An article by Cameron McNeish in a

German travel magazine enlightened me to this folly and by the time I moved to Scotland permanently I possessed my own copy of the SMC guide.' Isobel (4707) and Graham Murdoch (4708) 'started by accident. We drove to Glen Clova looking for casual walk and drove as far as we could. Only because it was such a nice day we followed the path which led to the Shank of Drumfollow and to the top of Driesh.'

TENACITY

Bagging Munros often illustrates the old adage regarding 'the best laid plans', usually falling foul of the weather. Andrew Wells (4498) reported that 'Sgurr a Choire Ghlas required three visits to Glen Strathfarrar, our first two visits being defeated by thick wet snow, strong wind and zero visibility.' Colin H. Wigston (4502) 'finished with Ruadh Stac Mor then A'Mhaighdean on a 2 day trip. This was my fourth attempt on these two summits.' James P. R. MacLaren (4602) Completed on Ladhar Bheinn 'at the fifth attempt!' No details, but he comments 'I have also climbed many peaks around the world – Alps, Elbrus, Mt. Kinabalu, Carstenz Pyramid and Mt. Cook but I consider Compleating the Munros to be my top achievement.'

LONGEVITY

The benefits to health and well-being of climbing Munros are well illustrated by many Compleatists. I am always particularly pleased to hear from 'Golden Munroists' who have managed to stretch their round over 50 or more years. Norman Hull (4506) 'climbed his first Munro (Ben Lomond) in 1956 when he was 17, finishing on Stob Coire Raineach at the age of 71.' His son Craig wrote to notify me as 'Norman is currently embarking on the TGO Challenge.' John Pope (4529) started with Dreish in 1959 'with Bell-Baxter Biological Society – without the benefits of map, compass, waterproof, leader or anything at all' and recalled being 'led round the Grey Corries at New Year by P. N. L. Tranter, in white out conditions, in 1966.' He also suggested that instead of issuing numbers and certificates free, the SMC should ask Compleaters to make a £50 donation for footpath repair. Iain Mackenzie (4581) started in 1958 and finished in July 2010 on Sgor an Lochain Uaine, reporting 'the day on my last Munro was marked by a unique experience. A group of about 20 deer appeared in the misty gloom and started trotting towards us. Our mood of disbelief was only dispelled when they came sufficiently close to discern that they were reindeer.' Andy Hosking (4618) climbed Beinn Alligin 'as a 16 year old in 1960... part of the Maidstone Grammar School Senior Scout trek.' David A. Wright (4630) 'climbed Ben Nevis by the tourist path with my father sometime in the summer of 1948, aged 9.' David Barraclough (4637) 'climbed my first Munro – Sgurr nan Gillean- as a 14 year old member of a school party in 1959. I walked (or cycled) about 2085 miles and climbed 680,000 feet in my 51 year campaign of 193 separate trips.'

REFLECTIVE

One of the pleasures of reading Compleatists letters is that many take the opportunity to look back over their bagging years. John Johnson (4511) observed 'I value my time in the mountains, a place of great experiences and fine people.

In some ways "finding" the Munros is an insubstantial event as setting the arbitrary height of 3000 feet does not condemn those of lesser height – now to seek other horizons.' Roddy J. Murray (4599) confided 'summiting on Sunday was a strange feeling... a curious mixture of joy and some sadness, all mixed up with a great sense of achievement – the beginning of something rather that the end. Plans are afoot to work my way through a list of all the three star Severes in Scotland as my next mission.'

FAMILY LOYALTY

Husband and wife Compleations continue to be popular, with other family connections cropping up occasionally. Dustin (4534) and Howard (4535) Bunyan, son and father 'both started our Munros with Ben Nevis.' Their hill-going ways diverged for a few years, before coming back together to Compleat on Càrn Mòr Dearg, 'before following the arête over to the Ben.' Mary C.M. Rogers (4577) and David A. Rogers (4578) 'have some family connections with earlier Munroists.' Mary's father is John Havard (352). A lot of his and Mary's Munros were done with Bill Myles (157). David's grandfather 'was a friend of Willie Docharty (13), the first person to do the Munros, Tops, Furths and Corbetts. Both served as officers in the King's Liverpool Regiment at Ypres in France in 1917 and 1918. My father and his siblings knew Mr Docharty as "Uncle Doc".' Lisa Bowman wrote 'My father Derrick Bowman (4654) and my Uncle, David Bowman (4655) both Compleated last year. They never got round to sending off for a certificate which is a shame considering it was such a huge achievement! It is my father's 60th birthday and thought this would be a nice surprise for them both.' Martin Wilson (4557) sent me a copy of a very interesting illustrated summary of some of the highs and lows of his round. He also noted 'I rented a cottage near Kirriemuir in August 2009. The lady owner told me that Sir Hugh Munro was buried nearby. Of course I visited his grave to pay my respects and found it completely overgrown. The family had clearly been neglecting its clearance. I borrowed a set of shears and for two hours cleared the area around the grave.' Trevor Dearnley (4659) Compleated on Meall nan Tarmachan and reported 'that I met Sir Hugh Munro's great great grandson in the Ben Lawers Visitor Centre car park at the end of our outing. A charming man from Suffolk who had also been up the same hill, his fourth Munro. He and his family had come up to see why his ancestor was so famous and were thoroughly enjoying themselves. In the excitement we never thought to ask his name – his mother was a Munro.'

DEDICATION

I am frequently reminded of my good fortune in being able to look away from my computer screen and out of the window see several Highland Munros. Mark Williams (4536) sums up the determination of those living further afield, with a brief summary of his final Munro weekend from his home in Suffolk. 'Leave Bury St Edmunds at 0600hrs Saturday 29 May... Breakfast A66... Coffee break Pam's Café, Newtonmore... Tiso's, Inverness for some kit. Arrive 1800hrs at Sheena's B&B, Lochluichart... 600 miles... dinner... bed. Up at 0700hrs for start of route... Loch a'Bhraoin to Beinn a'Chlaidheimh. 10.5 hours later back at car, job done. Celebrate at Altguish Inn. Back to Sheena's for dinner, bottle of fizzy stuff then bed. Off to Glencoe in the morning for Sgurr na h-Ulaidh... start at 1200hrs... back at car by 1800hrs... wash in river... fish & chips in Tyndrum, then home... arrive 0400hrs.' Another Highlander, Ken Wiseman (4514) who I met on Ben Wyvis a few months before finishing confessed 'although I have Completed my Munros I believe that I remain a lazy so and so. Often I think I would like to sleep longer on a Sunday morning rather that getting up early to go walking.'

TRUE GRIT

Every year I hear remarkable accounts from people who have used the challenge of climbing Munros to help recuperate from serious illness or overcome a serious disability. Allan Stevenson (4537) 'took up hill walking after retiring from Highland League Football. When I had completed 270 I discovered that I needed a triple heart bypass which knocked me back for 2 years.' Geoff L. Davies (4521) suffers from an inherited form of macular degeneration and has been a Registered Blind Person since 1991. He Compleated with the help of his wife, Julia Jackson (4520), who commented that 'for Geoff, who only has peripheral vision and no central vision, it was a herculean effort.' Gregory P. Lambert (4530) reported that 'in 2003 I was diagnosed with Idiopathic Pulmonary Fibrosis, a lung disease, with a median survival time of 4.5 years. The mountains of Scotland should be placed on the recommended treatments for patients under the NHS! They have given me life.' Larry Foster (4676) suffered 'a major accident in Coir a' Ghrunnda that resulted in a broken pelvis, head injuries and a substantial rescue by the Skye MRT and Coastguard helicopter. After a year off to recover I went back to Skye and finished the hills there.'

RECORD BREAKING

As ever, the occasional Compleater has an eye for the record books. Steven C. P. Cham (4538) made an unusual claim during his Round 'my longest stay at the summit was Ladhar Bheinn, over 5 hours, just watching the world go by!' Martin Sansby (4544) noted '26 Munros have been done using X-country ski gear.' Obviously a man of diverse interests, he also reported 'plans for the future include: taking up sea kayaking; drinking more Red Kite; hand diving my own scallops.' Pete Nienon (4546) reported a summit party of 102 on Ben na Lap, ranging in age from 72 years to 6 weeks. Stephen Pyke set a new record for the fastest round, a remarkable 39 days 9 hours 6 minutes. He has not yet written to register for a number.

INTERNATIONALISM

The challenge of climbing Munros continues to appeal to overseas visitors. Anne van der Wal (4517) and Jan Vijfhuizen (4518) became the first Dutch couple to Compleat and Anne the first Dutch female. French-Canadian Nicole Bourque (4647) became the second Canadian female Compleater, with an interesting story. 'My first Munro was the Inaccessible Pinnacle on my first weekend away with a boyfriend who was a mountaineer. I had no idea what I was doing... we had practised abseiling at a local crag before the climb. Sixteen years of Gortex later I arrived at the summit of Ben Lomond with the same mountaineer, Robert Wright (3508). As I pulled up to the cairn I heard some corks popping.' This

Coincident Compleation was Ali Odds (4651) who 'moved to Scotland 9 years ago from the flat lands of Flanders.' Nicole and Robert used the late Irvine Butterfield's map for their Compleation, given to them by his sister.

CELEBRATORY

Most Compleaters enjoy some form of celebration to round off the big day and like to fill me in on the details. Typically, after finishing on Ben Lomond, John Crascall (4524) 'stayed overnight to celebrate at the Rowardennan Lodge Hostel and enjoyed a bottle of 18 year old Dalwhinnie malt and a good meal.' A couple of weeks later, after receiving his certificate and number, he sent me a copy of the menu of a surprise celebratory lunch organised by his wife in The Blacksmiths Arms, Chichester, West Sussex, with a useful list of the Munros printed on the back. He commented that 'these sorts of things do not happen very often down south.' Fiona P. Duncan (4650) finished on Schiehallion then 'partied in Killiecrankie Village Hall which I booked through to the Sunday. There was a huge spread and a barrel of Schiehallion Ale. We danced into the wee sma hours. Next morning there was tea in sleeping bags and egg rolls all round.'

GREAT AND GOOD

Occasionally a familiar name appears. A certain David Gibson (4559) let slip that 'I work for the MCofS in Perth.' Paul Webster (4591) noted 'I also run the walkhighlands.co.uk website which has all the routes of ascent.' Jim Willsher (4598) the Webmaster's Assistant noted that 'I've had clear views from 261 summits, experiencing mist on only 22.' He even included a pie chart to prove the point, adding that 'I saw no point climbing hills unless there was a good chance of a view from the top.'

ECCENTRICITY

One cannot help but smile at the antics of some Compleaters. Les Reilly (4560) started 'when my big cousin took me out into the hills for the first time. Since July 2003 I have been climbing wearing my kilt. I am also known as the Kilted Munro Bagger.' Helen Hamilton (4705) enclosed a photo, noting 'hopefully you will all have noticed my pink shoes. This was the second time that I had them on. The first time was on the summit of Kala Pattar 18,514 ft in the Himalayas, when I raised £ 1,650 for breast cancer research.'

QUIRKY

Under this heading comes the growing phenomenon of the Contiguous Compleation , Munrosis contiguum, a carefully planned event, not to be confused with the entirely accidental Coincident Compleation, Munrosis coincidentalsis. Deborah (4600) and Andrew (4601) Ramage contrived an extreme form of the former, finishing both their Munros and Corbetts on the same day. With the help a couple of trains to Corrrour station, early birds accompanied them to the summit of Leum Uilleim, while a bigger group arrived later to join them on Beinn na Lap. Colin D. Smith (4686) held back from registering until he had Completed Chris Crocker's '600' (Munros, Tops and deleted tops as set out on biber.fsnet.co.uk).

CHARITABLE

Occasionally Munro bagging is combined with charity fundraising. Michael Howell (4624) used his Compleation as 'the final summit in a fund raising project for Afghan Action, a small training school in Kabul which is giving young men and women skills to become economically independent. The total raised is £21,000 so far.'

INVESTIGATIVE

David Barraclough (4637) set out to answer the old question 'So which is the most remote Munro?' With the help of a digital map wheel and 1:25000 maps he produced an interesting paper with data for 21 hills, giving distances for the 'shortest, most direct and sensible walking route from a public road or railway station.' His top 5 are:

1. Càrn an Fhidhleir	From Linn of Dee	11.40 miles
2. A' Mhaighean	From Incheril	10.98 miles
3. Beinn Bheoil	From Rannoch Lodge	10.46 miles
4. Ruadh Stac Mòr	From Corrie Hallie	10.37 miles
5. Ben Alder	From Corrour station	10.34 miles

AMENDMENTS

The eight columns give number, name and the year of each Compleation of Munros, Tops, Furths, Corbetts, Grahams, and Donalds.

Number	Name	Munros	Tops	Furths	Corbetts	Grahams	Donalds
152	Erlend Flett	1977		2010	2002		
2832	Richard A. Llloyd	2002			2010		
1930	Martin Scoular	1998	1998	1998	2010		
1147	Robert M. Robertson	1993	2010				
600	Hugh R. Shercliff	1987	2006	1990			
3552	Martin Richardson	2006		2003			2009
2474	Gordon Stewart	1988 2000 2009	2000	1995	2000		2009
73	Andrew M. Fraser	1967 1978 1986 1996 2001	1980	1977	1991	2010	
3438	Hazel Strachan	2005 2008 2010					
1841	Pamela Bridge	1997			2010		
3687	Dave Coustick	1989			2010		
2862	John Edward Casson	2002		2007	2010		
267	Martin Hudson	1981 2007	1981	1982	2010		2010
1611	Alex Smith	1996	1999	1999	2008		

		2003					
580	John Green	1988	1989	1989	2010		
768	Tony Rogers	1990					
		2010					
2444	Peter A. Haigh	2000	2000	2010			
3102	Charles McCartney	1988					
		2003					
		2010					
3103	Michael McCartney	2003					
		2010					
2534	Andrew J. Rook	2001		1995	2010		2004
1292	Julian P. Ridal	1994		1995	1999	2010	
		2005					
2795	Maria R. Hybster	2002			2006		
		2010					
2943	Donald R. Sutherland	2003			2006		2010
3366	Anne Butler	2005			2010		
		2010					
225	Alan L. Brook	1980	1980	1978	2004		2010
		2002	2002				
1891	Dave Marshall	1993					
		2010					
1061	Bill Fairmaner	1992	1995		2002	2009	2003
		1999					
		2010					
2422	David K. McRonald	2000			2010		
4193	Ron A. Brown	2008			2010		
1045	Steven Fallon	1992	1993	2010			
		1994					
		1995					
		1996					
		1997					
		1998					
		1999					
		2000					
		2001					
		2002					
		2003					
		2004					
		2006					
		2010					
1340	Andrew Balsillie	1993	1994				
		2010	2010				
1170	Elaine S. Fenton	1993		1994	2010		
1169	Garth B. Fenton	1993		1994	2010		
1333	Kenneth W.C.Stewart	1994			2004		1999
		2010					
2803	Jamie Brogan	2002					
		2009					

1925	Patrick A. Hamilton	1998		2010			
		2009					
3497	Richard Knight	2005			2010		
1806	Ross Jervis	1997			2010		
1995	Neil Hutton	1998	2010				
1319	Robert P. Gray	1994			2004		
		2010					
1801	Lindsay Boyd	1997	2002		2004	2009	2010
		2000					
		2002					
		2008					
1635	Eric Young	1996		2006	2001	2005	2010
3432	Sheila Simpson	2005			2010		
3433	Bill Simpson	2005			2010		
2771	Alex Stobie	2002					
		2010					
2268	Susan Henderson	1999		2005	2004	2010	2010
2269	George Henderson	1999		2005	2004	2010	2010
2955	Paul Brooks	2003			2010		
3271	Kevin Murray	2004			2010		
533	Leon D. Firth	1987		2002	2000	2010	2009
319	Ken P. Whyte	1984	1987	1987	2000	2000	2000
		2010					
2630	Euan J. F. Ross	2000	2000	2001			
		2010					
2959	Roger Squires	2003			2010		
3211	Margaret Squires	2004			2010		
3417	Paul R. T. Newby	2005		2010			
114	Donald Smith	1973	1982	1982	1997		
		1988					
		2010					
4691	Frank Baillie	1997	1999		2009	2010	2008
4692	Tim Weller	2007	2008	2010			
4696	Michael Feliks	1987	1992			2007	
166	Terry Moore	1978	1982				
		2010					
2610	Tony Smith	2001	2001	2001	2010		
4151	Norman Wares	2008	2010				
3465	Colin F. Morsley	2005	2009	2010			
108	Brian K. E. Edridge	1972			2010		
		1982					
		1986					
		1994					
1790	Robert Hopkin	1997					
		2010					

Recording Amendments continues to take up an increasing proportion of the Clerk's time. I have laid in a large stock of Corbett Compleation certificates and the Webmaster has set up a Corbetteers Photo Gallery.

I continue to be impressed and inspired by the enthusiasm of correspondents. Worthy of note include Andrew M. Fraser (73) who has Compleated a Munro Round in each of five separate decades while Steven Fallon (1045) registered his 14th Munro Round. Richard Knight (3497) 'noted that it took me 22 days more walking to achieve the Corbetts than the Munros with the average distance per Corbett being 1.3 miles greater than that required per Munro.' The number of different Lists seems to keep growing. Alan L. Brook (225) has compiled a number of 'Private Hill Lists' including 'Highlands & Islands Tops 2000' to 2999' + Hills with 500' drop (1634 Tops + 410 Hills)'. Ken Whyte (319) Compleated his second Munro Round 'as part of a quadruple Compleation of Slioch (Munros), Meall Fhuaran (Corbett Tops), Meall Daimh (Graham Tops) and also the last 2000' Top with a 30m prominence in GB & Ireland.'

This information is available on www.smc.org.uk along with the Munroist and Corbetteers Photo Galleries. To register a Compleation or amendment please write to Dave Broadhead, Cul Mor, Drynie Park North, Muir of Ord, IV6 7RP. If you would like a certificate for either Munro or Corbett Compleation, please enclose an A4 sae (with the correct postage please). Once you have received a number, a Compleation photo can be emailed or posted to the Webmaster. Alex Mayes (4644) waited 25 years before registering, so it really is never too late.

Enjoy your hills

Dave Broadhead
Clerk of the List

MOUNTAIN RESCUE COMMITTEE OF SCOTLAND

SCOTTISH MOUNTAIN ACCIDENTS

INCIDENT REPORT 2010

(Finalised 14 March 2011)

THE MOUNTAIN RESCUE COMMITTEE of Scotland Incident Statistics and the information therein, excluding logo/s, may be reproduced free of charge in any format or medium for research, private study or for internal circulation within an organisation. This is subject to the information being reproduced accurately and not used in a misleading context. The material must be acknowledged as Mountain Rescue Committee of Scotland copyright, and the title of the publication specified.

All enquires about the content of this report or any other matter associated with Incident Reporting should be directed to the MRC of S Incident Statistics Officer. The acting Officer is:

Dr Bob Sharp
31Craigfern Drive
Blanefield
Glasgow
G63 9DP

Tel: 01360 770431
Email: lomondbob@talk21.com

Introductory comments

The information reported here is based on the new Incident Reporting System, which was initiated at the start of the year and agreed by the MRC of S at its meeting in November 2009. Every attempt has been taken to ensure the accuracy and completeness of the information given in this report, but it is likely that as with previous years, a small number of reports for 2010 are still to be submitted.

The Statistician is in the privileged position of being the first person in Scotland to see the incident picture unfolding as the year progresses. As such, it is easy to draw conclusions about what is (or is not) happening. Whilst this cannot be avoided, it is dangerous for anyone to interpret and then publish their views based on what is limited information. The information given in this report should be examined in the light of past reports and judgements based on information gleaned over a period of time. It should be noted that any interpretative comments made in this report are those of only a single individual. Others may interpret the data differently.

Executive summary

1. Following a period of rising incidents over the past 8 years, 2010 shows a small decline.

2. The number of mountaineering incidents fell in 2010 compared to 2009.

3. The number of non-mountaineering incidents rose compared to 2009. The proportion of all such incidents was 36% which is the highest ever reported.

4. Around one third of all non-mountaineering incidents are searches for vulnerable people reported missing. These seem to apply more for some Police authorities than others. A small number of incidents were connected with community resilience activities.

5. There were a total of 534 incidents in 2010 during which the combined resources of all MRTs and SARDAs expended around 26,600 hours. The number of incidents and time expenditure varies considerably across Police authorities and areas (SMC defined) within Scotland.

6. A total of 659 people were assisted of whom 255 were injured and 45 died. Of these, only 16 people died in mountaineering incidents; the lowest number for over 30 years.

7. Helicopters were used for 39% of all incidents and dog teams for almost 20% of all incidents.

8. Hillwalking in summer conditions is responsible for more incidents than any other mountain activity.

9. The small number of rock climbing incidents is indicative of the general decline across several years. This has been reported elsewhere (The Scottish Mountaineer, August, 2008).

10. There are a small number of incidents due to avalanche and this also a continuing downward trend, which has been reported elsewhere (Mountain Rescue, April, 2010).

11. One third of all mountaineering incidents result from the simple slip. Poor navigation, inadequate skill and bad planning continue to be key factors associated with many incidents.

12. The most common injuries are to the lower leg and this follows the pattern observed over many years.

Incidents by SMC Region

It is tradition that the MRC of S Incident reports are published annually in the Journal of the Scottish Mountaineering Club (SMC). The categorisation of incidents mirrors the regions as defined by the SMC District Guides. The table below provides details of the incidents in which people are involved, the number of people involved and the most commonly cited contributory factors.

Table 4: Incident information for each SMC region.

Region	Mountaineering						Casualties			Major Contributory Factors					NM
	WALKING (SUMMER)	WALKING (WINTER)	SNOW/ICE CLIMBING	ROCK CLIMBING	SCRAMBLING	MOUNTAINEERING (Total)	PERSONS (INJURED)	PERSONS (FATAL)	TOTAL PERSONS ASSISTED	MEDICAL/ILLNESS	LOST/NAVIGATION	SLIPS/TRIPS/STUMBLES	PLANNING/TIMING	AVALANCHE	NON-MOUNTAINEERING (Total)
NORTH HIGHLND	25	2	3	-	-	33	17	-	43	5	21	15	15	1	16
WEST HIGHLND	20	5	-	1	-	26	10	1	29	2	5	9	9	-	2
BEN NEVIS	30	5	8	-	4	47	32	5	73	8	11	15	14	2	2
GLEN COE	35	14	4	-	5	61	35	7	83	7	20	24	10	2	9
OTHER CNT HIGH	1	1	1	-	-	3	1	-	6	-	4	1	2	-	-
CAIRNGM	27	16	10	4	-	57	33	1	84	7	35	13	24	2	36
SOUTH HIGHLND	50	16	-	1	2	71	51	1	110	8	41	37	18	-	65
SKYE	10	1	-	-	6	19	8	1	16	-	10	7	8	-	3
OTHER ISLANDS	10	1	-	-	1	12	7	-	15	2	6	1	5	-	9
STH UPLANDS	6	5	-	-	-	11	4	-	17	4	8	6	4	-	52
TOTALS	214	66	26	6	18	340	198	16	476	43	161	128	109	7	194

This report covers the period from 01/01/2010 to 31/12/2010
(Compiled from reports received by the Statistician)

NORTHERN HIGHLANDS

JANUARY 4 – Beinn Alligin (NG865612). Two pairs of climbers were climbing Diamond Fire (Grade IV). One pair had to abseil off due to deep powder sloughs. As they left the corrie they noticed the other pair half way up the route. They raised the alarm when their friends became overdue. Torridon MRT were alerted but decided to wait a while. The climbing pair eventually topped out at 2352hrs and walked out unaided. Torridon MRT. 4hrs.

JANUARY 24 – Liathach (NG930564). A member of the public spotted two lights descending Liathach around the Glen Cottage area. One light was considerably further down than the other. MRT informed Police that this sounded normal but would send members along the road. They met up with climbers in a parked car, who informed them that the light belonged to their friends and all was to plan. Torridon MRT. 1hr.

FEBRUARY 13 – Spidean a' Choire Leith, Poacher's Fall (NG928578). Two climbers (41yr old female and 53yr old male) from England were hampered by a broken hammer and poor weather. They had to change their descent route because of the bad weather which extended their day by eight hours. Both climbers eventually walked out unaided and uninjured. Torridon MRT. 15hrs.

MARCH 13 – Fisherfield Forest (NH007770). A 55yr old male walker from England was on a week-long camping trip. He spoke to his wife from the summit of A' Mhaighdean at 1430hrs and arranged to contact her when off the hill. The text message he sent did not get through so his wife raised the alarm as he had always been in touch before. The man was unaware anything was wrong when located in his tent having done nothing wrong. Dundonnell MRT, Kinloss MRT, SARDA (Scotland). 83hrs.

MARCH 18 – Fisherfield. A 55yr old male walker left Shenavall at 0745hrs to climb A' Mhaighdean and return to Corrie Hallie via Shenavall. When he failed to arrive on time his son raised the alarm. Team members searched in deteriorating weather until the man turned up safe and well at 2330hrs. Dundonnell MRT. 8hrs.

APRIL 30 – Gleann Bianasdail (NH032680). A party of five walkers left Incheril car park on the evening of the 30 April intending to camp at Lochan Fada to the north. By 2030hrs the party grouped near the summit of the pass to discover one member (50yr old male) missing. A search was undertaken and the man was found safe and well but much further on, off the path near the lochside. Torridon MRT, SARDA (Scotland). 73hrs.

MAY 5 – Beinn Dearg (NH259812). A 63yr old man called to say he was lost. A team member spoke to him to verify his location. This was difficult as the walker had only a vague idea about navigation. His position was identified when he called back to say he could see a road. He was eventually uplifted by vehicle at Loch Glascarnoch. Dundonnell MRT. 8hrs.

MAY 24 – Alligin to Diabaig path (NG801594). A party of four well equipped but inexperienced walkers were walking along the public footpath from Alligin to

Diabaig when a 63yr old female in the group tripped and fell whilst traversing a rock slab. Her husband walked out to Diabaig where he alerted the Police from a call box. The team was alerted, attended and treated the casualty but due to the nature of the terrain requested evacuation. The casualty was then transported to Broadford Hospital by helicopter. Torridon MRT, 35hrs.

JUNE 1 – Helmsdale (ND168032). A 28yr old male walker failed to return after climbing local hills near Helmsdale. Two Police Officers together with a local person searched the area and located the person safe and well. They escorted him off the hill and back to his brother's house in Navidale. No MRT involvement.

JUNE 8 – Ben Wyvis (NH462684). A 29yr old man alerted the police at 2100hrs to say he was cold and very tired and in the cloud somewhere on Ben Wyvis. He was located by a SAR dog at the summit, very cold and wet in challenging weather conditions. He was walked down by the team to waiting vehicles. The casualty was ill prepared for his trip and had no map, but had taken his laptop with mapping software. It would have been impossible to use his computer in the driving rain and it clearly added significantly to the weight in his pack. Dundonnell MRT, SARDA (Scotland). 132hrs.

JUNE 10 – Quinag (NC205290). A male walker limping heavily on the ridge between Sail Gharbh and spot height 745m was reported by another party of walkers when they left the hill. The man told party members that he would walk off slowly. The Police discussed this situation with Assynt MRT. Weather conditions were suitable for a helicopter but a car was dispatched to Quinag's John Muir car park from where the walker could be seen descending. Team members were not deployed and the man eventually reached the car park unaided. Assynt MRT. 5hrs.

JUNE 11 – Bienn Uidhe (NC297258). Dundonnell team members assisted Assynt MRT to carry out a search for six overdue DofE students. They were located at the indicted GR and accompanied by team members down to Glencoul bothy then by boat to Kylesku. The students handled the situation well but, in the view of team members, the expedition was poorly supervised and inappropriate for the planned expedition. Dundonnell MRT, Assynt MRT, SARDA (Scotland). 292hrs.

JUNE 15 – Letterewe to Poolewe path (NG925735). A male walker attempted to walk the Letterewe to Poolewe path (the 'Posties' path) but lost the path and then slipped down a small crag. He was unable to relocate the path and became progressively more disoriented on steep ground from where he called for help. He was located by team members about 4k NE of Letterewe close to the shoreline below Creag Tharbh, and then accompanied by foot and boat to safety. Dundonnell MRT, Torridon MRT. 57hrs.

JUNE 17 – Glas Bheinn (NC260261). A 76yr old man from England walking with a younger couple slipped near the summit of Glas Bheinn and suffered a badly swollen knee/suspected broken ankle rendering him unable to continue unaided. Assynt MRT called on Dundonnell and Kinloss MRTs for support to assist with the incident. Because of prevailing cloud conditions R137 dropped off first aid equipment and personnel some 250m below the casualty's position. Team members then carried the man down to a point (approx NC266254) where he and his two companions were uplifted by R100 (R137 had been recalled for another emergency service) and transported to Inchnadamph Hotel. MRT members made their own way off the mountain. Assynt MRT, Dundonnell MRT, Kinloss MRT, R137, R100. 185hrs.

JUNE 22 – Beinn na h-Eaglaise (NG908523). A 79yr old male walker left Torridon at 1030hrs on the 22nd to walk to the summit of Beinn na h-Eaglaise (an 8k round trip). He 'phoned Torridon YH were he was staying at 1830hrs to say that he was on the summit and would be back at the Hostel by 2230hrs. When he failed to arrive by 2300hrs the warden called the Police who called out Torridon MRT. Team members found the man unharmed around 0015hrs and took him back to the hostel. Torridon MRT. 5hrs.

JULY 2 – Ben More Assynt (NC324181). The Police received a 999 call from a 50yr old man on the southern peak of Ben More Assynt, to say that he was cragfast and 'clinging by his fingers in fear of his life'. R100 located and airlifted the man (minus his sac) safe and well to Inchnadamph. The man was subsequently cautioned by Northern Constabulary who reported him to the Procurator Fiscal (the same man was rescued in similar circumstances a year earlier). Assynt MRT, R100. 21hrs.

JULY 16 – Elphin (NC223120). A 60yr old woman slipped and broke her leg whilst walking locally to visit a burial cairn. Team members assisted the ambulance crew carry the casualty to the road. Dundonnell MRT. 6hrs.

JULY 24 – Loch a' Bhealaich Mhòr (NG801586). A family of four (husband, wife and two children) had just left the path to walk towards the loch where they planned to fish, when the lady tripped and sustained torn ligaments. She and the youngest child were evacuated along with team members by R100, to Torridon. Torridon MRT, R100. 12hrs.

JULY 24 – Gorm Loch Mor (NC310240). Two female walkers became separated from their friends in cloudy conditions. Unable to locate themselves and not having adequate clothing, they called for help. R100 located the two women before nightfall. Both were unharmed. Assynt MRT, R100. 4hrs.

AUGUST 9/10 – Eas a' Chual Aluinn waterfall (NC280277). Late afternoon on the 9th, a lone foreign female walker contacted the police requesting assistance as she was lost in mountains near Kylesku. Before any further information could be obtained, the mobile phone signal was lost and the call ended. It was established she only had an AA type road map, but had plenty of clothing in her pack. R100 was deployed to search and Assynt teams members covered the track between Kylesku and Inchnadamph. The operation was stood down at falling light without the woman being found. Teams re-assembled the following morning and the missing woman was spotted by a team member while he was travelling to the incident. She was walked to the post at Inchnadamph following a night on the hill. She indicated she had seen a helicopter the previous night on several occasions but had not believed it was looking for her. Assynt MRT, R100, SARDA (Scotland), Kinloss MRT. 100hrs.

AUGUST 11 – Midtown to Rubha Reidh (NG762917). A 70yr old woman set off at 10.20hrs to walk from Midtown to the lighthouse with a rendezvous at 1800hrs. When she failed to arrive, her husband raised the alarm and Dundonnell and Torridon MRTs were tasked to initiate a search. Unknown to the teams, the woman finally reached her destination cold, wet and disorientated. She flagged down a car, acquired a lift to Gairloch and then took a taxi to her holiday cottage, unaware that anything was amiss. When her husband went back to cottage he found his wife and reported her safe arrival to the Police. In addition to involvement by the two MRTs, Coastguard Rescue Teams were also dispached. Dundonnell MRT, Torridon MRT, SARDA (Scotland). 86hrs.

AUGUST 14 – Conival/Ben More Assynt (NC307201). A 48yr old female member of a party of three, tripped and twisted her ankle and was unable to continue. With a known location and favourable weather conditions it was decided to request R100 to collect the casualty. She was taken to a waiting ambulance at Inchnadamph Hotel. Once transferred to Raigmore it was established that the lady had broken her ankle in three places. Assynt MRT, R100. 3hrs

AUGUST 16 – Conival (NC294207). A 32yr old man was returning from the summit of Conival when he felt dizzy. He consequently felt anxious and concerned at his ability to return to Inchnadamph. At this point he rested briefly and phoned for assistance. He took rehydration liquids and some food, but the midges drove him to keep walking down. During this period he was in consistent communication with a local Police Officer with MRT assistance. Eventually, mobile contact was lost, at which point team members were deployed to assist the man. It transpired the man's ascent had been too fast (partly due to midges) and therefore he misjudged his fitness suffering dehydration and exhaustion. He had also misjudged the weather and had not reckoned on it being so wet. Assynt MRT. 12hrs.

AUGUST 24 – Liathach (NG935580). Two walkers (33yr old man and a 34yr old woman) had completed the Fasarinen ridge from west to east. On reaching Spidean a Choire Leith the woman became cragfast. The man dropped 200 metres to gain a mobile signal. R100 called but had to abort due to technical fault. R137 was then tasked and found the man with the help of night vision goggles. The woman was located by team members on top of Spidean and walked down beneath the cloud base where she and team members were airlifted back to the Torridon base. An example of bad planning, inexperience, inadequate clothing etc. Torridon MRT, R137. 48hrs.

AUGUST 28 – Beinn Alligin (NG857601). A 24yr old man had completed the Beinn Alligin ridge traverse but failed to find a decent path after searching for four hours. Team members found the man and walked with him back to the Torridon base. Torridon MRT, R137, R100. 25hrs.

SEPTEMBER 6 – Slioch. Team placed on standby for male walker overdue on Slioch. Turned out the man had failed to return to work because he was ill at home, and not on the mountain. Dundonnell MRT. 1hr.

SEPTEMBER 8 – Liathach (NG927577). A party of seven were completing the ridge from east to west when a 62yr old woman took a tumble and suffered head lacerations. Her husband called the police, and R100 carrying team members was tasked to assist. The casualty and two members of the party were winched off and the woman flown to Raigmore Hospital. Torridon MRT, R100. 8hrs.

SEPTEMBER 11 – Drumbeg (NC136324). A 47yr old man from England had been staying at the Drumbeg Hotel sightseeing in the area. He asked hotel staff to recommend a short walk and a laminated sheet describing the route was provided. As night fell, hotel staff became concerned and informed Northern

Constabulary. MRTs located the man on the road, confused and tired, walking away from Drumbeg just west of Nedd. He had become lost at some point on the way and walked untill darkness fell. He fabricated some protection from the weather by stuffing his outer clothing with heather, and then waited for daylight. He was checked by Dundonnell paramedic found to be OK. Assynt MRT, Dundonnell MRT, SARDA (Scotland). 203hrs.

WESTERN HIGHLANDS

JANUARY 7 – Affric (by Loch Beinn a Mheadhoin). Two men (40yrs and 15yrs) were on a camping/Munro bagging trip in winter conditions in Glen Affric. The Police received a worried call from the mother of the 15yr old as the pair had said they would report in every night but had failed to do so. Kintail MRT advised Police that deployment was not required immediately as the walkers were not, in fact, overdue and their failure to report was possibly due to poor mobile signal. Police decided to alert R137, which found the men walking back to their tent having had a good day on the hill. Kintail MRT, R137. 11hrs.

FEBRUARY 8 – Sgurr Coire Choinnichean (NG815004). A man had gone walking without telling his friends. At some point on his journey he slipped, became lost and lost all his equipment. He eventually made his way back to the bunkhouse at Inverie without reporting this to anyone. A search commenced through the night by a team member followed by helicopter back-up at first light. He was eventually located but nobody could make sense of his story! Glenelg MRT, R137. 6hrs.

FEBRUARY 9 – Skiary (NG962071). Two walkers were making their way from Barrisdale to their car at Kinloch Hourn. One became cragfast at Skiary. A team member launched his own boat from Arnisdale and guided the man down to safety then took both men to Kinloch Hourn. Glenelg MRT. 18hrs.

FEBRUARY 15 – Sgùrr Coire Choinnichean (NG795000). A male walker (69yrs) from England started to walk at 1230hrs and suffered a stumble/fall. He subsequently became disoriented and benighted. At daybreak he made his own way off the mountain. The team was stood down en route. Glenelg MRT, Lochaber MRT, R137. 33hrs.

FEBRUARY 20 – Glen Licht, Kintail (NH002175). A 51yr old female walker slipped on an ice-covered stalker's vehicle track and injured her right ankle. She was splinted and carried to a waiting vehicle and on to Broadford Hospital in Skye. Kintail MRT. 12hrs.

FEBRUARY 20 – Beinn a' Chapuill (NG826154). Search for a missing woman in her 20s reported overdue from climbing Beinn à Chapuill. She was located safe and well near Balvraid (NG847165). Glenelg MRT. 18hrs.

FEBRUARY 20 – Glen Shiel. A motorist reported seeing flashing lights on one the hills in the Glen. On investigation by team members it turned out to be mountaineers descending from the hill after dark. They were not in any difficulties. Kintail MRT. 3hrs.

MARCH 20 – Creag a' Mhàim (NH209807). Two men (44yrs, 31yrs) in a larger party of seven became cragfast on the east ridge of Creag á Mhàim and called for help. R100 airlifted them to rejoin the other members and the party then made their own way off the mountain. Kintail MRT, R100. 4hrs.

MARCH 21 – Sròn a' Choire Ghairbh (NN226938). A 41yr old walker fell about 100 metres over a cliff after slipping on snow covered rock. R137 traced the casualty and airlifted him to the Belford Hospital where he was diagnosed with multiple injuries. The rest of his party walked off unaided. Lochaber MRT, R137. 3hrs.

APRIL 19 – Garbh Bheinn Ardgour (NM915625). Two walkers (male and female) left Inversand to climb Garbh Bheinn via the SE ridge. The man was walking a lot faster than his partner and they eventually became separated. Following a search, he descended and called the Police for help. As team members were assembling, the missing person was seen descending safely to the road. Lochaber MRT. 3hrs.

APRIL 25 – Glenfinnan (NM948872). A male walker slipped on the path from Arkaig to Glenfinnan (just north of Streap) and suffered an ankle injury. Lochaber MRT. 44hrs.

MAY 18 – Falls of Glommach (NH017258). A 65yr old man had been reported overdue by a B&B landlady. His car was located at Killilan and a note indicated Glen Elchaig as his possible route with various options for destination. One member drove the road from Killilan to Iron Lodge checking buildings with one member at control. Police reported a call from the man that he had been to the Falls of Glommach and now had lights at Morvich in sight at around 0215hrs. At this point the team was stood down and the Police met him as he came off the hill. Kintail MRT. 4hrs.

JULY 3 – Polnish to Peanmeanach Bothy path (NM833725). A 65yr old walker from England took a wrong turn on the path and became lost. After attempting to relocate himself by climbing back up to the path he found he was unable to either climb up or down any further. R100 was in the area and uplifted him to safety. Lochaber MRT, R100. 11hrs.

JULY 9 – Morvich (NG961210) to Falls of Glomach. A 47yr old female walker and her dog left Morvich campsite at 10am to walk to the Falls of Glomach. Later in the day her dog returned un-accompanied and friends raised the alarm as the dog did not normally leave her owner. Team members set off to walk all the access paths when the missing walker arrived back. The dog had had become spooked by deer and run off. The woman was uninjured but somewhat embarassed. Kintail MRT. 8hrs

JULY 17 – Aonach Buidhe (NH058325). Team members were called to assist with a 30yr old male walker overdue at Dornie Hotel, from a walk in the area. The man eventually turned up safe and well having underestimated the duration of his walk. Kintail MRT. 5hrs.

JULY 21 – Shiel Bridge to Iron Lodge (NH043293). Friends of a 73yr old man reported him overdue from from a cycle and walking trip to three unspecfied remote hills beyond Iron Lodge. Team members carried out initial checks of the private road to Iron Lodge. The man subsequently arrived at his accomodation (Kintail Lodge Hotel) fit and well, having underestimated the time of his journey. Kintail MRT. 2hrs.

AUGUST 4 – The Saddle (NG934163). Two walkers (A 36yr old woman and a 25yr old man) failed to return from a day on The Saddle, and the alarm was raised by a friend. An initial search of the route was carried out in the dark and spotted flashing lights at NG934163. Both walkers had been trapped by rising burns due to heavy rain. With better lighting provided by the team, they were able to cross the burn and were then escorted off the hill by team members. Kintail MRT. 27hrs.

AUGUST 30 – Five Sisters of Kintail (NH984134). Two men in their 20s walking on the Five Sisters misjudged their route and the time required to complete their journey. They had no map, torch, compass, food or drink. Both were dressed in trainers, track suits and hoodies. One had a waterproof jacket but neither had gloves or hats. They descended off the path and dropped into difficult ground just as darkness came in. They sat down and called the police to report their situation and asked for help. Team members walked in and guided the two men off the hill. One was very cold but when given warm drink and food recovered quickly. Both men decided to sleep in their car in Glen Sheil before driving on to Portree the following day. Kintail MRT. 16hrs.

SEPTEMBER 1 – Falls of Glomach (NH015252). A 60yr old man slipped and suffered ligament damage, which rendered him unable to walk. He was with a party of three about one kilometre above the Falls of Glomach. Kintail MRT sent four members to the scene to assess the situation but lost communication with the hill party. The ARCC offered the services of R177, which was in the area at the time. The man was successfully lifted off and taken to Broadford Hospital. Team members walked the remaining members of the group off the hill. Kintail MRT, R137. 30hrs.

SEPTEMBER 10 – Sgùrr na Sgine (NG945114). A 28yr old male walker slipped and gashed his leg and couldn't walk. With regard to time and impending darkness R137 was deployed at the team's request to snatch the party from the hill before full dark. Two members of Kintail were on scene just in case R137 failed to find the party. All went well with the injured party delivered to Raigmore Hospital and partner delivered back to their car. Kintail MRT, R137. 6hrs.

SEPTEMBER 29 – Kintail. A 52yr old male walker was last seen at his accommodation (Great Glen Water Park) on Tuesday 21st Sept. He was reported missing on Saturday 25th when he failed to check out. He had left no route plan but was known as a hill walker doing Munros. His car was discovered late on Tuesday 28th in a little used car park at Dorusduain Forest in Kintail. A search was mounted at first light on Wednesday 29th by Kintail MRT, SARDA, Poilce handlers and R100. The search area was narrowed by information from the man's digs detailing Munros he had not climbed in the area and that those maps were missing from a collection of printed maps in his digs. Searching stopped overnight and resumed at first light on 30th with 40 extra personnel from RAF Kinloss, Glenelg and Skye MRTs and SARDA. All options within the search area were explored by ground troops, dogs and from the air. Additional areas were also checked as being options in bad weather if he changed his mind about doing a Munro on arriving at the car park. The search was put on hold at 1800hrs on the 30th with the commitment to resume if more info was received. Additional searches were carried out by Kintail, RAF Kinloss and Dundonnel MRTs during subsequent training exercises. Memebrs of Kintail MRT eventually found the man's body close to the Bealach an Sgairne (NH012213). The man appeared to have fallen a considerable distance down the north flank of Meall a Bhealaich. Kintail MRT, Kinloss MRT, Skye MRT, Glenelg MRT, R100, SARDA (S). 1004hrs,

BEN NEVIS

JANUARY 3 – Meall Cumhann (NN178697). The casualty (24yr old female) had climbed Ben Nevis but became lost on the descent. She slipped and suffered minor abdominal injuries. R177 was in the area and assisted with the evacuation of the casualty who was treated for minor injuries in the Belford Hospital. Lochaber MRT, R177. 1hr.

JANUARY 28 – Ben Nevis (Raeburn's Easy Route). Two experienced and well-equipped German climbers became disoriented in bad weather and decided not to continue. They alerted the Police and team members traced them and walked them down to the CIC hut where they spent the night. Lochaber MRT, R177. 198hrs.

FEBRUARY 4 – Ben Nevis (near path at Red Burn). Two males (26yrs and 28yrs) set off to climb Tower Ridge but due to snow conditions changed to Ledge Route instead. They left the summit around 1600hrs intending to go west to the north face car park. On the way down they triggered a slab avalanche falling approximately 300 metres. One suffered a neck injury and the other knee/elbow injuries. Team members stayed with the pair in an emergency shelter before uplift by R177. Lochaber MRT, R177. 16hrs.

FEBRUARY 24 – Ben Nevis (near CIC Hut). A lone walker was walking in the area of the CIC Hut when an avalanche carried him about 100 metres. He suffered limb injuries and was carried first by stretcher then airlifted to hospital in Fort William. Glencoe MRT, R177. 94hrs.

FEBRUARY 25 – Steal Falls, Glen Nevis. A 65yr old male walker had become tired and cold on reaching the Steall Falls in bad weather. Unable to continue, he alerted the Police who called out Lochaber MRT to assist. He was eventually airlifted out and taken to the Belford Hospital where he was rewarmed and discharged. Lochaber MRT, R137. 8hrs.

MARCH 3 – Ben Nevis (Gardyloo Gully). Two climbers (40yr old male and 45yr old female) were about to complete the route when the man slipped on unstable snow while leading. He fell, pulling out his ice screws and dragged his partner down with him. Both fell about 300 metres coming to rest in Observatory Gully. Team members and R137 were deployed but owing to bad weather, the injured man was carried to the helicopter. The female climber was able to walk unaided. The man received treatment at the Belford Hospital for a dislocated left shoulder. Lochaber MRT, R137. 56hrs.

MARCH 14 – Ben Nevis No 2 Gully Buttress (NN164716). Two experienced and well equipped men (58yrs, 36yrs) were abseiling down No 2 Gully Buttress when a peg came away. The elder climber fell about 300 metres suffering two broken arms. Team members attended along with R137 and airlifted both climbers off the mountain. Lochaber MRT, R177. 53hrs.

MARCH 27 – Ben Nevis No. 2 Gully. Two men started Raeburn's Easy Route and then traversed too far and ended up at the top of the cascades on much harder ground than the original route. The team climbed to the summit then lowered down the route to bring the climbers back up before walking them off the mountain. One climber was taken to the Belford Hospital where a broken coccyx was diagnosed. Lochaber MR. 174hrs.

APRIL 7 – Ben Nevis Tower Ridge (NN165714). Two climbers had completed the Italian Climb and were ascending Tower Ridge. One climber went ahead losing communication with the other climber. The lead climber subsequently became cragfast with the rope snagged between them. He detached himself and continued alone but became cragfast again and raised the alarm. Both climbers were winched to the summit plateau. Lochaber MRT, R137. 33hrs.

APRIL 19 – Ben Nevis Point Five Gully (NN169714). A male climber fell about 50 metres from above the third pitch, suffering suspected back, head and leg injuries. Both climbers were lowered about 600 metres. Two other climbers assisted. Lochaber MRT, R100. 138hrs.

APRIL 21 – Coire na Ciste (approx NM164719). Two climbers (male and female) had descended Number 4 Gully when they became cragfast above the CIC hut. Both were winched off suffering from hypothermia. Lochaber MRT, R137.

APRIL 24 – Tower Ridge Ben Nevis (NN165714). A mobile phone call was received at 2015hrs from a climber on Tower Ridge just below the Great Tower. His partner had 'had enough' and both were looking for a lift off the mountain! Both claimed to be experienced mountaineers. They called back again at 2200hrs and 0800hrs but nothing further was heard. Lochaber MRT. 2hrs.

MAY 1 – Càrn Mòr Dearg Arête (NN176715). A party was cragfast on the Arête. R177 attended. Lochaber MRT, R177.

MAY 20 – Coire Giubhsachan (NN880760). A 42yr old male walker became disoriented in mist and was talked down to the path by a team member. Lochaber MRT. 3hrs.

JUNE 9 – Ben Nevis (NN212772). Three walkers had just started along the tourist path from Achintee when the female member of the group (aged 60yrs) slipped on a rock suffering a suspected fracture to her left leg. Team members stretchered her to the road and a waiting ambulance. Lochaber MRT. 16hrs.

JUNE 11 – Ben Nevis (NN213483). A 44yr old woman was overcome with tiredness and asthma on the main path near the first steel bridge. Team members were not required as R137 was in the area at the time and airlifted her to a waiting ambulance. R137. 0hrs.

JUNE 23 – Stob Coire Bhealaich (NN204705). A 17yr old school pupil was unable to continue walking (no reason given) and assisted off the hill by team members. Lochaber MRT. 30hrs.

JUNE 24 – Ben Nevis (NN133720). A 51yr old male walker was descending the tourist path when he slipped and suffered a broken lower leg. Team members stretchered him to the road. Lochaber MRT. 16hrs.

JUNE 25 – West Highland Way (NN128706). An 84yr old woman was walking along the WHW when leg pain rendered her unable to continue. She was uplifted by team vehicle. Lochaber MRT. 10hrs.

JUNE 26 – Ben Nevis (NN14872). A 43yr old male walker collapsed and died on the path. R137 airlifted the body to the team's base. Lochaber MRT, R137. 21hrs.

JUNE 26 – Ben Nevis (NN147725). A 28yr old man descending the main path suffered an epileptic fit/exhaustion. R177 airlifted him to the Belford. Lochaber MRT, R177. 4hrs.

JUNE 30 – Ben Nevis (NN143723). A 61yr old man descending the tourist path experienced pain in his foot and was unable to continue. R177 attended and uplifted the man to hospital. Lochaber MRT, R177. 17hrs.

AUGUST 23 – Staoineag Bothy (NN295677). A man (21yrs) and woman (18yrs) took the train from Bridge of Orchy to Corrour with the intention of walking into Staoineag Bothy, staying the night and returning the following day. When they failed to arrive the following day, the alarm was raised. The pair turned up a day later having decided to remain on the hill a further day. They were enjoying themselves and decided not to inform anyone of their revised plans! Strathclyde Police MRT, Glencoe MRT. 1hr.

GLEN COE

JANUARY 2 – Signal Point, nr Clachaig Inn (NN122566). A female walker (62yrs) slipped and fractured her ankle. The team carried her out to a waiting ambulance. Glencoe MRT. 13hrs.

JANUARY 6 – Aonach Dubh (NN145555). Two men (24yrs and 22yrs) from Wales were climbing No 6 Gully. One of the climbers was known to suffer from diabetes and also chronic fatigue syndrome. During the climb he became extremely fatigued resulting in both becoming cragfast. Team members lowered both climbers off the route and then accompanied them to a waiting ambulance. Paramedics checked the man who did not require any medical treatment. Glencoe MRT. 90hrs.

JANUARY 8 – Clachaig Gully (NN128575). A 70yr old experienced and well-equipped male walker was descending the Clachaig Gully path on his own having completed the ridge. Whilst descending he recalls catching a crampon strap and falling forwards. The group behind who assisted him estimated that he tumbled for about 50 metres. He suffered bruising, chest and limb injuries and was evacuated by R137. Glencoe MRT, R137. 30hrs.

JANUARY 28 – Coire nan Beithach (NN214756). Two experienced men (31yrs and 22yrs) were climbing Stob Coire Nan Lochan when, by mistake, they descended into Coire Nan Beithach instead of Coire Nan Lochan where they became cragfast and benighted. Both were experienced but because of disorientation thought they should call for help. Team members located the pair and walked them to safety. Glencoe MRT. 55hrs.

JANUARY 30 – Stob Coire nam Beith (NN154546). A 56yr old woman slipped on snow and fell approximately 150 metres. She suffered cuts, bruises and a punctured lung. She was airlifted to the Belford Hospital. Glencoe MRT, R177. 24hrs.

JANUARY 31 – Ben Cruachan (NN072303). Three hill walkers (male 48yrs, male 24yrs, female 22yrs) were descending Ben Cruachan when they lost the path and descended onto steep icy ground and were unable to go up or down. They had no ice axes, crampons or torch. The team was called just before dark and members able to spot the location of the walkers using a light from their mobile. The team was deployed on the hill to find and rescue the group. R177 located and airlifted the three hill walkers who were all uninjured but very cold. They were dropped off at Control located at head of dam. Arrochar MRT, Oban MRT, R177. 51hrs.

FEBRUARY 7 – Stob Coir an Albannaich. Three male walkers from England (42yrs, 61yrs, 56yrs). One became separated and went on to the summit without incident. The others also summitted in white out conditions. A cornice gave way and one member fell 100 metres down a sheer rock face sustaining fatal head injuries. Team members were airlifted by R100 and the fallen walker taken to Belford Hospital where he was pronounced dead. Glencoe MRT, R100. 73hrs.

FEBRUARY 7 – Creag nan Gobhar. Two men from England (24yrs and 26yrs) had been kayaking the day before and one became injured. The same day they climbed part way up the mountain to camp. The following day the injured person was unable to walk. Team members stretchered him the 300 metres to the road. He had suffered a double lumbar spinal fracture in the kayak incident. Glencoe MRT. 9hrs.

FEBRUARY 20 – Hillside above Glen Orchy Farm. A member of Leuchars MRT slipped on ice whilst descending the mountain path above Glen Orchy Farm and sustained a dislocated shoulder. First aid was administered by fellow members, and the man escorted off the hill and then by team vehicle to the Belford Hospital. Leuchars MRT. 11hrs.

FEBRUARY 24 – Buachaille Etive Mor (NN214552). A party of three met up with a party of two descending the mountain. They decided to avoid Coire na Tulaich and descend via the west ridge. At a height of about 800 metres a small avalanche started above the group. Two of the group were knocked off balance and carried down to a height of about 400 metres. Their attempts to self arrest failed and they were eventually found by the others in the group, both buried just below the surface of the snow debris. It was snowing at the time with strong winds and freezing temperatures. Both died of their injuries. Members of Glencoe MRT carried the bodies off the mountain. Glencoe MRT. 110hrs.

MARCH 10 – Aonach Dubh (No. 2 Gully). Three males (62yrs, 65yrs 69yrs) from England were walking when one slipped and fell about 25 feet and suffered several scalp wounds. All three were airlifted and the injured man taken to the Belford Hospital. Lochaber MRT, R177. 22hrs.

MARCH 17 – Sgorr na Ciche (NN125595). Two walkers (42yr old male and 39yr old female) were descending from the summit when the man slipped and fell sustaining a dislocated shoulder. Both walkers were airlifted from the hill and the man conveyed to Fort William. Lochaber MRT, R177. 21hrs.

APRIL 4 – Ben Cruachan (NN074304). A woman slipped whilst descending eastwards from the summit of Ben Cruachan. She failed to arrest using her axe and continued to fall around 150 metres coming to rest on a small snow saddle. Team members who were training nearby attended but although the woman was shaken she was uninjured and able to rejoin her party. Oban MRT. 4hrs.

APRIL 4 – Ben Cruachan (NN074304). As team members were going to assist the fallen walker in the previous incident, one team member (65yr old man) slipped and fell a similar distance. Unfortunately, he came to a halt on rocky ground suffering multiple injuries. Team members were able to provide immediate medical assistance and he was then airlifted to the Southern General Hospital in Glasgow. Oban MRT, Arrochar MRT. R177. 90hrs.

APRIL 17 – Rannoch Moor. Two walkers (42yr old male, 36yr old female) were walking between Rannoch Station and Kingshouse across Rannoch Moor. The female was overtaken by muscle cramps and exhaustion and unable to carry on. Team members met the couple and assisted them seven miles back to their car at the Kingshouse Hotel. Glencoe MRT. 56hrs.

MAY 4 – Beinn Lurachan (NN173339). The Police received a 999 call from a man stating he was cragfast close to the summit of Beinn Lurachan in Glen Strae. Contact by mobile phone was made with the man and his condition (uninjured) and position on the hill confirmed. On arrival in Glen Strae the casualty could clearly be seen from the track by team members. A small party was sent to locate him and accompany him back safely to the main Glen Strae track. Oban MRT, Strathclyde Police MRT. 65hrs.

MAY 19 – Buachaille Etive Mòr (NN226546). A 53yr old man was walking with a friend and both became disoriented in the cloud, missing their intended route – Curved Ridge. The man subsequently slipped and fell approximately 150ft into D Gully sustaining multiple but not life threatening injuries. Team members were airlifted onto the mountain to assist and the casualty was then taken by helicopter to the Southern General Hospital in Glasgow. Glencoe MRT, R177. 59hrs.

MAY 22 – Lairig Gartain (NN200544). A call was received from another walker that the casualty (64yr old man) had fallen and injured himself (suspected dislocated shoulder). Another walker (a medical doctor) arrived on scene and assisted the casualty and helped him to walk out. Team members assisted with the walk out in the final stretch. The casualty was taken by ambulance to the Belford Hospital. Glencoe MRT. 14hrs.

MAY 29 – Beinn Fhada (NN163541). Two men from Germany (35yrs and 39yrs) decided to go walking with no plans, map or compass, food or suitable clothing. They called for help when lost in the cloud. They were met by team members descending the bealach into Coire Gabhail and subsequently escorted off the mountain. Glencoe MRT. 35hrs.

MAY 31 – Beinn Molurgainn (NN005385). A male walker was lost on Beinn Molurgainn. Mobile communications with the man were poor until he climbed back up the hill to gain a better signal. From this point he could see the road and flashing lights of a police vehicle. Team members acquired a GR of his position using his camera flashes as a reference point. Using this information they located him and accompanied him off the hill. The man was cold but otherwise able to walk unaided down. Oban MRT, SARDA (Southern Scotland). 85hrs.

JUNE 11 – Aonach Eagach Ridge (NN156579). Two men in their 50s were descending a gully on the south side of the ridge when both slipped and fell a short distance sustaining minor cuts/bruises. One of the men also suffered a recurring knee injury that rendered him unable to continue. Team members commenced a route search, but both men were subsequently located by R137 and airlifted from the hill. Neither required further medical assistance. Glencoe MRT, R137. 48hrs.

JUNE 15 – Aonach Eagach Ridge (NN151582). A man contacted the Police to say that he was stuck on the ridge and unable to continue. Prior to team members arriving to help, he was assisted off by another party on the ridge. Glencoe MRT. 12hrs.

JUNE 20 – Aonach Eagach (NN155583). The Police were called after a hillwalker heard cries for help from a woman cragfast on the Ridge. Team members mustered at Achtriochtan but prior to heading uphill another walker advised them that he had helped the woman safely off the hill. Glencoe MRT. 9hrs.

JUNE 23 – Ben Cruachan (NNB080281). A 62yr old male walker contacted his wife by mobile phone to say he was lost and disoriented on Stob Diamh and was in difficulties. His wife was worried and tried unsuccessfully to call her husband back. Unsure what to do she contacted Glenmore Lodge and was advised to contact the Local MRT and Police. Not wishing to cause trouble, she looked up Oban MRT on the internet and left an e-mail to the effect that her husband was in trouble on Stob Diamh. By sheer luck, the e-mail was picked up immediately, replied to, and the team placed on stand-by. This resulted in the man's wife phoning the deputy team leader and in turn the Police. A call-out was initiated and team members traced the walker close to Cruachan Dam. He was advised on a suitable descent route and made his way unaided and uninjured back to his vehicle at Cruachan Power Station. Oban MRT. 28hrs.

JULY 17 – Cruachan Horseshoe (NN072305). A 42yr old man was descending Ben Cruachan when he slipped, fell and sustained a broken ankle. Team members located the walker and carried him off the mountain. Strathclyde Police MRT, Oban MRT, Arrochar MRT. 32hrs.

AUGUST 1 – Ben Cruachan (NN083294). A 'casualty' working with Oban MRT on a training exercise became ill. She had been lying in water for some time but it was only when she arrived at the team's base having been 'evacuated' in a stretcher, that the seriousness of her condition (pallor, nausea, vomiting) became apparent. The team doctor examined the woman who was then taken to hospital in Oban. Oban MRT. 24hrs.

SEPTEMBER 21 – Ben Cruachan (NN064283). An initial report from police control was that a 35yr old man was lost but unhurt on the south side of Cruachan. The initial GR was wrong but when the police contacted the man by mobile again, his correct location was identified. A SARDA dog located the man and team members walked him back unhurt. Oban MRT, Strathclyde Police MRT, SARDA (Southern Scotland). 38hrs.

OCTOBER 11 – Beinn Sgulaird (NN048465). At 14.35 hours a 64yr old man was walking close to the tourist path on Beinn Sgulaird having reached the summit of the hill earlier in the afternoon. He was well equipped and experienced. He slipped on a steep, grass covered path and landed awkwardly on his left leg. He immediately realised that he had broken his leg. His collegues attained higher ground and contacted the Police for help. The man was picked up by R100 at 16.32 hours and conveyed to Oban Hospital. Oban MRT, Arrochar MRT, Strathclyde Police MRT, R100.

OTHER CENTRAL HIGHLANDS

FEBRUARY 15 – Creag Meagaidh (NN428885). A group of 24 scout leaders from Kent County Scouts ascended Creag Meagaidh in four groups of six. The first group of six summitted and then began to make their way along a ridge above 'The Window'. They were walking in a line unroped about 5/10m from the edge when the cornice gave way and one walker fell 2/300ft to his death. All others made their way off the mountain without injury. R137 winched the deceased from the mountain. Lochaber MRT, Kinloss MRT, R137. 42hrs.

FEBRUARY 7 – Creag Meagaidh, Staghorn Gully. Two male climbers began the route but were held up by slower climbers above them. They still had two pitches to go with darkness approaching. One torch failed as they reached the plateau. They tried to orient themselves but became disoriented and called the Police but they eventually made their own way back. Lochaber MRT. 1hr.

MARCH 11 – Sgairneach Mhor (NN518705). Three men in their 30s called the Police to say they were completely lost having left Dalwhinnie to climb the four Munros west of the Drummochter Pass. They added that they could see Loch Garry and the A9 but were three hours walk away. It was decided that given the clear conditions and lack of objective dangers, the men should be talked off the hill. This proved successful and the men were picked up by Police Officers at Dalnaspidal. Teams remained on standby pending their safe arrival. Tayside Police MRT, Tayside MRT. 4hrs.

MARCH 6 – Stob Coire Easain (NN334764). A 69yr old man was descending Meall Cian Dearg with two companions when he slipped on loose shale and fell around 70 metres down a gully landing eventually on a grassy outcrop. His companions made their way to him where they found he had suffered a serious scalp laceration but was still breathing. Emergency assistance was requested and he was airlifted to the Belford Hospital where it was found he had suffered a broken collar bone plus lacerations/bruises. Lochaber MRT, R137. 16hrs.

CAIRNGORMS

JANUARY 15/16 – Ryvoan Bothy. Police received a call at 02.30hrs to say that a party of five walkers who had left Glenmore Lodge at 22.30hrs had arrived at Ryvoan Bothy less one person whose whereabouts were unknown. A SARDA handler was requested but not required as the 20yr old student was found cold and wet bivouacking by the side of the track at 0510hrs. Lack of fitness was a possible factor, but the party still separated. Cairngorm MRT,12 hrs.

JANUARY 23 – Glen Muick (NO255853). A party of five (4 males and 1 female) left the Glen Muick car park at 10.30hrs heading for the summit of Lochnagar. At 1300hrs the party reached the col above Foxeswells where three stopped and two went on to the summit. They quickly became disoriented and lost their map. They attempted to relocate their friends to no avail. At 15.00hrs one of the pair called the Police to say they were lost on the Lochnagar plateau. MRT were alerted and discovered the party of three had made their way back to Aberdeen. At 17.06hrs the 'lost' pair phoned to say they had managed to make their way back to the car park with the assistance of other walkers. Grampian Police MRT, Braemar MRT. 8hrs.

JANUARY 24 – Lock Muick (NO284 822). Two walkers (male and female both 27yrs) left Loch Muick car park at 12.00 hours to walk round Loch Muick. Overestimating their ability, the weather conditions and having completely inadequate clothing for the time of year they encountered snow drifts on their way round. Instead of retracing their path they continued until the female member became exhausted and was unable to move any further. She began to show signs of hypothermia at which point the man contacted the Police. A group of four attended at the scene, treated the female and both were uplifted by helicopter. Suitable advice was given to both who did not appear overly concerned by their actions. Grampian Police MRT, Braemar MRT. 26hrs.

JANUARY 28 – Coire an t-Sneachda. The casualty and his climbing partner, both from England, were climbing Aladdin's Mirror. It was the casualty's first winter lead and he took a fall breaking his leg. Members of Cairngorm and Glenmore Lodge MRTs who were in the coire went to assist. The casualty was administered entonox and Sam splinted. As the rescue box was buried in snow, the Cairngorm Mountain Ski Patrol was asked to assist. The casualty was taken to Raigmore by R177. Cairngorm MRT, Glenmore Lodge MRT, Cairngorm Ski Patrol. R177. 8hrs.

JANUARY 31 – Coire an t-Sneachda. A party of two men and one woman in their 20s from England started to climb The Runnel. As they were making poor time they decided to abseil off the route. This took them so long that their friends raised the alarm. Cairngorm MRT was placed on standby and waited. The party eventually arrived tired but safe and well at the car park around 2115hrs. Cairngorm MRT. 16hrs.

FEBRUARY 5 – Coire an t-Sneachda (NH998035). A male hillwalker (41yrs) in a group of three walked over a cornice close to the exit of Jacob's Ladder and fell 200 m suffering minor facial injuries. He walked out accompanied by team members. Cairngorm MRT. 40hrs. (NB. Another walker suffered the same fate only 30 minutes later – see next).

FEBRUARY 5 – Coire an t-Sneachda (NH998035). A female instructor (age 37yrs) with two clients walked over a cornice adjacent to the exit of Jacob's Ladder. She slid all the way down (200m) without injury then climbed back to rejoin her party. Cairngorm MRT, Glenmore Lodge MRT. 40hrs.

FEBRUARY 7 – Ben Rinnes (NJ263337). A female walker (61yrs) set off to climb Ben Rinnes near Dufftown and walked up the path onto the summit. The conditions were misty with full snow cover. At 13.00hrs she phoned stating she was lost and needed help. Police were contacted and teams arrived on scene. Three parties accompanied by SAR dogs set off in search areas. She was found in a Bothy exhausted and cold due to walking through soft wet snow. She had crawled into some feed sacks for warmth and was treated with warm drinks and extra clothing. R137 arrived on scene but the woman did not require further treatment or evacuation. She travelled back to the car park in a tractor and trailer (not MRT supplied). Grampian Police MRT, Braemar MRT, Aberdeen MRT, SARDA (Scotland). 88hrs.

FEBRUARY 16 – Ben Vrackie (NN949626). A 19yr old man was part of a poorly equipped youth group from Edinburgh. Whilst glissading without an ice axe, the man struck a rock sustaining a serious leg fracture. The group leader alerted the emergency services and team members carried the man to a waiting ambulance. Tayside Police MRT, Tayside MRT. 50hrs.

FEBRUARY 20 – NN 891948. Two male walkers (both 25yrs) both planned to walk from Kingussie to Blair Athol up Glen Tromie and the Minigaig Pass. They became lost on the second day despite superb visibility and possession of a GPS receiver! Their eventual location was so remote and potentially involving three different MRTs that R137 was called to assist to uplift them from their location (height of 890m). Cairngorm MRT, R137, 4hrs.

FEBRUARY 20 – Shelter Stone Crag. A party of two males were climbing Postern when the leader fell 70m and broke his femur, hip and also suffered spinal injuries. His partner abseiled down, cut a bucket seat/scoop, put the casualty in warm clothes and secured him to the route with one of their ropes. He used the other single rope to abseil down further, traversed into Pinnacle Gully and then down climbed to safety. He then walked into Coire Domhain and contacted people in the snow holes who raised the alarm. Cairngorm MRT requested the help of R137 (for the third time that evening). On arrival at the team base, the helicopter uplifted team members including the team doctor. This was essential as the winchman did not have the qualifications to administer the required drugs. The casualty was lifted into the aircraft by a single strop under the arms due to the technical nature of the rescue. The winchman was asked to assess for severe hypothermia or unstable spinal injuries which would have prevented this. Whilst the casualty was in severe pain a strop was the best course of action at the time. The casualty was flown to hospital and operated on the following day. Cairngorm MRT, R137. 40hrs.

FEBRUARY 20 – Coire an Lochain (The Vent). Three climbers from England (51yrs, 34yrs and 19yrs). The older male climber was the only experienced member of the pair. There was a large cornice at the top and the father (quite rightly) made the decision that his son was not capable of completing the route. Their anchors (ice axe belays) were not safe enough to abseil from and both were very cold. The father raised the alarm and R137, which was on location at the rescue base dropping off two lost walkers from a previous rescue, was tasked to help. All team members were put on stand by in case a technical rescue developed but this was not to be the case as the three were air lifted from the route. They were all checked by one of the team doctors. All were fine but cold and the female casualty had a cut on the inside of her lip. The younger male suffered from ASA and his medication had frozen during the day. It was rewarmed at the team's base and self administered. Cairngorm MRT, R137. 40hrs.

FEBRUARY 28 – Glen Callater (NO178844). A party of two (male 35yrs, female 24yrs) from London had intended to wild camp overnight in the upper reaches of Glen Callater. The pair had not factored in the depth of snow on their proposed route and hadn't re-assessed their trip according. When they became exhausted beyond the end of the loch, they returned to the bothy at Callater. One incurred a minor ankle injury on the walk back to the bothy. To speed up things they left one of their rucksacks near the mouth of Coire Kander. Over the next three days the uninjured member attempted to walk out to get assistance but was forced back due to the depth of snow. Eventually a mobile signal allowed contact with Police and MRT attended to uplift the party. Braemar MRT, Grampian Police MRT. 16hrs.

MARCH 4 – River Findhorn (NJ004508). Kinloss MRT were tasked to assist a local ambulance crew with a fallen walker alongside the Findhorn River at Logie Steading. A full team callout was issued as a precaution due to the nature of the area. Upon arriving on scene and having located the casualty, a decision was made to request R100 as the optimum option for the casualty's recovery. The casualty was riverside, approximately 55m below the footpath down a snowed up steep craggy wooded cliffside. Using technical rescue techniques, the Team lowered the Bell stretcher to the site, the casualty was then placed in the stretcher prior to either the helicopter arrival or a vertical raise by the MRT. R100 arrived on scene and very swiftly recovered the casualty. Kinloss MRT, R100. 56hrs.

MARCH 8 – Coire an t-Sneachda. A party of three were climbing Finger's Ridge. The casualty (46yrs old male from England) fell 30 metres and his belay held but he suffered head and pelvic injuries. R137 was contacted and agreed to evacuate. Members of the ski patrol took three members of Cairngorm MRT to stabilise the fallen climber. R137 arrived shortly after and airlifted him to Raigmore Hospital. Cairngrom MRT, Cairngorm Ski Patrol. 15hrs.

MARCH 13 – Coire an Lochain (NH981028). Two men from England were climbing the route Oesophagus when the casualty (27yr old male) took a lead fall. His belay held preventing a more serious outcome but the man fractured both ankles in the fall. He was lowered to the loch by his partner and then airlifted by R137. Cairngorm MRT was placed on standby throughout. Cairngorm MRT, R137. 12 hours.

MARCH 30 – Fords of Avon (NJ042031). A party of four male students in their early 20s were involved in a multi-day expedition starting on the B976 Crathie to Gairnshiel Bridge road. On their third night they were camped about 1k north of the Fords of Avon refuge when they were overtaken by a severe blizzard. Two members managed to walk a short distance north to obtain a mobile signal to raise the alarm. Both MRTs were deployed, located the party and escorted them to safety. Grampian Police MRT, Braemar MRT. 294hrs.

APRIL 9 – Coire an t-Sneacda (NH995029). A party of two (female 19yrs, Male 19yrs) were finishing The Runnel in sunny, thawing conditions. The leader exited via a slot in the cornice, triggered a minor slide and was dislodged. She fell direct onto the belay (15m below) which failed. She and her partner then fell the length of the route (150m). The leader collided with her partner causing multiple crampon wounds. Both were walked off assisted by team members. Cairngorm MRT, Cairngorm Ski Patrol. 2hrs.

APRIL 25 – Ben Macdui (NN997982). Two walkers (a 57yr old male and a 41yr old female) were walking from the summit of Ben MacDui heading for the Sron Riach path. There was snow underfoot and visibility very poor. The man was walking in front following a compass bearing when he fell over the cornice edge and into the corrie of Lochan Uaine. He fell a considerable distance over snow, ice and rock but managed to arrest his fall with a walking pole. His partner called the Police and headed for the Allt Carn a Mhaim. The man, who was uninjured, began to climb back up towards the ridge but was defeated by the steepness of the headwall and, after sliding part of the way back down, decided to traverse across the corrie to the south. A party was uplifted to the Sron Riach and following a search the helicopter located the man. A dog handler and further team members mustered to search for the woman who could no longer be contacted by phone. The helicopter returned to the hill and uplifted the man and their winch-man and after a short search located and uplifted the woman from the vicinity of the Allt Carn a Mhaim. Both were taken to Braemar where they were examined by team doctors. Grampian Police MRT, Braemar MRT, R137. 28hrs.

MAY 9 – Meall Chuaich (NN713874). A group of eight walkers were on the summit of Meall Chuaich when an 84yr old male tripped and injured his head. Due to his age and the nature of his injuries, the party called 999. Aviemore police contacted Cairngorm MRT for advice. R137 was requested due to the location and casualty's age. R137 evacuated the casualty and flew him to

Raigmore where he was released after treatment for cuts and bruising to the head. Cairngorm MRT, R137. 15hrs.

MAY 23 – Ben Macdui (NH977033). A party of five were walking back from Ben Macdui when a 36yr old female tripped over a culvert suffering slight injuries (probable broken/bruised ribs). She was able to walk slowly. When asked for advice, team members advised her that she would probably be at the car park at the same time as us if she was able to continue under her own steam. Her friend thought this was the best option and agreed to call MRT when they arrived at the ski centre. They arrived safe and well. Cairngorm MRT. 15hrs.

APRIL 27 – Carn nan Sac (NO119769). A 58yr old retired teacher was undertaking a walk to pick up tops in the Glenshee area. Whilst returning from Carn a Gheoidh he began to experience breathing dificulties. Two walkers passing by came across the man and offered to help. Progress back to the man's car was slow and eventually the three had to stop near an area known locally as "The Bunny Run". The two men called the emergency services. Members of Braemar MRT used a vehicle to access the slopes and quickly located the man where he was walked a short distance and the transported to the road by vehicle. He was taken to Aberdeen Royal by R137 where he was diagnosed with a heart condition that required a stay in hospital. Braemar MRT, Grampol MRT, R137. 24hrs.

APRIL 30 – Carn an Tuirc (NO157802). A man undertook a one day walk to complete a number of Munros. He had a GPS receiver but not a map or compass. Late in the day and in poor visibility he became disoriented and contacted the Police. He was unable to give a GR as his GPS was still calibrated in Lat/Long but the Police were able to estimate his location from his known height and description of the terrain. From this, they were able to talk him down. Grampian Police MRT, 2hrs

JUNE 7 – Cairn of Barns (NO320713). A 78yr old man was used to climbing this hill every week. When he was reported overdue, MRTs were tasked and found the man at the summit in an unresponsive state. Team members carried him to a lower position where he was evacuated to Ninewells Hospital by helicopter. He had died from an internal illness. Tayside Police MRT, Tayside MRT, R137,149hrs.

JUNE 11 – Coire an t-Sneachda. A 36yr female old walker slipped and fell about 10ms onto snow whilst descending the ridge. She stopped awkwardly and broke her right leg above the boot. Her instructor (a member of Cairngorm MRT and Glenmore MRT) called the police who then notified CMRT. The weather was fine and R137 was able to assist. She was given cylimorph by the winchman and the improvised splint was replaced by a vacuum splint. She was then flown to Raigmore Hospital. Cairngorm MRT, R137, 4hrs.

JUNE 26 – Pass of Ballater, Creag an t-Seabhaig (NO367972). Two men (33yrs and 34yrs) were climbing a local crag when one slipped and fell about 10 feet. He landed heavily next to his partner who managed to grab his clothing thus preventing a longer fall. The man's injuries, whilst initially thought to be serious, turned out be soft tissue damage and deep grazing. Grampian Police MRT, Braemar MRT, 4hrs.

JULY 27 – Creag Choinnich (NO160917). A 64yr old female walker lost her footing and slipped and suffered a torn achilles tendon. With help from her husband she managed to shuffle some distance but was in too much pain to clear the mountain. Team members carried her to a waiting ambulance. Grampian Police MRT, Braemar MRT. 4hrs.

AUGUST 17 – Capel Mounth (NO285778). A Ranger in Glen Doll reported that an elderely couple had been seen heading slowly uphill from Glen Doll towards Capel Mounth late in the day. Due to a delay, this information was not picked up by the police for 12 hours. There had been no report of anybody overdue but a track search was undertaken as a precautionary mesure. Nobody was found. Grampian Police MRT, Braemar MRT. 8hrs.

AUGUST 19 – Shelter Stone Crag (NH999014). A man and woman climbing The Needle on Shelter Stone Crag were reported overdue. The man was known to members of the team and it was thought that the poor weather had delayed their climb. This was in fact the case as was discovered when both arrived safe and well the following morning. Cairngorm MRT. 4hrs.

AUGUST 27 – Cuidhe Crom (NO260849). Two walkers (55yr old man and 46yr old woman) were undertaking a day walk in order to take in a number of tops within the Lochnagar area, when they separated at the area of the top of Cuidhe Crom. The woman was not keen to follow her partner down the rough ground to Little Pap. The man began to make his own way onto Little Pap, with the woman intending to return north west to pick up the line of the Meikle Pap path to descend to the car park at Glen Muick. Unfortunately she turned the wrong way and descended towards the Glas Allt whilst the man made his way to the main path, intending to meet the woman as she descended. He waited on the main path but then began to descend when he failed to meet the woman as anticipated. Returning to the car park, he was surprised to find she had not yet returned so began to make his way to Cuidhe Crom again, hoping to meet her on the way up. In the meantime, the woman had made her way back to the car. Eventually, the man contacted the police for assistance. Prior to the search of tracks, the car park was checked, where the woman was found safe and well. Grampian Police MRT, Braemar MRT. 4hrs.

AUGUST 27 – Tolmount (NO204790). A walker called the Police to say that he and his brother were lost in the hills west of Glenshee. He stated he had a map but no compass. Teams were alerted and on speaking with the man it was ascertained he was possibly in the Cairn of Claise area. A three man party was sent out initially supported by RAF helicopter. Shortly after, both men were found between Tolmont and Fafernie and flown to Braemar. Both were cold but otherwise uninjured; poorly equipped for their journey. Grampian Police MRT, Braemar MRT, R137,16hrs.

AUGUST 30 – Beinn Mheadhoin (NJ008010). The casualty (a 62yr old woman) and her friend were walking from Loch Avon to Bheinn Mheadoin when she slipped close to Loch Etchachan. She was in considerable pain and unable to bear any weight. R137 was on a training flight close by and diverted to the location. The woman was taken to Raigmore Hospital where her injuries were diagnosed as a broken/dislocated ankle. Braemar MRT, Grampian Police MRT, R137. 3hrs.

AUGUST 31 – Lairig Ghru (no GR given). A 20yr old man was reported by his father as two days overdue from a walk. He was found by two other walkers who put him in a tent. The man had not eaten for two days and had been constantly sick. It was unclear exactly what his illness was but possibly linked to lack of food. R137 was training in the area and was tasked to take him to Aviemore Health Centre. Cairngorm MRT. 15hrs.

AUGUST 31 – Coire an t-Sneachda (Pigmy Ridge). A female climber was witnessed taking a lead fall by an off duty winchman from R137. He called the police who alerted Cairngorm MRT as the previous incident was ongoing. The woman had suffered a severe head laceration and minor leg injuries. Team members were deployed as R137 was en route to Raigmore Hospital with the previous casualty. When it returned to assist, team members were taken on board to effect what was expected to be a technical rescue. In the event, R137 managed to winch off the casualty and fly her to Raigmore. Cairngorm MRT, R137. 30hrs.

SEPTEMBER 3 – Lairig Ghru (NH973005). Aviemore police received a distress call from a 65 year old man reporting that he was ill. R137 located the casualty south of the Pools of Dee and transported him to Raigmore Hosptal safe and well. Cairngorm MRT, Braemar MRT, Grampian Police MRT, Kinloss MRT, Braemar MRT, R137. 8hrs.

SEPTEMBER 4 – Lairig Ghru (NN987931). A group from the Leuchars Air Training Corps was undertaking the first day trek of a three day Duke of Edinburgh Award expedition in the Braemar area. An 18yr old girl in the group injured her left ankle when in the Lairig Ghru resulting in considerable pain. There was no mobile phone reception at the locus but a passing walker undertook to phone the Police. Team members were deployed in an off road vehicle and were able to drive to within 2K of the incident. Because of the girl's pain, the rough journey by stretcher to the vehicle was considered best avoided. R137 was requested and airlifted the casualty to Raigmore Hospital where she was subsequently diagnosed as having torn ligaments on her left ankle. Braemar MRT, Grampian Police MRT, R137. 26hrs.

SEPTEMBER 11 – Glen Banchor behind Newtonmore. A 17yr old girl from Gordonstoun School was on an expedition with nine others. Members of the group alerted the Police when the girl collapsed and fell unconcious. R137 uplifted the girl and took her to the Belford Hospital. Cairngorm MRT, R137. 3hrs.

SEPTEMBER 21 – Cairn a' Claise (NO184790). Two 19yr old men had set out from Callater Bothy with a view of crossing Jocks Road into Glendoll. They had no map or compass, but they were carrying a tent and sleeping bag of poor quality, and waterproofs and footwear which were equally poor. On reaching the Plateau between Glen Callater and Glen Doll they became disorientated in mist and lost. Two team members were mobilised but the men were found by another walker at Cairn a' Claise who walked them down to Glen Callater where they were met by team members. Both men were unhurt and suitable advice was given with regards to future forays into the mountains. Grampol MRT, Braemar MRT. 4hrs.

SEPTEMBER 21 – Lairig Ghru (NO983960). Two students (male and female both aged 23yrs) set out about 07.00hrs to walk through the Lairig Ghru from Coylumbridge to Braemar where they were to spend the night in the Youth Hostel. They had arranged to phone one of their grandparents at 17.00hrs to say that all was well. About 19.15 hours, the woman called the police to say the girls had not phoned in as planned. Police MR confirmed they had not arrived at Youth Hostel. One member of Braemar MRT drove to Derry Lodge to check along last 10 miles of the intended route. About 20.10hrs hours the girls were found near the gates of Glen Derry where they had just been to a Gamekeeper's house to phone the grandmother to say that all was well. Braemar MRT, Grampian Police MRT. 6hrs.

SEPTEMBER 22 – White Hill Glen Clova (NO370760). A 24yr old man and 28yr old woman walked from the Clova Hotel to high ground in thick mist without proper clothing, footwear or navigation equipment. Once lost they called Police and MRTs were deployed to search high ground. Nobody was located that day, but the following day R137 joined search along with the two RAF MRTs. Both walkers were found suffering hypothermia and treated on scene. The woman was stretchered and both were evacuated by R137. Tayside Police MRT, Tayside MRT, Grampian Police MRT, Braemar MRT, Kinloss MRT, Leuchars MRT, SARDA (Scotland), SARDA (Southern Scotland). 1123hrs.

SEPTEMBER 24 – Glen Lui (NO057922). Three missing men in their 30s were reported as having no hill walking experience and being very poorly equipped. They parked their car at the Lin of Quoich and set off with another man. They walked towards Glen Lui and the fourth member of the party went into Glen Quoich. They were to meet at the end of the Clais Fhearnaig path in Glen Lui at GR 057 922 but the group never met up. The fourth man waited for some time before heading back to the vehicle and thereafter contacted the Head Ranger who drove up to Derry Lodge as an initial search but found no trace of the three men. Grampian Police and Braemar MRTs checked the Land Rover tracks in the area with negative result. Rescue 137 traced the males walking south in Glen Derry en route to Braemar. The men were not as badly equipped as first described but were cold and wet. They had missed the end of the Clais Fhearnaig path and continued north into Glen Derry. They had a 1:25000 scale map with them but were unable to read it. They eventually found the Hutchison Bothy in Coire Etchachan, where they spent the night. They met another walker who informed them of their position and gave them advice on how to return to their start point. Rescue 137 traced them walking out in Glen Derry. Grampian Police MRT, Braemar MRT, Leuchars MRT, R137. 186hrs.

OCTOBER 12 – Lochnagar (NO245856). A 75yr old man set out from the Spittal of Glenmuick car park with the intention of ascending Lochnagar and returning to the car park on the same day. After reaching the top he became disorientated and walked in the wrong direction before becoming benighted. He spent the night on the plateau and during this time was in mobile phone contact with his wife at home. The following day, concern was expressed that he was still out on the hill and apparently sounded confused and tired when spoken to by a relative. At this time, he was still unsure of his whereabouts and how to navigate off the hill. Grampian Police MRT members were contacted and made contact with the man by mobile phone. He was unable to establish his location. Around mid day a fell runner came across the man and was able to pass a location to Police. A former team member who was on the hill was requested to make contact with the man and begin to assist him in walking off the hill north towards Ballochbuie. Two members of Grampian Police MRT were deployed and met both men to provide further assistance off the hill. Grampol MRT. 10hrs.

OCTOBER 15 – Lairig Ghru (NO 018885). Two men were overdue from traversing the Lairig Ghru from north to south. They had left Aviemore at 0930hrs expecting to be at the Linn of Dee car park by 1630hrs. They were found at White Bridge at 2215hrs having been delayed by a lack of torches. Cairngorm MRT, Braemar MRT, Grampian Police MRT, 7hrs.

OCTOBER 18 – Coire Raibert (NJ005025). A group of four (two men in their 20s and two women in their 20s) were on a night traverse of the Cairngorm plateau. They were due to return by 06.00hrs but reported overdue by a friend. Cairngorm MRT was placed on standby and then called out at 12.00hrs due to limited light and deteriorating weather. Two of party were located at 16.05hrs in Coire Raibert, reporting that they had always intended to return by 18.00hrs and not 06.00hrs. The other two members of the party spent the day with an instructor and reported to base 17.19hrs. An extensive and manpower intensive search casued by a basic error in communication between the hill party and the informant. Cairngorm MRT, Kinloss MRT, Braemar MRT, SARDA (Scotland), R137. 195hrs.

OCTOBER 19 – Strathy Nethy (NJ023052). Three walkers (51yr old woman, 17yr old woman and 17yr old man) were lost on the Cairngorm plateau. The party reached Cairngorm summit at 15.15hrs. Their return took place in a blizzard. When interviewed they described a route which, in effect took them east into Strath Nethy rather than north back to Ptarmigan. Rescue 137 attempted to assist, but the weather was too poor. However, when they 'pinged' the casualty's mobile it gave a GR of NJ 014043. In contrast, when the man contacted control with a Lat/Long reference from his iPhone, it placed them at at NJ 023052 almost 2k from the first location. Eventually the three walkers were located at 20.32hrs and walked out unaided – cold but otherwise OK. Cairngorm MRT, R137, SARDA (Scotland). 104hrs.

SOUTHERN HIGHLANDS

JANUARY 17 – Ben Lui (NN266262). Two inexperienced winter hillwalkers (male 28yrs, female 28yrs) were climbing the east ridge of Ben Lui when the male fell. He was found 350ft below the crest with multiple injuries – unconscious with head wounds. He was given first aid (head wound dressed, guedel airway inserted and administered oxygen) and subsequently packaged in a vacuum mat and casualty bag and stretchered off the mountain. A helicopter was requested but due to the poor weather conditions was unavailable. CPR was administered on the way down and continued by ambulance crew once in the waiting ambulance at Cononish. He was pronounced dead by the crew. It was the casualty's first experience of winter conditions and of wearing crampons. His partner suffered mild hypothermia. Killin MRT,SARDA (Southern Scotland). 372hrs.

JANUARY 24 – Beinn Chabhair (NN361183). Two walkers (male and female aged 30yrs) were walking when the female slipped on ice and suffered a lower leg fracture. Neither were appropriately kitted for winter conditions (no ice axe, crampons, map, compass or whistle). They did have a GPS receiver which enabled them to provide an accurate GR. Killin MRT who were training in area attended. Both walkers were airlifted by R177. Killin MRT, R177. 30hrs.

JANUARY 28 – Ben Lomond (Tourist path). A walker descending from the Ptarmigan path reported two shouts. Subsequent interviews with walkers descending the main path suggested there were 3/5 'lads' on the path ill-shod and clothed and not prepared for the winter conditions. They had been advised by walkers on the hill not to continue but chose to ignore this advice. The team was tasked to climb via the tourist path and quickly encountered four young men fitting the description – dressed in jeans and trainers. The men were descending via the path and the team accompanied them to the car park. Lomond MRT, SARDA (Southern Scotland). 28hrs.

JANUARY 30 – Ben Ledi (NN564095). Two walkers (male and female in mid 40s) were descending from the summit when the man slipped on a steep icy section of the path sustaining a broken ankle. Killin MRT was deployed as the helicopter was initially unavailable. When it became available it uplifted the casualty and took him direct to Glasgow Southern Hospital. Neither walker had torch, map, ice axe or crampons. But they had a GPS receiver with built-in mapping that allowed them to give a GR of their location. Killin MRT, R177. 42hrs.

FEBRUARY 6 – Ben More (NN430247). A party of three men and two women in their 30s became disoriented on descending Ben More. They called the Police for assistance and the Killin Team Leader gave them instructions for a safe route off the mountain. The party commenced their descent but soon found the ground too steep and visibility very bad so they decided to wait to be rescued. R117 uplifted two teams of MRT members to below the cloud base, who then climbed up to the party and escorted them off the mountain to a waiting vehicle. No injuries and all well equipped for the conditions. Killin MRT, R177. 96hrs.

FEBRUARY 23 – Lochgoilhead (NN207009). A professional outdoor education instructor was setting up an abseil but failed to correctly tie into a safety line. When he tested the system, it failed and he fell, suffering fractures to his hip, ankle and elbow. Team members treated the man and evacuated him by stretcher to the Scout Centre from where a health service helicopter took him to hospital. Arrochar MRT. 35hrs.

FEBRUARY 27 – Beinn Achaladair (NN342432). Two walkers (male and female) strayed onto the west face of Beinn Achaladair. They heard the snow making a 'whoomphing' noise and became frightened to move in case the whole slope avalanched. R177 found both 150m below the summit sheltered by a large rock, and airlifted them to safety at Achaladair Farm. Oban MRT, Arrochar MRT. 34hrs.

MARCH 8 – Auchineden Hill (NS505809). A 48yr old female nurse and her uncle were descending the popular route from Auchineden Hill. The woman slipped on the ice-encrusted path and suffered a suspected broken right leg. The uncle called for ambulance assistance. The paramedics on scene struggled to cope with the icy ground conditions. Realizing they could not effect a rescue they asked for MRT assistance. There was a delay of an hour and a half between ambulance control receiving the initial call and Central Scotland Police/ Lomond MRT being alerted. Team members stretchered the woman one mile to the car park for evacuation by R177 to the Southern General Hospital. Lomond MRT, R177. 4hrs

MARCH 13 – Beinn Each (NN600170). A party of two (male 41yrs and female 35yrs) were climbing the NW flank of Beinn Each. The female slipped on snow covered heather and sustained a suspected twisted ankle. R177 located and winched both walkers. The uninjured male was dropped off with MRT at Glen Ample Farm and the casualty taken to Stirling Royal Hospital. Both walkers were well equipped for the conditions. Killin MRT, R177, 38hrs.

MARCH 13 – Beinn Achaladair (NN341447). A couple (male 66yrs, female 55yrs) had set off at 08.00hrs to climb Beinn an Dothaidh. Not wishing to descend too soon (especially since their campervan was parked at Achallader) they aimed for the col between Beinn an Dothaidh and Beinn Achaladair. They missed the col and ended up on Beinn Achaladair becomong tired and confused about their descent route. After several abortive attempts to find a route down the northern corrie they eventually braved the slope between Meall Buidhe and Coire an Lochain. By this time the female was exhausted and had temporarily collapsed. It was getting dark and they made a 999 call for assistance. They then continued their descent, saw police blue lights and made second contact with force control to confirm they were heading to lights. Oban MRT personnel met them on their descent. The couple were well equipped for the terrain and weather and the man seemed experienced and knowledgeable. A navigational mistake led to them losing their location, then their situation became compounded by tiredness. Oban MRT, Arrochar MRT. 47hrs.

APRIL 5 – Conic Hill (NS425920). Central Police called the team to assist in the evacuation of a 48 year old female walker near the summit of Conic Hill. Whilst walking on the West Highland Way she had slipped and injured her leg. Seventeen team members made their way to Balmaha. Subsequently, it became known that the SAS had contacted the ARCC and requested support from R177. A number of Lomond MRT members had reached the casualty's location when R177 arrived and evacuated the casualty to the Southern General Hospital. Once again, an initial 999 call went to the SAS Control and a delay in contacting Police/MR resulted. Additionally, SAS Control contacted ARCC direct without Police involvement in decision making. Lomond MRT. 17hrs.

APRIL 8 – Ben Chaluim (NN385322). A 52yr old male teacher from Edinburgh was reported having injured his ankle whilst descending Ben Chaluim. While he continued to struggle down the hillside, his walking companion had made his way to Kirkton Farm near Tyndrum where their car was parked and raised the alarm. One team member went to Kirkton Farm while the Team Leader started to assemble a couple of local members. The casualty was located by a team member using binoculars. He was seen hobbling slowly about 400m from Kirkton Farm. Assistance was gained from a local shepherd to uplift the casualty using an agricultural vehicle. The casualty refused further medical treatment for his twisted ankle and managed to drive home. The injury was sustained as a result of a simple slip on rough ground. Killin MRT. 2hrs.

APRIL 11 – Ben More (NN429247). A 45 year old man from Fife and his 12 year old daughter were hill walking on Ben More in winter conditions. The man phoned the police and reported that he had twisted or broken his ankle and needed help. The couple were poorly equipped for the conditions and terrain.

No ice axe or crampons, poor quality canvas boots (non-vibram soles), poor waterproof clothing. They did have a map, compass, torch and whistle. Rescue 177 and Killin MRT were alerted. The helicopter picked up the injured man and his daughter and dropped them at Ben More Farm. The man, who could hardly walk on the hill stepped out of the helicopter and walked to his car with no apparent problem. The Police gave the gentleman counselling on the cost of running helicopters. Killin MRT. 4hrs.

APRIL 17 – Craigmore Crag Nr Blanefield (NS528798). Two young men with some experience on a climbing wall, were now climbing rock for the first time. Having completed a short route, the leader was being lowered off when the top runner (that was taking his full weight) ripped out. The casualty hit the ground with his lower back hitting rocks. He was using very new rock climbing equipment and was inexperienced at leading rock climbs. The ambulance service received the emergency call and sent an ambulance to the incident. Police contacted Lomond MRT when the ambulance crew realised that they couldn't evacuate the casualty by themselves. The team carried him to the roadside and the waiting ambulance transferred him to the Glasgow Western General Hospital. Lomond MRT. 32hrs.

APRIL 25 – Meall nan Aighean NN688490). A husband and wife in their 30s planned to complete the four Munros comprising the Cairn Mairg group. After the last top they descended in mist from Meall nan Aighean, lost the path and found themselves on steep ground in the approaching dark. They contacted the Police who alerted the teams. Both walkers had appropriate navigation equipment. They reported their GR and were then advised by mobile of a suitable way off the mountain. Two team members climbed to meet the pair but, in the event, both made their own way down. Tayside Police MRT, Tayside MRT. 8hrs.

APRIL 25 – Ben More (NN421253). A 43yr old man was hill walking with two male friends. During their descent of Ben More the casualty slipped on snow and tumbled approximately 100 feet sustaining leg, head and rib injuries. The party was poorly equipped for the conditions and terrain: no ice axe or crampons, poor waterproof clothing, no map, compass, torch or whistle. R137 and Killin MRT were alerted and went to Ben More Farm. From here they could see the injured person and one of his friends who had stayed with him. Team members went to the casualty, administered first aid and loaded him onto a stretcher. R137 winched up the casualty and his friend and took them to a waiting ambulance. Due to the nature of his suspected injuries, the casualty was flown to Paisley Hospital. Killin MRT, R137. 43hrs.

APRIL 25 – Ben Vorlich (NN615201). A party of three hill walkers reached the summit of Ben Vorlich and then became lost. They called Central Scotland Police who informed Tayside Police. Killin MRT members were redeployed from the Callander area (having just returned from another incident on Ben A'an) along with additional team members from the Ben More incident (see above). The group eventually made their way down to a cottage and the owner agreed to take them back to their car at Ardvorlich. The Police indicated that they were ill equipped for the prevailing conditions and had poor navigational skills. Killin MRT, Tayside Police MRT, Tayside MRT, SARDA (Southern Scotland), 24hrs.

APRIL 25 – Ben A'an (NN502082). A 19 yr old man (member of eleven Air Cadets from Glasgow) fell approximately 12 feet whilst scrambling on a crag and sustained a suspected broken leg. On examination by one of the team doctors it appeared to be a gash to the leg that was painful and bleeding (note, the casualty went through two bottles of Entonox). A helicopter was unavailable due to low cloud conditions so the casualty was packaged and stretchered off the hill to a waiting ambulance and then transferred by road ambulance to Stirling Royal Infirmary. The casualty's clothing was suitable for the conditions but no climbing equipment was being used nor was he an experienced climber. Killin MRT, 110hrs.

APRIL 30 – Ben Lomond. The team received a call from Central Scotland Police requesting Lomond MRT's help in response to concerns raised by a member of the public. A walker had passed an elderly man making his way to the summit of Ben Lomond but had missed him on the descent. While were making their way to Rowardennan, news came that the elderly gentleman had turned up safe and well. Lomond MRT. 7hrs.

MAY 1 – Weem north of Aberfeldy (NN845500). A 28yr old man was bouldering on the crags just north of Weem with friends when he fell and injured his back. The Scottish Ambulance Service was initially called and then requested MR assistance. The man was eventually carried off by team members to a waiting ambulance. The man was under the influence of alcohol whilst bouldering. Tayside MRT, Tayside Police MRT, 35hrs.

MAY 8 – Ben More (NS138854). Team members were alerted to a party overdue from Benmore Outdoor Centre. A police helicopter spotted the group making their way back to the Centre. Arrochar MRT. 14hrs.

MAY 24 – Ben Venue (NN485060). At 16.30hrs two female hill walkers (aged around 21yrs) called the Police to say they were lost descending the summit of Ben Venue. The walkers were contacted by Killin MRT and given guidance and advice on how to reach the path. They then made their own way off the hill to the car park with progress monitored by team members by regular mobile phone calls. Neither walker had a map or compass. Killin MRT, 2hrs.

MAY 27 – Dumgoyne (NS541 827). The team was contacted just after 1300hrs to go the aid of a walker who had fallen near the summit of Dumgoyne. The 65 year old man was in a party of four when he slipped on the path, fell and twisted his knee. He was in such pain that his companions telephoned the Police for help. The first team member was on scene at just before 14.00hrs. The casualty was administered pain relief before being packaged into the stretcher. The casualty and his three companions were taken off the hill and the casualty taken to a waiting ambulance and then to Glasgow Royal Infirmary. Lomond MRT, 35hrs.

MAY 29 – Beinn Narnain (NN267064). A male walker descending Beinn Narnain took a fall and suffered two broken ankles. He alerted his wife who called the emergency services. R177 located the casualty and evacuated him to the Southern General Hospital. Arrochar MRT, R177. 8hrs.

MAY 30 – Ben Venue (approx. NN480075). Police contacted the Team Leader at 18.55hrs in response to a call for help from a man in difficulty descending Ben Venue. In talking with the casualty, he described his position, which was in the Bealach Nam Bo area on the southern shore of Loch Katrine. He also indicated that he had a hamstring injury. Whilst the team was responding, the Police called to say that the individual had been picked up by a Scottish Water Board boat and that he was safe and well. Lomond MRT, Water Board personnel. 14hrs.

JUNE 3 – Ben Vorlich area (NN611192). At 21.45hrs a group of five youths on a Duke of Edinburgh expedition were reported overdue on a walk from Glenartney to Ardvorlich. A local team member carried out a search of the hill tracks on the west side of Ben Vorlich without success. At 23.15hrs the party made contact with their organisers to report they had made a navigation error and were back on track to reach Ardvorlich safe and well. Killin MRT. 2hrs.

JUNE 4 – Ben Oss (NN288251). At 08.15hrs a call was received from Central Scotland Police to report two men needing assistance on the summit of Ben Oss. R177 was alerted and three members of the team went to Cononish Farm. The two walkers were uplifted by helicopter and taken to Glasgow for a check up. Both were very poorly equipped (shorts and jogging bottoms), whilst poor planning and lack of experience were contributing factors. Killin MRT, R177, 7hrs.

JUNE 9 – Gleann Ach-innis Chailein (NN343378). A male walker alerted the Police that he had fallen against a boulder and was suffering back pain. Teams were called to assist a road Ambulance as the man was several kilometres up the track. He was loaded onto a spinal board and evacuated across the river to a waiting Hospital helicopter. The casualty was known to the Police as a persistent instigator of false alarms and call-outs by the emergency services elsewhere in the UK. Arrochar MRT, Oban MRT. 43hrs.

JUNE 20 – Campsie Fells (NS645812). A female left the car park on the Crow Road and began to walk up Lecket Hill. She quickly encountered steep ground, became scared and phoned her friend at the car park. She, in turn, called the Police and R177 was alerted and lifted her to safety. Strathclyde Police MRT, R177. 3hrs.

JUNE 20 – Beinn Bhuidhe (NN222182). Teams were called out in response to the report of an overdue walker. The walker (a 53yr old male from Glasgow) had left home the previous day at 09.00hrs with the intention of climbing Ben Bhuidhe. The man had a history of epilepsy and had had brain surgery some years before. The man's car was located in the car park at the head of Glen Fynne and he was located after a search of known routes up the mountain. He had fallen into a burn and sustained head, spine, rib and knee injuries. Following full immobilisation he was evacuated by helicopter to the Southern General Hospital in Glasgow. Strathclyde Police MRT, Arrochar MRT, Oban MRT, SARDA (Scotland), SARDA (Southern Scotland). 285hrs.

JUNE 23 – Clachan Hill (NN187131). A 45yr old man took a bus from Paisley intending to walk from Dalmally to Arrochar. He had no rucksack, map, compass, food or waterproof clothing, nor had he informed anyone of his intentions. The Police received an emergency call from him to say he was crag-fast near Clachan Hill. He had managed to wander down steep ground and ended up in a deep ravine with a burn running through it. He was able to describe in part his location before his mobile phone battery died. Workers at the Clachan Power Station heard shouts for help. A Police helicopter was called to assist and discovered the man trapped in a deep ravine. MRT's were directed to his position and effected a technical rescue. He was then walked off the hill safe and well by team members. Oban MRT, Strathclyde Police MRT, Arrochar MRT, SARDA (Scotland). 177hrs.

JUNE 27 – Ben Chaluim (NN384310) A 45 year old male was reported missing by his wife. Both were staying at the Strathfillan 'wigwams' near Tyndrum and had been drinking brandy all night and then decided to walk up Ben Challum at 04.30hrs. At approximately 06.30hrs the woman returned to the campsite leaving her husband to continue to the summit. He had no hill equipment, clothing, food or water. Around mid-day he phoned his brother to say he was lost, dehydrated, out of breath and distressed; his last words to his brother were that he was "dying" and the phone then cut out. The Police were contacted and Killin MRT deployed. Rescue 177 arrived, the casualty was located on the path just below the summit and flown to Stirling Royal Infirmary. He was suffering from dehydration, heat exhaustion and low blood sugar level. Killin MRT, R177. 48hrs.

JULY 5 – Campsie Fells (NS553836). A 48yr old man – properly equipped and clothed – called the Police to say he was disorientated on Garloch Hill in the Campsies. He had planned a walk from Glengoyne Distillery along the north ridge to Earl's Seat and back but had became disorientated in the cloud. He made attempts to find his way off the hill and finally, when the cloud lifted, recognised Dumgoyne and managed to make his way back to the car park from where he drove around to the Kirkhouse Inn in Blanefield. Team members had begun a search when the Police received a call from the man indicating he was safe and well. Lomond MRT, SARDA (Scotland). 26hrs.

JULY 6 – Menstrie Glen (NS847983). A 25yr old local woman was reported missing by her family. Initial enquiries revealed that she was despondent and fearful for her future. She had been very quiet on previous days and had packed a rucksack which was kept at the side of her front door. On 6th July her family returned home to find a note written by the woman intimating she was low and depressed. The police were informed at 18.20hrs and initial enquiries indicated she may be in the Menstrie area and possibly heading into the Ochil Hills. Team members were alerted that evening and carried out a search of Menstrie Glen by vehicle and foot. The search re-commenced the following morning when the woman was found safe and well camping in the glen. She was well prepared and unaware that any concerns had been raised. Ochils MRT, SARDA (Southern Scotland). 86hrs.

JULY 11 – West Highland Way (NN333130). The team was called to locate a 36yr old walker lost on the WHW. Contact with the man by mobile phone confirmed his position somewhere north of the Inversnaid hotel. With help from the Loch Lomond Rescue Boat, team members were deployed to the expected location and found the man, distressed and very apologetic, about a mile north of the Hotel. The man was cold, very poorly dressed with a tiny rucsac and little in the way of backup gear. He and his three companions had camped out the night before and the man had assumed his companions had all the gear. As the group made their way along the path, the man began to trail the others and eventually slipped, hurt his ankle and lost contact with his friends. Contact was made with Ben Glas campsite to inform his companions of the situation and the man was taken to Ardlui and a waiting ambulance. Lomond MRT. 27hrs.

JULY 16 – Conic Hill (NS426918). The team was called in response to a request from Ambulance Control to help an injured walker (63yr old man) on Conic Hill. The man was descending from the summit when he slipped on a steep section of the path and suffered a leg injury rendering him unable to continue. Members of his party raised the alarm but there was a delay of over an hour before the SAS, unable to complete the job, alerted the Police/MRT. Team members arrived on scene, relieved a National Park Ranger who had arrived earlier to assist, and administered first aid. As the man was being packaged for evacuation by team members, R177 arrived and took the man to the Southern General Hospital in Glasgow. Lomond MRT, R177. 18hrs.

JULY 17 – Cruach Ardrain (NN413206). A 41 year old female hill walker became disorientated in the mist as she was descending the south side of Cruach Ardrain and found herself in an outcrop. When questioned by mobile she described seeing a farm in the distance and a loch (which she thought was Loch Lomond, but was in fact Loch Voil). One group of team members drove up the Inverlochlarig Glen hill track whilst others met with police officers at Inverlochlarig Farm. The woman eventually walked off the hill unaided, to join team members at the farm. Her clothing was suitable for the conditions and she had a mobile phone, map and whistle, but no compass or head torch. Killin MRT, SARDA (Southern Scotland). 64hrs.

JULY 24 – West Highland Way (Balmaha to Rowardennan). The team was placed on standby just before 18.00hrs to assist with an incident on the West Highland Way. A man with seven youngsters, aged between seven and 17, were 'stuck at a steep bit down by the lochside'. Having started at Balmaha they were making their way to the Youth Hostel at Rowardennan. The man initially phoned in around 16.00hrs but then radio contact with him was lost. The Loch Lomond rescue boat and the Park Ranger's boat had been searching but with no success. A helicopter was unavailable because of bad weather. Given the time of day and the relative ease in which the man ought to have found his way to Rowardennan the Police decided to wait and, if at 19.00hrs there was still no news, ask the team to assist. Just before the 1900hrs deadline, reports came in that the party had arrived safely. Lomond MRT. 2hrs.

JULY 25 – Conic Hill (NS444924). The Scottish Ambulance Service contacted the Police to request the team's assistance just before 06.00hrs. A party of eight teenagers were stuck on the eastern slopes of Conic Hill when one fell suffering a suspected broken ankle. Another member who hadn't eaten or drunk anything for 24 hours fell ill. A hospital helicopter was despatched to the scene, dealt with the casualties and evacuated them to the Southern General Hospital in Glasgow. Team members began to escort the remaining members of the party off the hill until, en route, they decided to carry on with their intended plan. At this point the team stood down. Lomond MRT. 14hrs. (Statistician's note – this incident is another in a whole line of incidents over many years in which the initial call for help was directed to Ambulance Control with a subsequent delay in the MRT being notified and hence deployed)

AUGUST 1 – Beinn Chabhair (NN363182). A 52yr old male was in a party of four hill walkers coming off Beinn Chabhair when he twisted his ankle. His friends raised the alarm. R177 was scrambled and Killin MRT called out and assembled at Beinglas Farm near Inverarnan. R177 located the man, uplifted him and flew him to Glasgow Southern General Hospital. The three remaining members walked off the hill unaided. Killin MRT, 30hrs.

AUGUST 5 – West Highland Way (NS375958). The team received a call around13.30hrs regarding a couple who were lost in the "Rowardennan Forest". The eighteen year old and his girlfriend had spent the night at Cashel campsite and were heading up to Doune Bothy along the WHW. When questioned, they recalled the last feature they remembered was the University field station. They had then lost the path somewhere near Ross Point. They were given instructions by phone and told they would eventually pick up the WHW at Mill of Ross. They eventually reached the path and were reassured by other walkers they met subsequently that they were only a couple of kilometres from Rowardennan. This is the second incident of this type and Central Scotland Police confirmed they have approached the National Park to look at the signage. Lomond MRT. 2hrs.

AUGUST 5 – Ben Venue (NN477061). A man reported that his 54yr old sister had fallen on the summit of Ben Venue and sustained a head-injury. The Police confirmed that a request had been made for Rescue 177. Whilst the team was assembling, confirmation came through that the helicopter had winched the casualty and her brother off the mountain and was en route to the Southern Royal Hospital. Lomond MRT, R177.15hrs.

AUGUST 7 – Lossburn Reservoir north of Menstrie (NS833990). The father of one of five men in their early 20s contacted the Police to notify that his son plus four friends had failed to return from a walk from Mentrie Scout Hall to Lossburn Reservoir (where they planned a drinking session). He was concerned because no contact could be made by mobile phone, it was dark and the group were not dressed or equipped adequately. Contact was made with group who reported they were making their way back down and that nobody was suffering any ill effects. In view of the good weather, the team was placed on standby only. All members of the group arrived safely just before midnight. Ochils MRT. 1hr

AUGUST 16 – Conic Hill (NS432923). A 52yr old female walker was part of a trekking group tackling the West Highland Way. The group were making their way off the summit of Conic Hill when the lady fell on the steep path leading down and suffered a spiral fracture of her left ankle. The group leader contacted the Police who, in turn called the team. Due to the location and the approaching bad weather, a helicopter was also requested. The casualty was packaged, carried to the awaiting helicopter which arlfited her to Paisley Royal Hospital. Lomond MRT, R177. 29hrs.

AUGUST 22 – Bridge of Orchy. A 43yr old man left the Bridge of Orchy Hotel the previous evening leaving a route card of his plans which indicated an ETA of 1800hrs. When he had not returned by 19.30hrs the Hotel Manager contacted Oban Police Office to report the man overdue. Failed attempts were made to contact the man via mobile phone at which point Oban MRT was asked to assist. Just after 21.00hrs mobile contact was established and the man reported he was SAW at his home address in St. Andrew's. He had made it off the hill in good time, had a meal at the Bridge of Orchy Hotel but forgot to mention he had returned to reception. The man was suitably advised of the resources deployed to help in the search, and he agreed to contact Oban MRT to apologise for the inconvenience caused. Oban MRT, Strathclyde Police MRT. 51 hrs.

AUGUST 19 – Ben A'an (NN509074). A 40yr old woman in a party of three started to walk up the Ben A'an footpath when she collapsed, felt nauseous, lightheaded and began shaking. Her friends thought she was having a fit and called the Police for assistance. Eight team members attended, administered oxygen and stretchered her down the path to the car park where she was transferred to an ambulance and taken to Stirling Royal Infirmary. Killin MRT. 16hrs.

AUGUST 22 – Beinn Dorain (NN325378). Two walkers (28yr old man and 25yr old woman) set off to climb Beinn Dorain late in the evening. They began their descent without any navigational aids at 22.00hrs in the dark and quickly became lost. Both were found by team members. The woman was cold and very tired and evacuated to the Southern General Hospital in Glasgow by R177. Strathclyde Police MRT, Arrochar MRT, Oban MRT, R177. 79hrs.

AUGUST 29 – Ben Lomond (NN374012). The team was asked by the Police to assist in the rescue of a 46yr old female who had fallen on Ben Lomond. The lady had sustained a deep cut below the left knee and was unable to continue. With it being a bank holiday week-end coupled with fine weather, the roads to Rowardenan were very busy and it was creditable that the first team members were on the hill within an hour. At this time, R177 was en route to the casualty's location. Whilst waiting, other hill users came to the aid of the injured walker's party including a qualified mountain instructor who was able to provide an accurate grid reference and an update on the casualty's condition. Whilst the stretcher party was making their way up the hill, R177 arrived and evacuated the casualty to awaiting MR and Ambulance at the landing site adjacent to Rowardenan Youth Hostel. She was then taken to Stirling Royal Infirmary by ambulance. Lomond MRT, R177. 32hrs.

SEPTEMBER 12 – Cruach Ardrain (NN403212). A 53 year old female hill walker (GP by profession) stumbled as she and her walking partner were descending from the summit of Cruach Ardrain. The injured walker was unable to weight-bear and suspected that she had broken her leg. They phoned the Police who alerted Killin MRT and also requested helicopter assistance. Team members met on a forestry road near a clearing suitable for helicopter landing. R137 collected the injured walker and her friend from the mountain. The aircrew splinted the casualty's injury, but she refused Entenox. The Pilot offered to take the casualty to Stirling Royal Infirmary, but she declined the offer (and the option of Ambulance transport to hospital) so both walkers were brought down to the team's location and then taken by team Landrover to the casualty's own vehicle. Her friend drove her to hospital in Glasgow. Both walkers were well equipped and suitably experienced for the conditions. Killin MRT, R137. 51hrs.

SEPTEMBER 12 – Ben Ledi (NN565105). A party of walkers from the Monifeith Hillwalking Club were descending Ben Ledi when one member (a 60yr old woman) slipped in Stank Glen between the bealach and the stile and suffered a fractured leg. The party was able to deal with the casualty's injury and helped her to walk off to the top of the Stank Glen track where she was met by police and ambulance crew. A Callander group of Killin MRT members were re-deployed from the completed rescue on Cruach Adrain (see above) and stood by at Ben Ledi car park until police and ambulance crew arrived with casualty. The rest of the hillwalking club made their own way off the hill with no further assistance required. All walkers including the casualty were well equipped and suitably experienced for the conditions. Killin MRT. 4hrs.

SEPTEMBER 18 – Glen Devon (NN295703). An 18yr old man in a larger party slipped and exacerbated an old ligament injury. He was unable to walk and placed in a sleeping bag and survival bag by group members. He was stretchered by team members to the team ARV and conveyed to a waiting ambulance. Tayside MRT, Tayside Police MRT. 59hrs.

SEPTEMBER 18 – Beinn Narnain (NN290052). A 46yr old male walker slipped on rocks whilst descending the mountain, and sustained a lower leg injury. He was carried by team members to the road and a waiting ambulance. Arrochar MRT, Strathclyde Police MRT. 37hrs.

SEPTEMBER 23 – Ben A'An (NN505079). A party of four were descending the mountain when a 66yr old man in the group slipped on loose, steep gravel and sustained a fractured left ankle. He was wearing light, flexible soled boots. Team members attended then R100 winched the casualty by high line into the helicopter and transferred him to a land ambulance at he foot of the mountain. Killin MRT, R100. 27hrs.

SEPTEMBER 24 – Ben Lomond (NS361998). Central Scotland Police contacted the team leader following a request from the Scottish Ambulance Service, to help extricate a 27yr old male walker on Ben Lomond who had fallen and injured his leg. This followed a delay of one hour twenty minutes while the SAS tried to evacuate the casualty first to the ambulance then by hospital helicopter without success. The casualty was descending Ben Lomond via the Ptarmigan ridge route. He was nearly down when he slipped on wet rocks and fractured his right lower leg. Team members quickly arrived on scene, splinted the casualty and carried him off the hill to the waiting ambulance. Lomond MRT. 10hrs.

OCTOBER 10 – Conic Hill (NS424918). Following a request from the Scottish Ambulance Service, the team was asked to help evacuate two females (18yrs and 25yrs) who were apparently having 'seizures' on Conic Hill a short distance from the main car park. The two women were members of a group of youngsters from Glasgow with troubled backgrounds. At least one of the casualties had allegedly taken '10 yellows' (!) that morning. R177 was also tasked to attend. Team members were sent up the hill to support a paramedic who was already tending to the casualties who were actually further up the hill than at first thought. Helicopter evacuation was hindered by the fact that the winch was out of action forcing the aircraft to 'land-on'. This meant that the two casualties had to be loaded into stretchers then carried to where the helicopter had managed to find room to touch down. Successfully loaded, the casualties and a group leader were taken to the Glasgow Southern General for treatment. Lomond MRT, R177. 14hrs.

OCTOBER 15/16 – Ben Chaluim (NN386322). At 16.30hrs on Friday 15th October a party of three male walkers in their 30s became separated whilst descending from the summit of Ben Chaluim. A pair retraced their steps to try and locate the third member. When they could not find him they returned to their accommodation at the Wigwams in Auchtertyre to find that their friend had not returned. At this point they raised the alarm. Killin MRT searched the summit, paths and potential hot spots with the help of R177. The search was called off at 03.00hrs with the aim of resuming the search in daylight. It turned out that the poorly equipped (no map, compass, torch, whistle or waterproof clothing) and inexperienced walker had become lost near the summit and headed north east into Glen Lochay, where he spent the night sheltering in a disused property (Badour NN 430 352). He left this location at first light and headed back into the hills. At 08.00hrs the search recommenced with assistance from Lomond and Ochil MRTs. The man was eventually located by R177 during one of its many up lifts of MR personnel. Not for the first time, the team leader was inclined to provide some advice to a walker on the use of appropriate equipment for the hills. Killin MRT, Ochils MRT, Lomond MRT, R177, SARDA (Scotland), SARDA (Southern Scotland). 262hrs.

OCTOBER 19 – Ben Vorlich (NN629188). A woman in her 50s was overdue from walking up Ben Vorlich having started from Ardvorlich. Her husband raised the alarm to the local estate owner who then called Killin MRT direct, after he had called Police. Team members checked a couple of hill tracks when the woman phoned in. She had planned to walk to the summit of Ben Vorlich but due to a navigational error (probabaly not helped by the prevailing weather at the time), ended up at Glenartney to the south. In view of the conditions, she was fortunate to have ended up unhurt. Killin MRT. 4hrs.

OCTOBER 25 – Coire an Dothaidh (NN318399). A 57yr old man was walking on the path into Coire an Dothaidh when he slipped on ice and suffered a broken ankle. Strathclyde Police MRT, who were training in the area, carried the man off the hill to a waiting ambulance. Strathclyde Police MRT, Oban MRT. 125hrs

OCTOBER 30 – Beinn Achallader (NN344432). A 22yr old female walker was feeling unwell and was left by her party. When she failed to arrive at the car park the alert was raised. She was located safe in Glen Lyon. Strathclyde Police MRT, Oban MRT, Arrochar MRT, Leuchars MRT, SARDA (Scotland).

SKYE

APRIL 9 – Sgùrr a Mhaidaidh (NG448235) A group of three were climbing the north ridge when one (a 21yr old male) slipped and fell onto snow suffering a back injury and cuts/bruises. His friends summoned help and Skye MRT was alerted. R100 went straight to the casualty who was winched aboard and taken to Broadford Hospital where he was released following treatment for minor injuries. Skye MRT, R100. 24hrs.

MAY 10 – Sgùrr nan Gillean (Tooth Chimney NG469253). A 70yr old man staying at the Sligachan Hotel was reported missing when cleaners found that he had not slept in his room. Information from the hotel indicated that he had left, on his own, for a two hour walk at approx 14.00hrs the previous day. The team, assisted by R100 carried out a search of potential routes within an hour's walk of the Hotel and checked the Camasunary Bothy and JMC Hut at Coruisk. At 14.30hrs the police received a telephone call from a Mountain Guide reporting that he and his clients had discovered a body at the foot of Tooth Chimney. Due to low cloudbase, team members were airlifted to the lochan in Coire a' Bhastier, then made their way up the hill to recover the body which was identified as the missing person. Evacuation was carried out to below the cloud base by stretcher then by R100 to Broadford Hospital. Skye MRT, R100. 200hrs.

MAY 23 – Sgùrr Dubh Mor (NG456205). Two walkers (64yr old male, 57yr old female) set off late from Glenbrittle to climb Sgurr Dubh Mor. After summitting they made a navigational error on the descent. When they discovered their error they retraced their steps but, in failing light were unable to find the route back up onto Sgùrr Dubh an Da Bheinn. They elected to stay out overnight but, later decided to ask for assistance. They gave a GR and four team members ascended to the location and walked them off the hill. Both walkers had previous experience of the Cuillin but this had been in the company of more experienced friends whom they relied on for route finding. This lack of experience, the lack of time due to a late start and their choice of route (they could have done a more accessible Cuillin given the late start) were contributory factors. Skye MRT. 42hrs.

JUNE 4 – The Quiraing (NG453690). A man and his 16yr old son were scrambling on rocks adjacent to the Quiraing when the son lost his footing and fell about 50m onto a boulder field, suffering a suspected broken ankle. The boy was ill-equipped with only shorts, T-shirt, light cagoule and tennis shoes. Team members carried the boy to the road from where he was conveyed to Broadford Hospital. Skye MRT. 35hrs.

JUNE 4 – Allt Dearg Beag (NG475278). A man in his 50s was practising abseiling into the gorge when he fell approx 4m to the burn bed below. It would appear that he may not have set up his abseil correctly. He suffered a suspected broken pelvis. Team members attended on foot and prepared the casualty for evacuation by R100 which winched him from the bottom of the gorge. Skye MRT, R100. 45hrs.

JUNE 6 – Coire a' Ghrunnda. The casualty (a 57yr old man) and his companion were descending Coir' a' Ghrunnda. Rather than take the normal route out on the western side of the corrie they ended up on the east side of the burn and 'boiler plate' slabs. The casualty slipped on a wet section causing him to slide/fall some 15m into the bed of the burn. His companion descended to Glenbrittle to raise the alarm and the team was called out. Members were deployed by R100 and the casualty was immobilised, packaged and stretchered a short distance to a position where he could be winched and flown to Broadford Hospital. Skye MRT, R100. 56hrs.

JUNE 9 – The Storr (NG487512). A 61yr old woman was walking on the Trotternish Ridge. She intended descending from the Storr via Bealach Beag but, in fading light she missed the Bealach and raised the alarm via her mobile phone. She then continued south along the ridge until she came to Bealach Mor and began to descend. When team members arrived they spotted her head torch, now on the moor, and went out to meet her and walked her off the hill. Skye MRT. 7hrs.

JUNE 16 – Sgùrr Dubh na Dà Bheinn (NG534223). In misty conditions a 58yr old man left his rucksack, containing his map and compass on Sgurr Dubh na Da

Bheinn and headed out to climb Sgurr Dubh Mor armed with only his GPS. On his return he couldn't find the way back up onto Sgurr Dubh na Da Bheinn. Thinking he should traverse rather than re-ascend he became cragfast and raised the alarm via mobile phone giving a grid reference of his position. The team leader gave the man instructions as to how to get back to the summit of Sgurr Dubh an Da Bheinn, whilst team members set off for the man's last known position. A short time later the man contacted the team again to advise he was now back with his rucksack and the mist appeared to be lifting. He was given instructions on the route to take to descend to Lochan Coir a' Ghrunnda. The man was located above a large drop to the east of the waterfall in upper Coir a' Ghrunnda. Team members ascended the short scramble to the west side of the waterfall, made contact with the man and accompanied him off the mountain. Skye MRT. 19hrs.

JUNE 18 – Clach Glas (NG534231). Two men in their 20s were scrambling on Clach Glas when one fell approx 10m and suffered a serious lower leg injury. R100 uplifted team members en route to the incident but, due to a lack of space at the incident location, they were not deployed onto the hill. The casualty's leg was splinted by the winchman and the casualty airlifted to hospital. Skye MRT, R100. 25hrs.

JULY 10 – Glenbrittle (NG413205). A man took off up the hill from the campsite following an argument with others. When he hadn't returned after two hours his colleagues raised the alarm. Team members were placed on standby, but the man returned to the campsite at 01.00hrs. Skye MRT. 6hrs.

JULY 11 – Trotternish Ridge (NG479557). Three female walkers from Belgium (20yrs, 22yrs and 23yrs old) left at 09.00hrs to walk the ridge. As nightfall approached they contacted the Police for assistance as the weather had deteriorated markedly. Unsure of their location, they were soaked through and running low on supplies. The team leader managed to contact them via mobile and advised them to camp where they were and descend at daybreak. They were forced to spend the night on the hill and were met and escorted off the hill by team members the following morning. All three walkers were adequately equipped for the conditions. Skye MRT, SARDA (Scotland). 64hrs.

AUGUST 3 – Elgol to Camasunary coastal path (NG521157). A woman walking on the path from Elgol to Camasunary fell and suffered a broken ankle. Members of her party (15 in total) effected a self rescue by improvising a stretcher from a ladder. Another person, independent from the group, raised the alarm. Team members met the group and the casualty just as they arrived at a waiting ambulance. Skye MRT. 37hrs.

AUGUST 12 – Beinn Dearg Bheag (NG597317). Two 20yr old men were climbing the Beinn na Callich horseshoe when cloud descended. Neither had a map or compass. On descent, they became unsure of their position and concerned for their safety. They raised the alarm and as they were unable to give a clear indication of their position, a full team call-out was initiated. As the team assembled at Torrin, a brief lifting of the cloud base permitted the pair to get a glimpse of the lower ground. After describing what they had seen to the team leader, their possible location was narrowed down and the team ascended Strath Suardal. Just as a dog handler was setting off, the men contacted the team again to advise that they were now below the cloud base, could see their car, and didn't actually need help! They were met at their car by the local policeman and the Team Leader. Skye MRT, SARDA (Scotland). 38hrs.

AUGUST 16 – Trotternish Ridge (NG473558). A party of two men and one woman in their 30s set off at 06.30hrs to attempt the Trotternish Ridge. The weather forecast was poor and the party only had photocopied sections of a guidebook for a map. As the light was fading the party realised they were not going to reach their B&B in Portree. They called the team with information they were at Bealach a' Chuirn and asked for advice on how to descend via Corrie Scamadal. They were informed this could be a tricky descent, particularly as their exact location was unknown. Instead, they were advised to follow a SW bearing and descend via either Glen Haultin or Romesdal, depending on what Bealach they were actually on. A dog handler set off up Glen Haultin, followed by a party of five team members. Another member ascended Romesdal on a quad bike followed by another five members on foot. The party was eventually located in upper Romesdal at approximately 21.30hrs and escorted off the hill. Skye MRT, SARDA (Scotland). 68hrs.

SEPTEMBER 26 – Am Basteir (NG466263). A man in his 70s climbing Am Basteir slipped and fell suffering a compound fracture of his right leg. A member of his party raised the alarm and he was evacuated by R100. The remaining members of the party, some of whom were very cold, were also flown out to Sligachan.

OCTOBER 10 – King's Cave Chimney (NG466253). Two men in their 40s were descending from the Am Basteir Tooth via King's Cave Chimney. The second was very inexperienced and had not abseiled before; the slightly more experienced leader elected to abseil down first leaving his second to tie into one end of the rope for lowering. After a few metres of the lower the rope jammed in the chimney crack leaving the second man stuck on the end of the rope but, thankfully in contact with the rock so he could take some of his weight on his legs. The leader was unable to exit the system and effect a self-rescue and the team was called. R100 lifted three team members deploying them by winch into King's Cave before returning for more team members. They found a lot of loose stones at the head of the pitch and after securing/removing these, were able to free the rope allowing the man to be lowered. Skye MRT, R100. 35hrs

OCTOBER 16 – Glen Scaladal (NG522164). Two 37yr old brothers were reported missing when they failed to return by nightfall from a walk to Camusunary, and the Coastguard were called out. R100 searched the route with its heat detection system but found nothing. At this point the MRT were asked to assist while R100 proceeded to check the bothies at Camusunary and Coruisk. There were two people at one of these. It was established that they were not the missing persons but had spoken to them when on the south ridge of Blàbheinn; they had said that they intended to climb Blàbheinn, descend to Loch Slapin and return to Elgol via the road. R100 carried out an air search of Blàbheinn before returning to Stornoway. R137 was then tasked and the MRT stood by for deployment via R137. At 22.45hrs one of the missing persons contacted his wife to advise that they were at NG523200 and had unsuccessfully been trying to alert R100. According to the wife of one of the party, who reported them missing, they had no map or compass, no head torches and were not carrying sufficient kit (extra clothing/bivvy bag) for a night out. Both men were taken off the ridge by helicopter. Skye MRT, R100, R137. 63hrs.

ISLANDS OTHER THAN SKYE

March 6 – Ben More Mull (NM535333). In the morning two men and a woman set off on an unplanned walk up Ben More. It would appear they headed to the summit of A Chioch on the Ben More ridge. They had no idea where they were going and had no winter gear of any description. They had no map or compass and were unable to give their position when asked. The party headed up till they could climb no further because of steep craggy ground covered in a mix of ice and snow. It was at this point they discovered they couldn't go down either because of the steepness of the ground. They called 999 and were subsequently winched from the crag by R177. Oban MRT members attended but were not required. Oban MRT, R177. 21hrs.

MARCH 8 – Ainshval Rum (NM378914). A 63yr old woman was overdue walking from Kinloch to Ainshval. She descended via Dibidil but failed to meet up with her colleagues at Kinloch. She was found the following morning on the path west of Dibidil by SNH staff after spending a cold and wet night alone on the hill. Lochaber MRT. 15hrs.

MARCH 14 – Ainshval Rum (NM378943). A 41yr old male walker was walking alone in the Rum Cuillins and whilst descending Ainshval a rock from above fell and struck him on the head causing him to fall/slide some 5ms. As a result, he sufferred face, rib and hand injuries. He was evacuated by R100 which was in the vicinity at the time. Lochaber MRT, R100. 3hrs.

APRIL 25 – Arran, Goatfell Tourist path. Two walkers (30yr old male and 23yr old female) reached the summit of Goatfell and on descent became lost in the cloud. They alerted the Police who called the team. As team members were making their way onto the hill, the cloud lifted and they met the walkers on the path. Both were adequately dressed but neither had a map or compass. Arran MRT. 20hrs.

MAY 1 – Arran, A'Chir Ridge (NR699423). A woman fell and broke her ankle on the A'Chir Ridge. As the team were making their way to the scene, R177 arrived and uplifted the casualty and transferred her to Crosshouse Hospital. Arran MRT, R177. 22hrs.

MAY 26 – Glen Rosa (NR976417). A 20yr old male walker fell whilst crossing the burn in Glen Rosa and suffered ankle and facial injuries. As team members were making their way up the glen, R177 located and uplifted the man to Crosshouse Hospital. Arran MRT. 9hrs.

JUNE 2 – Goatfell (NR997414). A 21yr old male walker complaining of numbness and feeling unwell, collapsed on the tourist path. Team members located the man and administered first aid. R177, returning from another incident, uplifted the man and took him to Crosshouse Hospital. Arran MRT. 17hrs.

JUNE 30 – Glen Rosa. A 51yr old male walker was reported overdue after walking from Glen Rosa to Glen Sannox. As team members were gathering to begin a search, the man was located by Police, on his way home. Arran MRT, SARDA (Southern Scotland). 7hrs.

JULY 31 – Ben More (Mull). A young man left home to travel to Mull with the intention of climbing Ben More. His father alerted the Police when his son failed to make contact. Local enquiries confirmed that the son was safe and well, camping by a roadside. Strathclyde Police MRT. 1hr.

AUGUST 17 – Goatfell (NR990414). A 55yr old man contacted the police to report he was lost on the Goatfell range. He had mistaken North Goatfell for Goatfell and started to make his way down via an old scree path. The team argocat was deployed and the walker spotted. Exhausted, he was carried down in the vehicle and met by police at the road head. Arran MRT. 9hrs.

AUGUST 23 – Goatfell (NR999400). Report came in of a male walker turning blue and suffering from the cold. Team members found his group who were able to rewarm the man, and walked everyone off the mountain. Arran MRT. 5hrs.

AUGUST 29 – Cir Mhòr (NR974434). A walker reported that he was cragfast in the Saddle area of Glen Sannox. He was located by team members on the lower slabs of Cir Mhòr, lowered to safe ground and then walked off. Arran MRT. 58hrs.

SOUTHERN UPLANDS

JANUARY 22 – Bewcastle Fells (NY577821). The team was asked to assist Penrith MRT search for a couple missing between Bewcastle and Newcastleton. Team members from both MRTs worked together to estimate where they might be located. A helicopter was deployed to the predicted location where the missing persons were found and evacuated. Tweed Valley MRT, Penrith MRT, R137. 18hrs.

MARCH 30 – Pennine Way (NT879200). The team was asked to assist with three experienced male walkers in their late 20s on the Pennine Way (nr Yetholm) who had called the Police to say they were cold, etc. All three were wearing lighter waterproofs than demanded by the weather. They weren't lost but had overestimated their capabilities and the time needed to complete the last leg of their journey. When they called for help, they had found shelter en route (Auchope refuge hut – NT879200) but may well have been benighted in poor weather had they not been assisted. Groups of team members responded and one party took a vehicle to Mounthooly in case all other exit routes were flooded. All three walkers were eventually uplifted by vehicle some three hours following the alert. Borders SARU. 76 hrs.

APRIL 3 – Castle O'er Forest. Two girls were reported overdue from a walk around local forest tracks. The team was called to look for the girls but they turned up safe and well within minutes of the call. Moffat MRT. 0hrs

APRIL 7 – Glen Trool A husband and wife (50yrs) were walking a trail in Glen Trool when the woman had an asthmatic attack. By the time team members arrived the couple had reached a house at the head of the glen. The team's paramedic checked out the casualty and gave both walkers a lift back to their car. Galloway MRT. 12hrs.

MAY 4 – Queensberry (NX988997). A 55yr old man was separated from his three friends who reported him missing. The man turned up as the team were about to be deployed. Moffat MRT, 6hrs.

JUNE 4 – Wanlockhead (NS872129). An 88yr old man walking the Southern

Upland Way was overdue at Wanlockhead Pub. The landlord called the Police but by the time team members arrived, the man turned up having taken a tumble and suffering minor facial injuries. He was checked out by the ambulance crew but remained at the pub to continue walking the next day. Moffat MRT. 20hrs.

AUGUST 16 – Glen Trool (NX433817). Husband and wife on a walk when the husband made a detour to examine an aircraft wreck. On return his wife was no where to be seen. The team was alerted but the woman turned up safe and well. Galloway MRT, SARDA (Scotland). 33hrs.

SEPTEMBER 28 – Loch Doon (NX497883). A 67yr old man went to walk the high tops of Loch Doon in Ayrshire. He calle his wife at 17.30hrs to say he was lost after ascending Carlins Cairn. Following a search, he was located at 08.00hrs by Dumfries and Galloway Police. Strathclyde Police MRT, Lomond MRT, SARDA (Southern Scotland). 35hrs.

NON-MOUNTAINEERING INCIDENTS HAVE NOT BEEN INCLUDED.

IN MEMORIAM

GERRY PEET j. 1966

I FIRST MET GERRY at a J.M.C.S. Glasgow Section meet in October 1964. He was one of the clubs more experienced members, prepared to take several younger novices under his wing, and I remember well being tutored for the first time by him in the art of step cutting in *Gargoyle Chimney* on Lochnagar. A few weeks later I was allowed to lead a pitch of *Number Two Gully Buttress* on Ben Nevis whilst he prompted and encouraged from below.

In the summer of 1965 in company with others we climbed several classic rock climbs in Scotland, Wales and the Lake District, with the highlight, a weekend in the Cuillin of Skye. Initially the plan was for four of us to travel to Skye, however two called off and Gerry and I ended up on our own. This was my first visit to Skye and I was extremely lucky to have Gerry as my mentor in an area which he knew well following earlier visits commencing in 1949. On this first visit we climbed from dawn to dusk, climbing in Coire Lagan in the morning and Coire a' Ghrunnda in the afternoon with large parts of the Ridge thrown in for good measure.

We returned to Skye for our last visit together in 1982 when we completed the traverse of the Ridge which surprisingly had eluded Gerry on many previous visits. At that time, following a visit to the hills, Gerry would calculate the cost of provisions, travel, and hut or camping fees and divide this with the total length of snow and ice or rock climbed to give a cost per foot climbed and claimed the most expensive climb he ever made was a winter ascent of *Comb Gully* on Ben Nevis when en route to Fort William he had an incident in his car requiring the

Photo: Margaret Peet.

sump to be replaced before the journey could be completed. He also claimed that the most inexpensive climbing was recorded on our first visit to Skye due to the number of routes completed over that weekend. When I met Gerry he had a reputation as a manufacturer of climbing equipment, this was mainly rock and ice pitons, however he did experiment with an early model of an all metal ice axe. Unfortunately at his first attempt with the ice axe the head and shaft parted company whilst climbing on the Brenva Face of Ben Nevis leading to a benightment on the upper part of the *North-East Buttress*.

Although Gerry was never a tiger and visited the Alps only twice, the second time with myself, when poor weather restricted climbing to an ascent of Piz Palu in white out conditions, he was a very competent mountaineer with excellent rock and ice technique and an enthusiasm for the hills which knew no bounds.

The legacy Gerry leaves to Scottish climbing will be his work to S.M.C. Huts and this interest in huts first manifested itself in 1965 when he proposed that the Glasgow JMCS. build a hut in Coire Ardair on Creag Meagaidh.

The story of the building of the Meagaidh Hut was an adventure spanning five years with several spectacular failures, including carrying a glass fibre workman's hut the five miles into Coire Ardair, and was an early testament to Gerry's resolve to see a difficult job through to completion. The hut was finally completed in October 1969 and, although a Glasgow JMCS venture, from the work party would eventually emerge four SMC hut custodians, three hut convenors and one treasurer.

Gerry became custodian of the CIC Hut in l967, a post he would hold until 1980, and immediately instigated steps to improve and secure the hut, relying almost entirely on young Glasgow JMCS members as a volunteer workforce. At that time there was a history of misuse of the hut with gate crashing and non payment of hut fees a major problem.

The first major work party involved the hire of a mobile welding plant and welder to fit horizontal metal bars across the existing vertical posts to the windows, this was before the use of helicopters, unfortunately on arrival at the hut the welding plant refused to work. The welder spent the weekend sunbathing whilst the work party laboured. The following weekend Gerry and I returned alone with the welder and a new welding plant, to find the new equipment was twice as heavy as the previous faulty equipment, and although we attempted to carry it up to the hut the weight defeated us. Fortunately the RAF Mountain Rescue Team was in Fort William that weekend and they rescued the day, carrying the plant up to the hut on a stretcher.

In the early to mid seventies volunteer work parties to the huts peaked with the renovation of Lagangarbh, upgrading to the Ling Hut, and the installation of a drying room and extension to the CIC Hut and Gerry was involved in all these projects. With the improvements in the huts, revenue increased, and this eventually led to the use of professional labour to carry out major works in the huts giving Gerry the opportunity to develop his management skills which proved considerable.

Following a thirteen year period as CIC Hut Custodian Gerry was Hut Convenor from 1980 to 1998, following this with a further two spells as Custodian of the Raeburn Hut between 2001 and 2008. During his period as Huts Convenor he managed the building of the club's two new huts, the Raeburn and the Naismith.

For his service to the club Gerry was awarded an Honorary Membership in 1977, was Vice President 1985 to 1987 and became an Honorary Vice President in 2004.

George Wilkinson

MIDNIGHT MARCH 1968 the door of the CIC hut burst open and a group of Glasgow JMCS members enter the hut, among them the much loved custodian Gerry Peet. They were booked in, we two non members were not. We cowered down in our corner and tried to be invisible. Nothing was said and after a short period of tea making etc. peace reigned. In the morning I met Gerry for the first time and we hit it off from the start so much so that within a week or two we along with Bob McMillan made the first ascent of the Pumpkin on Creag Meagaidh.

After that we became good friends climbing, hillwalking, skiing, socialising and even playing squash together. A friendship which lasted until his death. Gerry was one of life's great characters, full of enthusiasm and ideas. Life was never dull when around Gerry. He was a glass half full person and I count it a great privilege to have been counted among his friends. One of the amazing things about Gerry was his energy. I would be coming home from a day hill walking looking forward to a seat by the fire and a dram, Gerry would be off to play squash or tennis.

Gerry's great service to the SMC was his work on the club huts which has already been covered and which in the early days involved most of his friends.

He was probably a very underrated climber. Most club members tended to think of him mainly in relation to club huts and work parties but he was a very competent climber and the advent of front pointing tended to suit his neat style of climbing originating from climbing in nails.

In the seventies Gerry began climbing more and more with what has loosely been called the Dundee group. He probably did some of his best winter climbs at that time with Gordon McKenzie, Doug Lang and myself, among them *Zero* and *Point Five Gullies* on Ben Nevis and an epic winter day in the Garbh Choire on Beinn a' Bhùird climbing *South-East Gully*, not a day for the faint hearted.

In the early eighties we both got involved in cross country skiing and then to a lesser extent downhill skiing and ski mountaineering. We had some super days such as skiing the four Cairngorm high tops and traversing from Glen Shee to Invercauld on skis. After 10 years of skiing while we enjoyed ourselves it lacked the bite that climbing had and we both resumed winter climbing and continued climbing together until the general debilities which come with old age took there toll, on me in particular.

Gerry had a very enquiring mind, always interested in what was going on in the world around him. I last met him a few weeks before his death when he came to Dundee to see the plans for the Victoria and Albert Museum building. We had lunch afterwards and he was the usual Gerry full of criticism for most of the plans.

It was almost symbolic that the day of Gerry's funeral was probably the worst blizzard to hit Scotland for a generation and dozens of people, myself included, didn't make it to his funeral. To his wife Margaret and his son Duncan and daughter Rhona we offer our deepest sympathies.

Neil Quinn

Photo: Margaret Peet.

I FIRST REALLY GOT to know Gerry when we became involved in the construction of the Raeburn Hut just north of Dalwhinnie. Gerry was then the Convenor of the redoubtable Huts Sub-committee. I knew he was suspicious of professionals, especially architects, but as this most unfortunate view was not uncommon among the general public I didn't let this trouble me overmuch. As it turned out things went well from the beginning, and soon we were arranging days out on the hill.

As both of us were semi-retired, we devised a series of day-trips – Gerry called them – mainly during the week, which required little notice, a reasonably good weather forcast and did not clash with his evening tennis fixtures. We also agreed to use as little gear as possible when climbing. Thus freed from the tyranny of the rack, this was an exhilarating experience, with not an E or a V in sight and no queues either.

We seemed to go all over the place: A trip of particular interest and enjoyment started with an early morning boat to Arran. Once aboard, the thought of a MacBrayne's Scotch Breakfast was simply irresistible. The boat often drifted into Brodick through a thin sea-mist with a light blue outline of peaks floating magically above. The prospect of sun-warmed rock in Glen Rosa or Sannox seemed like the promised land to me. Needless to say the climbing was always superb, with the added frisson of Arran granite's unique and sometimes humbling challenges thrown in. What a place to be on a good summers day!

Other memorable times were spent in or around the Ardnamurchan Ring above Sanna Bay. This involved a two day trip which Gerry finally conceded was a much better way to fully appreciate this enchanted peninsula. Here it was difficult to avoid the Es, but somehow we found enough to our liking. Modest performances maybe by today's standards, but then the ambience was truly stunning, the sea views were indescribably beautiful and that seemed compensation enough.

Then there was Lochnagar in winter. This trip started for me in the wee small hours and finished nearly 24 hours later back in Glasgow. The crags that day were certainly 'wild and majestic' and amply plated with snow and ice. *Parallel Gully A* seemed a good idea and soon I was able to note Gerry's innate ability when front pointing on ice. He really made it look easy that day! On this occasion we had both 'agreed' to use 2/5mm ropes; this of course, was never a good idea from the outset. I won't bore you with the convolutions these ropes put us through, but they seemed to develop an infuriating life of their own; we never used them again ! In spite of this obvious drawback, the plateau was gained in reasonable order and so we were able to totter downwards into the gathering gloom of Glen Muick thinking our own thoughts of a good day out.

Another day trip was made to Nevis and starting from the Glen, Gerry was particularly pleased with this ascent of *Comb Gully* climbed in a very reasonable time, with himself doing the hard bit. As far as I was concerned, I knew this was difficult when my nose touched the ice, but was heartened by cheery noises from above and the knowledge of a bomb-proof belay to come. The gully now opened out easily onto mixed snow, and with no cornice it was up and over with the satisfaction of a good finish to a short and exciting climb. Walking across the plateau, we remembered how we had all been put off on a previous attempt due to tiring underfoot conditions and a form of lethargy which can so easily overcome the cautious Salvationist.

Later on The Borders became a regular destination for some of our trips. Perhaps it was a change of scene, more likely it was due to gathering years and the inviting number of reasonably harmless quad-bike tracks made by shepherds which allowed for much easier walking over the many rough patches found in these hills.

I think I can honestly say that these outings were memorable, enjoyable and of lasting value to us both. We learnt a lot from each other and a great deal about ourselves. Gerry was a good friend and a good companion on the hill. He cheered me up especially when I had the black dog on my back. I am greatly indebted to him in so many ways.

Gerry finished his days learning to fly a micro-lite 'aircraft'. My wife and I visited him at an airfield in East Lothian doing a flying exercise sometime called 'circles and bumps' – taking off and landing – which he appeared, to my untrained eye, to carry out rather well.

En avant, Gerry, Biggles was surely watching you.

Douglas Niven

DOUGLAS F LANG j. 1960

IN 1965 WHILE on a Cam Dearg MC winter meet to Creag Meaghaidh the weather was so awful Tony Viveash and I decided to explore the south side of Binnien Shuas. While dripping wet, I immediately recognised the climbing potential. Tony, being a hardened hill walker had no aspirations to rock climb so I sweet-talked Dougie Lang into making a visit with me in the summer of 1967 with the promise of sun-kissed virgin rock, and a perfectly dry Howff to overnight.

That first weekend in June 1967 was perfect, Doug and I set off from the Keeper's Cottage, having hidden Doug's rather conspicuous white Volvo 122s behind a shed, out of sight of prying eyes.

The route up to the crag from the sandy beach at Loch na h-Earba was heavy going through the heather as there was no path in these days. We dumped our gear at the big cracked boulder Howff, where Doug was horrified to find that not only was there no level sleeping area, it was full of old animal bones. He was always a bit fussy, as I was to find out. After a good brew-up, we reconnoitred the crag. The most conspicuous direct line on steep slabs in the centre took our immediate attention. I had a small stalker's telescope that we used to spy the line; the rock looked pretty thin and compact, so it looked hard. Anyway, the first route was climbed at Mild Severe, a really enjoyable classic climb with belay ledges in all the right places, 550 feet of perfect rock and stunning situations. Doug and I agreed that the route name should also be classic in nature so *Ardverikie Wall* was named, after the Estate.

The partnership was cemented and over the next two years we climbed a total of 16 new routes on Binnien Shuas before we published in the 1968 SMC Journal. This seemed to cause quite a stir, even the illustrious Tom Patey who had visited the crag on a grotty wet day in 1964 is quoted as saying 'It was the best route I ever walked past'.

Dougie and I continued our activities in Creag an Dubh-Loch where we climbed most of the existing hard routes, some second ascents, and added a few of our own during 1968-70: *Sword of Damocles* (E2), *Falseface* (E2) and *A Likely Story* (HVS) on Eagles Rock (now considered 'An unsung Cairngorm Gem').

Doug and I loved feeding the Etive Slabs midges but managed to complete most of the existing routes over a couple of years. However, probably our biggest expedition in Scotland was the first ascent of 'The Great Stac of Handa' with Hamish MacInnes with the able support of Alistair Munro the RSPB Warden for Handa and expert seaman (Died at sea off Handa in 1972). Patey and Bonington had had an unsuccessful attempt on the Great Stac the previous year, so things were getting interesting.

Compared to me, Doug was always quite a natty dresser in the hills, so he hated the smell, noise and mess of seabirds. He particularly enjoyed the delight of puking fulmars. Doug and Hamish claimed to be non-swimmers so I was elected to step off the boat onto the rock, weighed down with the usual ironmongery. It had occurred to me that if I slipped off, I'd be more like a deep-sea diver than a rock climber. I never did find out if Doug was a non-swimmer, or just a crafty delegator. However, the route turned out to be a rather sporting, mega-exposed affair. The final decent was a dramatic 50 metre free abseil off a jammed nut from an overhanging platform directly into a small boat which was a moving target being buffed around by the swell.

When I left the UK in 1971 for South Africa, our close climbing partnership sadly came to an abrupt end. However, Doug continued climbing with Neil Quinn mainly in Winter. Together they were one of the strongest winter partnerships in the 1970–80s, completing several classic winter ascents on Ben Nevis and Lochnagar. It was only 4-5 weeks before Doug's death that he was in Norway ice climbing with Colin Stead, who was a regular rock and ice partner spanning many years.

We were both members of the Carn Dearg MC in Dundee before joining the SMC in 1969. Doug became president of the Scottish Mountaineering Club in 1992 and had been heavily involved in the affairs of the club ever since, attending almost every spring and summer meet, and always prominent at the long-standing series of winter meets at the club's hut on Ben Nevis.

Doug contributed over 60 first ascents on rock and ice throughout Scotland, many of which are classic routes today. We were privileged to have the opportunity to climb on virgin rock of such scale and quality, a unique pioneering experience no longer available to climbers of today.

Doug's tragic death on 19 March 2011, in the easy *A Gully*, Coire Fee, Glen Doll at the age of 69 is so sad. He was built like a whippet, not an ounce of fat, and still very fit and hyper active. Hence the reason he was out on his own, investigating new opportunities for winter routes in such inappropriate conditions. Doug was a totally dependable partner and friend. While his conversation was always informed, it was enthusiastically restricted to Climbing, Cars and Tool Designing. He was very popular and will be greatly missed by all who came into contact with him. We treasure the memories…

Graeme N Hunter

Photo: Neil Quinn.

I FIRST MET DOUG LANG at a Carn Dearg Mountaineering Club meet to Creag Meagaidh in May 1961. Everyone was going hill walking except Doug and his friend Dave Crabbe. They went off with ice axes and ropes to climb Raeburn's Gully, returning late, faces glowing with excitement full of tales of walls of old snow and ice and through routes up water covered rock. This was typical Doug full of enthusiasm for the hills and climbing in particular. He was the most enthusiastic climber I ever met. After a long winter climbing together I would be looking forward to a long lie and a spot of fishing while Doug would be bouncing about desperate to go rock climbing.

Doug was born in Dumfries but moved to Dundee when only one year old. He attended Harris Academy in Dundee and when he left school trained as an engineering draughtsman with the Timex factory. In 1967 he and a friend started up their own business, Tool Design Company, which he helped to run and worked in until he retired. Outside of climbing, his family and work were his main interests although in later years he enjoyed working in his garden. After our first meeting we would occasionally meet on Carn Dearg meets and climbing on the Red Craig up Glen Clova. It was on a trip to Stob Ghabhar that we did our first winter climb together, the *Upper Couloir,* and it was the start of a winter partnership which lasted nearly 40 years.

Doug did several notable first ascents in winter, *Slav Route, Left Edge Route* (Observatory Buttress) and *Indicator Right-Hand* on Ben Nevis, *The Wand* on Creag Meagaidh, *Winter Face* of Black Spout Pinnacle on Lochnagar, *The Flume Direct* in the Garbh Choire Beinn a' Bhùird. Besides first ascents he did most of the established winter climbs of the day, notably an epic winter ascent of *Eagle Ridge,* Lochnagar, which he wrote about in the SMC Journal number 160. He also did the first free ascents of *Parallel Buttress* and *Tough Brown Ridge Direct.* One thing he was very proud of was doing the only traditional ascent of *Orion Face Direct* other than the first ascent.

Doug joined the SMC in 1969 and over the years was a good servant to the club being a member of the committee for three years, two years as Vice President and two years as President. He was also Distribution Manager of the Journal for 36 years. Besides these duties he was always keen to help on work parties on the huts such as painting the inside of the CIC and helping dig out the foundations for the first CIC extension. Doug was a gregarious character he loved meeting other climbers and talking climbing late into the night. He was also an excellent companion on the hill always ready to help if you were struggling a bit. He was a regular attender at Club meets particularly the CIC winter meets and in recent years the Easter meets where he enjoyed the social side of the meet as much as the hills.

Doug enjoyed solo climbing for the freedom it gave him, he soloed climbs such as *Parallel Gully A* on Lochnagar and *B Gully Chimney* in Glen Clova. It is ironic that just when he seemed to be realising that he wasn't a youngster any longer that he should be killed in an area as innocuous as *A Gully* in Glen Clova. To his wife Denise and his daughter Hilary we offer our deepest sympathy.

Neil Quinn

Doug at Rjukan 2008.

Photo: Rosie Goolden.

I FIRST MET DOUG in the late sixties when we were both members of the first generation Rannoch Mountaineering Club. He had an impeccable pedigree as a rock climber with many first ascents to his credit and repeats of the existing classics. I once got a postcard from him while I was on a family fishing holiday and all it said was 'Did NEEDLE!', a much sought after route. He did not mess around on rock. Recently doing a climb on Stac Pollaidh, I helpfully suggested a left handjam on the crux. 'Handjam! Handjam! I've never done a handjam in my life' as he grabbed a convenient runner and completed the move. We climbed on and off on rock over the years and had one successful trip to the French Alps together. Doug had other trips to the Alps but details are lacking.

He was quite bold and would solo climbs regularly both rock and ice including some first ascents. He hated climbing walls and preferred to train by using a shunt in two of the less frequented quarries near his home in Dundee.

He was quite a natty dresser and would sometimes turn up at climbing huts in a collar and bow tie. His trademark tweed bunnet with ear flaps was always with him and was worn under a helmet in winter. He was unfailingly courteous and would be mortified if he forgot his little ritual of shaking your hand after completion of an ascent. He was a great companion on and off the hill.

Winter climbing was his forte and he transferred seamlessly from step cutting to front pointing and continued pioneering new routes throughout his life. We climbed together in winter after Neil Quinn hung up his axes. Doug was always receptive to the suggestion of a new route. On *Roaring Forties* on Nevis on a day of storm and blasting spindrift when my ambition ground to a halt in the dreadful conditions, Doug gave a masterly display as he sang his way up the big groove which is the climb's highlight. On another occasion he made a brilliant lead of the crucial second pitch of *Edge of Beyond* because he was in such a rage with my inept rope handling that he never paused to think, the only time I ever saw him lose his cool.

A regular attender at the CIC meets, the whole weekend mattered to Doug, not just the climbing but the craic around the table on a Saturday night fortified by steak and wine followed by his customary rhubarb crumble and custard. This was Doug in his element.

He just loved climbing and anything to do with it. 'I am not a hillwalker' he would say but inevitably climbed many hills with friends and family. His enthusiasm was legendary and if he was down for a meet, go he would even in the face of the most dire weather forecast and a partner's withdrawal. Only in the last two years were there signs of mellowing in this regard.

Doug's contribution to Scottish climbing and the SMC was immense. He was a much loved character because he related so well to people. It was rare not to meet someone he knew in a gathering of climbers anywhere.

If he was pleased with a climb, one was treated to a rendition of some country classic as on our last day at Rjukan this year as he completed 1500 feet of grade 3 ice. Country music hall of fame he was not but if there is a winter climbing hall of fame, Doug is right up there with the best of them. Should the faint strains of *American Pie* assail your ears when you think you are first in a Nevis ice gully, do not fear. It will just be Doug's restless spirit on a half day pass from heaven.

Denise and Hilary have suffered a huge loss but so too have those of us who knew and loved Doug.

CS

PROCEEDINGS OF THE CLUB

The following mountaineers were admitted to the Club in 2011.
We welcome:

DEREK J BUCKLE (67), Consultant, Redhill, Surrey.
IAN D CROFTON (56), Writer and Editor, London.
DAVID CROOKES (52), General Practitioner, Edinburgh.
CHRISTOPHER J DICKINSON (55), Outdoor Instructor (retired), Spean Bridge,
    Inverness-shire.
MARTIN FITZSIMONS (45), IT Consultant, East Kilbride.
KENNETH GRANT (34), Mountaineering Instructor, Corpach, Inverness-shire.
ADRIAN J HART (52), Dental Surgeon, Cawdor, Nairn, Morayshire.
ROBERT M JAMIESON (24), Science Graduate, Tain, Ross-shire.
JAMES R RICHARDSON (36), Sales Executive, Aberdeen.
SANDY SIMPSON (23), Joiner, Inverurie, Aberdeenshire.
TONY V R STONE (35), Climbing Instructor, Linlithgow, West Lothian.
TIMOTHY WALKER (40), Project Engineer, Aberdeeen.
ALAN WILSON (47), Rope Access Technician, Callander, Perthshire.

The One-Hundred-and-Twenty Second AGM and Dinner

For those not out on the hills during the afternoon, Greg Strange gave a talk
based on his new book *The Cairngorms, 100 Years of Mountaineering*. Maybe it
was the slides of just a small selection of routes the book includes, that have
inspired the committee to propose that the next Dinner should move east again.

The AGM closely followed the end of the talk and seemed a particularly
business like meeting although it did have to take place without the presence of
the Club Treasurer (stuck at home by snow). A number of members raised
concerns over the benefit of the MC of S and the increase in subscriptions.
Others voiced concerns over the quality of the windows at the recently renovated
CIC hut. The club were also asked to approve constitutional changes to the
number of members on the committee and to time limits to the length of service
by office bearers. However the meeting concluded that the proposed changes
were not clear and the items were returned to the committee.

At one time, Dinners in Fort William meant mild wet weekends. However this
year we had a significant change and the whole of the UK was hit by heavy
snow. Numerous members were keeping me updated by e-mail on their progress
at clearing their cars of snow and the likelihood of them making the Dinner. Even
the Guest Speaker, Peter Gilmour couldn't get his car out from his house in
London and decided not to risk the trains as they were only running as far as
Edinburgh/Glasgow. Despite these testing times we had a nearly full dining room
and President Des Rubens kept us entertained in place of the speaker. Amongst
his report was the sad news of the very recent death of one of our Honorary Vice-
Presidents, Gerry Peet.

With Des Rubens time as President coming to an end, the Dinner proceedings
closed with the handing over of the President's regalia to new President, Andy

Nisbet. He gratefully accepted the offering and then invited us all to attend the President's Meet on Stob Ban the following morning. I've added comments from Andy below.

President's Walk

The President was joined by two members and a guest for a walk up Stob Ban (Mamores) by its north ridge. The weather was near perfect and there was snow from the road. Once above the steep initial pull to 650m, the ground eases in angle but the snow deepened. Near where the east ridge joins, there is a short tricky section (scrambling in summer) but by here the snow was taking your weight and all found it interesting but not taxing. There follows a fine narrow crest leading to the top. With light winds, we could stop, have lunch and try to identify numerous white peaks, including Ben Cruachan, Ben More and Ben Lawers. Descent was by the icy regular path up the valley to the east. A lovely day enjoyed by all.

Chris Huntley

SKI MOUNTAINEERING MEET, GLEN SHIEL
12–13 FEBRUARY 2011

Venue: The Cluanie Inn, Glen Shiel.

The 2011 Scottish Mountaineering Club ski mountaineering meet was a joint meet with the Eagle Ski Club. Members and guests gradually accumulated by the fireside at the Cluanie Inn on the Friday evening. The weather forecast meant that travel was undertaken more in hope than expectation!

Earlier during Friday Jim Thomson and Ian Ferguson had lugged skis up from the shores of Loch Quoich (circa 200m) to Sgùrr Coire nan Eiricheallach and Sgùrr a' Mhaoraich (1027m). They reached meagre snow from about the 550m contour, enjoying a good ski back down although the cover remained thin. Bob Reid and Ian Crofton had wisely opted to walk up Gleouraich (1035m). Two Eagle members, Alan Sloan and Angus Armstrong, also skied up Sgùrr a' Mhaoraich confirming reasonable snow cover above 600m.

Saturday dawned...somewhat overcast, but a substantial full Scottish breakfast allowed time for everyone to deliberate on the best approach to the conditions.

The ski team active on Friday, Ian Ferguson and Jim Thomson, started from the shores of Loch Cluanie to ascend Càrn Ghlusaid (957m), donning skis from 600m. They headed west out to point 998m and around to Sgùrr nan Conbhairean (1109m); off with skins and a good run down to the col, then out to Sail Chaorainn (1002m). Here they enjoyed flapjacks and fine views in all directions in contrast to the earlier conditions. They reported a good ski back to the col and up to 1060m to contour around to the top of the gully looking south into Gorm Lochan. There followed an excellent ski down the top of the gully and on down to 600m on ribbons of spring snow. From there it was a walk down the Allt Coire Lair and back along the road to pick up the car. A group of walkers had beaten them back, but then anyone can walk it...

Chris Ottley and Paul Cook tackled the North Cluanie Ridge finishing in Shiel Bridge, then catching a late bus back to the welcoming Inn. Friday night's snow had resulted in some minor slides aiding downhill travel. The weather was generally clagged-in but cleared late on giving some fine views including north over to Torridon.

Dave Crookes and Pauline Kell put up a possible new route on Creag Coire an t-Slugain or Mid-way Buttress – *Radio Ham* (III,4). This was after a forced retreat from the original plan to climb on the Slugain crag due to the avalanche hazard. Tense and gnarly, this route, they enthusiastically assured us, is sure to become a crag classic. Bob Reid and Ian Crofton for the same safety reasons ascended an unnamed Grade II gully a little further to the right – if new, then they suggest the name *Cluanie's Kipper*?

Brian, Amy and Graeme went left of *Mid-way Gully* up a diagonal snow ramp and finished up the left-hand end of the crag. Interesting, they reported, but not too technical. They then headed west and met Colwyn and Ann MacDonald on the South Cluanie Ridge. There followed an excellent and atmospheric descent down the north ridge Aonach air Chrith (well worthy of a star) then onto A' Chioch with snow down to 580m, before a wet river crossing and directly back to the hotel arriving at dusk.

Anthony Walker and Christine Watkins reconnoitred west from the road and spotted good snow cover in an unknown corrie. Carrying skis up to 500m delivered them onto good snow. An ascent of Sgùrr Beag yielded such good skiing that they skinned back up to the summit for a second descent.

A party led by Alan Sloan, with John Gay, Angus Armstrong, Dan and Glynis Carron, propelled by repeating Orkney Blackpudding, and carrying skis and boots, went up the stalkers' path to the Lochan at 550m above the hotel. With skis on there was a tenuous traverse east round the corries of Gorma and Eich Bhric, with improving snow cover. There followed a direct ascent up Coirean an Eich Bhric to the ridge at point 868m. The corrie had 4" of fresh snow on a hard base and after testing, appeared sound. They achieved the ridge through the only gap in the cornice, more easily found from below! From there it was up to bag Creag a' Mhaim (947m) then back to the col. Plans to traverse round for a direct descent into Coireachan Gorma were ditched in light of the conditions and that they 'knew' conditions on the ascent route. They describe a 'whooping' descent and traverse back to the lochan to boot back down the stalkers' path laden by skis.

Saturday night was spent dining at the Cluanie Inn with each individual claiming that they had enjoyed a far better day than everyone else!

Sunday dawned, somewhat wet. The Vice President drove east to sea level at Shiel Bridge then headed south up Glen Undalain to ascend the mighty Corbett; Sgùrr Mhic Bharraich (781m) with Graeme, Ann, Amie and Brian. As they ascended, sleet replaced the steady rain and there was a good 10 centimetres of fresh snow on the summit which provided a pleasant descent back down the path.

David and Pauline reported that it was well worth the effort of slogging through the rain for about 30 minutes to climb a route called *Deceptive Chimney* on the west face of Druim Shionnach. It gave a wet start with rain turning to snow at about 350m. The freezing level, with some ice forming, was around 500-600m with approx 6" of fresh snow overnight; a further 4" or so falling during the day. The corrie was isolated and they saw no-one all day. Initially cloudy, it cleared during the afternoon with no wind! The route was done in three pitches of steep turfy climbing with much clearing of deep snow required. They reported a poor belay at the top of pitch 1 and a noticeable lack of good gear where needed (tied off warthogs for runners). The guidebook undergrades the route, which was thought Grade IV on the day. [Confirmed by an independent note in the New Climbs section.] A good quality route worthy of 1 or 2 stars.

Many of the Eagle Ski Club members decided to depart early in search of quieter conditions elsewhere, whilst those who remained enjoyed low level walking and the occasional glimpse of the local scenery.

Members present: Colwyn Jones, Ann MacDonald, Bob Reid, Brian Shackleton, Jim Thomson, Graham Tough, Anthony Walker, Christine Watkins.
Guests: Ian Crofton, Dave Crookes, Amie Goodill, Pauline Kell.
Eagle Ski Club members: Angus Armstrong, Dan & Glynis Carron, Paul Cook, Ian Ferguson, John Gay, Chris Ottley and Alan Sloan.

Colwyn Jones
Vice President

Easter Meet, Kinlochewe   28 April–1 May 2011

With our return to the excellent Kinlochewe Hotel, this became the Easter Meet that had everything. Continuously glorious weather, which brought out Club members and their guests in numbers, a Royal Wedding with no televisions in the hotel and headline news as the mountains of Torridon burst into flames around us.

Friday evening saw us enjoying John Hay's splendid hospitality at Annat with salmon, champagne and venison consumed outside, wihout the unwanted attention of culicoides impunctatus, watching the smouldering flanks of the mountains across the loch, as the sun set redly in the west.

Duly fortified, ascents were made of Fuar Tholl, Slioch, Beinne Eige by various routes, Beinne Liath Mòr, Sgòrr Ruadh, Beinne a' Chearcaill, Ruadh-stac Beag, Meall Mheinnidh (a fine wee hill) and Beinn Dearg (Torridon).

This meet was however, memorable for its rock climbing on the established and popular crags of Stone Valley, Raven Crag, Slioch, Seana Mhellan, Ardheslaig, Waterfall Buttress, the Shieldaig Slab and the Cioch in Applecross. There was also new route activity, with the President correcting earlier piton misdemeanours on a new combination E3 on the Eastern Ramparts of Coire MhicFhearchair, and others reporting success on mysterious Crag X. Many of these routes offered sightings of the helicopters bringing water to aid the numerous firefighters trying to prevent the fires from spreading to houses, as the smell of smoke drifted in the air.

Another splendid meal took place in the hotel on Saturday where Dick Allen was thanked for his organisation of both this event and also the organisation of some ten previous Easters as he stepped down from the post of Meets Secretary. As persuation of various Past Presidents had come to no avail, the Hon Secretary John RR Fowler picked up the mantle that Dick had worn so urbanely, to take charge of the Easter Meet 2012.

Easter Meet 2011 – Kinlochewe

(L to R) John Hay, Dick Allen, Roger Robb, Bill McKerrow, Calum Anton (Guest), Marion Moffat (Guest), Raymond Simpson, Noel Williams, Andrew James, Peter Moffat, Paul Brian, Phil Gribbon, Gordon Macnair, Helen Forde, Gail Staddon (at window), David Stone, Peter Macdonald, Douglas Niven, Simon Fraser, Charles Rose, John Temple, Dick Balharry. Sitting/crouching: Robin Chalmers, Iain Smart, Andy Nisbet, Des Rubens, John Fowler, Peter Biggar, Geoff Cohen. Photo: Andrew Staddon (Hotel Proprietor).

Members present: AD Nisbet (President), new Honorary Member R Balharry, ER Allen, PJ Biggar, PV Brian, RDM Chalmers, G Cohen, HGS Forde, C Forrest, JRR Fowler, S Fraser, PWF Gribbon, JYL Hay, AM James, DM Jenkins, PF Macdonald, G Macnair, WS McKerrow, PR Moffat, DMG Niven, RJC Robb, CS Rose, DW Rubens, RJ Simpson, IHM Smart, AC Stead, D Stone, DJ Temple and DN Williams.

Guests of the Club included C Anton and M Moffat. Resident at Shieldaig were S & J Murdoch (guest) and a club Vice-President was also spotted in the vicinity.

Helen G S Forde

Skye Meet, Allt Dearg Cottage 11–18 June 2011

The month of May was extremely wet this year – a lot wetter than the wettest May on record – so we were glad that we had a later than usual booking. However, the week was disappointingly damp overall and we ended up snatching routes in the better spells. With the manuscript for the new *Skye Sea-cliffs & Outcrops* guide to hand a little last minute feedback was also accomplished.

The main road was blocked for many hours after a fatal accident east of Broadford on the Saturday, so no one arrived until very late. Tom Prentice and guest Nick Kemp kicked off proceedings on the Sunday with some classic routes on Sròn na Cìche including *Joker* and *Direct Route*, and Alan Smith and Peter Wilson had an evening walk up Bruach na Frithe.

Monday was wet but Tom and Nick managed to zoom up both Ben Tianavaig and Belig. On Tuesday numerous climbs were done at Flodigarry and Kilt as well as a scramble on Marsco. The following day John Mackenzie and Eve Austin climbed several routes on the upper tier at Neist, and James Hotchkis and Peter Macdonald climbed *Odell's Route* on Marsco.

On Thursday Alan and Peter ventured into the Cuillin and traversed over Sgùrr na Banachdaich and Sgùrr na Ghreadaidh. John and Eve climbed several more routes at Neist including *Tailgate Substitute*, while James and Peter ascended *Boswell's Buttress*. Tom met up with Duncan Tunstall and did *Minch and Tatties* and *Master of Morgana* at Rubha Hunish. Duncan made an on sight lead of a new direct start (E2,5b) to the latter – up the wall to the left of the chimney.

Alan and Peter snatched *Bridging Interest* and *Midas Touch* in the Financial Sector at Neist on Friday before rain stopped play around midday.

The meet organiser was crocked all week with a bad knee and only managed to hobble along the start of the upgraded path to Rubha Hunish.

The cottage is a delightful base and the week was enjoyable enough, but we still look forward to our stay coinciding with heatwave conditions one of these years.

Members present: James Hotchkis, Peter Macdonald, John Mackenzie, Tom Prentice, Alan Smith, Duncan Tunstall, Noel Williams and Peter Wilson.

Guests: Eve Austin and Nick Kemp.

Noel Williams

Lake District Meet, Robertson Lamb Hut, Langdale – September 2011

Back row, standing on benches (L to R): Noel Williams, Rob Collister (Guest), Max Biden (Guest), Bob Richardson, Derek Buckle (Guest).

Front row: James Hotchkis, Roger Robb, John Wood, Mike Cocker, Peter Macdonald, Hamish Brown, Nigel Suess, Maureen Suess (Guest), Robin Campbell, Jane Murdoch (Guest), Ian Grey (Guest), Stuart Murdoch, Peter Dixon (Guest & Past President Wayfarers), Pippa Cocker (Guest), John Temple.

Missing: Dick Allen who took the photo.

Lake District Meet   9–11 September 2011

The Lake District Meet seems to attract extremes of weather. A firmly established event now, it is always popular and always enjoyable come rain or shine – this year we had the former! The venue as usual was the Robertson Lamb Hut in Langdale, the oldest climbing hut in the Lake District and surely one of the most atmospheric. One party climbed *Original Route* on Raven Crag on Friday before the heavens opened and left the crags awash for the rest of the week-end. On Saturday three members reached the top of Scafell Pike while others explored White Ghyll and Pavey Ark, all returning soaked through and testing the drying-room to its limit. The highlight, as always, was the Saturday night banquet, inaugurated in 1997 by the late Oliver Turnbull and for many years now produced by Dick Allen with his usual style and good humour. His efforts were much appreciated by all concerned, as was the hospitality of our hosts, The Wayfarers' Club. The weather was the same again on Sunday but after an evening like that, who cared?

Members present: Dick Allen, Hamish Brown, Robin Campbell, Mike Cocker, James Hotchkis, Peter Macdonald, Stuart Murdoch, Bob Richardson, Roger Robb, Nigel Suess, John Temple, Noel Williams and John Wood.
Guests: Max Biden, Derek Buckle, Pippa Cocker, Rob Collister, Peter Dixon (Wayfarers' Club Past President), Ian Gray, Jane Murdoch and Maureen Suess.

PFM

JMCS REPORTS

Edinburgh Section: September 2011; as the drizzle falls and an exceptionally poor summer comes to an end, one would not be surprised if a motion were to be proposed at the Club's AGM to the effect that we should emigrate and become the JMCS Costa Blanca, or some other suitable destination with a greater number of climbable days per season. Many folk taking up climbing nowadays tend to regard it primarily as an indoor sport and one cannot blame them after the 'summer' we have just had. Our summer weekend meets were particularly badly affected: on several occasions planned visits to mountain destinations far afield fell through in favour of a hastily arranged day trip to Kirrie Hill or Northumberland, or some other lowland location. Our long-suffering Meets Secretary, Sue Marvell, finally concluded that she must have offended the weather gods in some way and stood down from the post which she has cheerfully and efficiently filled for some time; it remains to be seen whether her successor attracts more divine favour.

However the wet summer should not obscure memories of the preceding winter, which was one of the best on record, although the rapid thaw in April cut short activities on the Ben and our meets did not always coincide with the best of the weather. But on a memorable weekend we found Lochnagar in prime condition, with the sun shining, and this enabled some long held ambitions to be fulfilled.

We always welcome new faces. Come along to our Monday or Wednesday night activities and meet some of the existing members. It is probably best to contact Terry Lansdown, the Membership Secretary, beforehand to make sure there has been no last minute change of venue. We go to Ratho on winter Wednesdays and Alien Rock on winter Mondays. During the summer we tend to climb outside on local outcrops on both days; you can see where we are going by looking at our website which also lists our forthcoming weekend meets. Just Google 'Edinburgh JMCS'.

Our huts are available for booking by kindred Clubs; please contact the Custodians whose names are shown below. We have 'the Cabin' in Balgowan, between Laggan and Newtonmore, and 'the Smiddy' at Dundonnell in the North West.

The present committee is; *Honorary President:* John Fowler, *Honorary Vice-President:* Euan Scott, *President:* Chris Eilbeck; *Vice President and Smiddy Custodian:* Helen Forde (30 Reid Terrace, Edinburgh EH3 5JH, 0131 332 0071), *Secretary:* David Small (5 Afton Place, Edinburgh, EH5 3RB, <secretary@ edinburghjmcs.org.uk>), *Treasurer:* Bryan Rynne, *The Cabin Custodian:* Ali Borthwick (01383 732 232, before 9pm please); *Membership Secretary:* Terry Lansdown <t.lansdown@hw.ac.uk>

David Small

SMC AND JMCS ABROAD

NORTH AMERICA
Kenai Mountains, Alaska – June/July 2010

Jas Hepburn, Graham McDonald and Niall Ritchie accompanied a group of 12 students from Banchory Academy to the Kenai Mountains of South Central Alaska. After arriving in Anchorage and sorting equipment, provisions and transport we headed south to Seward and the nearby Exit Glacier trail to camp and travel on the Harding Ice Field. (The largest ice field solely in the USA) Despite fairly mixed weather the party succeeded in climbing one of the many unnamed nunataks at 5,000 feet above sea level and marvelled at the vast and beautifully unspoiled wilderness. Grim conditions akin to the Cairngorm plateau on a good day, forced a lengthy spell tent bound and subsequent return to the valley; however a fantastically rich experience was had by all. Some of the groups' only previous camping experience had been at 'T in the Park'!

After a couple of days rest in the typically rainy town of Seward, the group headed to Soldotna to team up with the United States Fish and Wildlife Service to take part in a conservation project in the Lake Tustamena area. This remote and seldom visited area in the Kenai National Wildlife refuge provided the opportunity to view the Harding Ice Field from a different angle. The five-day project involved restoring the tin roof of the Andrew Berg Hunting Cabin and the clearance of the Emma Lake trail from Lake Tustamena's shoreline.

Although quite different, both parts of the three-week expedition were equally satisfying and hugely rewarding. The skills gained have had a big impact on all the young group members, two of whom recently scaled Kilimanjaro as part of a gap year experience.

The Banchory Academy Alaska expedition was generously supported by the Scottish Arctic Club which is greatly appreciated.

Niall Ritchie

Kenai Fjords National Park, Alaska: Sunrise on Banchory Academy camp on the Harding Ice Field looking to the Exit Glacier. Photo: Niall Ritchie.

HIMALAYA
Scottish-American Sikkim Expedition, 2010

In late April 2010 a group of SMC stalwarts might have been observed lingering in the duty-free shop at Glasgow airport. What were they doing? Were they on a trade mission to promote Scotland's most important export? Maybe, though an observer who had noticed their cover-up game involving heavy rucksacks, double boots, ice axes etc, checked in some time earlier at the 'outsize luggage' counter might have been given pause despite the many hundreds of pounds worth of 'water of life' in their trolleys.

Some twenty-four hours later a sweating Steve Kennedy, Bob Hamilton, Dave Ritchie and Geoff Cohen, holed up in a somewhat drab Calcutta hotel, celebrated the late arrival of American Paul Swienton by broaching one of the 'trade samples', and indeed entirely demolishing it. But it was only after a rendez-vous with lead 'refreshment expert' Dick Isherwood at Bagdogra airport next day that the mission could be said to be fully on its way to Sikkim.

We were met by our agent Barap Namgyal and the guide he had assigned to us, Sanjeev Tamang. Barap, who had been recommended by Roger Payne, a recent expert on Sikkimese mountaineering, would probably have been quite happy if our mission truly had been devoted exclusively to whisky. Though commendably efficient and supportive throughout our trip, one had the impression he could very comfortably adapt to the playboy lifestyle of the successful entrepeneur once his trekking business expands sufficiently. He arranged for us to visit a Buddhist monastery, helped us look over the tents and food he had provided and very kindly invited us to his home to dine and sample Sikkimese spirits. Much as we enjoyed the evening our feeling was that the trade balance in spirits is likely to remain in Scotland's favour for some time.

From Gangtok, we drove for six hours over wooded ridges to Yoksam the ancient capital of Sikkim. Though not much more than a village, it had a very comfortable and well-run hotel where we were royally treated. Barap's staff did everything for us, the organising of yak loads, camp cooking tents and so on; all we had to do was pack our personal gear, enjoy the scenery and keep well – something Steve unfortunately failed to do as he spent most of his time in Yoksam with his head over the toilet. Despite this he bravely kept up with the party next day as we trailed through very steep forest to a height of about 3000m. Here Dick, a veteran of many years in Nepal, introduced the party to the delights of 'tumba', and gave the locals the first hints of his drinking prowess.

What is tumba? Many will have heard of chang, the millet beer that is drunk widely throughout the Himalayan regions. Apparently 'tumba' refers to the receptacle as well as the drink it contains – a section of bamboo into which the warmed beer is poured, together with a bamboo straw that has a clever feather at its base to prevent the drinker sucking up solid matter. Dick had an unerring instinct for the low huts where such drinks could be found, and always made certain he had a spare one warm by his side for when the drink in progress became exhausted.

We were following an old and popular route to a viewpoint at Dzongri (4100m) where a magnificent panorama of Kangchenjunga and its satellites can be seen. Another day took us to base camp at Thangsing (3960m), a flat plain in the Prek Chu valley, with a few stone huts, staffed in summer by a diminutive chowkidar

Tangshing (3600m): Basecamp in the Prek Chu valley of west Sikkim, with a view to Pandim (6691m).
Photo: Geoff Cohen.

(caretaker) who kept an interesting collection of libations in the depths of his den. It took us a few more days to establish an advanced base camp among moraine boulders at about 4900m, with our sherpa Karma and liaison officer Bhai-Chung for company.

Above us was Jopuno (5936m) which has had a number of attempts and at least one ascent. It was first claimed in 1883 by W.W. Graham who later climbed Kabru (7317m) the highest peak ever climbed at that time. More recently an American party climbed its attractive west ridge, following a long snow arête, then a band of golden rock and finally a less steep section of loose black rock. The nominal objective of our expedition was exploration of the east side of the Jopuno range, which has never been visited. However we started our campaign with a climb on neighbouring Lama Lamani (5600m). The lower North top of this peak had already been climbed by Roger Payne in 2005, but Kennedy's eagle eye spotted an alternative route which four of us enjoyed on 11 May. We had pleasant mixed climbing at about Scottish grade II/III finishing by a very elegant snow arête in perfect condition. Unfortunately, like Roger Payne, we didn't have time to traverse to the higher South top.

Further exploration did not reveal any obvious way to get over to the east side of the range. And at this time Dave, though he climbed a small peak of about 5500m with Bob, was suffering from high altitude oedema, while Dick had important seminars to conduct with the chowkidar in his den. The remaining four of us, helped by our formidable sherpa, carried to a small camp at about 5100m under the west ridge of Jopuno. We had hoped to attempt a new route on the north-west face, but a day of poor weather together with a bit of illness for Bob

North-west face of Lama Lamani (5600m) in Western Sikkim: The SMC route climbed the couloir leading to the col below the right-hand ridge and finished up the elegant snow arête.
Photo: Geoff Cohen.

and my lamentably laboured breathing persuaded us that our best hope of reaching the summit was to repeat the American route. This we attempted on 18 May, and had a very good Alpine day, involving some icy slopes and good quality mixed climbing on the golden band. However we were too slow to get up and down safely in the day, so retreated from the foot of the black band, well short of the summit.

Indifferent weather prevented further ascents, though Bob and Dave stayed high as long as possible; while down at Tangshing the chowkidar provided singing, dancing and local spirits in exchange for our malts. The programme that Barap had organised for us (unasked) involved several days of sightseeing and meant that in the end we only had 12 days above base. We were taken on a tour of old Sikkimese palaces and monasteries, ending up at Darjeeling, where the Glasgow-built steam engine was much admired.

Our thanks go to the Mount Everest Foundation and the Mountaineering Council of Scotland who gave generous financial support; to Barap who was not just an agent but a generous friend; and to Roger Payne who was a mine of information and advice.

Geoff Cohen

EUROPE
Punta Baretti, Mont Blanc Range

In early September 2009, Duncan Tunstall and I spent a week in the Mont Blanc Range where we made the first ascent of the South-West Spur of Punta Baretti (ED1).

Punta Baretti (4013m) is situated on the Italian side of Mont Blanc and is considered to be the most remote of all the 4000m peaks. The peak is rarely climbed and access to the huge 1200m-high South-West Spur that drops directly from the summit, is guarded by the chaotic Mont Blanc glacier.

Global warming has caused significant retreat of many alpine glaciers in recent years creating increasingly difficult access to many alpine routes. The retreat of the Mont Blanc glacier however, has turned its lower icefall into a smooth glacier snout that has opened up access to this major but isolated alpine face. Inevitably the great extreme skier Pierre Tardivel was the first to notice, and with Jeremy Janody and Sebastian de Sainte Marie he climbed and then skied the TD+ central couloir on the SW face in May 2006. The couloir was repeated as a summer climb last July.

On 7 September Duncan and I climbed 400m up the lower glacier on easy but brittle ice to reach the foot of the spur. This gave 40 pitches of absorbing climbing over a series of difficult towers, a whaleback ridge and a final steep headwall that was turned by a knife edge ridge on the left. We reached the summit on the third day and descended to the Eccles Hut. Difficulties were sustained at V and V+ with a couple of pitches of VI and the route was comparable in difficulty and character to the North-East Rib of the Finsteraarhorn in the Bernese Oberland.

Simon Richardson

French and Swiss Alps, Summer 2010

This year, eschewing that rare climatic phenomenon, the Scottish summer, I was able to tempt our esteemed President to the Alps – compounding the sins whereby he has spent most of his term of office climbing outwith his native land. Our warm up climb was a very pleasant ten pitch bolted limestone route on the Tour Termier (close to col Galibier), only slightly delayed by my forgetting the sack at the bottom, and then wandering off route onto something a wee bit beyond me. The scene was then set for our first ambition, a traverse of the Meije.

My proposal was to climb directly up the west ridge from the Breche de la Meije and bivouac beside the Glacier Carre, thus getting ahead of the morning rush on the normal route and enjoying a true 'union with the mountains'. Des, who knows my ways, was naturally suspicious; he recalled all too well some long nights shivering on tiny ledges, but I told him all that was ages ago. His misgivings were certainly not improved when after a five-hour ascent to the Breche we found the initial rocks of the west ridge to be extremely loose overlapping slabs. Once over these and a loose gully we were on a delightful ridge of firm rock, albeit snow-covered on its north flank where some excursions were required. Weather was fine, though a cold wind from the north and the late hour (by now after 8 p.m.) no doubt raised Des's foreboding. At last coming round a sharp corner at the end of a very narrow crest he let out an ecstatic whoop. The perfect bivvy site was awaiting us – a sheltered back wall, cleared ground and a protective wall built up around to keep us cosy and prevent us dropping things. There was just enough snow left after a recent storm to allow us to cook and thus conserve our water bottles for the morrow. Once in our sleeping bags we enjoyed a magnificent sunset behind Le Rateau, with Venus shining on long afterwards in the evening sky.

Geoff Cohen climbing on the traverse of La Meije.
Photo: Des Rubens.

Next morning the earliest French parties had climbed 500m from the Promontoire Hut and were past us while we were still getting ready. But we managed to keep up a reasonable pace, well ahead of the slower second wave of climbers. The ridge was in fine condition and gave as splendid a day as we could have hoped for. The initial view of the Doigt de Dieu from the Grand Pic was formidable, but in fact the climbing was straightforward, though the icy section after the Breche Szigmondy would be very time consuming without the in situ cables. Descending from the Doigt we had to make a rappel over the last rimaye, about which I was rather apprehensive, having heard some horror stories. Des launched himself into space over the undercut upper edge, and fortunately the ropes just reached! We rested in the Aigle Hut and then made the long 6000ft descent to the valley. We were down early enough to dine in La Grave and toast our success.

We then went to Switzerland, with an eye on the Weisshorn. Our initial plan to climb the Schalligrat was frustrated by information about glacier change on the Tasch side and a full Rothorn hut preventing a traverse from that direction. Des then had the bright idea of climbing the mountain by the normal route and descending the Schalligrat. However our last few hundred feet up the peak were in cloud and snowfall that felt a bit like a poor Scottish winter day, so we didn't really consider trying to find an unknown descent route from the summit, but just reversed the normal route – only to see the weather clear beautifully again in the evening.

Our final climb was the traverse of the Obergabelhorn from the Arben bivouac hut. This can be thoroughly recommended. The hut is in a fantastic position under the south face of the mountain with stunning views of the Matterhorn

Geoff Cohen on the summit of Obergabelhorn, with Dent Blanche behind.
Photo: Des Rubens.

right opposite. It is very well designed and maintained, apparently, by the Biner family of Zermatt. We were lucky to have the place to ourselves, and to be able to enjoy a feeling of remoteness unusual in this popular Alpine region. The Arbengrat was as good as it is made out to be, an excellent friendly rock climb, mostly soloable. The descent of the normal route provided a pleasant contrast with some nice down climbing on mixed ground at about grade III, followed by the elegant arête to the Wellenkuppe.

Geoff Cohen

Chaukhi Mountain, Eastern Caucasus, Georgia

In April 2010, Graham Dudley visited the Eastern Caucasus and made a ski ascent of Kazbek (5,034m) with Ewan Clark (SMC), Dave Coustick and Dave Howard. He noticed an attractive range of lightly glaciated rock peaks about 30km to the southeast, and was determined to come back for a 'look', so he persuaded me to join him for a seven-day visit last September (2010).

Research revealed these were the Chaukhi mountains, which lie close to the Russian border and are known as the Dolomites of Georgia, boasting fine alpine rock routes. The massif consists of a ridge of unusual, metamorphic, volcanic rock, with four separate summits, surrounded by grassy hills rising to 3500m. The highest point is Asatiani (3820m). The area can be reached in a three-hour taxi and 4WD journey from Tbilisi, followed by a two-hour walk with horses.

The Chaukhi region is breathtakingly beautiful and very much unknown outside Georgia. Our stay caused a little local excitement, as apparently we were the first foreign visitors to climb technical routes. The area is popular with trekkers and non-local climbing parties, who have either hill walked or made simple Grade I scrambles. However, we were certainly not the first overseas party as we were told that the mountain was first climbed by an American woman in the 1930s. Russians must certainly have climbed here also, and there was mention of a Czechoslovak team in the 1980s.

Since we knew nothing of the area, we spent our first day climbing the Normal Route on Javakishvili (3650m), Chaukhi's second highest summit, with Georgian guide Tito Nadiratze. Graded 3A, this was about Alpine PD, following an easy snow/scree couloir, and then V Diff rock to the summit. Next day we climbed the Normal Route on Asatiani. This took a long couloir, then climbed four, long, protectionless pitches up slabs at Hard Severe. Graded 4A, the route equated to Alpine D⁻.

We then took a rest day and our run of good weather ended – unlucky because the previous eight weeks had been perfect! We made three attempts to climb a 5A rock route on the 600m-high north face of Javakishvili but on each occasion were beaten by cold and rain. However, we managed a route on the south face, which Nadiratze had pointed out to us as unclimbed. On 10 September, starting midway between the Nadiradze-Gujabidze route and the ridge of the Normal Route, we followed weaknesses up the face at VS (not sustained) to join the Normal Route a little before the summit. Our line, named *Perseverance*, was 320m (around six pitches) and grade 4A.

Despite the weather, we managed to do something every day. After our various failed attempts we would go off walking in the rain, eventually reaching the tops of almost all the surrounding 3500m peaks. Although the unsettled weather was a surprise (it certainly felt very Scottish), we returned back to Aberdeen after a short but very satisfying trip.

Postscript: A few months later I was talking to Robin Campbell about the trip at the SMC dinner. Robin was intrigued by the suggestion that the peak was first climbed by an American woman, and suggested that it may have been Una Cameron who first climbed Chaukhi. Robin kindly sent me a photocopy of Cameron's book (*A Good Line*, 1932, published privately), and sure enough she made a visit to the Eastern Caucasus with two Courmayeur guides in 1932.

Their experience was far tougher than ours, and just reaching the mountains was a journey of epic proportions. After travelling south across Europe, they took a steamer along the Mediterranean and the Black Sea to reach Batum on the western border of Georgia where the Russians treated them with utmost suspicion. Their journey to the mountains was hampered by uncooperative horsemen and infestations of lice. Eventually they reached Chaukhi (spelt phonetically as Tschauchee), but frustratingly only a handful of pages in the book (which reads more like a travel diary than a mountaineering account) are devoted to details of their climbing. Over the space of four days they made first ascents of the four major summits in the massif. They climbed Asatiani by almost the same route that we followed in the remarkably fast time of four hours.

So the Georgians were incorrect, that Graham and I were the first non-Georgians to climb technical routes on Chaukhi. (In hindsight, the peak name Kameron, the third highest summit in the range, should have given us a clue!)

The redoubtable Una Cameron had been there nearly 80 years before. As is so often the case in the ways of the world, a Scotsman (or woman) had been there first!

Simon Richardson

Turkey, Antalya Region

An old climbing friend of mine, Andrew Wielochowski, and his wife Fay have a holiday home in south-west Turkey. In early April this year I took up an invitation to stay with them. I flew directly from Glasgow to Antalya, and from there I was driven some 65km south-west to their house in Bejcik. I was immediately impressed with the scenery. There are delightful sandy beaches on the coast with impressive ancient ruins at Phaselis, but just a few kilometres inland there are 2000m high limestone peaks. There is very pleasant walking in the beautifully wooded countryside, including the 509km long Lycian Way. About 3 km north of Çıralı, are famous features called *chimera* – where escaping natural gas burns continuously from numerous vents in the ground..

There is much sports climbing to be had at several venues west of Antalya as well as deep water soloing at Olympos. An excellent Turkish/English guidebook is available for the area (*A Rock Climbing Guide to Antalya*, 4th edition 2011) with over 600 routes recorded at Geyikbayiri, for example, 25km west of Antalya.

During my stay Andrew and I had two particularly enjoyable outings of a more mountaineering nature. The first was a fun traverse of a prominent ridge west of Çıralı called Omurga Dağ, which means 'backbone mountain'. This long ridge is mainly scrambling, but it also has a few short sections of interesting albeit easy

Omurga Dağ (Backbone Mountain), near Çirali, South-West Turkey.
Photo: Noel Williams.

Andrew Wielochowski leads the key pitch on the south-west face of Tahtali Daği.

Photo: Noel Williams.

climbing. It is best to complete the whole ridge and descend from the higher southern end rather than drop down the western flank, as we did, and fight through dense thorn bushes.

The second outing was a longer day. Fay dropped us off around 6 a.m. on a forest track at about 960m below the south-west face of Tahtali Daği (also called Mt Olympos). After a long and vegetated approach slope we took a direct line up a ridge feature in the centre of the face. This was mainly scrambling, but there were three or four climbing pitches of Severe standard. Route finding was not entirely trivial, and we took a couple of false turns. A steeper section of buttress, undercut at its base, looked quite intimidating from below, but proved fairly straightforward after a crucial leftwards traverse. We eventually finished at about 12.30 p.m. on an extensive and complex boulder terrace (2080m), still some distance below the summit (2365m). Our route may well have been new.

It would have been easier to continue up to the summit and then descend the other side by cable car. Instead we traversed a long way north and then west, much of the time on snow, and from a col at 1750m we descended by the Lycian Way back to Beycik. This took longer than the ascent. .

There is much to interest climbers in the area, not least the good weather. The main summer months are rather hot, so the best times to visit are probably April and October.

Noel Williams

Argentiere to Zermatt – High Level Ski Traverse

Ann MacDonald, Colwyn Jones, with Moira Baptie and Adrian Hart, completed this traverse on skis in 2011. Starting in bright sunshine on 15 April, we used the busy Grand Montets lift to reach the Glacier des Rognons and spent the first night in the refuge d'Argentiere (2771m), ideal for early acclimatisation. Early next morning we skied up the Glacier du Chardonnet arriving first at the Col du Chardonnet, descended by abseil. The sunshine was unrelenting up the Fenetre de Saleina, but we had a superb ski in Spring powder over the Plateau du Trient to the Cabane du Triente (3170m). In the afternoon we skied up the Pointe d'Orny (3271m) behind the hut just for the view.

Next morning the meagre snow dictated skis off for climbing the crumbling rock of the Col de Ecandies and after the icy snow a long but pleasant walk through the pine woods of the Val d'Arpette to Champex. The excellent bus service allowed an early arrival in Bourg St Pierre for lunch in the continued sunshine.

On 17 April Ann and I walked for a couple of hours up the Val Sorey to reach the treacherous snow below the Cabane de Velan (2569m); hotels seem to result in a late start! We stayed the night in the modernistic cabane and next morning enjoyed a fine ski down the glacier du Tseudet to then skin up to the Cabane de Valsorey (3030m). Moira and Adrian arrived shortly afterwards directly from Bourg and sunbathing again filled the afternoon. Next morning, in moonlight, we joined the modest queue up the Plateau de Couloir, which was in benign condition. The shortage of low level snow seemed to have prompted a few cancellations in the huts. The Glacier du Mont Durand provided excellent skiing and we arrived at the Cabane de Chanrion (2462m) for more sunbathing, although the poor snow cover involved carrying skis.

An early start up the Glacier d'Otemma and over the Col du Petit Mont Collon allowed an early arrival at the Refuge des Bouquetins (2980m) on the Friday. We had booked this excellent hut, but it is unwardened and by nightfall it was full to overflowing resulting in various international territorial incidents breaking out. The planned early start next morning involved climbing over the sleeping dossers to get out of the door and we were the first party over the Col du Mont Brule (3213m). The day was made interesting by the first cloud of the trip and careful navigation in the white-out up the Haut Glacier de Tsa de Tsan slowed progress allowing some of the guided parties to overtake us; although there was a suggestion that this had been planned! Thereafter we had a track to follow between the gaping crevasses on the east side of the Col de Valpelline (3557m). Once below the cloud we had a fine ski down the Zmutt glacier, a long walk off the moraine, then an intermittent ski on deteriorating piste to Furi and the telecabine down to spend Saturday night, 23 April, living it up in Zermatt. Ski mountaineering doesn't come much better than this.

Colwyn Jones

REVIEWS

George Ingle Finch's *The Struggle for Everest*: Edited by George W. Rodway (Carreg Ltd, 2008, hardback, 232pp, ISBN 978-0-9538631-6-7, £20.)

Whilst the name of George Leigh Mallory is well-kent that of George Ingle Finch, in contrast, can be considered to be comparatively obscure. Yet, of the two accomplished mountaineers it is Finch, arguably, who is the more intriguing character especially if you find nonconformists more fascinating than romantics. Finch's story becomes even more compelling as events surrounding his involvement in the three Everest expeditions of the 1920s also include allegations of perfidy and skulduggery.

George Finch was born in Australia in 1888 and at age 13, whilst out pursuing wallabies on his pony, scrambled to the top of a rocky hill where he made up his mind to see the world thenceforth from the tops of mountains. In 1902 the family moved to Europe where George and his younger brother Maxwell inspired by Whymper's *Scrambles in the Alps* made an audacious and thoroughly dangerous ascent of Beachy Head followed, a few weeks later in Paris, by an ascent of Notre Dame Cathedral by an unorthodox route. A clash with the authorities was narrowly avoided but the unconventional nature of this colourful start set the tone for the way his climbing career developed, particularly when this forthright antipodean came into contact with the English mountaineering establishment.

Finch studied physical chemistry in Zurich where he became fluent in German and French. All spare time was spent climbing extensively in the Alps, and in his splendid book *The Making of a Mountaineer*, he describes how his experience was gained by 'good climbing, adventure and untrammelled fun'. He became an outstanding alpinist and continued his scientific career at Imperial College, London, until enlisting in the Royal Field Artillery during the First World War, seeing action in Europe and Egypt and being awarded an MBE for his bomb disposal work. After the War he was an automatic choice as a member of the first Everest Expedition in 1921. Intended primarily for reconnaissance this expedition was to be followed by a full assault on the mountain in 1922.

Finch was excluded from the expedition at the last minute on extremely flimsy medical grounds, despite demonstrating his quite unusual powers of endurance in a low pressure chamber which simulated the effects of high altitudes. The case for Finch's inclusion in the 1922 expedition could not be ignored and he duly took part that year. He was a strong believer in the advantages to be gained by the use of bottled oxygen at a time when many, including Mallory, argued forcibly against it and he was heavily involved in the design of the equipment. His ideas were vindicated by practical demonstration when he and Geoffrey Bruce reached an altitude of around 8300m on their summit bid, the highest anyone had reached at that stage. The expedition ended in disaster with the death of seven porters in an avalanche, subsequently to be followed by acrimonious recrimination, although no blame could be attached to Finch.

Finch did not take part in the expedition of 1924, well known for the sensational disappearance of Mallory and Irvine. Once again, the controversial Finch was blackballed, this time because he had become embroiled in a dispute with the Mount Everest Committee, particularly its disagreeable secretary Hinks, about book and lecture rights. Finch went on to become an eminent scientist, was elected President of the Alpine Club in 1959 and died at the age of 82 in 1970.

*

Finch's *Der Kampf um den Everest* was published in German in 1925 but never in English in its entirety until now. George Rodway, an American alpinist and physiologist with an interest in high altitude mountaineering, has commissioned an English translation of the book and acted as overall editor by including relevant extracts from Finch's personal diaries, plus a comprehensive overview by Dr John B. West (originally published in *The Journal of Applied Physiology* in 2003) and a reprint of a 1988 review by Stephen Venables of a new edition of Finch's 1924 book *The Making of a Mountaineer*. That particular edition is significant for the inclusion of an extended introduction by Finch's son-in-law, Scott Russell, filling in biographical gaps and revealing then newly researched information about Finch's shabby treatment.

Inevitably, then, it is the bringing together of this evidence which provides the spice in this book, particularly the issue of Finch's exclusion from the 1921 expedition and the allegation that the two medical reports that sealed his fate were biased and inconsistent and that a favourable report was deliberately suppressed. This may well have been the case but I don't like the use of the words *presumably* (pp.23, 24) or *possibly* (p. 24) by a scientist who should know better than to present suppositions in support of his case. However, it is difficult not to believe that Finch was cheated in 1921 and, to a lesser extent, in 1924 although in the latter case he contributed to his own misfortune.

Of course, Finch was not present on the 1921 or 1924 expeditions and his accounts of these are little more than revamped summaries taken from official versions. The more interesting section of the translation is his much fuller description of the 1922 expedition of which he was a member. Finch's reputation as an awkward oddball accompanied him but prejudices faded as the team bonded and he confided to his diary (p.96) ...*we are all settling down well and I am glad to feel how most of the legacy of hate that Howard Bury* [expedition leader in 1921] *left behind for me has ...vanished.* One of the advantages of reading a piece of historical writing such as this is the ability to know the answers to earlier theories. For example, one might mock at Finch's statement (p. 184) that it is generally known that *breathing takes place to a certain degree through the pores of the skin* but for every dubious idea there are plenty with which one would agree, particularly his scientific approach to high altitude clothing and the benefits of oxygen. Forever the innovator, he designed and produced eiderdown clothing for himself which proved completely successful and was the envy of his initially-sceptical companions. Similarly, his humanity is revealed by his attitude that the Nepalese porters who in the past *had often been regarded equal to pack animals and treated accordingly* (p. 43) should be treated with dignity and respect.

The main enchantment of Finch's account is that it takes the reader to a time before airlines and instant communication and back to the austere challenge of a Himalayan giant when you had to trek for weeks even to approach the mountain. This long walk had its own fascinations; Finch states that *an old Tibetan of royal descent once proudly told me that he had only bathed twice in his life ...*

positioned downwind, to this day I am convinced that the man had greatly exaggerated the number. I find this type of humorous observation more entertaining than factual descriptions of expedition life.

Of particular interest to SMC members are the references to Alexander Kellas and Harold Raeburn, both of whom were members of the 1921 team. Kellas' pioneering work on the use of oxygen is fully described and the importance of his work given due credit. Raeburn had always thought that the North-East ridge of Everest, from a col called the Rapiu La, was a potentially better route than that from the North Col as proposed by Mallory. He based this opinion on the theory that it would provide more shelter from the prevailing winds. In 1922, Finch had the opportunity to visit the Rapiu La and concurred with this view (p. 137) reckoning that the menacing rock towers high on the ridge could easily be circumnavigated. It is now known that those towers, where P. Boardman and J. Tasker lost their lives, provide a nasty sting in the tail and the ridge wasn't climbed in its entirety until the 1980s by Brice and Taylor.

Although the book is a bit of a hotchpotch I enjoyed reading it. I liked the artwork at the head of each chapter and the inclusion of many relevant photos, diagrams and post-expedition lecture adverts and, importantly, an index. However, would I spend £20 on this book of just over 200 pages? No. I would rather pay half the price for nearly 400 pages of Holzel & Salkeld's *The Mystery of Mallory and Irvine* which provides a more gripping, better written and completely authoritative overview of the 1920s attempts on Everest.

Mike Jacob

Mountain Magic, Britain's Mountains in Photographs: Van Greaves. (Francis Lincoln Ltd, 2009, 192pp, ISBN978-07112-2858-0, £25.)

This is a lifelong photographic record of an enthusiastic mountain voyager to many parts of the UK with a good eye for capturing mountain landscapes, unusual rock formations and landforms. Van Greaves has been prepared to visit the country's unique landscape in all seasons and weather conditions, ready to capture the varied colour schemes and atmosphere which are special to mountain areas and in this volume he has assembled a collection of images which the armchair mountain walker will enjoy.

I particularly liked the arrangement of the images: it allows the viewer to see the country more as a whole rather than a series of disconnected parts and helps us to wander at will around the country's mountains. There are many mountain images here with a well captured atmospheric feel to them as well as good light quality and subtle colouring. There are, however, a few that have, I feel, lost some of the punch that Greaves was trying to capture because of a strong colour cast pervading the image.

The narrative attached to each image is sufficient and well addressed with the possible exception of the title which supports the picture Figures on Hart's Ledge where clearly they are well above Hart's Ledge and approaching King's Chimney. In addition, some readers may be a little concerned by the use of higher instead of lower case in parts of some Gaelic spellings; of course these may simply be publication errors and do not in any way detract from the presentation of the images. Again, although technical details are not necessary for the general reader, amateur mountain landscape photographers would have found a basic technical detail of each image useful as an appendix.

There are many good, mountain and wild landscape Coffee Table books on the market, generally rather expensive. *Mountain Magic* is, I feel good value at the price and would sit attractively on many a mountain visitor's coffee table.

Roger Robb

The Cairngorms – 100 Years of Mountaineering: Greg Strange. (Scottish Mountaineering Trust, 2010, hardback, 400pp, ISBN 978-1-907233-11-1, £27.50.)

There were rumours that Greg Strange had been writing a book on the Cairngorms, so when this hefty tome fell into my lap there was an immediate feeling that it meant business, and the subtitle, *100 Years of Mountaineering*, reinforced that. It is definitely a book that will last a lifetime on any Scottish mountaineer's bookshelf. I stroked the polished hardback cover as I stared down Loch Avon and fixed my gaze onto the fine turret of the Shelterstone Crag lit by the morning sun, as though it was my long lost sweetheart.

On opening the book, I flicked through the pages, staring eagerly at the photos, perhaps looking for inspiration, or memories as any human being would. Then I searched for snippets of information in the text which was of foremost interest to me. I would then normally store the book on the shelf for reference or inspiration at a later date, but this was different as I had to do a review. I was not sure how to do one and was rather nervous about reviewing Greg's *magnum opus*, and I felt unqualified for the task, but I started reading from cover to cover.

Firstly, I must mention that the Cairngorms aren't just the remnants of a decaying mountain massif of granite, but are an exclusive set of remote mountains, corries, lochans and glens that have become a lifestyle to many; to none more so than Greg who has been climbing in the Cairngorms for over forty years. The Cairngorms are devious entities, sometimes warm, heather-clad, happy hills, and at other times, snow-draped, windswept mountains depending on the season and their moods. That is why they are enjoyed by so many, be it by climbers, walkers, skiers or naturalists. Perhaps more than anywhere in the UK, the Cairngorms have space – room to disappear amongst the landscape.

I find it fascinating how history is archived so well over a hundred years ago, as the old black and white photo of Lochnagar in 1893 pays tribute to the start of mountaineering in the Cairngorms. Greg has done a good job of weaving first ascent accounts of climbs taken from the SMC journals (and other works) along with his own text to produce a readily readable tale of climbing adventure and development throughout the Cairngorms. In some ways I preferred the text from the earlier days of mountaineering more so than the modern times, but sometimes history dictates that: the lack of road infrastructure, transport, poor equipment and really no knowledge of the cliffs give rise to big adventures that are no longer available to us. Imagine having an epic climb on Lochnagar, returning to Loch Muick in the darkness, and since there was no road there then, continuing for a further eight miles into Glen Clova (as per Raeburn) – these stories should certainly open up our perspective about those early days of pioneering.

The pages are neatly laid out with a wide margin on each page where photos of cliffs and portraits of climber's sit, also there is an occasional quote or 'mini headline' too, which I liked, but sadly they became fewer and further between towards the end of the book. More importantly, the book is set out into twelve chapters that divide the development of climbing tradition into well thought out, short epochs. Most interestingly is the period around the two world wars, where exploration of the Cairngorms suffered quite substantially due to the young men and women called up for war, and worse, those who never made it back to enjoy the hills once more. The chapters are of manageable length, but being a slow reader, I struggled to read the longer, later chapters, which is due to the marked increase in climbing development.

Throughout the book Greg has written with fairness and understanding about the climbs and climbing, the result is an unbiased and balanced view that is plainly honest, which makes for a pleasant read. In the same vein, the climbing characters have been assessed in a fair way, without stripping them bare, but enough to get a feel of the character, which is sometimes mirrored in their achievements on the cliffs. Many of the great Scottish climbers have had a small part to play in the development of climbing in the Cairngorms, the likes of Raeburn, Bell, Patey and so on… but let us not forget that there are many climbers who have shared a rope or a bothy with those legends who have also played their part in the development, and that haven't had a mention in the book. However the book has unearthed some un-sung legends who certainly aren't known to the wider climbing community. One such character that struck me was Charlie Ludwig, who was obviously brave, athletic and talented, but died during the Second World War. If he had survived, the climbing history of the Cairngorms would probably have been significantly different, and if he lived today, he might have revolutionised climbing like Ron Fawcett did in the 1970s or Johnny Dawes in the 1980s.

Outwith the technical climbing, there are other important aspects of the Cairngorms that need to be brought out, and these have been delicately added to the text. Firstly, dare I say it, are the tragedies. Tragedy is a weird phenomenon, it's like the news, and people are fascinated by it. On the other hand it gives sad, albeit intriguing reading. I for one was not aware how many climbers had died in the Cairngorms – ropes snapping, poor equipment etc… and then there were the cruel sagas of mountainous misadventure such as the school kids that froze to death on the plateau when they couldn't find the hut, and the miraculous event when Robert Burnett survived a 22 hour avalanche burial. All these scenarios along with the rise and demise of the bothies, which have been at the centre of many trips into the mountains, have given the Cairngorms a macabre and almost Alpine mountaineering feel.

The book surely convinces one that the Cairngorms aren't a climbing backwater, as has sometimes been thought and it's good to read how the climbing development fitted in with the more renowned climbing areas of Glen Coe, Ben Nevis and Skye, although I felt a little more could have been done here so that we could understand the broader picture a little better. For example: Derek Haworth is mentioned in the text, but there was no relating him to his pioneering of his route *Integrity* on Skye. It does seem that the Cairngorms did lag behind other areas in the pushing of standards of rock climbing, but by contrast it has always had its nose ahead when it comes to the pushing of ice climbing standards.

Even if you are not into climbing history this book gives a definitive, subtle account of the evolution of the sport of mountaineering and of how climbing dirty gullies evolved towards the scaling of clean, blank open walls; it shows how combined tactics evolved to modern free climbing, hob nailed boots evolved into crampons or sticky rubber, a wooden shafted ice axe for cutting holds evolved into front pointing technique, a hemp rope around the waist evolved into nylon rope and a comfortable harness...etc... all this evolution in a hundred years.

However, I did find out towards the end of the book that it was veering towards a drawn out first ascent list. This, I can imagine would be very hard to avoid as the pace of climbing development was becoming exponential. To add to these woes is the fact that not all today's climbers write their tales in the Journal as they did in the past, so good epic stories will be lost in the mists of time. My last point is that I feel rather let down that the text finished in 1993 and not in the present day (almost 20 years on), but I presume that it has taken Greg that amount of time to gather all this information and present us with what is such a fine and valuable offering to the history of mountaineering in the Cairngorms.

Now just sit back and try and imagine if the Cairngorms didn't exist – Scottish mountaineering would be vastly poorer for it and we would never have been blessed with the beautiful lifestyle of the Cairngorms which is portrayed in this volume.

Julian Lines

The Ultimate Guide to the Munros Volume 3: Central Highlands North including Ben Nevis: Ralph Storer. (Luath Press, 2010, 232 pp, ISBN1-906817-56-1, £14.99.)

I have never been a buyer of hill walking guides. If I pick one up it is usually to look at the pictures. The real pleasure in hill walking is to look at a map and conjure up your own routes. A picture of a ridge can inspire but if it's not a technical ascent I'd rather find out for myself. I'd really only consult one to see what the best point of access is for leaving a vehicle. I have managed to survive all these years with Poucher's *The Welsh Peaks* and Butterfield's *The High Mountains of Britain and Ireland*, again only really for the photos, in several cases quite inspirational.

Scotland now has a growing plethora of hill walking guides, a disease which has been sweeping areas south of the Border for some years now.

Ralph Storer is a well known name on the guidebook writing scene. The book is full of relevant information for climbing the Munros in the proscribed area. With Ben Nevis, Creag Meagaidh, the Grey Corries and Ben Alder to name a few, there are some very fine hill days covered. It is fully illustrated with colour photos and the relevant sections from OS maps. There are star ratings and a Route Rage Alert for the less inspiring outings. Main routes and interesting options are all covered.

Information is accurate and exhaustive with labels on the photos but the red arrows marking the way on several pictures are surely a case of overkill. Many of the pictures are of obviously very fine shots in themselves but the size of the book means they can never be fully appreciated.

If I was to buy one of these books I would be looking for a more personalised approach to the subject matter. Hamish Brown's *Hamish's Mountain Walk* and Craig Weldon's *The Weekend Fix* are good examples of this genre. According to the quoted reviews of the other books in the series this is what marks out Storer's style. He has a number of associates with nicknames who offer their own personal slant on a particular walk. However this is usually in the form of more information (albeit useful) but with no stamp of an individual, original voice. This guide is a functional pocket size with good production values. If it was quirky and too idiosyncratic, it probably would have a much smaller market.

In summary, not the kind of book I'd buy, but if you want a detailed informational text which gives you it all on a plate it will do you very nicely. Sadly, there is obviously a continuing demand for this kind of work. Despite the intervening years, Butterfield's original work (1986) on high ground over 3000 feet has still to be superseded.

Mike Dixon

Seton Gordon's Cairngorms. An Anthology: Compiled by Hamish Brown. (Whittles Publishing, 2010, hardback, xxii and 193pp, ISBN 9781904445883, £25.)

Like Tom Weir, Dick Balharry, Jim Crumley and numerous others, Hamish Brown admired the late Seton Gordon's books on the Highlands. In 2005 he delighted readers with his book *Seton Gordon's Scotland. An Anthology* (Whittles Publishing). Now he has compiled an Anthology of Gordon's writings about the Cairngorms.

It was soon after 1900 that Gordon began to visit the Cairngorms, studying and photographing wildlife. His first book was published already in 1907, when he lived at Aboyne. Having corresponded with him since 1939 and valued him as a friend since 1944, I know he regarded the Cairngorms as the finest part of Scotland.

To the many inspired by his writings, all the books in their entirety are desired. However, larger numbers of less specialised readers should find this Anthology attractive. As Hamish writes in his Preface, 'These selected essays and observations on this special landscape are for dipping into rather than reading straight through'. Although I have all of Gordon's books, in this Anthology I appreciated some writing published outside them. Also, Hamish searched the Gordon archive at the National Library of Scotland and used some photographs that I had not seen published before.

Gordon excelled at describing hills, weather, plants, birds, fish, mammals, snow patches, local people, folklore, history and place names, descriptions so vivid that you feel you are standing beside him, watching what he tells so well. He loved the high tops of the Cairngorms more than anywhere else, and pages at random in the Anthology reveal good examples. Brown has chosen well, serving readers with a wide variety and choosing some of Gordon's best pages. He has tended to give short chapters or even shorter separate bits within chapters. Again this is justifiable for wider readers.

A frequent result of anthologies is that they do not reveal the characteristics of the original author. When writing, Gordon tended to hide his personality. To those who knew him, he was a complex character, caring and friendly with all, whether laird or gillie or crofter, and yet with a mischievous sense of humour. It is not a serious loss for the Anthology to lack this, however, because his writings are now more important than his past personal relationships with others.

His writings tend to be free from anthropocentric attitudes, one of the features that always attracted me. Another aspect of his writings which attracted me as a boy was that he never exaggerated or over-wrote the risks. He was lucky to enjoy a freedom that is now foreign in these days of political correctness and health and safety. When I first went on a long walk to visit an eagle's eyrie with him in April 1944 when I was 13, he seldom mentioned himself and spoke to me as if I were an adult. The hill, the birds, even the water skaters and water beetles in the bog pools, all delighted him, and he imitated bird calls excellently, although already largely deaf.

In the Anthology I spotted very few errors, and these minor. I mention them here for use if there is a second edition. The photograph three pages before page 105 shows not Coire Bhrochain of Braeriach as in the caption, but Coire an Lochain of Cairn Gorm, as correctly captioned by Gordon opposite page 36 in his book *The Cairngorm Hills of Scotland*. On page 177 of the Anthology in a note by Brown is the typographical error 'unbowlderised', and another has 'Lochnager'.

An erroneous claim appears in the Afterword by James Macdonald Lockhart, who asserts '....for the first three decades of the twentieth century Gordon was the only full-time practising naturalist in Britain'. In England this is certainly incorrect for vegetation and ornithology. Even in the Highlands, Desmond Nethersole-Thompson was more active than Gordon from 1932 onwards. From 1921 onwards, Carrie of Whitewell, an indigenous Rothiemurchus woman who later married Desmond, made more intensive studies of the breeding behaviour of greenshank, dotterel and crested tit than anyone had done before, internationally. Frank Fraser Darling began a full-time study of red deer in Dundonnel after 1933 and later in the 1930s switched to seals on the isle of Tanera.

I have a criticism of this Anthology, relating to Brown's Preface, where he writes on page xv 'Gordon was a prolific writer of both articles and books and, while captivating, the writing could sometimes be hasty, particularly early on where, for instance, the dead adjective 'beautiful' appears three times in two sentences or 'very' seven times in one chapter.' Apart from questioning what is wrong with 'beautiful' or 'very', some may suggest that the above sentence might well be regarded as clumsy as well as hasty! Brown continues later, 'Selections have only been edited to avoid repetitions, standardise layout and punctuation, and prune circumlocutions whether in a word, sentence or paragraph'. The drawback is that readers will not know whether what they read is always exactly what Gordon wrote, and will be unable to tell when something has been omitted. The standard convention for giving quotations but leaving out certain parts is to print three or four full-stops to indicate a part left out. This might be helpful if there is a second edition.

I am pleased that Hamish Brown has given us this Anthology. Take for example his Epilogue, *Sunrise on Cairngorm*, where readers will see three outstanding pages. Gordon appreciated his summer night on Cairn Gorm and the day that followed so much that every sentence makes you feel you are there, hearing red grouse crowing at dusk, seeing far-distant Tarbat Ness lighthouse flashing orange, and then in the half-light of dawn the 'Ptarmigan, awakening, called to the young day. The light strengthened and mysterious objects revealed themselves....No pen could describe the beauty of the early morning'. Seton Gordon's pen, however, certainly described it well! His words reminded me strongly of what it is like being alone on the high tops through the night at midsummer, always a memorable experience.

A defect of the photographs in this Anthology is their poor quality, generally of greyish hue, lacking black and white crispness, and not sharp. If readers compare them with the published originals in Gordon's books, such as *The Cairngorm Hills of Scotland*, they will see the better contrast and sharpness of the originals. A better result would be helpful in a second edition.

However, Brown delights with photographs that may not have been published before, such as Seton in his first car, sitting on a boulder in the middle of Poll an Eisg in Glen Dee, lying in the doorway of Corrour Bothy beside a deer-watcher, sitting on the parapet of the former Luibeg footbridge beside a stalker, camping in Old Caledonian pine-wood, camping with friends on the high tops. These are gems to be treasured.

Adam Watson

Cool Britannia – Snowier Times in 1580-1930 than since: Adam Watson & Iain Cameron. (Paragon Publishing, 2010, 64pp, ISBN 978-1-907611-48-9, £12.99.)

This book is the result of a painstaking gathering of snow information from many and varied sources. Early travellers are quoted giving their observations as they journeyed through Britain's mountain areas. According to the authors' research these same 'tourists' would behold a totally different snow aspect today. For example, R. P. Dansey wrote in the SMCJ of 1920, that: 'There are two snow beds beneath the cliffs of Aonach Mor facing North-east, which seldom, if ever, entirely disappear, though one of them succumbed in 1918. These snow beds are conspicuous from Roy Bridge Station, which is probably the only station in Britain from which snow is always visible.' This has not been the case in many recent years.

Judging by the extensive accounts collated it is fair to say that prior to 1930 winters were expected to produce large volumes of snow. Whereas in recent decades it's been: 'Do you think we'll get some decent snow this winter?' Adam Watson seems to have been born with a fascination for snow, and for many years has kept an accurate record of how long patches have lasted in the Cairngorms and other parts of the Highlands. His book is not perhaps aimed so much at the general reader it is rather for those who are seriously interested in the complexities of climate change.

Derek Pyper

Scottish Paragliding: An Introduction & Selected Sites Guide: Cliff Smith & Gary Williamson (Blurb Bookstore, 2010, softcover, 240pp, £40.95.)

I came across this volume by chance, Cliff Smith being one of our members. I am not competent to judge the technical aspects of the book, although the guide has been favorably welcomed elsewhere. However, what makes this book worthy of mention in our Journal are the outstanding full page photographs.* Being taken from a paraglider, most of them are views from above the mountains, but not at jet plane sort of height. However, Gary Williamson has a flair for composition which is demonstrated even in his photographs taken at ground level.

For both landscapes and more intimate studies it is not too much to make comparisons with Yann Arthus-Bertrand's *Earth From Above*. See, for example, the single tree in an island of green surrounded by heather in bloom. However, mountaineers will be delighted with fresh views of well-known and less well-known peaks, from stunning views of the Ben to the Liathach ridge to the more gentle landscapes of the Southern Uplands. The Cairngorms and the Assynt peaks are also well represented.

Now that the ski-touring and painting meets are well established, when will the first Club paragliding meet happen?

Des Rubens

*You can get an idea of the quality of the photographs in this book by checking out the preview at this link <http://www.blurb.com/books/1510814>.

Hamish's Groats End Walk: Hamish M. Brown. Revised Edition. (Sandstone Press, 2011, 280 pp., ISBN 987-1-905207-59-6, £14.99.)

Sandstone Press have recently published new versions of *Hamish's Mountain Walk* – the record of our Honorary Member Hamish Brown's round of the Munros in a continuous traverse in 1974 (the first such traverse), and the present book. Whereas the former book is a more or less straight reprint, this one incorporates some new material (mostly bracketed addenda bringing walking or bagging records up to date) and new photographs. Brown's walk from John o' Groats to Land's End took place in 1979. This was the year of the sabotaged devolution referendum, the advent of Margaret Thatcher, a summer of provisional IRA atrocities, the disastrous Fastnet yacht race, and the year without the Times newspaper – a good year to take a long walk perhaps.

Brown's walk crossed to Cape Wrath, worked down through the Western Highlands, deviated into a canoe for a traverse of the Forth, then down through the Borders to the Pennine Way (with a diversion to the Lake District) and into North Wales. Then came another diversion across to Killarney and back, before traversing Wales into Somerset, and so along moors and coast to Land's End. In the course of the expedition he completed a sixth round of the Munros, all the Furths, and a host of lesser hills. His wanderings stretched from snowy May into dank October. Throughout he was accompanied by his Shetland collie Storm, a companion who offered company and friendship, but caused continuous difficulties with accommodation, obliging Brown to carry not only dog food but cumbersome camping equipment everywhere. In the spirit of this annus horribilis, an angry god beset the party with plagues of midges, flies, boils, downpours and hailstorms, and set their feet in bog and mire.

The book follows the inevitable diary format bracketed by preliminaries and tailpieces. The diary entries are almost everywhere augmented by nuggets of local history, literary references, reminiscences of previous visits, and Brown's mostly negative opinions about the manners of the citizens encountered along the way and the customs of the times (presumably all added later). I don't feel that this works very well. If too much of this sort of thing is inserted, the reader loses the thread of the journey, and begins to wonder why he is not reading a proper book about the town or region. If too little, then the reader begins to wonder why anyone would want to undertake a walk like this one. And Brown's opinions are apt to irritate. They often irritated me on account of their inconsistency, and I am just as averse to modern life as Brown. To give two examples: 'As usual I could not face the powdered soup. All reconstituted things seem to taste uniformly revolting . . . . Apple flakes finished the meal. I never tired of them' (p.118 – on the same page!); in the early part of the book he makes several compaints about the din of the ubiqitous transistor radio (then a novelty), but in Lynmouth he buys one, and marches on to the strains of Beethoven and the like. The text is well illustrated by effective and well-drawn maps – especially the clever 'Contents Map', and the photography is well-chosen. One might complain that the inclusion of 17 portraits of the dog amounts to idolatry. The dog doesn't feature in the photo of the C.I.C. Hut interior where Brown and his friend Ray made a day visit (p. 65): presumably he was tethered outside, in accordance with Hut Rules.

What remained with me after finishing the book was strong admiration for Brown's logistic skills. Almost every other day the timetable had to be shaped around the appalling opening hours of Post Offices, so that parcels (carefully sent out beforehand) could be opened, refilled with unwanted objects, and re-posted. If Brown had been in charge of the Moscow campaign in 1812, it would have had a different outcome.

Robin N Campbell

It's a Fine Day For The Hill – Hill Folks and Wild life 1935-62: Adam Watson. (Paragon Publishing, 2011, 181pp., ISBN 978-1-907611-58-2, £29.99.)

The facility Google is something I use, like many others, as an information source, but when there is something pertaining to the Cairngorms, that needs some clarification, I e-mail Adam Watson. Time and time again it has proved a method very speedy – but more importantly – very informative. He knows everything that needs to be known about this range of hills.

This book is not an autobiography – it is a vast collection of Adam's experiences, walking and skiing his beloved Cairngorms. Author and devotee of the Cairngorms, Seton Gordon, was the man who lit Adam's fire. Adam says: 'The Highlands that Seton Gordon wrote about were utterly different, a place of endless beauty and variety with a wonderful wild life and fine people. From then on I saw Scotland, its wild life, weather, skies, people and culture, with this different eye.' There was no turning back for the young Adam – his life was taken over by the lure of the Cairngorms.

It is right and proper to say that Seton Gordon, Tom Weir, Bob Scott and Tom Patey had a great influence on Adam, but in the Fifties and Sixties there were so many characters who frequented the Cairngorm bothies who contributed in all different ways to the culture of the area. Adam has an obsession with everything associated with the Cairngorms, but it is his affinity with people – whether it is the walker, climber, birdwatcher or the inhabitants of the glens – that comes to the fore in the book. He highlights Freddie Malcolm and Alex (sticker) Thom who built the first howff in Glen Slugain; Mac Smith, who wrote the first rock-climbing guide to the Cairngorms, which was a model for all future guides to the area, and of course, Tom Patey.

The chapter entitled 'With Tom Patey', tells of Patey's early days when he was a schoolboy 'Munro-bagger' who frequented Luibeg Bothy with a group which Luibeg keeper Bob Scott labelled the 'Horrible Heilanders'. Nights are recalled when Tom would play his accordion in Braemar's Fife Arms public bar where the grumpiest of locals would be generous with their applause. The bar manager even offered free whiskies if he came back next Saturday, so, yes, you guessed, he was back next week, but only after having completed a few new routes.

Adam's exploits on skis are remarkable expeditions – through the Lairig Ghru, Gaick to Luibeg and his Cairngorm Langlauf. The latter was his amazing trip over the six high tops of the Cairngorms. His record of trips (mostly alone) in North Iceland, and Swedish Lapland, where he travelled on ski over dangerous terrain, makes exciting reading. They were all good training for his later exploits with the various characters who frequented the bothies.

The photographs – featuring stalking days with Bob Scott, trips with Tom Weir, Iceland and climbing with the Cairngorm stalwarts – are superb.

Derek Pyper

Isles at the Edge of the Sea: Jonny Muir. (Sandstone Press, 2011, 235pp, ISBN 978-1-905207-61-9, £8.99.)

In the summer of 2010 Jonny Muir embarked on a three month tour of the Scottish islands, starting in Arran and culminating in the islophile's El Dorado, St. Kilda. The book tells the story of the trip, with a chapter dedicated to each of the 18 islands visited.

Inevitably, what he writes about is selective but does do justice to the range of interesting aspects that these places offer. So for instance we have historical events such as the 'murder' of David Rose on Arran and the evacuation of St, Kilda as well as contemporary issues like Sunday sailings on Lewis, buyouts and eco awareness on Eigg and the invasion of the camper van on Tiree. The tragedy of Lena Zavaroni and anorexia is sensitively covered in the Bute chapter. Along the way are midges, distilleries, wildlife and the vagaries of the Scottish weather. Unsurprisingly, Boswell and Johnson are name checked but then so is Will Self taking a pot shot at goatee hill runners. During his journey Muir takes part in hill races in Arran and Jura and describes the purgatorial nature of the sport very well before having an epiphany on Harris and deciding to give it up for good. He gives an honest, non- heroic account of climbing the In Pinn.

The author shifts seamlessly from the sublime of the machair fringed beaches to the karaoke kitsch of Flower of Scotland and Caledonia. He is candid and successful in describing the effects of drink (Eigg ceilidh) as well as the false bonhomie it can foster (Berneray party). The book's a potpourri but a very interesting one and not without structure.

Muir was previously a journalist and he has learned to condense an issue and deliver it in a well-paced, snappy style. He is a good observer of incidental detail which he weaves into the main flow. He can surprise by producing an arresting phrase for the commonplace, such as when the ring pulls on beer cans 'hissed like a chorus of pistons'. The only real dud chapter is the one on Mull where he fails to achieve much in 24 hours and pads it out with retelling an amusing hoax story. Canna fares only slightly better, however his enthusiasm for Colonsay, Coll and Rum (before it starts raining) will get anyone who hasn't been there consulting maps, guidebooks and websites. I've already made a note to visit Berneray in the near future.

You will probably get more out of this book if you have already visited these islands as, apart from St Kilda, his descriptions don't paint a topographically vivid picture. His expectations concerning the latter are suitably fulfilled as they are for the majority of visitors but he has nothing original to say about the archipelago. In future island books it would be refreshing to see the Shetland island of Foula getting due recognition. Although it possesses nothing like Stac Lee and Stac an Armin, the main sea cliffs exceed anything on Hirta.

It was pleasing to read an account of a journey not overly confessional, nor linked to a charity stunt, and one which was not one of those dreadfully earnest trips as a metaphor for life type of books. The moment he realizes he misses his fiancée, on a ferry to Coll, is nicely understated.

For a general introduction to possibly Scotland's greatest scenic assets Jonny Muir has written a very readable piece and an excellent primer.

Mike Dixon

Mountain Views, A Lifetime's Enjoyment: Rupert Hoare. (Vertebrate Publishing, 2011, hardcover, 212pp, ISBN 9781906148331, £22)

I felt very privileged to be asked by Jay Turner, Rupert Hoare's widow, to review this book.

Rupert died at Roxburghe House, Aberdeen early on Tuesday 20 September 2011, eight months after the diagnosis of pancreatic cancer. Within the first six months, Rupert had written his book *Mountain Views* for friends and family. The book was fortunately published some weeks before Rupert passed away.

Mountain Views is a superb autobiography of a mountaineer's life, climbing all over the world and particularly in the Alps. Rupert's enthusiasm for the mountains shines through virtually every page of the book. Although the book is almost entirely about mountaineering exploits, often on some of the most iconic mountains in the world, Rupert's character and personality leap out from his distinctive style of writing.

The book adopts a chapter by chapter approach. The chapters are often short but the quality and content is impressive. Words are not wasted; each chapter gives a clear and honest account of a particular area, alpine holiday, Scottish adventure or the like. I would also mention that the book is divided into four parts, namely 'The Early Years', 'Peak Years and Alpine Classics', 'The Far East' and 'Recent Highlights'. Each of those parts starts with a quotation which is particularly apposite. Each part is broken down into chapters and most chapters are broken down into particular expeditions, exploits and days out illustrated by relevant photographs.

Rupert had an abiding interest in photography from early years and the photographs almost entirely taken by him are an extremely fine collection.

The book covers mountaineering from his expedition with the British Schools Exploring Society to Arctic Norway/Sweden after leaving school, his mountaineering whilst at Exeter University, numerous expeditions and 4000m peaks in the Alps, climbing, mountaineering and skiing in Scotland, Greenland, the Pyrenees, the Karakoram, Malaysia and Indonesia, Japan, New Zealand and all places in between! Rupert was also a highly accomplished ski mountaineer and many of the accounts are of ski tours, some more serious than others along with a wonderful collection of photographs.

One of Rupert's messages which shines through the book is to make the most of life, to enjoy every day in the hills and to take nothing for granted. Rupert had a great love for the mountains. I remember having a phone call with him not very long before he died when he told me 'remember it is a huge privilege to put your hands on the rock'.

I would recommend the book to anyone who has an interest in mountains. The book has a particular and poignant interest to all those who knew Rupert, many of whom are mentioned in the text.

James Hotchkis

ERRATA

There was an unfortunate problem with the Mountain Accidents section last year (pp. 229–73). In the files supplied to the editor many longer lines of text had words missing from the right-hand side. This was not spotted at the time. Unfortunately the number of lines involved are too numerous to itemise.

On p. 230 the broken bone should have been the 'humerus'.

Several other typos have also been identified:

1. On the Contents page (inside the Front Cover) the correct titles of the articles concerned should be:

THE SEPARATION OF MOUNTAINS REVISITED [No apostrophe]

and

TRILOGY OF MOUNTAIN TRAGEDIES

2. P. 1

Photo captions (top & bottom): The skier's name is Finlay Wild.

3. P. 161

Photo captions (top & bottom): The climbers are Heike Puchan and Mark Fitzsimons ['z' was missing].

OFFICE BEARERS 20010–11

Honorary President: W.D. Brooker
Honorary Vice-President: I.H.M. Smart
President: Andrew D. Nisbet
Vice-Presidents: James Beaton and Colwyn M. Jones

Honorary Secretary: John R.R. Fowler, 4 Doune Terrace, Edinburgh, EH3 6DY. **Honorary Treasurer:** John A. Wood, Spout Close, Millbeck, Keswick, CA12 4PS. **Honarary Membership Secretary:** Geoff Cohen, 198/1 Grange Loan, Edinburgh, EH9 2DZ. **Honorary Meets Secretary:** (Acting) John R.R. Fowler. **Honorary Editor of Journal:** D. Noel Williams, Solus Na Beinne, Happy Valley, Torlundy, Fort William, PH33 6SN. **Honorary Librarian & Honorary Archivist:** Robin N. Campbell, Glynside, Kippen Road, Fintry, Glasgow, G63 0LW. **Honorary Custodian of Slides:** David Stone, 30 Summerside Street, Edinburgh, EH6 4NU. **Honorary Reporter on Accounts:** Nigel M. Suess, 35 Woodhall Road, Edinburgh, EH13 0DT. **SMC Webmaster:** Kenneth V. Crocket, Glenisla, Long Row, Menstrie, FK11 7EA. **Convener of Publications Sub-Committee:** Rab Anderson, 24 Paties Road, Edinburgh, EH14 1EE. **Convener of Huts Sub-Committee:** Andrew M. James, 41 Urquhart Road, Dingwall, IV15 9PE. **Representative to the MCofS:** Brian R. Shackleton, 4A Campbell Road, Edinburgh, EH12 6DT. **Committee:** Susan L. Jensen, Neil McGougan, Heike Puchan, John T.H. Allen, Ross I. Jones, Colin A. Moody and Bruce Kerr.

Journal Information

Editor:	Noel Williams, Solus Na Beinne, Happy Valley, Torlundy, Fort William, PH33 6SN. **e-mail** <noel@beinne.plus.com>
New Routes Editor:	Andy Nisbet, 20 Craigie Avenue, Boat of Garten, PH24 3BL. **e-mail** <anisbe@globalnet.co.uk>
Photos Editor:	Andy Tibbs, Crown Cottage, 4 Crown Circus, Inverness, IV2 3NQ. **e-mail** <teamtibbs@hotmail.com>
Distribution:	Roger Robb, Blaven, Upper Knockbain Road, Dingwall, IV15 9NR. **e-mail** <roger07robb@btinternet.com>

INSTRUCTIONS TO CONTRIBUTORS

The Editor welcomes contributions from members and non-members alike. Priority will be given to articles relating to Scottish mountaineering. Articles should be submitted before the end of April if they are to be considered for inclusion in the Journal of the same year. Material is preferred in electronic form and should be sent by e-mail direct to the Editor.

Acceptable file formats in order of preference are (best) Open Document Format (odt), Rich Text Format (rtf), Plain Text (txt) or MS Word (doc/docx). *Open Office* is an open-source, multi-platform productivity suite which is free for individuals to download from http://www.openoffice.org/

Those without access to e-mail can send hard copy (typewritten and double-spaced) by post to the Editor's home address.